THE ORIGINS OF

ORIGINS OF MODERN WARS
General editor: *Harry Hearder*

Titles already published:

THE ORIGINS OF THE FIRST WORLD WAR
  James Joll
THE ORIGINS OF THE ARAB-ISRAELI WARS
  Ritchie Ovendale
THE ORIGINS OF THE RUSSO-JAPANESE WAR
  Ian Nish
THE ORIGINS OF THE FRENCH REVOLUTIONARY WARS
  T. C. W. Blanning
THE ORIGINS OF THE SECOND WORLD WAR IN EUROPE
  P. M. H. Bell
THE ORIGINS OF THE KOREAN WAR
  Peter Lowe
THE ORIGINS OF THE SECOND WORLD WAR IN ASIA AND THE PACIFIC
  Akira Iriye
THE ORIGINS OF THE VIETNAM WAR
  Anthony Short

THE ORIGINS OF
THE VIETNAM WAR

Anthony Short

LONGMAN
London and New York

LONGMAN GROUP UK LIMITED
Longman House, Burnt Mill, Harlow
Essex CM20 2JE, England
and Associated Companies throughout the world.

Published in the United States of America
by Longman Inc., New York

© Longman Group UK Limited 1989

First published in 1989

BRITISH LIBRARY CATALOGUING IN PUBLICATION DATA
Short, Anthony
     The origins of the Vietnam War. –
     (Origins of modern wars)
     1. Vietnamese wars, 1954–1975. Causes
     I. Title   II. Series
     959.704′2
     ISBN 0-582-49080-4 CSD
     ISBN 0-582-49081-2 PPR

LIBRARY OF CONGRESS CATALOGING-IN-PUBLICATION DATA
Short, Anthony.
     The origins of the Vietnam War.

     (Origins of modern wars)
     Bibliography: p.
     Includes index.
     1. Vietnamese Conflict, 1961–1975—Origins.
     2. Vietnam—History—20th century.   3. United States—
     Foreign relations—Vietnam.   4. Vietnam—Foreign
     relations—United States.   5. United States—Foreign
     Relations—1945–   .   I. Title.   II. Title: Origins
     of the Viet Nam War.   III. Series.
     DS557.6.S53   1989   959.704′32   88-27194
     ISBN 0-582-49080-4
     ISBN 0-582-49081-2 (pbk.)

Set in 10/11pt Linotron Times

Produced by Longman Singapore Publishers (Pte) Ltd.
Printed in Singapore

CONTENTS

EDITOR'S FOREWORD

With the publication of this, the eighth, volume in the series, the short lull which has followed Akira Iriye's *The Origins of the Second World War in Asia and the Pacific* is over, and it seems likely that a second wave of volumes is beginning. It is therefore an appropriate moment for the editor to reiterate the aims of the series, and perhaps he will be forgiven for indulging in the first person.

When I first had the idea of editing a series of books on the causes of individual wars – long before I found a publisher who was wise enough to undertake the project – I was asking myself why it was that academics in other disciplines – political science, sociology, psychology, even zoology – were prepared to speculate on the causes of wars in general, while historians were inhibited from doing so. T. C. W. Blanning, in his *The Origins of the French Revolutionary Wars*, discussed shrewdly and amusingly the speculations of anthropologists, ethnologists, sociologists and psychologists. It seemed to me that what historians could contribute were specific analyses of the origins of individual wars, using a knowledge and understanding which the other social scientists would inevitably lack. Historians (whether they teach in departments of History, Politics or International Relations, or are, indeed, outside the academic world altogether) would bring to bear on the problem their scholarship and their research into the history of various countries and societies, and their understanding of the operation of international relations in the immediate, and not so immediate, past. In doing so they would contribute to a revival of what used to be called 'diplomatic history', by placing it into a much deeper perspective than it had enjoyed in the writings between the wars. That 'diplomatic history' has something to offer in this deeper perspective, which can better be termed 'international history', can hardly be doubted. Already in 1965 Jacques Godechot referred to 'the lack of favour which has unjustly been shown towards diplomatic history in recent years' (*Les révolutions 1770–1799*, Presse Universitaire de France). The injustice is now being to a great extent eliminated.

To encourage academic historians to provide an objective view of the origins of the wars in fields in which they were specialists seemed to me a worthwhile task. The series could have a double purpose. It would bring to the university public a series of syntheses of the literature on the subject and of the author's individual research and interpretation. It would thus serve on the one hand a strictly academic, scholarly, purpose. But on the other hand, I hoped that the series would contribute a body of writing which would enlighten our understanding of the causes of war in general. Dr David Gillard was kind enough to say in a review in the *THES* that the series 'will be of the utmost value to all scholars, politicians, diplomats and journalists with a professional interest in why some international crises are resolved by war rather than by negotiation'. If only a very few politicians and journalists read only one or two of the volumes something will have been gained in international understanding.

I felt that the two aims were not contradictory or mutually exclusive. The author would usually view his task in writing the volume as a purely academic one – the acceptance of a challenge to get at the truth of one particular historic tragedy. But the very fact that his search was an impartial and dispassionate one would validate his work in the more general context.

Anthony Short's splendid book on *The Origins of the Vietnam War* takes us from the early days when the American government at first genuinely wanted to mediate between the French and the Vietminh, to the culminating tragedy of full-scale American involvement. Mr Short shows that de Gaulle's government believed Vietnamese 'freedom' could be obtained within the French Union, and was unaware of the significance of the word 'independence' for the emerging third-world countries. The French never used the word 'independence' with regard to Vietnam, and in this respect showed a greater inability to adjust to the post-war world than that displayed by the British. On the other hand Short makes it clear that the Americans (notably Acheson) went through a process of thought with regard to Nationalist China, and the probable ultimate success of communism there, with the Communists exploiting a revolutionary spirit in the midst of the poverty and misery of centuries. But the Americans failed to recognize an analogy between what was happening in China and what was likely to happen in Vietnam.

As the thunder clouds of the cold war gathered, the Americans evolved their domino theory, and in Short's interpretation their attitude emerges as something akin to the attitude of Christendom during the crusades of the middle ages: the infidel must at all cost be stopped. But the Communists, for their part, also believed in a 'just war'. Short shows that the 'just war' concept was used by Khrushchev in a speech in 1961 with reference to Algeria, but at a time when the USSR was sending military help to Laos. In Short's words, 'All members of his administration were apparently directed by Kennedy to read the Khrushchev speech and to consider what it portended'. If the ideological clash between the two worlds was thus in as uncomplicated a form as it had been since at least 1792, it would still be facile to assume that a confrontation in South-East Asia was in some way inevitable. When, by the summer of 1964, Johnson had in Short's words 'reached the point where the decisions would finally have to be made, whether to fight or to let Vietnam go', the second option was still open. Some individual political figures realized that wrong paths were being taken. All too often they were in a small minority, but that they existed at all shows, once again, that the human mind and imagination could prevent the 'inevitable' if it were present at the right time, in the right place, with the right powers. When Johnson in 1964 finally seemed ready to launch major American intervention in Vietnam, Short tells us that Senator Morse said: 'We should never have gone in. We should never have stayed. We should get out.' But the men in power – Johnson and his advisers – lacked the will, or the imagination, or the ability, to assess the possible consequences of their decisions.

A lack of imagination in political leaders is emerging in this series as a very common factor in the outbreak of war. Often it takes the form of an excessive optimism about the ease with which ends can be achieved. The Prussians in 1792, the Russians in 1904, the Germans in 1914, believed that a quick victory was attainable. Such a belief is often linked with the fear that there is danger in missing an opportunity. The need for a pre-emptive war is often given as the justification for aggression. Again the Germans in 1914 claimed that Russian armament was proceeding so quickly that Germany could not afford to postpone the conflict. The Israelis may claim that they have fought pre-emptive warfare successfully – though this may be true only in the short term. A policy which would secure more permanent peace takes a correspondingly greater leap of the imagination. Sometimes a lack of imagination leads to a simple miscalculation. Anthony Short quotes the American Assistant Secretary of State, Chester Bowles, declaring, with reference to intervention in Laos, 'that America was going to have to fight China anyway in 2, 3, 5 or 10 years' time, and it was just a question of where, when and how'. That was 27 years ago.

But if American administrations at least avoided war with China once the Korean war was over, they regarded involvement in Vietnam more lightheartedly, in spite of warnings like that of Democratic Senator Russell, who is quoted by Short as saying: 'it was going to be one of the worst things this country ever got into', or Vice-Admiral Davis who wrote: 'One cannot go over Niagara Falls in a barrel only slightly'.

But I am yielding too readily to the temptation of quoting from the text which follows – a text which adds impressively to the value of the series which I have the privilege of editing.

HARRY HEARDER

PREFACE AND
ACKNOWLEDGEMENTS

As a temporary soldier in Malaya in 1948 I became more immediately aware, through some contact with the French navy and listening to the immensely confident French broadcasts from Saigon, of the war that had started in Vietnam. Fifteen years later, in January 1963, by coincidence again in Malaya, sharing a bivouac during an exercise of the Jungle Warfare School with an American colonel, John Paul Vann, rekindled my interest in what was happening in Vietnam, and at the same time, abruptly changed my perspective. John Vann, one of the most remarkable and impressive men I have met, had, a few hours before, taken part in that shameful fiasco of a battle at Ap-Bac which, like many that followed, was declared to be a victory for government forces. The reality, described by Vann, who later died in Vietnam, was very different and was a direct challenge to the assumptions and comparisons I had made.

At that time I was engaged in a study of the communist insurrection in Malaya, a comparatively small and self-contained war in a colonial context, and it subsequently became obvious to me that the struggle in Vietnam was of an entirely different order. What the American dimension would be had not yet become clear when General Westmoreland visited Kuala Lumpur the following year but the overwhelming impression was of the power of an immense American war machine that was about to engage itself when it had found the co-ordinates and could quantify the data of the Malayan experience as a means to this end. Again, it was impressive; somewhat mechanical; and rather frightening.

What happened in the end, what good, if any, came of it and the lessons to be drawn are questions that are still being discussed but a question which is almost as difficult to answer, because it is spread over such a long period, is when and how the war began. As with Scottish hills the approach may seem interminable, and rather wet, but almost before one realizes it the climb, and the struggle, has started.

Professor Harry Hearder and Longman, who suggested the ascent, must often have wished they had not, or at least, that a shorter route had been taken. One similar perhaps, to that of Professor George Herring who has dealt with the entire war in a masterpiece of compression and lucidity without losing any of the salient features. I am particularly grateful to him for an early, and continuing, source of information and ideas and wish also to record my thanks to a number of people who have contributed to my understanding of what happened in Vietnam; the misunderstandings, of course, are entirely my fault and responsibility. Individually, they are: Professor David Anderson, Sir James Cable, Mr Dacre Cole, Dr Vince Demma, Professor William Duiker, Dr Dennis Duncanson, Mr Michael Forrestal, Professor Gary Hess, Dr Edward Keefer, Mr Charles B. MacDonald, Dr Douglas Pike, Professor Douglas Ross, the Honorable Dean Rusk, the Honorable Blair Seaborn, Dr Ralph Smith, Colonel Herb Schandler, Colonel Hugh Toye, Professor William Turley, Dr Stein Tønnesson, John Cloake and Professor Geoffrey Warner.

Institutionally, I have to thank the staff of the great American Presidential Libraries in Abilene, Austin and Boston: particularly Dr David Humphrey. The National Archives in Washington: in particular Mrs Sally Marks and Dr John Taylor. The Public Record Office in London; the Library of the Department of External Affairs, Ottawa; and the Queen Mother Library of Aberdeen University, notably Mrs Gillian Johnston. Aberdeen University, The British Academy, The Carnegie Trust and the Canadian High Commission were all kind enough to support my travel and research and it is a pleasure to acknowledge the generous hospitality of Mrs Margaret Learnard in Washington, Professor and Mrs Joseph Silverstein at Princeton, and Dr and Mrs Michael Leifer in London. My thanks, too, to all of them for their encouragement. Undergraduate and postgraduate students, both of Aberdeen and the freemasonry of the Public Record Office, have either corrected or ungrudgingly shared ideas and information. My former student, Dr Myles Robertson, went out of his way in attempting to standardize the wilder inconsistencies of the manuscript. Mrs Catherine Walker has borne the brunt of the typing and my wife, Agnes, thinned out some of the denser thickets and has put up with the moods and bad temper of a much less fluent writer.

Dunbar Hall
Old Aberdeen

Age after age their tragic empires rise,
Built while they dream, and in that dreaming weep.

(Hymn 84, *The Church Hymnary*)

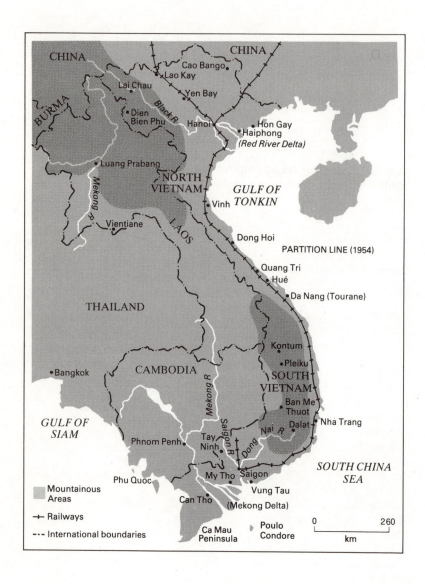

PROLOGUE

It is now a little over a hundred years since Vietnam had its first, major impact on Western politics. On 31 March 1885, three days after reports of a French military disaster in Tonkin had reached Paris, the French government fell. Thus ended the ministerial fortunes of Jules Ferry, already known as 'le Tonkinois'; but this setback to the Tonkin expedition, while it had helped to bring down his government, had done nothing to diminish the importance of this, the most northerly part of Vietnam. 'Marseilles and Toulon', Ferry proclaimed, 'would be defended quite as much in the China seas as in the Mediterranean.' And, in justifying the strategic importance of France's colonial possessions, and in calling his fellow countrymen to greatness, he declared, 'Nations, in our time, are great only according to the activity they develop; it is not by the peaceful extension of institutions that they are great any more . . . . Extension without acting, without becoming involved in the affairs of the world . . . is to abdicate, and in a shorter time than you would believe possible to descend from the first rank to third or fourth'.

By 1885 France was, in fact, consolidating her position in Vietnam, her most populous and perhaps most important overseas possession. Seventy years earlier her domination of Europe and what certainly passed as a Napoleonic empire had ended at Waterloo; and although her immediate, and in a sense, tactical political interests were first diverted by opportunities that lay nearer to hand in North Africa, French interest in Vietnam had existed since the time of Louis XIV. Much of the practical interest was kept alive by the French church which, from time to time, had got itself involved in political as well as in literary affairs. Indeed, French clerical support in the shape of a small unofficial expedition mounted from Pondicherry, a French possession in India, had already been given to a deposed prince, Nguyen Anh who, restored to power, proclaimed himself Emperor Gia Long.

His mentor, the man to whom he owed his life, Pigneau Behaine,

1

bishop of Adran, had returned to Vietnam in support of his protégé ten days after the French Revolution had begun. His interests, like most of the Society of Foreign Missions, were supposedly religious: the conversion of rulers and their subjects. In practice, it proved impossible to separate religious and political activities. Already, by the 17th century, in addition to a prodigiously successful conversion rate, French priests were sometimes involved in arms procurement for their various clients although the European presence became not so much an assault upon, as an undermining of, traditional Vietnamese society.

When Nguyen Anh proclaimed himself Emperor Gia Long in 1802 and founded the last of the Vietnamese dynasties which would continue until the abdication of the Emperor Bao Dai in 1945, it was both a supreme achievement and a supreme irony. It was, as Woodside points out, the first time in history that a single Vietnamese court governed a united polity that stretched from the Kwangsi–Yunnan border all the way south to the Gulf of Siam. Hitherto the predecessors of the Nguyen dynasty had never truly controlled both the Red River delta and the Mekong delta simultaneously. In 1802 it can be said that the Vietnamese state stood on the brink of a golden age unparalleled since the late 15th century.[1] For the Nguyen dynasty, once in power, the supreme purpose was the perfection of the Confucian state in a land which already gave the appearance of 'a miniature Chinese civilisation'.[2] From its court ceremonial to its Chinese-style law code the Vietnamese imperial system was 'a calculated imitation of the more useful institutional features of the Ch'ing empire'.[3] From the imperial palace at Hué, itself a replica of the Forbidden City at Peking, 'the Mandarin road' conveyed imperial couriers to the northern capital of Hanoi and south to the frontier lands and the southern capital of Saigon. The sophisticated dyke systems of Tonkin, in themselves a mark of the 'hydraulic civilisation' of China, were repaired; and French mercenary volunteers stayed on to help build the walls around the citadel at Hué as well as other fortifications. They represented the public works of a court and society which, however, has been condemned for its inability to conceive of any civilization other than that of the Celestial Empire and which deliberately shut its eyes to the outside world and the immense progress being made by Western people in science and technology.[4] The supreme irony, therefore, lies in the fact that while under Gia Long's chosen successor, his fourth son, the Emperor Minh Mang, appeared to preside over the incipient consolidation of the Vietnamese state, at the same time he was presiding over its incipient dissolution. Already, within it, it contained the intellectual if not the political seeds of its own destruction.

Anything which challenged the intellectual premises of the Confucian state challenged its authority. The principal challenge came in the doctrines of Christianity and in the form of the French missionaries of the Catholic church. In spite of native converts, Christianity was obviously a foreign idea and one that was in association with foreign powers which might occasionally be of service to one dynasty or another but from whom demands were to be expected. That exposure to foreign influence might be disruptive to the bases of the Confucian state had been seen when the young prince who had accompanied Pigneau to Paris refused, after his return, to prostrate himself before the altar of his ancestors. This particular prince died before he could succeed the Emperor Gia Long and, in his place, the Emperor Minh Mang was notably less sympathetic to Christian beliefs and their foreign associates. In 1825 Christianity was proscribed by what was in effect an exclusion act and, although not applied consistently, more general persecution followed a few years later. Had it succeeded in removing the handful of Catholic missionaries from Vietnam, preventing their return and excluding others, and in confining the existing Christian villages to tolerable limits in their departure from prevailing beliefs and behaviour, then the policy might have been effective at least for a while in sealing off Vietnam and in maintaining isolation: a theme that was common to China and Japan, as well as to Korea whose uncertain relationship with the Chinese empire resembled that of Vietnam itself. Minh Mang is reported to have studied Japanese policy as a model of exclusion[5]; but his great fault, says Buttinger, was not that he abandoned the allegedly pro-western cause of his father but that he failed to recognize that after 1820 non-involvement had become obsolete as a defensive policy against the West.

> In an entirely new world of international activity, and against previously
> unknown dangers that threatened Asia from the West, Vietnam's policy
> toward Europe remained in fact fundamentally unchanged. What
> Gia Long had preached while France was non-existent as a political
> and military factor outside of Europe, Minh-mang and his successors,
> Thieu Tri and Tu Duc, tried to practise against a France that soon was
> able to destroy Vietnamese harbours and warships at will.[6]

That France had such a military capacity was soon to be shown. Whether she had the intention to use it had yet to be proved; nor could she be said to have had the occasion. However, when the direction of policy becomes obvious, occasions often suggest themselves; and in the first half of the 19th century a major factor in France's relations with Vietnam seems to have been frustration. Attempts to persuade the Vietnamese court to enter into either commercial or political relationships with France were rejected and requests to receive a French consul were repeatedly refused. On the other hand, from a Vietnamese point of view, it might be argued that the French were importunate rascals; and, already, by 1825, in the final report reaching Paris of one of the Emperor's French 'mandarins', one finds the ominous conclusion and the principle that would be familiar for the next 150 years that, in order to obtain the necessary concessions, armed force was indispensable. Before that policy became fact, however, a cause for concern to both sides presented itself. A revolt that began in Saigon against the Emperor and his policies was supported by large numbers of Christian Vietnamese, as well as by Siam, but ended with defeat and death for practically all who had taken part or were taken prisoner. An exception was the unfortunate Father Marchand, a French priest, who not only represented the perverse and proscribed religion of the Europeans 'which corrupts the heart of man', but open rebellion as well. After atrocious torture he was put to death: to become a symbol of outrage for Catholic France and, for imperial Vietnam, a somewhat lesser symbol but practical reminder that 'a philosophy which rejected Fate altogether . . . therefore presented a challenge to the whole of Vietnamese civilisation.'[7]

Outrage in France, however, did not yet manifest itself in policy; but at a time when the government of King Louis Philippe was generally rather cool to the advancement of the Church's interests in Vietnam, and when the Foreign Minister, M. Guizot, was a Protestant, the French navy maintained its reputation as a Catholic bastion and added to it an understandable desire that somewhere in the Far East there should be a port in which French ships could anchor in sight of French territory. Not only was this desirable in itself but also as a comparable mark of importance to the Dutch in the Indies, the Spanish in the Philippines, even the Portuguese at Macao; if not yet to the British who had already established themselves at Singapore, were now about to take Hong Kong and were on the point of monopolizing the China trade through enforced acquisition of facilities at a string of Chinese ports from Shanghai to Canton. Two years after a demonstration of ruthless acquisition and naval power had secured Britain the treaty of Nanking – signed on board a British warship which had penetrated three hundred miles up the Yangtze – a treaty which France also extracted from China, ensured the removal of all Chinese restrictions on the practice of Christianity. By this time, the Pope had already recognized France's primacy in the Far Eastern mission field and it was perhaps not unreasonable and certainly not unthinkable for her to imagine that the commercial and religious openings that had been conceded by China, 'the Greater Dragon', should also be made available by Vietnam, 'the Lesser Dragon'. Particularly since, at least when it suited her, Vietnam still acknowledged the tributary relationship to China.

Every two years or so French warships had been appearing off Tourane – better known today as Danang – the nearest port to the Imperial capital at Hué and had engaged in 'demonstrations' on behalf of imprisoned or tormented missionaries. Considering the opportunities that had opened up in China, it was desirable from a French point of view that a French fleet should now be stationed in the Far East; although the question of where they were to find a base had still not been answered. One possibility that was recommended by the French navy depended on support for a rival claimant to the Vietnamese throne who could count on Christian converts in the North; and, although this was not accepted, the French government was now prepared to authorize the navy 'to afford protection to French missionaries threatened with personal violence' but only 'if it could be done without involving the French flag in any altercation'.

French naval officers in the area had already engaged in rescuing French missionaries from Vietnam – some of whom withdrew the better to return – and the case of one of them, Monseigneur Lefèbvre, under sentence of death, provided the occasion for further intervention. This time there was no happy outcome and, unaware that M. Lefèbvre had been released and had already left the country, having waited two weeks at Tourane for an answer from the Emperor and having already as a precaution immobilized five Vietnamese corvettes in the proximity, the French ships eventually opened fire: apparently under the impression that they were themselves about to be attacked.

Probably, as has been suggested, it will never be known for certain who fired the first shot[8]; and almost a hundred years later another French cruiser opened fire at Haiphong under not entirely dissimilar circumstances and caused even heavier casualties in the immediate prologue to the outbreak of the first Vietnamese war. But on this occasion, and in this early example of what might charitably be called prophylactic fire, it was virtually an end in itself.[9] The French ships withdrew leaving the French missionaries and the Christian converts to their unhappy fate and the Emperor at Hué in paroxysms. Nevertheless, aware of the encroaching European presence in Asia, his predecessor, Minh Mang, had sent an embassy to Paris in 1840 with the offer of exclusive trading rights in exchange for a defence agreement. Had it been accepted it would have had intriguing possibilities and could have cast France in the role of defender of Vietnamese independence against neighbouring kingdoms such as Siam or even Britain, rather than that of predator; but in the event Catholic feeling in France ensured that it got nowhere.[10]

Perhaps French naval intervention would have taken place sooner had not two French warships been wrecked in the course of a clandestine operation to put missionaries ashore in Korea in the summer of 1847. As it was, under mounting clerical pressure at home to do something about the new wave of Christian persecution in Vietnam, ten years later the government of Louis Napoleon was moving towards a new policy even before what Hall has called 'a piece of crass stupidity' on the part of the Emperor Tu Duc which would afford France the pretext for an international response: although in this case the only other power involved was Spain.[11] The execution of the Spanish Bishop of Tonkin, Mgr Diaz, at any rate focused attention once again on the disorders of Vietnam. A few years earlier it was claimed that Christians were implicated in a rebellion in Tonkin, led by the Emperor's disaffected brother, and this had led to the execution of two more French priests. At that time France itself was still in a period of transition from the disorders of 1848 but, as Cady puts it, the advent of the Second Empire in 1852 had marked a decisive stage in the development of French policy towards Vietnam.[12]

A mood of intervention may indeed be sensed although not so much in the character of the Emperor Louis Napoleon himself. His entourage, however, seemed always ready to quarrel on matters of protocol and, on the matter of the unfortunate Mgr Diaz, Louis Napoleon's Spanish-born Empress, Eugénie, who, as a girl, had known the Bishop in Andalusia, was likewise in favour of intervention. One who would also have known the Bishop but who certainly did not know Vietnam, having never been there, was Abbé Huc, a former missionary in western China, described by Cady as 'the principal protagonist of a forward French policy in Annam'.

In a secret memorandum prepared for Louis Napoleon in January, 1857, Huc argued that the Pigneau de Behaine treaty of 1787 gave France an incontestable right to occupy the port of Tourane, an action which could easily become the beginning of a new and glorious role for France in the Far East. The occupation, he said, could be achieved by French forces already in the Far East. The suffering Annamite population would receive the French as liberators and benefactors, and only a short time would be required to make them entirely Catholic. France must move quickly, however, because the English already had their eyes on Tourane.

Huc's proposal was first submitted to the keeper of the archives at the French Foreign Office, Pierre Cintrat, for examination. On March 20 Cintrat came up with a strongly negative opinion. He reported that France had never fulfilled its part of the 1787 bargain; seizure of Tourane would therefore be an act of war without legal justification and one which could entail for France ruinous embarrassment and costs far exceeding the advantages to be realised. He expressed the opinion that France already had enough interests abroad to engage their energies without throwing itself into a hazardous and largely profitless venture in the centre of the China sea.[13]

The 'special commission' on Vietnam to whom this opinion was referred concluded that no rights in fact existed under the unexecuted treaty of 1787 but 'the opportunity to act was afforded France by her association with the movement on behalf of progress, civilization, and commercial expansion for which China was going to be the principal theatre'.[14] The commission recommended, therefore, that the three principal ports of Indo-China be occupied as chastisement for the treatment of French missionaries. A few months later Louis Napoleon was presented with a petition which declared that the preservation of Christianity in Annam was at stake and, in asking that the memorandum be forwarded to the Foreign Minister's office for examination, Cady concludes that 'Louis Napoleon was obviously preparing to use the forces sent to the Far East under cover of joint intervention with Britain in China to gain the long-sought French foothold in Annam'.[15]

In the event, the decision to mount the French expedition to Vietnam, in which the Spanish were subsequently invited to join, was taken before news of Mgr Diaz's death had reached Paris; and it is significant that, instead of being dealt with by the French Foreign Ministry, it was handled by the Minister of Marine. The objective was to establish a French protectorate over Cochinchina (the southern part of Vietnam); but while the taking of Tourane was to be the first step, it could, in any event, be held as a bargaining counter in exchange for a treaty that was to be extracted from the Imperial court at Hué.

Taking, and holding, Tourane was also to be the first and irretrievable step in Western commitment in Vietnam. Previous contacts were essentially skirmishes. French warships would appear, hostilities would often ensue and the ships would eventually withdraw: indeed they could hardly do otherwise. But such demonstrations were leading nowhere in Vietnam. In China, however, and in spite of occasional reverses, UK trading interests were being advanced by similar tactics even though they represented a challenge to a much greater, and potentially at least, much more powerful established order. Trading opportunities involved and to a large extent depended upon opium: which was perhaps just as likely to undermine Chinese society as any Western ideas or beliefs, but at least they did not require anything more than limited settlement. To begin with, too, in Vietnam limited French ambitions hardly seemed to require more than limited outlay although it was difficult to see what exactly would be involved.

As it happened, the Franco-Spanish force that arrived in Tourane in 1858 was mostly French but altogether incapable of reaching Hué, where, conceivably, it might have persuaded the Imperial court to make concessions. It was in fact incapable also of doing more than barely maintaining itself in Tourane after the decision was made to switch the point of attack to Saigon. This, too, was captured without great difficulty but, as in Tourane, there were none of the expected manifestations of popular support and, again, a small garrison was left behind when the fleet sailed back to Tourane. Here it once again failed to have any effect on the court of Hué with the result that the position was finally abandoned. The French fleet sailed on to take part in joint operations with the Royal Navy along the China coast which were offering much higher dividends, at least to Britain, and it was this relationship, part ally, part rival, which was one of the factors that kept French interest in Vietnam alive. The Tourane/Saigon expedition while not quite a fiasco could hardly be presented as a success or as something of great consequence. But if it failed completely then, in the opinion of the disgruntled French naval commander at Tourane, it would be the British who would move in to take over and France would once again be trailing behind.

This in itself was a possibility that aroused certain traditional French feelings, but an equally powerful argument was that French blood had already been shed and French lives were in danger: although, to be callous and as Buttinger points out,[16] 80 per cent of the French troops were in fact Senegalese and Algerians. Nevertheless, a French force had been left holding Saigon, French lives were in danger and by 1860 France was becoming accustomed to intervention. In an area and to some extent a pattern that is similar today, in that year French troops had also landed at Beirut after Maronite Christians had been massacred by Druze; and a spectacular demonstration of joint imperialism occurred when a substantial Anglo-French force, by way of reprisal and putting pressure on the Chinese empire, destroyed the Summer Palace at Peking. This violent opening up of the Chinese empire to Western contact was now to be repeated in Vietnam.

In a sense the French already had a commitment to a commitment – the garrison they had left behind at Saigon – and one which, given the direction of French policy and the forces that now became available from the China theatre, was unlikely to be liquidated. French power was no longer to be confined to what came out of the mouths of naval guns and a substantial French force fought by land and sea to occupy the surrounding provinces. To French surprise, but in part because the enfeebled imperial forces had lost control of the granary in the south and in part because they were threatened by rebellion in the north, the Emperor Tu Duc sued for peace and offered not only freedom of religion but the cession of three eastern provinces of Cochinchina. Skirmishes, however, were endemic, punctuated by rebellions on a larger scale and, already, there was the problem of conflict with the contiguous 'unoccupied' territories. This took France not only into the rest of Cochinchina but, claiming to have inherited rights and privileges from the court at Hué, into the neighbouring kingdom of Cambodia as well.

Where, and when, interests and resolution may have wavered in Paris or were diverted, for example, by the Mexican adventure, there were always a substantial number of activists, usually in the French

Navy, on the spot in Asia who were ready and anxious to keep up the momentum of French expansion. Among them was the heroic but impetuous figure of Lieutenant Garnier, an early exponent of manifest destiny, who believed that France had received a higher mission from Providence[17] and that with France now installed at one end of the Mekong river there were dazzling prospects, if not glittering prizes, if China could in fact be opened up by means of an inland waterway. The Mekong, unnavigable to the extent that one can hop across it in the dry season from one sand bank to another, and thus from Laos into Siam, unfortunately was not the river that would lead to China's unbolted back door; but, it became obvious, the Red River in Tonkin was.

In concluding a treaty with France the Emperor Tu Duc had, in spite of second thoughts, been prepared to sacrifice the South and allow the French to create their enlarged colony of Cochinchina, in order to hold on, as best he could, to the middle and the North. His country's independent but tenuous existence might have continued (although the example of Cambodia was unpromising) and with a different temperament perhaps some sort of accommodation might have been reached with France. Independence, however, or its formal equivalent of sovereignty, did not have the same conceptual sharpness in Asia as it did in Europe and the attraction, for the French, of Tonkin had always to be balanced by the question of how far they could go without bringing in the Chinese. Where French and Western incursions into Vietnam were transient, the presence and proximity of China was immutable. It may be that 'the Vietnamese in general regard the Chinese as their traditional enemy'[18] and that, in halting successive incursions of China's expansionist dynasties the Vietnamese had secured their own independence. But, whether or not the Vietnamese had, in the past, saved the whole of Southeast Asia from a gradual but unrelenting process of 'Han-hwa', or 'Han-isation',[19] from a Vietnamese point of view it was the French who were now attempting to reverse the natural flow by moving upwards through the narrow tube of Annam into the cone of the funnel and at some point, therefore, a collision was to be expected. Not least because, when China was able or inclined to assert herself, or Vietnam chose to acknowledge the relationship, the latter was seen not as a state in its own right but as a tributary of the Chinese Empire. Under mounting pressure from China, (at least for tactical reasons) the Vietnamese court now chose to reassert this relationship if not its dependence.

French exploration in the 1860s had already taken them up the Mekong into China and when they were published the accounts of this epic journey, comparable to that of Livingstone, aroused great interest in Paris. The author, eventually leading the expedition, was Lieutenant Garnier who, in the course of extricating his expedition via the Yangtze, after a period of over two years, met up with an equally remarkable character, Jean Dupuis, a French entrepreneur who had adopted Chinese customs and traded in guns or salt with equal facility. When Dupuis, after a gun-running trip from Hanoi to Yunnan, under more or less official Chinese auspices, found himself in difficulty he appealed to the French in Saigon for assistance. The Emperor Tu Duc, for the opposite reason, did likewise. Again, as far as France was concerned, it was an extraordinary opportunity. Lieutenant Garnier was dispatched with the ostensible purpose of removing Dupuis; but in spite of the size of his expeditionary force – he had less than 200 men – he may well have been entrusted with more ambitious projects. At any rate, after a propaganda battle with the local Vietnamese authorities, Vietnamese fears and suspicions would have been confirmed when Garnier's force stormed the citadel and routed what was apparently a garrison of 7,000 men.

There then began what was called one of the most remarkable episodes of French colonial history.

> In about three weeks a region containing 2 m. inhabitants and a number of fortified towns was subdued by a force which never exceeded 180 men, commanded by officers none of whom, apart from Garnier himself, was older than 25. Some of their exploits would sound hardly credible if they were not admitted to be historical fact. Thus for instance the citadel of Ninh-Binh, defended by 1700 soldiers, surrendered to a canoe load of seven Frenchmen. It was as if the Vietnamese were hypnotised by the spell of these terrible invaders.[20]

Whether they were or not, or whether they were demoralized by a bombardment from French gunboats there must, on the French side, have been an equally terrible contempt for the fighting qualities of the Vietnamese forces, if not for the extraordinary irregular Chinese forces who were operating in Tonkin, the Black Flags. These veterans of the Taiping and other rebellions in China characterized the endemic disorders of Tonkin: the absence of government, tribal disaffections, an uncertain frontier and an equally uncertain relationship between China and Vietnam. In almost his last words, it is said that Garnier identified the Black Flags as the only real enemy that France had to face in Tonkin. A few minutes later, having misjudged his distances and his bravery notwithstanding, the 'Great Mandarin Garnier' as he had styled himself, was cut down by them, his head and his heart removed from his body, and his assailants believed, mistakenly, that they had dispatched the son-in-law of the Emperor of France.

Garnier's impetuosity, although almost certainly connived at, was officially disowned in what might be regarded as an exercise in higher statesmanship. Intent on consolidating in the south and with a government in Paris that was not yet prepared for the entailed risks of Garnier's exploits, the French withdrew from Tonkin in exchange for a treaty which appeared to recognize the 'legitimacy' of their possessions in Cochinchina.

This treaty of 'peace, friendship, and perpetual alliance' was signed at Hué on 15 March 1874. French sovereignty over Cochinchina was confirmed and, nominally, the Red River was open to navigation while Christianity became a permissible option for the Emperor's subjects. Leaving behind, in the course of a controversial evacuation of the territory which had been obtained by Garnier's exploits, essentially defenceless Christian communities, it was perhaps not surprising that they once again suffered under the vengeance that was exacted on 'collaborators' with the French. On the day that Nam Dinh was handed over, 14 neighbouring Christian villages were burned and the total eventually reached several hundred.[21] Nevertheless, a French Resident was to be permitted at the court of Hué; it was agreed that Imperial foreign policy would be aligned to that of France; but French military assistance was qualified in that it could only be given upon Imperial request.

Did this constitute a French protectorate? In so far as it was a matter of custom, as much as of law, the issue was now complicated by the fact that the Emperor in Hué chose to send, once again, tributary missions to Peking. France itself was diffident enough not to raise the matter with its chargé-d'affaires in Peking for over a year and although the issue seems to have been skirted, on both sides, it was becoming a matter of far more than academic interest. The Chinese Marquis T'seng in his European mission had already reminded the French Foreign Minister that Vietnam was a vassal of China. As the evidence of impending French operations in Tonkin grew he wrote again, on 10 November 1880, from St Petersburg to a new Minister of Foreign Affairs in Paris:

> I need not tell Your Excellency that the Chinese Government could not look with indifference on operations which would tend to alter the political situation of a country on its frontier, like the kingdom of Tongking, whose ruler down to the present day has received his investiture from the Emperor of China.[22]

The French position was that in the treaty of 1874 they had recognized 'the entire independence' of the ruler of Vietnam as regards any foreign power and had promised him aid and assistance to maintain peace and order in his dominion and to defend him against any attack. Conditions were not mentioned – it might be assumed he would get French assistance whether he wanted it or not – and when, in the uncertainty of these relationships, the new French Foreign Minister, M. Gambetta, asserted on New Year's Day 1882 that 'Vietnam was formerly a Chinese dependency' it was a misreading of an earlier Chinese message which read 'Vietnam has been for a long time a Chinese dependency'.

Whether or not France chose to confront China in the last quarter of the 19th century it was, without any doubt, Vietnam which drew the two countries into war and for the next hundred years established a context if not an extra dimension to the origins of war in and about Vietnam. The outcome of the Tonkin affair therefore has to be seen as much in a relationship between France and China as between France and Vietnam. Indeed, one might argue that, for the moment, Vietnam was itself only of secondary importance. To begin with, at least, it is the mood and impetus of French imperialism which must be considered.

In the early 1870s Garnier's intentions, no matter how widely acclaimed in France, hardly represented a national impulse towards further territorial acquisition. Ten years later, in what was a virtual reprise, French national sentiment may be said to have been aroused to the point where exploits or misadventures such as his were to be sustained rather than disowned. What had happened in the interval takes on the form of and can best be explained as France's recovery, moral and material, from the national disaster of 1870. When it came, this 'manifestation of the desire for rehabilitation, of the yearning to regain the former great power status, became almost a ritual in public gatherings, in political meetings, during scholarly banquets and the like',[23] and the desire for self-assertion and for assertion to the world remained powerful enough to impart strong impulses to imperialism: to the point where colonization and imperialism were regarded as a means of moral and national regeneration. As Cady puts it: 'By 1880 imperialism and patriotism were virtually synonymous.'

If only in view of her reluctance to disengage from empire it would seem important to establish the principal motive of French imperialism, at least in the later 19th century, and although one hesitates to contradict the assertion of Professor Duiker, who has made formidable contributions to Vietnamese studies, and without wishing to venture into the conceptual controversies of imperialism, one must at least look twice at the proposition 'From the beginning there was little question that the primary objectives of French colonial policy in Indo-China were economic'.[24] Perhaps that simple, and misleading, assertion is to be understood in a certain way. More particularly, because a few lines further on there is the apparent contradiction that 'for officials in Paris the main purpose of the French colonial venture in Southeast Asia could only be to enhance national security and prestige'. Compared at least to the weight of other received opinion about the nature of French imperialism there would seem to be little evidence of mercantile adventurers which would account for French involvement in Vietnam. After the event, an imperial adventurer such as Jules Ferry would, as Zeldin points out, develop a neo-mercantilist doctrine to justify his actions and to argue that France needed colonies for her economic growth and her political prestige but, in fact, just as Britain acquired much of her empire at the very time when colonies were considered to be useless, so France acquired hers when population was falling, her colonial trade minute and her people had practically no interest in overseas expansion.[25]

It seems more likely, as Dr Christopher Andrew suggests and as the French colonialists themselves complained, that the most characteristic attitude of French business towards colonial expansion in general was indifference; that the French colonialist movement represents the highest stage, not of French capitalism, but of French nationalism.[26] 'France' said Zeldin, 'exported its national pride in its most arrogant form, undiluted by universalism and its capacity for self-doubt; it was a similar national pride which rose up to expel it from its colonies'.[27]

To return from the general to the particular, the treaty of 1874 had given France a foothold in Tonkin. A small number of French garrisons was each to be limited to 100 men. When more than double this number arrived at Hanoi on two French ships from Saigon it was an obvious violation of the agreement. It could be, and indeed was, argued that the disorders of Tonkin required an enhanced French presence and when the conquest of Tonkin was fully under way Prime Minister Ferry argued its necessity because of the potential threat to Cochinchina from such an unfriendly and turbulent neighbour.[28] Power, as Acton also observed, 'tends to expand indefinitely, and will transcend all barriers, abroad and at home, until met by superior forces'. In the case of Vietnam at this time most of the counter force in one form or another was provided, intermittently, by the Chinese Empire of which, it will be remembered, Vietnam was still considered to be a part. In 1883 Captain Rivière's repeat performance of Lieutenant Garnier's exploits ended in the same way: he was killed in action against Black Flag guerrillas who were operating with at least the tacit approval of the Imperial courts in Peking and Hué. Even before this untoward event the French had begun a campaign of remarkable savagery with the wholesale hanging of Chinese mercenary prisoners from the yard-arms of their ships. After Rivière's death the French responded with an equally remarkable ultimatum, from Commissioner-General Harmand, which seems utterly to confirm Zeldin's attribution of 'national pride in its most arrogant form'.

> We could, for we have the means, destroy your dynasty from top to bottom down to its very roots, and seize for ourselves all the kingdom as we have done in Cochinchina. You will be perfectly aware that this would present no difficulty to us. You are incapable of putting up a serious resistance to our armies . . . you are at our mercy. We have the power to seize and destroy your capital and to cause you all to die of starvation. You have to choose between war and peace. We do not wish to conquer you, but you must accept our protectorate. For your people it is a guarantee of peace and prosperity: it is also the

only chance of survival for your Government and your Court. We give you forty-eight hours to accept or reject, in their entirety and without discussion, the terms which in our magnanimity we offer you. We are convinced that there is nothing in them dishonourable to you, and, if carried out with sincerity on both sides, they will bring happiness to the people of Vietnam. If you reject them, you must expect the greatest evils. Imagine the most frightful things conceivable, and you will still fall short of the truth. The Dynasty, its Princes and its Court will have pronounced sentence on themselves. The name of Vietnam will no longer exist in history.[29]

Backed up by the now familiar bombardment, a new Emperor in Hué was persuaded to sign a treaty which gave France a comprehensive protectorate: extensive rights to intervention in Annam and complete control of Tonkin. There remained, however, not only the disputed question of Chinese suzerainty but the matter of Chinese forces which might be encountered in Tonkin. Partition was unacceptable to the French; neither side could agree a neutral zone. And the French minister was warning that China was prepared to fight. It was a risk, although French ministers denied its existence, which the French Assembly for the most part was prepared to take. Success in Vietnam now depended on the defeat of Chinese forces. At the same time, paradoxically, it was something which would be much more difficult to achieve if the French were to engage not only Chinese regular forces but a spirit of Chinese resistance which, with comparatively unlimited space and numbers at its disposal, might have been of an entirely different order of magnitude from that hitherto encountered in Vietnam. Both sides were now building up their forces and in December 1883, after due notice had been given, French forces attacked the citadel at Son-tay, one of the principal Chinese bases in Tonkin, and regarded by them as a key to the defence of Yunnan. On this occasion, after heavy fighting, and with superior French firepower, the fortress was captured at the cost of under 100 French dead but more than 1,000 killed on the Chinese side. It prompted superb Chinese defiance, rhetorically at least the equal of Harmand's ultimatum, and, more ominously, the entry of some 12,000 Chinese troops from Yunnan. Other things being equal, then, the French were now faced with at least a potentially formidable adversary. What were the costs of an encounter likely to be and would they prove acceptable?

At this point one may note interesting but ultimately perhaps rather promiscuous historical parallels with American as well as French policy in 20th-century Vietnam. For example, it began to look expensive. With parliament having a remarkably tight hold on the appropriations that were necessary to sustain French policy, it was necessary for the government, usually in the person of Jules Ferry, to make increasingly frequent public requests. Even before they were in serious difficulties with China the question of how much French policy cost came up twice in the course of one week in December 1883 when an appropriation of 9 m. francs was debated and was followed by a request for a further 20 m. When the assertion that French honour was at stake was made, patriotic arguments always carried the day although there were some, like Clemençeau, who claimed that French colonial expansion was not only contrary to revolutionary principles but that it was weakening French defences in Europe. Most of the 25,000 troops in the Far East were in fact Algerian, which may have weakened this argument, but another one soon developed when the French foreign minister, perhaps unwisely, said that France was at war with Annam. If so, said his opponents, it was a violation of the constitution because only parliament could declare war and, moreover, as it looked as if France was becoming involved in a war with China, they had not been kept properly informed.

Ferry, like President Johnson, claimed 'It is not I who first undertook an enterprise which is based on national traditions.' 'Tonkin' he said, 'was not a personal affair for one Minister or another . . . from the beginning to the end it is a French affair and a national question.' On a later occasion he turned on his outspoken critic in the Senate, the Duc de Broglie, and told him to 'stop repeating that we are conducting an arbitrary, capricious, colonial policy. We are conducting, in this affair, the colonial policy to which the precedent created by you yourself condemned us.'[30] By then, in spite of what might be called a local success in Vietnam, France was in real difficulties. The local success was in two parts. In Tien-Tsin the ascendant 'peace party' in the person of Li Hung-Chang agreed to recognize all existing and future treaties between France and Vietnam. By implication, at least, this meant that Chinese claims were renounced and in a symbolic act 'the most important physical symbol of Chinese suzerainty . . . a seal presented 80 years ago to Gia Long, the founder of the dynasty, by his overlord the Emperor Chia Ch'ing' was ceremonially destroyed.[31] The difficulties arose out of the way in which the agreement between France and China was put into effect; and at about the same time as the Emperor's seal was being melted down French troops, attempting to enforce the evacuation from Tonkin of their Chinese counterparts (acting with what was later excused as 'patriotic haste') suffered a bloody nose at the hands of Chinese armed with Remingtons and retired with over twenty dead. It was obvious that in China there had been serious second thoughts about the Tien-Tsin treaty; and with Li Hung-Chang under threat of impeachment and with the new Chinese negotiating instructions being, 'The most important thing is that the King of Vietnam should continue to be enfeoffed by Us and to pay Us tribute', it was obvious that this was a very fragile agreement. France demanded the immediate evacuation of Chinese forces from Tonkin, plus an indemnity of 200 m. francs.

One commentator on these events[32] says it is a little hard to understand why Ferry was so rash, for such an ultimatum, if it were refused, was certain to lead to war. It was just possible that the true story had been withheld from the premier by those most anxious to move energetically. But it seems more likely, as Power concludes, that the Bac-le 'ambush' had become a matter of French prestige; French honour was at stake and it was difficult to stop short. Nevertheless, Power concludes, (writing in 1944) that all his advisers and Ferry himself misjudged China's will and capacity to resist, even though Ferry himself realized that his local commander, Admiral Courbet, was 'devoured by a desire for glory' and would do anything he could 'to lead us to Peking'.

Having ruled out that option, the problem for France, rather like that of Britain in the Crimean War, was how and where she could strike at her adversary and affect his policy. Another implicit question was whether France could ever command sufficient force to impose herself on China. While the Chinese could hardly have accepted with equanimity the bombardment of Foochow, the destruction of a Chinese fleet and a rather abortive French operation in and against the island of Formosa, (the possession of whose coal mines anticipated a later French demand for 'productive guarantees' from Weimar Germany) nevertheless these actions had no effect whatever on China's continuing refusal to pay anything at all by way of indemnity for an action which the Chinese attributed to French folly. 'We are not', said Ferry, 'in a state of war with China: we are in a state of negotiation.' To which one of his critics added 'With cannon-balls!' A couple of months later Ferry allowed that France was 'recalling China to the observation of its international duties'.

Throughout the autumn of 1884 there was deadlock. In early 1885, with a new and energetic French War Minister and the French army having taken over command of operations in Tonkin from the navy, a Chinese force was defeated and after another engagement the French captured the border citadel at Lang Son. Encouraged by this success the French commander decided to push on and, having crossed the border into Kwangsi, ran into what might be called an ambush on a large scale. Nothing loath, the French general mustered all his forces and again advanced towards the symbolically named 'Gate of China'. This time, after a two-day battle, and after the general himself was wounded, an alcohol-induced decision of his subordinate led to the abandonment of Lang Son and a wholesale but temporary French retreat. News of this setback, together with messages which suggested that the army hoped to hold on to the Red River Delta, reached Paris when the government was already defending its policy in Tonkin. Whether one were to regard it as the Lang Son skirmish or a great national catastrophe – and there were those who went so far as to compare it to Waterloo – it produced at least the occasion for the overthrow of Ferry's government (it has been suggested that it was his domestic rather than colonial policy which consolidated the vote against him) and he went down to defeat having demanded an appropriation of 200 m. francs to enable France to avenge her honour.

It was not one of the Assembly's more heroic moments; and comparisons were made with much greater reverses that had been suffered in Algeria and even with contemporary reaction in the House of Commons to the fall of Khartoum. It was nevertheless an example of stoical reserve on the part of Ferry himself who, as a result of negotiating behind the back of the official French representative in China, knew that he was on the brink of success but had pledged to reveal nothing until the treaty was signed.

In one sense the treaty of Tien-Tsin that was signed in June 1885 between France and China was an anti-climax: it did little more than confirm the treaty that had been signed a year earlier. But this time the Chinese effectively and finally gave up their historic claims on Vietnam and withdrew their forces. To that extent at least the French objective had been realized. The tide of Chinese imperialism had gone out: that of French imperialism had come in. Yet, as McAleavy points out, the 'war party' in China, muddle-headed and ignorant as they had been, were right in believing that by protracted resistance China could exact a price which no French government could ask its people to pay. And that, after Ferry's collapse, it was quite inconceivable that any French government would have been voted the enormous increase in expenditure that would have been considered necessary for a full-scale war with China.[33] Had Chinese resistance continued it is conceivable that France would have withdrawn, at least temporarily, from Tonkin, based itself on Cochinchina, and hoped that it would not run into too many difficulties with what was left of Vietnamese power based on the court at Hué. As it was, both China and Vietnam were in a state of debility. For the time being France assumed the role that in the past had belonged to Vietnam: to define the southern limit of Chinese power. In short, France was now engaged in the containment of China; and her continuing success in Vietnam would depend in part upon the maintenance of this regional balance of power.

In spite of its asserted and demonstrated political differentiation from China as a state, Vietnam had succumbed to the same problems which had weakened China in its confrontation with the West. The old order was breaking down. A static if not stagnant society which was obsessed with the past was capable of spasms of resistance but in China, certainly, and in Vietnam probably, there was a feeling that foreign aggression had been made possible only by the weakening of dynastic leadership and efficiency.[34] Unlike China, Vietnam had the added misfortune that the enemy was not only within the gates but about to capture the citadel itself.

Studies of 19th-century Vietnam asking, explicitly or implicitly, what had weakened resistance to the French have noted that it was the French invasion which prompted the first serious proposals for internal reform in Vietnamese society.[35] One of the most prominent but ultimately unavailing series of reforms would have committed Vietnam to a policy not of protracted war but of protracted negotiation with the French. At the same time it was proposed that the Court should model itself on Thailand, rather than China, and send its ambassadors abroad to seek diplomatic support; military academies, perhaps run by Germans or British, would help to modernize the Vietnamese army; and, in effect, it was proposed that the Emperor should lead an institutional revolution in Vietnam.[36] In the event none of this happened and it was, ironically, not until peace had just been concluded between France and China and the last chance had gone of co-ordinated and effective Sino-Vietnamese operations, that the standard of royal resistance was raised when the young Emperor Ham Nghi was prevailed upon to flee from Hué and to provide at least a symbol of national resistance until he was finally captured and exiled to Algeria. The episode produced a sort of romantic and despairing royalism – *Can Vuong!*: Aid the King! – on a level, perhaps, with the Jacobite cause after Culloden; and although one may resist the assertion that, because it was 'ethno-centric without having any real concept of Vietnam as a nation state in competition with other nation states', it did not therefore qualify as authentic nationalism, it may be agreed that the causes of nationalism, revolution and resistance that were shortly to be found in the 20th century would be of an entirely different order.[37]

REFERENCES AND NOTES

1. Alexander Woodside, 'Vietnam, 1802–67' in David Joel Steinberg *et al. In Search of South East Asia* (New York 1971), p. 123.
2. King C. Chen, *Vietnam and China, 1938–54* (Princeton 1969), p. 3.
3. Woodside, op. cit.
4. Hoang Van Chi, *From Colonialism to Communism* (London 1964), p. 8. 'In reviewing Vietnam's history', says Hoang, 'one is forced to conclude that the Han culture, although beneficial to the Vietnamese in the beginning, eventually became, with the Chu Hi school of Confucianism, the formula which conditioned every brain to the same conventional mould, deterring all independent thought and all spirit of innovation. It must be seen as the main cause of the national disaster at the end of the last century. The submission of the Vietnamese to

western colonialism was in great measure the consequence of their long enslavement to China's fossilised culture.'

5. With added urgency after one of his French 'military advisers' presented him with a set of prints depicting Napoleon's victories.
6. Joseph Buttinger, *The Smaller Dragon* (London 1958), p. 274.
7. Ralph Smith, *Viet-nam and the West* (London 1968).
8. Stanley Karnow, *Vietnam. A History* (London 1983), p. 70.
9. In case one should be tempted to believe that the French reserved their violence for other people it may be remembered that a year later, in the upheavals in Paris, General Cavaignac slaughtered Frenchmen as he had Algerians: to the extent of some 3,000 civilian dead.
10. From Paris the mission went to London, where it was received by Lord Melbourne, but had no more effect.
11. D. G. E. Hall, *A History of South East Asia* (London 1958), p. 559.
12. John F. Cady, *The Roots of French Imperialism in Eastern Asia* (Cornell 1967). See also the recent study by Yoshiharu Tsuboï. *L'Empire Vietnamien Face à la France et à la Chine* (Paris 1987).
13. Cady, op. cit. pp. 178–9.
14. Ibid.
15. Ibid. p. 180.
16. Buttinger, op. cit. p. 348.
17. Quoted in Milton E. Osborne, *The French Presence in Cochinchina and Cambodia* (Cornell 1969).
18. Hoang Van Chi. op. cit. p. 6.
19. Ibid.
20. Henry McAleavy, *Black Flags in Vietnam: The Story of a Chinese Intervention* (London 1968).
21. Cady, op. cit. p. 287.
22. McAleavy, op. cit. p. 184.
23. Winfried Baumgart, *Imperialism, The Idea and Reality of British and French Colonial Expansion 1880–1914* (Oxford 1982), p. 56.
24. William J. Duiker, *Vietnam . . . Nation in Revolution* (Boulder, Colorado), 1983.
25. Theodore Zeldin, *France 1848–1945 1. Ambition, Love and Politics* (Oxford 1973) p. 630. Most of Zeldin's commentary on French imperialism, in this magnificently idiosyncratic study of French history, is contained in Volume 2, *Intellect, Taste and Anxiety* (Oxford 1977): in the chapter entitled 'Hierarchy and Violence'. In Volume 1, however, he allows himself an aside on Constans – 'this bankrupt manufacturer of lavatory systems who had then become . . . Governor-General of Indo-China'.
26. C. M. Andrew, 'The French Colonialist Movement during the Third Republic: the Unofficial Mind of Imperialism' in *Transactions of the Royal Historical Society,* first series Vol. 26 1976. 'Jules Ferry and the colonialists of the Third Republic wanted a great French Empire, as Bethmann-Hollweg wanted a great German Navy, "for the general purposes of French greatness, for reasons of national prestige"; and it was the nationalism of French society which made it vulnerable to a colonialism with which it was fundamentally out of sympathy.' pp. 149–50.

27. Zeldin, op. cit. Vol. 2, p. 942.
28. Thomas F. Power, *Jules Ferry and the Renaissance of French Imperialism* (New York 1966), p. 170. It was, Power notes, the same argument he had used in the case of Tunisia, justifying a new acquisition as necessary not for markets but for the defence of French possessions.
29. Excerpts in Georges Taboulet *La Geste Française en Indochine* (Paris 1956). Vol. II pp. 805–6.
30. Power, op. cit. p. 182. Broglie was a former foreign minister.
31. McAleavy op. cit. p. 239.
32. Power, op. cit.
33. McAleavy, op. cit. p. 284.
34. See e.g. John K. Fairbank *et al. East Asia The Modern Transformation* Chapter 2 'Invasion and Rebellion in China'.
35. See e.g. Duiker; Steinberg; and David G. Marr *Vietnamese Anti-colonialism, 1885–1925* (Berkeley 1971).
36. Steinberg op. cit. p. 132.
37. Ibid. p. 303. One notes in passing that Kedourie in his study of nationalism maintained that it was a doctrine invented in Europe in the 18th century: in which case, in Scotland, there was a remarkable 14th-century prefiguration in the Declaration of Arbroath and the Battle of Bannockburn.

Chapter 1

HO CHI MINH AND THE FRENCH: NATIONAL COMMUNISM? 1920–1946

THE NATURE OF FRENCH COLONIAL RULE

In 1885 France was in possession of a colonial empire which, in 25 years, had grown to three times its original size. For the time being, and for many this looked like the foreseeable future, she had at least defined the territorial limits and the constituent parts of Vietnam. Together with the kingdoms of Laos and Cambodia Vietnam was now to be joined in the Indochinese Union although the country itself was divided into three parts. Cochinchina was a colony; Tonkin was a protectorate; while in Annam there was still an Emperor: with a French *résident-supérieur* at his shoulder who represented indirect but unmistakably sovereign French power. Now that traditional Vietnamese fortunes had fallen to their nadir, was there any chance that France could have transformed the country and diverted the course of Vietnamese history? That is to say, would 'collaboration' have been possible? Or was there something about the nature of French rule that made revolution inevitable? And that predetermined the nature of the revolution when it came? Perhaps the greatest danger for France lay in what has been called 'the suppression of Vietnamese political life', a theory expressed by Jules Harmand (French Commissioner General in Cochinchina whose ultimatum has already been recorded), in his book *Domination et Colonisation* (1910). The first duty of the conqueror, he wrote, 'is to maintain his domination and to assure that it will last; everything is good which has the effect of consolidating and guaranteeing it, everything is bad that may weaken or compromise it'. And thus ended, in effect, the doctrine of 'assimilation', a Revolutionary principle asserted in the French constitution of 1795 which declared that colonies were integral parts of the Republic.

It was of course an argument that carried with it a certain invincible logic. Convinced, like the even more outspoken Gustave

Le Bon, that 'Out of a hundred Hindus educated in English schools, there are a hundred who are irreconcilable enemies of British power' and that the export of democratic institutions would simply be a form of national suicide, for Harmand it was the lesson of Santo Domingo that counted: the Caribbean negro slave revolt of 1795 which, ten years later, led to the surrender of a French army. Given these premises, then, anything which allowed native populations to challenge the principle let alone the practice of assimilation was to be avoided; and the ultimate argument was that French culture would simply make the native 'an enemy better armed against us'.

This was, of course, an extreme statement of the principles of French colonial policy and in practice it was impossible not to export French culture, including political culture, at almost every point at which French administration touched on the life of Vietnam. Nevertheless, simply to take one influential American book of the 1930s, Virginia Thompson's *French Indochina*, there are enough echoes to make one wonder whether Harmand's characterization was that much of a caricature. There is intensified in a colony, she said 'the French state's perennial anxiety to keep control of every activity and its jealous husbanding of power. Ever in the presence of a potentially hostile population, the administration must perforce dominate: and the mechanism by which this is accomplished is the régime of decrees. The result is almost despotic power for the central government and this is as much resented by the colonials as by the natives themselves.'[1]

While one may note that these are observations that may be drawn as much from first principles as from pragmatic induction, studies by other authors who are not averse to imperialism and all its works tend to convey an impression in Vietnam not only of pervasive French presence but of almost total control. Thus, for example, Duncanson:

> Like the Gendarmerie, the Sûreté was a pan-Indochina service, owing loyalty to the state interests of France, not of the native sovereigns, of whose territories it had nevertheless a free run . . . .
> In practice the bulk of the work done by the Sûreté was not criminal investigation at all but political control . . . and its agents, not trained as professional detectives with clearly-prescribed answerability before a judicial authority, generally stood in low public esteem; they were never concerned with safeguarding the personal safety and private property of Vietnamese villagers and seem to have considered themselves primarily as a network of agents to watch over the interests of the French state. The scope for graft latent in many Asian societies was aggravated in Indo-China by the dependence of French police officers, in their almost universal ignorance of the native languages, upon the inquiries and operations of a class of Indian, Chinese, Eurasian, and other non-native informers whose venality became a byword. Worst of all, the Sûreté was not averse to operating for 'reasons of state' beyond the

terms of the law itself and tended to bring the legal and judicial system of the French administration into disrepute as hardly preferable to the arbitrary Chinese system which it had supplanted. The system proved little suited to dealing with subversion through intimidation.[2]

Elsewhere, Duncanson tempers his wide-ranging criticism of French rule with strictures on the incompetence and dishonesty of the mandarinate in Tonkin and on the lack of civic virtue of the educated professional class of Vietnamese; but to this theme of what he calls 'political disabilities' Lancaster adds what are equally heavy economic burdens. When the energetic Governor-General Paul Doumer ended his five-year term of office the Vietnamese contribution to public expenditure had increased from an estimated 35 m. gold francs at the time of the French conquest to something like 90 m. In the course of economic development there were, as one might expect, some outstanding French achievements. For example, by the time the Mekong had been drained the excavations were comparable to the construction of the Panama canal and in the sixty years before the Second World War there were 4½ m. acres of new land brought into cultivation and correspondingly prodigious increases in the exports of rice. Nevertheless, the cost of providing an economic infrastructure was one which seemed to bear heavily upon the people and, as far as the rural communities were concerned, it may be argued that the French occupation brought little positive benefits. The peasant, says Lancaster, would thus seem to have paid a high price for protection from foreign invasion and for increasing immunity from epidemics: which probably represented the principal benefits derived from the French occupation.[3]

In terms of long-range revolutionary potential it was what Lancaster calls the progressive pauperization of the countryside which would have the most ominous consequences, with a rural indebtedness in Cochinchina alone rising from 31 m. *piastres* in 1900 to 134 m. *piastres* in 1930. By the following year, as a result of mortgage and foreclosures, the manifest favouritism shown to French squatters and the pressures of population, peasants in Tonkin were having to feed themselves on average from the product of just over one-third of an acre of *padi* per head: in some localities barely a fifth.[4]

For the moment, however, and on the assumption that peasant-based revolution takes years of quiet combustion before the fire breaks out, the number of flashpoints increased as the cities grew. For example, as Duncanson points out, in the public services there was the principle that natives could not aspire to higher posts whatever their technical qualifications. Thus Indochinese with top marks from the *Grandes Écoles* in France returned home to serve under Frenchmen with much lower qualifications, or none at all, on a salary which was approximately a fifth of what would be paid to a European doing the same work. There were in fact three times as many

Frenchmen employed in 1937 to run Indochina, with 30 m. inhabitants, as there were Britons to run India which had more than ten times the population. At the same time, as late as 1938 there were still only 2,500 Vietnamese who had acquired French citizenship in the whole of Vietnam, three-fifths of them in Cochinchina. The fact that the Minister of the Colonies had to examine each application personally suggests a degree of caution that verged on the obsessive.

Nevertheless conditions in which limited but often intense urban nationalism would flourish were being created and would provide a catalyst of future revolution; although for a long time fears that educated Vietnamese would rise up against their French masters were certainly not encouraged by the numbers of children in school. In the mid-1920s only a little over 1 per cent were receiving a formal education. Higher education was available at the University of Hanoi where some Vietnamese students were introduced to revolutionary nationalism/national communism: although many more were able to ingest ideology and political doctrines in France itself. In Vietnam, other complaints centred on the lack of industrial development, the stranglehold of French companies and, especially, of the Banque de l'Indochine – a consortium of Paris banks which had a monopoly of banking services – but while one may say that the nature of colonial development or colonial repression in itself created the necessary conditions for revolution or national liberation, it is obviously time to consider how these, and other, factors influenced the forms of Vietnamese resistance. Here one may note that while, eventually, it was France who not only defined Vietnam but also the character of Vietnamese resistance, it can also be argued that in the impact of the first two revolutionary events of the 20th century experienced in Vietnam, the inspiration came from Asia itself.

The extraordinary achievements and transformation of 19th-century Japan, at least as a model for other parts of Asia, had to some extent been tarnished by her conflict with China and her consequent appearance in the ranks of the imperial powers. Victory over the disintegrating Manchu dynasty was perhaps to have been expected; victory over Imperial Russia was quite sensational. On its fateful journey from the Baltic the Russian battle fleet had, fortuitously, anchored in Camranh Bay. Nothing like this concentration of naval power had ever been seen in Vietnam; and we know that it was at least inspected by Vietnamese nationalists who may also have tried to make contact with Russian sailors. The annihilation of the Baltic fleet a few days later in the Straits of Tsushima was almost unbelievable and was the first defeat of a great power in modern history by an Asian state and for that reason alone Japan's success might have been an example for Vietnam.

The most immediate and exuberant assumption, that of Prince Cuong Dé, pretender to the throne and a descendant of Emperor

Gia Long, was that the Japanese army would help him to recover his throne and his country; but the example of Japan gave rise to different interpretations. Was it an example which showed that the power and position of France had first to be destroyed? Or was it to be an example of 'self-strengthening', of, essentially, successful reform? The alternative inferences are usually associated with the nationalist expositions of two contemporary Vietnamese 'scholar patriots'. The first, Phan Boi Chau, believed that the French had to be removed – and that this could only be achieved through armed struggle. The second, Phan Chu Trinh, did not believe in violence. Instead, he believed in a sort of reverse assimilation by which Vietnam would emerge as a modern nation assisted, or at least not impeded, by a beneficent France. Vietnam's weakness was, he believed, endemic to the people and its society, and the first task was to remove the feudal structure so that Vietnam could emerge as a modern state. Essentially an admirer of France, he exposed the Achilles heel of a French republic founded upon revolutionary principles: but he did not strike at it. This was an attitude which, long afterwards, was to put him in second place to Phan Boi Chau in the opinion of the Communist Party which, although stressing the patriotism of both men, especially Phan Boi Chau, declared that Phan Chu Trinh had mistaken the principal enemy. Bourgeois, even liberal, France, would never have given up without a fight. Reformism could never have succeeded. In any event, in colonial Vietnam reformists did not fare much better than revolutionaries. Phan Boi Chau had been sentenced to death. Phan Chu Trinh was sentenced to life imprisonment. Neither sentence was carried out and, ironically, both of them ended their lives as virtual pensioners of the French colonial government.

THE INFLUENCE OF JAPAN AND CHINA ON VIETNAMESE NATIONALISM

Of the two Asian models for Vietnamese independence, China and Japan, China was always more immediate and when at last the Chinese Empire fell to pieces and the Manchu dynasty ended in 1911, the impact of this revolution was full of promise for Vietnam. Not least because of the assumption that the conditions were approximately the same – modernization and foreign domination – and that China might once again be in a position to affect the course of Vietnamese history. Up until the eve of the First World War resistance and insurrection, although limited, had persisted particularly in the wild hill country of the Sino-Vietnamese border and when the war began in 1914 and the reserves of power available to France, both French and Vietnamese, began to be drained off there was at least a local opportunity for revived resistance. In the hope that deteriorating wartime conditions in Vietnam would spark insurrection, a liberation army of sorts was being formed on the border; but when the attack went off at half-cock (leaders executed or arrested and followers dispersed) another threat to the French position was removed and it must have become clear that the only credible threat to French power lay in France itself, at least until the forces of nationalism were able to attract some effective outside sponsorship or else embed themselves in the people to the point where they became an organized national resistance.

Of the 'scholar patriots' perhaps one can say that, instead, they helped to awaken the national consciousness; and in the evening of his life Phan Boi Chau, in a moving analogy in which Vietnam was likened to an orphan child which by this time should have learned to walk and France to a tutor who felt that the child was easier to control when he was unable to run, talked of a people whose traditional values had been destroyed and who were thus a generation of uprooted people on their own soil. It was no wonder that the Vietnamese, he said, were willing to turn to anyone who offered them a helping hand; and for the time being, for him and perhaps for most Vietnamese, it was China, and the Kuomintang, not surprisingly, which exerted the greatest influence on the development of Vietnamese nationalism: and especially a Kuomintang which still included communists as well as nationalists.

Phan Boi Chau ended his life wondering whether the Vietnamese people understood communism any more than he did himself; but even if, in the 1920s, they did not, and if international communism at least did not understand the Vietnamese people all that well either, one could argue that at a time when the prospects for Vietnam were still fairly evenly balanced between peaceful reform and revolution and even though, in 1924, a government of the Left had taken office in France, the failure of a constitutional Party helped to turn political forces in Vietnam in the direction of a radical nationalism. At one point, in December 1925, with a liberal Governor-General in Vietnam, the Vietnamese were told that they could aspire to a fuller and higher life to become one day a nation; but a few months later it was predicted that, while an independent Vietnam (in the indeterminate future) was a possibility, the bonds between it and France would become sufficiently strong so that nothing would ever break them.[5] It was obvious that France was determined to keep the lid on. It was becoming equally obvious that, with the build-up of pressure, some sort of explosion was likely. The original explosion had come in Petrograd in 1917. After this it was, for Bolsheviks, a moot point whether revolution in Europe would mean independence for the colonies, as Trotsky believed; or whether, as Marx had originally argued and Stalin now suggested, colonial revolution, particularly in Asia, could hasten the overthrow of European capitalism.[6] When the Second Congress of the Communist International met in 1920 the basic query, says McLane, was how *much* attention was to be paid to the East. And whether it was to be considered more important than the West. As *rapporteur* of the Commission which was considering national and colonial questions, Lenin made it clear it was essential to achieve the closest alliance of all national and colonial liberation movements with Soviet Russia: indeed the former were learning from bitter experience that their only salvation lay in alliance with the revolutionary proletariat and in the triumph of Soviet power over world imperialism.[7] And yet, on the matter of whether the colonial or the metropolitan revolution had priority, the statement was equivocal. On the one hand it was essential to try to make the peasant movement more revolutionary in character by uniting the peasants and all the exploited, wherever possible, into Soviets; on the other, the obligation to render the most active assistance to revolutionary-liberation movements rested in the first instance with the workers of the country on which the backward nation was colonially and financially dependent. Making concessions to Lenin's Indian and 'Asia-First' opponent, M N Roy, the Commission had, throughout the theses, replaced 'bourgeois-democratic' by 'revolutionary' and the result was, as one may see in the sixth thesis, that the revolutionary-liberation movement in backward countries or among backward nationalities was invited to determine what forms this alliance should take. Specific targets were to include landlords, large-scale landholders, the reactionary and mediaeval influence of the clergy and Christian missions, and all manifestations or survivals of feudalism.

HO CHI MINH

Even though, by 1920, the world revolution was notably behind schedule the prospect for revolutionaries, national or communist, of alliance with Soviet power in the struggle against world imperialism was dazzling. And for the self-styled Vietnamese patriot, reading these theses in Paris in the French Communist paper *l'Humanité*, it amounted, in his own account, to a religious conversion. It also approximated, in time, to the formation of the French Communist Party, of which Ho Chi Minh was a founder member, and one may, conveniently and conventionally, present him as a communist from 1920 onwards. The nationalist goes back much earlier, even though, as one of his biographers says, 'Everything that touches on his life until 1941 is fragmentary, approximate and controversial.[8] Born, apparently, in 1890 in Nghe An province of central Vietnam, Ho's father was at least an acquaintance if not friend of the veteran nationalist Phan Boi Chau. His uncle, sister, and brother can all be described as nationalists and although Ho seems to have been attracted at one point to the China of the 1911 Revolution, he chose instead to make his way to France where, having led an intellectually enriched but materially impoverished existence in Paris, he achieved some fame, or notoriety, among his fellow expatriates by attempting to present a list of Vietnamese grievances to Woodrow Wilson and the European statesmen who had gathered in 1919 at Versailles. When he made what may be argued were his next intellectually significant appearances, in 1923 at the Peasant International and in 1924 at the Fifth Congress of the Communist International, he had moved on from the French Communist Party and was now accepted in Russia as a revolutionary of considerable promise. But the matter of priorities had still to be settled and Ho threw his weight unmistakably behind the primacy of colonial revolution. He told the delegates: 'All of you know that at present the poison and vital capacity of the imperialist viper are concentrated in the colonies rather than in the metropolitan countries.' And yet, he said, hearing the speeches of comrades from France and Britain he had the impression that they all wanted to kill the serpent by beating its tail.[9]

As Ho and other communists noted, amongst the European proletariat the issue of colonial emancipation was very much an also-ran in the 1920s; and even after a bona fide Vietnamese communist party had been formed, it was just as irksome to them to have to accept the tutelage of the French Communist Party. It was not in fact until ten years after Ho's conversion to communism that the Indochina Communist Party itself was formed in 1930. In the meantime Ho's contribution to the cause continued to be made from outside Vietnam and most effectively, from Canton. His appointment to the staff of the Borodin mission to the Kuomintang in 1924 brought him into contact with hundreds of young Vietnamese for whom Canton was the centre of Chinese nationalism; and communism which, at this time, was still included in the Kuomintang.

When the Vietnamese Revolutionary Youth League was formed by Ho in 1925 its nucleus consisted of Vietnamese terrorists, the *Tam Tam Xa*, who had already attempted the assassination of a French Governor-General on a state visit to Canton, and Canton became a staging-post for the return of young Vietnamese revolutionaries who might now declare themselves to be Marxists as well. What Ho himself understood by Marxism at this stage can perhaps best be seen in the first Vietnamese Marxist revolutionary text: *The Road to Revolution*, published in 1926. While the idea of the two-stage revolution: liberation first, communism later: could be described as primitive Leninism, it may be seen that Ho's approach to Communism was also two-track: town and country: not necessarily in that order: and his Revolutionary Youth League also functioned on two levels: the mass nationalist party and the inner core of *Tam Tam Xa* hotheads who were to be the nucleus of a future communist party.[10] In its promotion of conjoint nationalism and communism the League resembled the Kuomintang at this time: and it lasted only as long as the Kuomintang managed to contain the two movements.

In addition to their ideological training, many Vietnamese also attended the Whampoa Military Academy in Canton where they were instructed by, among others, Chiang Kai Shek. By the time Chiang fell upon his Chinese communist rivals and destroyed the Canton commune in the spring of 1927, and thus terminated the League's existence also, it has been estimated that something like 200 'graduates' of Ho's Canton course had returned to Vietnam and although many of them were arrested, it was a significant infusion to be added to what might be called the natural sources of discontent. In Tonkin it has been suggested that the majority of young revolutionaries belonged to the working class: but that the party machine generally was composed predominantly of teachers and intellectuals.[11] If this is so then it was probably less of a proletarian organization than its principal rival, the Nationalist Party, or, in its fuller title, the *Vietnam Quoc Dan Dang*. This was a party which, created in 1927, reckoned to be the Vietnamese counterpart of the Chinese Nationalists who were now untainted by communist membership of the Kuomintang. To confuse the issue, however, the VNQDD was apparently conceived 'as a vanguard party, an adaptation of the Bolshevik model in Indo-China, and to that extent it reflected the impact of Marxism'.[12] As a party it is described, variously, as characterized by its insurrectionary mentality and always hovering on the brink of insurrection. As a vanguard, in spite of one or two sensational assassinations, it was not going to get very far unless and until it managed to co-ordinate widespread resistance to the French. To some extent both it and its communist rivals were able to take advantage of increasing misery and frustration once the effects of the world economic depression were felt. Wages fell; export markets collapsed; and, perversely, because the Vietnamese *piastre* was now linked to the metropolitan franc, the cost of living rose. The VNQDD as well as the communists had already been involved in fomenting strikes but on the whole they do not seem to have attached themselves to any cause other than nationalism and, while they were particularly active in attempting to subvert the army, when they finally and out of desperation, having been heavily penetrated by the Sûreté, attempted to begin their armed struggle, many of the Vietnamese riflemen in the battalion, which was induced to mutiny, rallied instead to their French officers.

ABORTIVE REVOLUTION

The Yen-Bay mutiny did not, as it was intended, form part of a co-ordinated attack on the French position in Vietnam and in the event it turned into disaster for the VNQDD. French repression, including aerial bombardment, was unsparing and as a result of wholesale arrests and executions they were practically wiped out. Almost incredibly a month later, the Communist Party attempted a repeat performance. Or, at least, it attempted to capitalize on similar conditions in other parts of the country. It was, now, a single if not entirely united party. It had been born out of a clandestine meeting in Hong Kong in February 1930 at a time which there were in fact three communist parties in Vietnam. The unifying factor was Ho Chi Minh, acting as agent of the Comintern, and while it would not manage to suppress its nationalist tendencies indefinitely it was for the moment clearly identified with the Vietnamese working class. Who they were, and whether the party's appeal should be confined to the quarter of a million or so who might be described as 'proletariat' was something that had yet to be defined. In the meantime, in the turmoil of Vietnam in 1930 and perhaps remembering Lenin's rather ambiguous call for soviets, the Party committed itself to what was essentially an agrarian revolt.

The Soviets of Nghe-Tinh are, obviously, one of the first landmarks of Vietnamese communism. There was a 'worker' element but for the most part it was a peasant revolt, described in James Scott's study of rebellion and subsistence in Southeast Asia as one of the 'Depression rebellions' of 1930.[13] But if not initiated by the Communist Party it was at least orchestrated by them although, as Scott notes, the destruction of land and tax records was virtually a peasant tradition in colonial Vietnam. A simple cause was the fact that, in the words of one observer, 'For two years the land has produced nothing'. This, plus tax demands and a steady loss of communal land to corrupt mandarins and village notables, would seem to have been enough to produce this peasant revolt in whose heartland both Phan Boi Chau and Ho Chi Minh had been born. The aftermath was even worse than Yen-Bay; 2,000 dead and the virtual destruction or disintegration of the existing party apparatus. From Ho Chi Minh, however, it was a matter on which apparently no opinion was ever recorded and it may serve to illustrate the dangers to which communism in Vietnam was exposed when decisions and even understanding were subject to foreign direction. By its insistence on the generalized imminence of revolution – more an article of faith than a result of pragmatic observation – the Comintern was at least partly responsible for the Nghe-Tinh disaster. Conceivably, if the revolt had spread to take in substantial parts of the country then, to anticipate Maoist precepts of the future, the countryside would have surrounded the cities; but at this time not only were there no 'sympathetic detonations' in other parts of the country but there was practically no challenge whatever to French power in the cities. And although he was not directly involved in the Nghe-Tinh débâcle, one may assume that, Ho, too, had 'overestimated the capacity of the communist leadership to transform spontaneous revolt into a nationwide uprising, and had underestimated the ability of the colonial régime to quell any challenge to its authority'.[14]

Whoever had taken the decision to commit the party to armed insurrection in 1930, what was now to be called in question was whether the party had any right at all to make such decisions for itself. During his time in Paris Ho Chi Minh had discovered that the French proletariat was not totally committed to the cause of Vietnamese independence: indeed the problems of France's colonies were much less immediate than their own. Nevertheless, it was the French Communist Party which had been given the task of encouraging communism in Vietnam; and, it appears, where necessary, correcting its faults. In this it may have been little more than a mouthpiece for a Russian directorate but in an article, which, says Sacks, amounted to a reading of the riot act to the ICP, one finds this clear and unmistakable instruction in the French journal *Cahiers du Bolshévisme*:

> If they [the Vietnamese comrades] find that certain points in the programme do not fit the concrete situation of the country, they can ask the Comintern to add or subtract something. But if they allow themselves to correct the Party programme of action elaborated by the Comintern without asking its opinion, such action is incompatible with the principle of democratic centralism, with iron discipline, and with the Comintern.[15]

Similar advice was apparently given by the Central Committee of the Chinese Communist Party, i.e. that 'the gate to victory is a disciplined and powerful Bolshevik Party' and it goes without saying that in Stalin's Russia deviation by small and not exactly successful communist parties abroad was not encouraged. On the whole, during what Duiker has called 'the Stalinist years', this was something that was accepted by the Vietnamese Communist Party but one can imagine that it was not always so easy to accept the advice which came to them from their French comrades. Thus, the French Communist Party leader Maurice Thorez explaining that, while French colonies of course had a right of self determination, they did not need to exercise it. Calling on Lenin for support he claimed that the interests of French colonies, including the Indochinese, were best served by a 'free, trusting and paternal union with France'.[16]

When the Popular Front, including the French Communist Party, came to power in France in June 1936 there was at least the hope that, by their actions, significant improvements, political as well as economic and social, might be achieved in Vietnam. But if, as Thorez implied, the Vietnamese and French Communist Parties should work together, would it not mean that the campaign for national liberation would have to be abandoned? Moreover, not only would Vietnamese interests be subordinate to those of France but the French Communist Party in turn was expected to follow a policy which was subordinate to that of international communism: in a word, Comintern policy. If the Comintern, too, decided that the anti-fascist coalition would be weakened in Vietnam by national independence, itself something of a bourgeois concept, and if the Indochina Communist Party followed suit, no matter how reluctantly, it would at a stroke lose a very significant part of its political appeal. Not that the national cause formed the only basis of the Party's support and it seems that by 1937 or so something like 600 action committees had been formed to organize the workers in Cochinchina, principally in the Saigon–Cholon area. Ironically, it was here, says Sacks, that he Trotskyists were most active and most effective and their significant increase in strength may at least in part be attributed to a sense of frustration and anger with the ICP who had, willingly or not, abandoned the cause of independence. Nevertheless the Trotskyists themselves split, on the issue of whether or not to co-operate with the ICP, and, just as the VNQDD had been destroyed as a competitor with the Communist Party by French repression after Yen-Bay, so the French colonial government, shortly after war had begun in 1939, rounded up virtually the entire leadership of the Trotskyist International Communist League, as it was then called: a coup from which the movement never recovered.[17]

PATRIOTISM AND THE PEASANTRY

From the experience of the 1920s and 1930s, therefore, it would appear that there was nothing overwhelmingly certain about the success of communism in Vietnam or, at least, about the success of the Indochina Communist Party. But the French had not managed to divert or to accommodate the forces of nationalism. The nationalists as a party capable of national leadership – that is to say the VNQDD – had admittedly been destroyed but while the ICP was not much better off the difference was that the VNQDD never really recovered from French repression. The ICP did. Their resilience and in part fortuitous revival may have been due to the slightly more permissive policies of the Popular Front government in Paris – thousands of political prisoners were released although thousands more remained in gaol – but much more seems to have been the result of the ability to rebuild an organization from the bottom up even though the advice and instructions they received from international communism meant acquiescence in policies which did not give them pre-eminent appeal as a revolutionary party. In all of this Ho Chi Minh is to be seen bobbing about like a cork on the tides of international communism, sometimes lost from sight for long periods, surviving life in Stalin's Russia and the manifest uncertainties of the purges and, when war broke out, still remaining as an experienced if not entirely successful figure in the communist world and a distant although still immanent leader of Vietnamese communism.

The almost immediate effect of the outbreak of war in 1939, following the almost entirely unexpected Nazi-Soviet pact, was that the Communist Party, in France as in Vietnam, announced its opposition to the 'imperialist' war and, in both countries, this was followed by swift government repression. Even before the collapse of France in June 1940 was to provide the Vietnamese communists with their golden opportunity, the Sixth Plenum meeting in November 1939 was looking towards national liberation in the foreseeable future as France's efforts and resources were obviously being diverted to maintain her position in Europe. Once again the Party was preparing for armed struggle and the stunning German victory of 1940 would have appeared to many Vietnamese to be 'the moment of great opportunity'. In the event, when insurrections were attempted both in the area of Lang Son, on the Chinese border, in September, and in Cochinchina in November, they were repressed with little difficulty by the French colonial government which still deployed enough effective power to ensure that these were rather rash, forlorn, and certainly premature insurrections. The following year, however, the Party took what was perhaps its most momentous decision in the mountains a few miles south of the Chinese border. In the history of the Vietnamese communist movement, as Duiker says, the Eighth Plenum is traditionally regarded as the moment when nationalism and a rural strategy of people's war became identified as the two pillars of Vietnamese revolutionary doctrine.[18] It is no less important in that it marked the return of Ho Chi Minh to Indochina after an absence of 30 years. Ho and the Indochina Communist Party had literally, and once again, found each other.

Since about 1938 Ho had been in China, first at the communist headquarters in Yenan then, apparently, with Chinese Nationalist forces, finally in Kwangsi and Yunnan which were close enough for him to attempt to resume contact with the Party inside Vietnam. At about the same time the Party was attempting to make contact with him and finally did so in the persons of two of its eventually outstanding members, Vo Nguyen Giap and Pham Van Dong.

Now, at Pac Bo, under Ho's chairmanship, the Party cleared its ideological decks and prepared to take advantage of the even more extraordinary opportunities that would be presented to it by the Second World War.

This, in fact, was the theme of the Eighth Plenum: to prepare for the *thoi co*, 'the moment of great opportunity'.[19] Instead of class analysis and the more obvious communist objectives the Party was to advance on a broad front as the dominant power of the League For The Independence Of Vietnam: the *Viet Nam Doc Lap Dong Minh* or, in its more memorable form, the *Vietminh*. Ho's appeal in his 'Letter From Abroad' was comprehensive: 'rich people, soldiers, workers, peasants, intellectuals, employees, traders, youth and women who warmly love your country!'. National liberation was the most important problem and the opportunity had come. It was time 'to follow the historic example set by our forefathers in the glorious task of national salvation'.[20]

If the patriotic appeal was designed to be all-embracing, the platform of support was obviously narrower. In its flight from the French security services once the war in Europe had broken out, the Party had, if only inadvertently, operationalized its interest in the peasantry; if only for the fact that, in leaving the towns, they were now living amongst them. Hitherto it had largely been a matter of intellectual interest and the best-known example was the study of the *The Peasant Question (1937–1938)* by two of the Party's foremost members, Truong Chinh and Vo Nguyen Giap. The inference that was clearly to be drawn from their study was that land reform/land redistribution was the critical factor in the peasant problem: even if the peasants' lot could be improved by less drastic means.[21] When it was first published in 1937-38 the authors had suggested points in the colonial government's peasant policy which might have been reformed – 'landlord rent oppression', the seizure of peasant land, heavy taxation – but the French response, apparently, was to ban the work after the second volume had been published. In class terms the peasants were identified as part of the rural petty bourgeoisie: generally speaking, not members of the proletariat because they usually owned some means of production to support themselves. In spite of an apparent natural distaste for many of the customs and superstitions of peasant society the most important discovery was of their revolutionary potential.

> Whenever they become conscious, or organized and have leadership, *they are an invincible force*. When they are ready they will flatten any obstacle to their progress and that of the nation. The whole problem is *consciousness, organization and leadership*.[22]

Essentially, the long-term problem of mobilizing the peasantry, as of mobilizing Vietnam with its 90 per cent peasant population, was one on which the success of the Vietnamese revolution would eventually turn. In the shorter term, the kaleidoscope of the Second World War was going to accelerate the process and would present opportunities both for independence and revolution. To begin with, however, the moment of opportunity that was presented in Vietnam by France's defeat in 1940 was taken by the Japanese; and although Ho might conceivably and eventually have been right in his optimistic assertion that 'if the entire people were united and single minded they would certainly be able to smash the picked French and Japanese armies', the vicissitudes of war and politics would ensure that, for a while at least, they would not be required for such a formidable task.

Having been engaged in an undeclared war with China since 1937 Japan took advantage of the French defeat in 1940 both to close one of China's last remaining links with the outside world, the Haiphong–Yunnan railway, and to begin her advance into Southeast Asia. Those of the French, the majority, who at least implicitly gave their allegiance to Vichy France, were prepared for a wary collaboration with the Japanese and as Admiral Decoux, the French Governor-General appointed by Marshal Pétain, always maintained, they were determined, no matter what happened in France, to preserve the French position in Indochina. Implicitly, it may be argued, this turned them into collaborators with the Japanese; although the latter, for their part, were content to maintain the superstructure of French administration even if, as events were subsequently to show, the realities of power were theirs. Did this mean therefore that in some way France had forfeited her position in Indochina and was she to be treated as an opponent rather than an ally? The question at the time, in May 1941, when the Vietminh was founded and Ho was talking bravely about taking on the combined French and Japanese armies in Vietnam was, of course, anachronistic: the two principal Allied powers had not yet entered the war. When Hitler invaded Russia in June 1941 and the war, for communists, abruptly changed its character, there was at least the prospect – in principle at least – of enhanced support for the revolutionary and patriotic cause in Vietnam; but until Russia had withstood the German onslaught this in practical terms meant nothing. In the meantime it was the Japanese attack on the US which would prove to have the most rewarding consequences as far as the Vietminh were concerned. One may indeed go so far as to assert that the Japanese occupation of Indochina was the key issue in the conflict between Japan and the US which led to the attack at Pearl Harbor[23]; and after what was, initially, a rather lofty approach to the problems of Indochina and Southeast Asian security, America's final demand that Japan remove its forces from both China and Indochina (26 November 1941) was met with the equally final Japanese rejection which manifested itself at Pearl Harbor and the invasion of Southeast Asia.[24]

American entry into the war had the effect of a second transformation. No matter what reservations Churchill might have
entertained about the Atlantic Charter and whether or not freedom
was meant to apply to colonial territories, the unworthiness of France
to return to Indochina was soon to become one of Roosevelt's fixed
ideas on colonialism and an issue that would bedevil relations between
all the Allied powers in Southeast Asia with the possible and ironic
exception of the Soviet Union. At least Churchill is on record that
Roosevelt had been more outspoken with him on the subject of
Indochina than on any other colonial matter: 'I imagine it is one of
his principal war aims to liberate Indochina from France'[25]. And while
Roosevelt was to some extent restrained by the State Department and,
even more, after the US had recognized de Gaulle's government in
October, 1944, by considerations of reconstituting France as at least
a European power, there was, on the operational level, a situation
developing in southern China, in which the US was involved, which
would affect the fortunes of the Vietnamese revolutionaries, their
appearance, their standing with other Vietnamese patriots, and their
ability to influence future events.

Shortly after the US had entered the war Ho's personal fortunes
had reached their lowest ebb. Having returned to China to work in
and among the numerous but fragmented Vietnamese independence
factions, Ho's position as an acknowledged communist in what was
an essentially anti-communist Kuomintang was always precarious
and for whatever reason he was imprisoned (in conditions of great
hardship) it seems likely that he had been close to the point of death
before he was released thirteen months later: Chen suggests because
of communist sympathisers in the local Kuomintang hierarchy. As a
matter of self-preservation, he changed his name from 'Nguyen the
Patriot' (Nguyen Ai Quoc) to 'He who enlightens' (Ho Chi Minh):
the name by which he is immortalized.

CHINA AND THE UNITED STATES: SPONSORS OF VIETNAMESE INDEPENDENCE

Part, at least, of Ho's enlightenment was the approximation and
future projection of political power in Vietnam, the need to maintain the appeal to Vietnamese patriotism, and, most of all, a
temporary but overwhelming necessity for Chinese support. By the
time Ho had been released by the Chinese in September 1943 the
US was beginning to make its major contribution to the war against
Japan and various strategies were being considered for a drive on
Canton or Hanoi. In either case principally Chinese armies would

have been involved and, in the short run at least, Vietnam's political future seemed to lie in Chinese hands. The Chinese, for their part, needed reliable intelligence on conditions in Vietnam – some genuine Vietnamese support, too, if they could get it – but not simply that which was promised by emigrés who had lived in China for years and who had little or no contact with or contemporary knowledge of Vietnam. While he was in Chinese captivity, and apart from writing poems in classical Chinese (some of which, while they may not have been of the highest order classically, are nevertheless moving and rather beautiful) Ho had also translated Dr Sun Yat Sen's modern political classic the *San Min Chu I* into Vietnamese and this expedient flattery of China and Chinese continued after Ho's release. Although admitting to the Kuomintang General Chang Fa-k'uei that he was a communist, he apparently persuaded him that it would take fifty years for communism to work in Vietnam; and, in any event, it appeared that, of all the groupings of Vietnamese nationalists, patriots, emigrés and revolutionaries who were to be found in Southeast China, none of them was as dynamic as the Vietminh. When the Chinese made their first attempt, in preparation for the invasion of Indo-China, to bring the various Vietnamese factions together and create a Vietnamese Revolutionary League (abbreviated to *Dong Minh Hoi*) members of the ICP were specifically excluded. Eighteen months later, in March 1944, at a second Chinese-sponsored conference at Liuchow, Ho had not only manged to slip back under the nationalist umbrella of the *Dong Minh Hoi* but, as one of its representatives, was named as a member of a Provisional Government which was expecting to enter Vietnam in the wake of the 'liberating' Chinese armies.

At this point, then, the Chinese were the indispensable sponsors of Vietnamese independence and Ho himself is supposed to have assured them that he would work under their auspices and as a member of what might be described as the Vietnamese patriotic front. In China, at this time, Ho and his communist supporters were only one among rival groups of Vietnamese nationalists. In Vietnam, they were probably pre-eminent and could certainly lay the largest claim to 'control' of operational areas on the other side of the Chinese frontier in Tonkin even though their simultaneous claim to the status of 'resistance' forces needs to be looked at more closely.

In August 1944, having enlisted Chinese support, Ho crossed the border into north Vietnam to make contact once again with the Vietminh forces who, by this time, and in the absence of any other administrative control or military power, were extending their influence in the mountains of northern Tonkin in the area known as the *Viet Bac*. Revolutionary armed forces were supposed to be growing and there was apparently enough revolutionary enthusiasm to support the idea of launching another insurrection from there within a couple of months.[26] Ho, cautiously, turned down such a premature example of left-wing adventurism and instead, and as a bridge between the political and military phases of the revolutionary struggle, the first armed propaganda unit was set up in the mountains of Cao Bang – and was to have primarily political duties.[27]

THE JAPANESE COUP

At the time Ho was discouraging thoughts of instant insurrection on the part of the Vietminh it was obvious that as far as French fortunes were concerned the wind had changed. Rather ingenuously it appears that, with the liberation of Paris, the French in Vietnam asked for Japanese permission to celebrate the event; and it must have been obvious to the Japanese, too, that the uneasy but *de facto* alignment between them and the French was liable to break down sooner or later. For de Gaulle, apparently, the sooner the better and, although this may be straining the comparison, on the analogy of Badoglio's Italy, the French in Vietnam might at least have been allowed to work their passage towards the status of a fully fledged ally rather than endure the uncomfortable ambiguities of a compromised position. According to his memoirs de Gaulle willingly envisaged that hostilities would commence in Indochina: 'French blood shed on Indo-Chinese soil would give us an important voice . . . since I did not harbour the least doubt as to Japan's ultimate aggression, I desired that our troops should fight, no matter how desperate their situation.' When, however, the hostilities did begin, for most Frenchmen they ended, ignominiously, with imprisonment by the Japanese while for those in the north who together with their Vietnamese riflemen fought the Japanese with exemplary heroism, dying in beleaguered garrisons or making a fighting retreat to the Chinese border, their fate precipitated the most unpleasant or at least the most unfortunate disagreement between the Allies.

By the time of the Japanese coup on 9 March 1945 the US had already become an important actor in the play that was to determine the future of Vietnam. A large part of the trouble lay in the overlapping and by no means clearly defined responsibilities for operations in Vietnam between US forces operating in support of the Chinese in the 'China Theater', and Southeast Asia Command: more particularly, the disagreements between the US General Wedemeyer and Admiral Lord Louis Mountbatten. Although his attitude towards the French seemed to change somewhat before he died, Roosevelt had effectively delayed the French in their attempt to return to Indochina. Whether or not his opinions actually percolated down to subordinate commanders many of them seemed to share his beliefs about keeping the French out, or at least, in an interesting reversal of roles in the First World War, treating France as an associated rather than an allied power. Small numbers of French had been parachuted into Indochina under SEAC auspices before the Japanese coup but a much larger and perhaps more effective intervention by the French *Corps Léger d'Intervention*, a specialist unit of some five hundred men recruited and waiting in Algeria, was frustrated for various nominal reasons; the effective one being that the US, until the very last moment, was unalterably opposed to French units participating in the war against Japan, and especially, if this involved Vietnam.

The result, in the aftermath of the Japanese coup, was that immediate help to the French, who were now fighting the Japanese in Vietnam, was denied to them at a time when the US 14th Airforce in southern China could be seen by the French in Laos and Vietnam as they flew on their predetermined attacks on the Japanese elsewhere in Southeast Asia. It would, of course, be far fetched to compare the plight of the French fighting the Japanese in Vietnam with that of the Polish Home Army who had been destroyed fighting the Germans in Warsaw in 1944 although, in one respect at least, the failure of the proximate military power to lend assistance meant that others, who were more responsive to the plight of the Poles and the French, did what they could from a distance to help. Again, in the case of Vietnam, this was accompanied by bitter political acrimony, at least on the operational level, between the Americans on the one side, the British and French on the other, about whether or not the French fighting in Vietnam were to be regarded as allies and whether or not the French had any entitlement to resume their pre-war position in Indochina.[28]

Although it was not appreciated at the time when the Japanese swept away the administration, the power and the remaining claims to sovereignty of the French in Indochina, the Second World War in Asia had entered its final six months. In this period, and before the events which may be described as 'the August Revolution', there were in retrospect, at least two others which assume a momentous character. The first was that on 11 March 1945, two days after the Japanese coup, the Emperor Bao Dai proclaimed 'That from today the protectorate treaty with France is abrogated and that the country reassumes its rights to independence'. It was of course a somewhat limited independence with the government of Vietnam announcing its trust in the loyalty of Japan and considering itself to be part of Japanese Greater East Asia. It was also limited in the sense that the Japanese appointed a Governor of Cochinchina, a resident-superior of Tonkin and advisers to Annam, Cambodia and Laos. Nevertheless it had broken the thread by which the country had been tied to France and although it might be claimed that, as in Burma during the war or in Indonesia at the end of the war, it was a spurious independence and part of Japanese mischief making, nevertheless Vietnam was now in a formal sense independent if not exactly free.

The French, too, responded to the Japanese coup with a formal declaration of their intentions for Vietnam. To some extent perhaps they were the victims of their own official attitude to what was happening – as when the French Ambassador in London told Eden that a French civil and military resistance organization in Vietnam had the general support of the army and the civil population: whether this was the French or the Vietnamese population was apparently not specified[29] – but in their Declaration of 24 March 1945 the Provisional French Government implied that all the peoples of Indochina were fighting for a common cause; which was that of the entire French community. It was thus acquiring additional rights 'to receive the place for which it is destined' but instead of independence, there was the rather less exciting prospect of an Indochinese Federation which would 'enjoy the liberty and the organization necessary to the development of all its resources'. Not only was France here, and on many subsequent occasions, unable to pronounce the word 'independence'. On this occasion she did not even pronounce the name 'Vietnam'. It would, by implication, be one of five constituent parts of the Indochinese Federation – which meant that Vietnam itself would be divided into three parts – and they, together with other parts of what were called the 'French Community' would form a French Union. The interests of the Indochinese Federation outside the Union would be represented by France. Inside the Federation, 'in the interests of each the Governor-General would be arbiter of all'. (As Irving points out it was, frankly, anachronistic; more or less what Edouard Daladier had demanded after the disturbances in Indochina in 1930.)[30] In any case the interests of Vietnam – or, one might say, the non-interest in Vietnam – had been subsumed and constrained in France's Brazzaville Declaration of January 1944 which said, unequivocally,

> Whereas the aims of the work of civilization accomplished by France in her colonies rule out all idea of autonomy and all possibility of development outside the French Empire; [therefore] the eventual constitution, even in the far off future, of self-government in the colonies is out of the question.[31]

As the most advanced part of the French colonial empire Vietnam in 1945 might, perhaps, by a sort of inductive leap, have been the first French colony to become independent. In hindsight, that is. At the time, however, in France it was practically unthinkable and one may surmise that while France itself might have recovered from the débâcle of 1940 there was added point to her recovery of Vietnam after the humiliation and tragedy of March 1945. One may also argue that the situation was increasingly beyond her control.

In Vietnam the loss of a small intelligence network to the Japanese had made it essential for operational purposes that it should be replaced and it is at this point that Ho Chi Minh and the American OSS found each other. The practical services rendered by each side to the other do not seem to have been all that large although there is still considerable speculation about the volume of weapons with which the Vietminh were supplied.[32] Of equal importance, it can be argued, to the Vietminh cause was the half dozen Colt 45s which Ho had obtained from US sources, together with a signed photograph of the US 14th Airforce Commander, General Chennault. Charles Fenn, the American OSS agent whose instructions were to disregard Franco-Vietnamese politics and re-establish an intelligence rescue network, reckons that the three months after the Japanese coup were perhaps the most significant in Ho's career.[33] Divergent political objectives notwithstanding, the obvious goodwill between Ho and the Americans, the limited but successful training teams that they provided for Vietminh guerrillas, and the obvious sympathy which many Americans – in particular, it seems the OSS – had for the cause of Vietnamese independence, not to mention corresponding doubts of the French title to Vietnam, all of these understandably encouraged the Vietminh in their political objective of the accomplished fact. As Truong Chinh is said to have told the 'People's Congress' in August 'We must wrest power from the hands of the Japanese and their stooges before the arrival of the Allies in Indo-China, and, as masters of the country, we shall receive the Allies who come to disarm the Japanese.'[34]

THE AUGUST REVOLUTION

In his biography of Ho Chi Minh, David Halberstam says that Ho realized what few others did: that it would all derive from August 1945. 'For it was then that the Vietminh had in one quick stroke taken over the nationalism of the country, that Ho had achieved the legitimacy of power.' The 'nationalism of the country' would seem to be an acceptable figure of speech but in practice it was centred on Hanoi. Twelve months earlier, when Paris had been liberated, communist members of the Resistance in France had wanted to strike before the French army and de Gaulle arrived and thus present them with an accomplished fact. Such a capture of French nationalism would probably have been impossible in Paris; but, in Hanoi, circumstances were combining to make it a reality. At least, in those extraordinary days between Hiroshima and the declaration of Vietnamese independence, hardly anyone, except the French garrison who were still imprisoned, first by the Japanese and then by the Vietminh, could be found to contradict this assumption of power and by the time it took place, or at least was claimed, another thread in the French connection had been broken. On 25 August 1945 the Emperor Bao Dai had abdicated. At the point of a gun, says one author[35] but not according to Bao Dai himself. 'The people', he said, 'possess a very sure instinct which, in historic hours, conducts them towards those whose mission it is to guide them. The Vietminh had seemed to bring it off as if by a miracle. Was not their incontestable success the sign that they had received the mandate of heaven?'[36]

Even before Bao Dai's abdication, his nominal government which had taken office after the Japanese coup, had resigned. Instead of government there were now centres of power; and it was to one of these, in Hanoi, that Bao Dai addressed his reply to the Vietminh. Not knowing their address, he says, he addressed it simply to 'The Committee of Patriots'. For Ho Chi Minh, formerly 'Nguyen the Patriot', it was an accolade that corresponded to reality but of all the 'objective circumstances' which might be held to account for even a temporary communist victory in August 1945 at least the most striking and immediate was the political vacuum into which they moved. The general insurrection was proclaimed on 14 August by the Central Committee of the Vietminh. It was, they said, the moment for the people to rise up in arms and obtain independence, and even though this begged the question against whom they would use these arms, there was no doubt, as the Central Committee said, that it was a moment of exceptional opportunity.[37] A fortnight later they announced themselves as the Provisional Government of the Democratic Republic of Vietnam and a few days after that, on 2 September, as the climax to weeks of stupendous political demonstrations, Vietnam declared its independence. How had it been achieved? In what sense was it a reality?

Perhaps, and perhaps contentiously, it was because the general insurrection had *not* taken place at this time: at least not in the sense that it involved trial by battle. What had been happening was an assumption of power on the part of the Vietminh and the demonstration that a communist party could seize the opportunity to capitalize on the power of nationalism at a moment of unparalleled opportunity. Like Leclerc's forces waiting outside Paris in 1944, Giap's forces hurrying towards Hanoi in August 1945 discovered that the city was in the process of liberating itself. But the appearance of Giap's armed guerrillas marching in more or less regular military formation seemed to confirm that, already, the Resistance had won. The spectacle of tiny little Vietnamese dressed in boy scout uniforms, even though they may have been 'Vanguard Youth', carrying placards bigger than they were which said 'Independence or Death' was just another element in the enthusiasm which can equally well be described as revolutionary nationalism or national revolution. Was it, because it was orchestrated by the Communist Party, invalid? Certainly, there were examples of transparent deception: for example, when, as proof of their transcendental patriotism, the ICP dissolved itself and announced it had become the Association for Marxist Studies. It was also obvious that the Vietminh were running rings around the rather remote and ineffectual nationalist parties who had appeared, as it were, as returning emigrés in the baggage train of the occupying Chinese armies: although nominal partners in the great enterprise of securing national independence the nationalists were in reality excluded from any partnership in a coalition government. Much of the success, perhaps, was due to superb stage management, as in the organization of demonstrations, but the fact that the Vietminh emerged as leaders of Vietnamese nationalism may be attributed to their sheer ability as a revolutionary party.[38] Under this heading one must include a capacity for malevolent violence which, in Duiker's rather chilling and non-committal words meant that where power was seized, people's liberation committees were established and 'class enemies were punished'.[39] In many places there were at least elements of spontaneity and although Duiker compares it with Trotsky's description of the Bolshevik revolution as, for the most part, being a 'revolution by telegraph', Khanh says that most places acted without instructions from the Central Committee. Where revolutionary committees existed much of their impetus reflected the organizing ability of the Party which, by capitalizing on the natural and man-made disasters of flood and terrible famine which may have left at least a million dead, and on Vietminh seizure and distribution of rice from guarded granaries, was able to discredit existing authority, both French and Japanese. The number of their supporters, if not activists, was enormously enhanced by the way in which the Vichy régime had mobilized the country's youth in patriotic but hitherto innocuous associations which now underpinned the revolution, perhaps even to the point where youth was as critical a factor in the Vietnamese revolution as it was, at the same time, in Indonesia.

Another factor of immense importance was the widespread availability of arms; but to understand how and why these became available one must first look, as Ho did, at the balance of international forces which had created this moment of opportunity. Here, as was done at Potsdam in July 1945, one may divide Vietnam into north and south. For Truman, Stalin, and Churchill it was an operational decision so that the Chinese armies could operate in the north and SEAC forces in the south. Hardly anyone had expected the Japanese to surrender quite so quickly and, when they did and for the moment, as far as the Allies were concerned, hardly anything happened. It was this temporal hiatus, as much as anything, which allowed the Vietminh to assume power, particularly in the north, but when the Kuomintang Chinese armies of occupation moved in, nominally to take the surrender of Japanese troops but in fact to remove almost everything of value that was portable, they existed side by side in fruitful collaboration. That is to say, although the Chinese did not recognize the new People's Republic, the Vietminh assumption of power was not challenged. It may be said, then, that it is China who again, and at this point, determined the fortunes of Vietnam. In exchange for large quantities of the only acceptable currency, gold, the Chinese armies also provided considerable quantities of their own weapons, presumably surplus to requirements, and were less than meticulous in their recovery of weapons from the Japanese armouries.

From all this, as from Potsdam and Yalta, the French were absent. To all intents and purposes, that is, because although the French garrison in Hanoi was still there it was imprisoned in the citadel and guarded, first by the Japanese, and then by the Vietminh. When, after notable delays, the first Free French representative, Jean Sainteny, arrived in Hanoi from Kunming he had apparently already been informed by his travelling companion, Major Archimedes Patti of the American OSS, that as the Postdam agreement made no mention of French sovereignty over Vietnam the French therefore had no right to intervene in affairs which were no longer their concern.[40] For the time being at least this was almost exactly how the French were regarded by the Americans in Vietnam: of little or no account and if not exactly in the 'out' tray at best their position was 'pending'. In the meantime, genuine US sympathies for Vietnamese independence were much in evidence. As it claimed to be the functioning government of Vietnam it was hardly surprising that US officers, particularly OSS, maintained fairly close contact with the Vietminh and perhaps there was a genuine basis for the American–Vietnamese Friendship Association; and when the senior US officer, General Gallagher, was persuaded to sing at one of their meetings and, apparently, broadcast on Vietminh radio, this too was in itself a comparatively innocent exercise. Cumulatively, however, the aura of association with the US was of immense political benefit to those who called themselves a provisional government but who were still skating on the thin surface of political respectability and had by no means attained a state of acknowledged legitimacy. As is now widely known, when, on 2 September, Ho Chi Minh made his declaration of Vietnamese independence, his opening and acknowledged quotation was from the American original. What is less widely known is that at this moment two P-38 Lightnings, (distinctive, long-range US fighters) appeared, their star insignia clearly visible, and although it may have been coincidence even to the sophisticated in a crowd of some hundreds of thousands it must indeed have appeared that the mandate of heaven had assumed its newest form.

CONFLICT IN THE SOUTH

As Ho Chi Minh presented the case the people who had fought side by side with the Allies, as well as against the French for more than eighty years, were entitled to their independence. For the moment, in the north, it could be maintained by Chinese approval or at least complaisance and by keeping the French out. In the south, it was to be a different story and with Vietminh claims recognized neither by the British/Indian forces who arrived first nor by the French who followed not long after, and with Japanese forces for the most part under much tighter control, the reassertion of French sovereignty, at least in so far as this might be done through the possession of Saigon, did not have long to wait. General Gracey, who commanded the 20th Indian Division, has been presented as a no-nonsense sort of general. For example, he was unimpressed by Vietminh claims to be the *de facto* government and to have resisted the Japanese; and for a while at least he believed, mistakenly, that they were in fact Japanese puppets. He, no more than General Christison in Java, was able to operate in a political vacuum but at least the French in Saigon were treated as allies rather than as one-time enemies although, in the absence of sufficient numbers of Frenchmen, Japanese troops were required to fight Vietnamese who, as in Hanoi, were intent on the politics of a *fait accompli*.

Apart from taking the Japanese surrender and recovering Allied prisoners of war, General Gracey's third task was to maintain law and order; and in this he was to recognize the sole authority of the French. Unprepared for the circumstances which he would encounter he was assured by them that the Vietminh would not resist and that Cédile, the French Commissioner in the South, had tight control of his forces. Neither, unfortunately, was true. The southern Vietminh, no less than those in the north, were to resist both principle and practice of the French return to power; the French were unprepared for any alternative and Gracey's forces were effectively caught in the middle. On 17 September 1945, a fortnight after Gracey's arrival, the Vietminh attempted to paralyse Saigon by calling a general strike. On the 22nd Gracey's forces assisted the French in what, despite what was claimed at the time and subsequently, was an almost bloodless coup by which they occupied the Town Hall and other central points; and two nights after that about a hundred and fifty French civilians, including many women and children, were massacred by Vietnamese who burst into the Cité Heraud district past indifferent Japanese guards.[41]

Whether it was the Vietminh, the Binh Xuyen,[42] or, most likely, Trotskyists, who were responsible, it obviously shattered any confidence that the restoration of French power could be achieved without such savage resistance.[43] On the British side there was a string of adverse comments on French performance and attitudes from newspaper correspondents; although the *Daily Telegraph* correspondent was not being particularly sensational when he reported on the unnecessary brutality of the French and concluded 'The solution of the problem of rule in Indo-China will depend primarily upon French ability to exercise tact and conciliation'.[44] Much more remarkable, however, were Gracey's comments when it became obvious that his earlier hopes – 'If only the French would promise progressive sovereignty . . . say two or three years *and* the Annamites would be equally ready to meet them . . .' (an almost exact parallel, so he thought, with Burma) – stood little chance of fulfilment. General Leclerc's troops had shown great skill and speed, Gracey said, but much unnecessary brutality. A Divisional Intelligence Summary described the senior French officer as 'small-minded, lacking in imagination and pig-headed' and, more important, said that the Indian other ranks had begun to distrust both the French troops and the civil authorities.[45]

In the preface to another intelligence report, the SEAC Assistant Director of Intelligence addressed himself squarely to some of the political problems which were being faced. For example, that it was hard to explain to the Vietnamese how large numbers of Vichy French were back in positions held during the war. Although he was convinced that there was conclusive evidence that Japanese intelligence organizations were behind the Vietminh and their revolt, he also said that throughout their handling of the situation the French appeared to lack every vestige of imagination but, 'provided the French are prepared to deal with the Annamites as human beings and not as chattels for exploitation as in the past, there is every reason to believe that the leading Annamites will not only listen to them, but will help them . . .'[46]

When the French and the Vietminh came face to face in the south there was, apparently, no room for compromise and conflict was almost immediate. On the rare occasions when French and Vietminh met and when local concessions might have helped at least to improve the atmosphere – for example the release of hostages taken by Vietminh – the Vietminh for their part denied all knowledge that any had been taken while violent incidents were either attributed to the forces outwith their control, which may well have been true, or else to the anger of the people which, again, may have been true but did not improve matters. Behind this, and the Vietminh demands for the complete restoration of their government and the disarming of French forces there was, as Dunn puts it, the insoluble problem: 'The Vietminh wanted full sovereignty and the French delegates could not negotiate it.' Furthermore, 'Both sides were stuck – neither was empowered to negotiate without instructions'.[47] In the meantime fighting continued both in and around Saigon and, increasingly, as more and more French troops arrived, throughout Cochinchina. Gracey's British Indian forces eventually totalled over twenty thousand men; and by December 1945 the French had about the same number in Vietnam. Much of the fighting, however, involved the Japanese forces who were acting under Gracey's command but there were significant numbers, too, fighting for whatever reasons on the Vietminh side. Apart from armoured columns the French navy had joined in as well and on at least one occasion the battleship *Richelieu* was in action against land targets.

Whether it would have been possible against this background of practically continuous fighting in the south, more than a year before the first Vietnam war between France and the Vietminh is usually reckoned to have begun, for either side to have modified its objectives to the point where compromise could have been reached is obviously a question which is relevant to the origins of the Vietnam war and one must therefore look for the characteristics which, at least after the event, suggest a remarkably high risk of collision.

On the French side one may begin in Paris with the emotional response of the Consultative Assembly to the cable which de Gaulle read out on March 20 1945 from one of the French garrisons fighting for their lives in Tonkin. As the Assembly rose to its feet 'amid shouts and tears' few of them would have realized that it was sixty years almost to the day since the Assembly of the Third Republic had responded in much the same way to the Tonkin crisis of 1885. Then, it had produced the tide of feeling which landed France in Vietnam. Now, it was responding to what de Gaulle had called the solemn pact which was at the moment being sealed 'in the suffering of all and the blood of the soldiers' between France and the peoples of the Indochinese Union and to his belief that 'not for a single hour did France lose the hope and the will to recover free Indo-China'.[48]

FREEDOM AND THE FRENCH UNION

Of equal importance, perhaps, was the assumption that France would, as a matter of course, recover Indochina and, although it might be described as 'free', the status of Indochina or Vietnam or, as it happened, part of Vietnam, would, as the French saw it, be determined by its membership of the French Union. This was a concept that was formally introduced in the declaration of the Provisional French Government of 24 March 1945. And it was to be within that Union that 'Indo-China will enjoy appropriate liberty'. A year later the issue of 'appropriate liberty' and indeed the nature of the French Union itself was still unresolved but by this time a Preliminary Convention had been signed between the Government of the French Republic and what was described, and recognized, as the Government of Vietnam. The Republic of Vietnam was accepted as a free state having its own government, parliament, army and finances. At the same time, it was recognized as 'forming part of the Indo-Chinese Federation and the French Union'. As far as either side was concerned, were the two concepts of freedom and membership of the French Union compatible? And, most important of all, by freedom did one mean independence? If not, conceptually, was there any prospect of real agreement?

Almost everything about the French mood in 1945 suggests that unqualified independence was just about the last thing that anyone envisaged for any part of the French colonial empire. The pattern may look more obvious after the event, but it is worth pointing out that the French war in Vietnam in 1946 is sandwiched between their bombardment of Damascus and the eruption at Sétif in Algeria in 1945 and their violent repression of the nationalist revolt in Madagascar in 1947 after similar claims had been made for independence within the French Union. At the same time as they were re-establishing themselves in Vietnam the French were finally being evicted, as they saw it, from Syria and the Lebanon and while these were League of Nations mandates rather than parts of the French Empire proper, their loss was no less bitterly resented. An attempt was made, at least by de Gaulle, to link riots in Syria in May 1945 with what happened in Algeria on VE Day; but the scale of the French reaction in Algeria to the murder of over a hundred European settlers and associated atrocities left at least a thousand and perhaps as many as six thousand Algerian dead.[49] Although Algeria would later prove to be the scene of last-ditch French resistance to decolonization, in the mood of the country in 1945 independence for Vietnam was equally inconceivable. It seemed, as much as anything, to be a matter of principle. Not only was France a republic, one and indivisible, but so was the French 'community' which comprised France and its colonies. In any event, and no matter what reforms were contemplated, the issue that was posed by Marius Moutet, pre-war Minister for the Colonies in the Popular Front and shortly to become Minister for Overseas France, was whether or not France really considered herself to be a nation of 100 m. and whether or not she was to be a great power. Others, like Bidault or de Gaulle, had no doubt: but for this even to be approximately true the contribution of her overseas territories was indispensable.[50] De Gaulle, at Brazzaville in 1944, may have believed that France, of all the imperial powers, would choose nobly and liberally in a new era; on a more mundane level and on the same occasion it was also agreed that 'access to the riches of all that bears the French name is the most certain measure of our country's return to grandeur'.[51]

It would seem from the record, therefore, that France was not prepared to dismantle her colonial empire. That is to say no French government and probably no French political party at this time was willing to concede the principle of secession; and the permanent loss of Indochina would obviously have made it harder to hold on to French North Africa and even to Black Africa. In Vietnam, however, after the war had ended, half of the problem was how to regain half of the country that was still under Chinese occupation and here one might argue, cynically, that the French Union was indispensable. And even if it was not it allowed both sides an extra nine months in which to strengthen their positions.

AGREEMENT OR DISAGREEMENT?

The agreement of 6 March 1946 reached between Jean Sainteny and Ho Chi Minh in effect postponed the basic disagreement between France and the Vietminh. The situation that produced it was comparable to that which was to lead to a similar agreement between the returning Dutch and those who had proclaimed the Republic of Indonesia: in both cases neither side was prepared, there and then, for all-out war when the last British forces left Indonesia or when the Chinese armies in Tonkin were finally persuaded to leave. In Indonesia a large part of the argument which led on two occasions to undeclared war turned on the federal nature of the new state. In Vietnam, it was the same argument, and with many of the same features, that underlay the nature of the French Union.

In so far as the French Union was a federation which would group Indochina, Black Africa, and North Africa it was, as Raymond Aron pointed out, a grandiose objective[52] but at least in the original proposals of the drafting committee which included a former governor general of Indochina, Alexandre Varenne, it was to be a union based on free consent. To that extent it might in principle have been acceptable to the Vietminh government: but probably only to the point where, in practice, it was powerless to circumscribe the sovereignty of the Democratic Republic. In a memorable analogy the black African nationalist (and socialist) leader Leopold Senghor had said that the French Union must not be built like a cage that no one would care to enter; but in the Ho–Sainteny agreement the Vietminh were in effect being asked to take up the tenancy of a building that had not yet been constructed. Perhaps with a generous spirit on both sides some sort of accommodation might have been reached but before the possible constraints of the French Union became important there were more ominous developments, first in Vietnam, then in Paris, which would make a full-scale confrontation more likely.

The Ho-Sainteny agreement, momentous in that it allowed a temporary re-occupation of Tonkin by French forces, was nevertheless reckoned to be a preliminary. When the two sides met again at the hill station of Dalat in April 1946 it was obvious that the immediate disagreement was on the nature of the Indochina Federation and whether or not the Government of Vietnam, which the French had already recognized, was anything more than the Republic of Tonkin. Both sides had agreed that the unification of the three parts of Vietnam would be subject to a referendum. It was now becoming increasingly clear that the French were determined at least to hold on to the richest party, namely Cochinchina: or at least this was the unmistakable objective of the new French High Commissioner, the implacable Admiral Thierry d'Argenlieu. As much if not more Gaulliste than de Gaulle, d'Argenlieu, a regular naval officer, was also the former prior of a Carmelite monastery. Practically unstoppable in pursuit of his ideas about France's place in Indochina, he was also, apparently uncontrollable, at least by the government in Paris. Although his actions were widely condemned at the time and subsequently, it is a more open question whether his objectives were so much at odds with those of his government.

When they returned to Cochinchina the French began by treating it as a restored colony and with Cédile, the French Commissioner in the South, and Moutet in Paris both anticipating, or frustrating, the results of the promised referendum there were increasing prospects that it would be retained for French economic interests in the form of a nominally autonomous government. The creation of such a 'free state' of the same order as the one which the French already recognized in Hanoi was bound to reflect on French good faith and again to call the unity of Vietnam into question. When the negotiations began at Dalat it was Giap who assumed the principal role on the Vietnamese side and while, as communists, they *might* have accepted a smaller but communist state that could conceivably have been free of the French, it was as nationalists that the Vietminh argued their case for indissoluble national unity. To lose Cochinchina, they said, would be like France losing Alsace-Lorraine; and with the French stepping up their efforts to create the impression of autonomy in Cochinchina the conference ended in total disagreement. In Cochinchina, as in Tonkin, French, Vietminh, and nationalist forces were in close proximity and as long as Vietnam's political future was in doubt clashes were almost inevitable. The Vietminh argued that the French in Cochinchina had never observed either the spirit or the letter of the Ho–Sainteny agreement. The French replied that the devastation and terrorism that continued was not all the fault of 'dissident' nationalist Vietnamese or bandits and although it might not have the status of an 'official' armed struggle the results were indistinguishable. And it was to restore order, as much as anything, that a nominally Vietnamese administration provided at least the façade of an 'independent' Vietnamese government

Admiral d'Argenlieu, who regarded the Ho–Sainteny agreement as the equivalent of Munich, was temperamentally opposed to negotiation and was obviously ready if not anxious to put differences with the Vietminh to the test of battle. General Leclerc, as a soldier, was not, at least not to begin with, and believed not only that the reconquest of Tonkin, even in part, was impossible but that a negotiated settlement was essential even if it conceded independence.[53] For the moment, however, there was still an outside chance that when the nationalist and communist members of what was described as a good-will parliamentary mission from Hanoi – and Ho as President – arrived in the more liberal and relaxed atmosphere of Paris an understanding might have been reached. But by the time the delegation set out for Paris, the French Draft Constitution had already been rejected – and with it the principle of free consent on which the French Union was to be based – and while he was still en route to France Ho learned that a Provisional Government of Cochinchina had been announced.[54] By the time negotiations finally got under way at Fontainebleau, elections for the new Constituent Assembly in France had resulted in a victory for the Catholic MRP, with the Communists in second place, and heavy losses for the French Socialist Party. Neither d'Argenlieu nor Ho led their respective sides at Fontainebleau but an agreement seemed no more likely between their substitutes: Max André, with his interests in the Banque de l'Indo-Chine, and Pham Van Dong.

One, the friend of the new French Prime Minister, Georges Bidault, had apparently been told that he could not concede the fundamental issue of independence[55]; for the other, who was to succeed Ho on his death, and for the large and varied delegation which came to Paris under the title of the Popular National Front (*Lien Viet*) everything, practically, turned on the question of Cochinchina. In what might conceivably have been the last chance of a diplomatic settlement, with the encouraging or surreal touches of a personally popular Ho walking up the Champs Elysées to lay a wreath on the Tomb of the Unknown Soldier and standing beside Bidault on the Fourteenth of July, these were the fundamental issues. Perhaps, as Ho said later, all that was needed was for the French to pronounce one word: independence; but on both sides this was the most fraught and emotional issue. It was unlikely to be conceded by Bidault and the MRP; Thorez and the Communists were not particularly interested; and the only Socialist member of the French team at Fontainebleau resigned after two hours.[56]

As at Dalat in April, the Fontainebleau conference failed entirely on substantive issues. Bidault, it has been said, leader of the Resistance in occupied France, may have been unaware how the world outside had changed during the war; but in any event distrusted Ho as a communist as well as a nationalist threat to France's post-war international position. Pham Van Dong in Paris, as well as Giap in Hanoi, had a comparable distrust of French intentions and, since elections of a kind had been held in January 1946,[57] the Vietminh had been busy consolidating communist power at the centre of a nationalist movement which, in its external aspect, impressed many observers with its moderation. Internally, it was a different matter where ultra-nationalist rivals and critics of even temporary accommodation with the French, as well as those who were suspected of favouring them, were being liquidated in purges which were probably as bloody as most in Eastern Europe and on some occasions it seems the former were killed as a result of Franco-Vietminh collaboration.[58] In most other respects, however, joint efforts, such as they were, to keep the peace, let alone to share the responsibilities of government, were coming to an end. In Tonkin as well as in Cochinchina both sides at best ignored the other as well as the general terms of their March agreement. Thus, and apparently removing all doubt about French intentions to dismember Vietnam, when d'Argenlieu convened another conference at Dalat on 1 August 1946 to discuss Indochinese problems, there were representatives of Laos, Cambodia, and Cochinchina as well as the dubious entities of 'Southern Annam' and the *montagnards* of the Southern Plateau – but no Vietminh.[59] This was to provide the occasion on the Vietnamese side for terminating the Fontainebleau exercise. After their return to Vietnam a Constitution was approved for the Democratic Republic which completely ignored the Indochina Federation and all mention of the French Union – but which affirmed that 'The territory of Vietnam . . . is one and indivisible'.

Years later, when Sainteny returned to Hanoi, Le Duan recalled these words, which he attributed to Ho Chi Minh, and which may stand as his memorial inscription: 'The Vietnamese nation is one and indivisible.' As much as anything it represents the conviction which took the communist leadership of a proto-state into and through two cataclysmic conflicts with a tenacity and disregard of human life that has characterized religious, revolutionary and patriotic wars. It was opposed, on the French side, by virtually the same principle which, for all the emotional resurgence of Jacobin principles that may have suffused France at the end of the war, had faded by comparison with the raw and remorseless nationalism that was waiting to engulf the French from one end of Vietnam to the other. Given these irreconcilable purposes it is Pham Van Dong and Giap, to take two symbols of Vietnamese intransigence, rather than Ho Chi Minh, who represented the reality of Franco-Vietnamese relations in the four or five months before the all-out war began in December 1946; even though it is tempting to consider how, up to the last minute, conflict might have been averted – or at least postponed.

Although the Fontainebleau conference failed and the Vietnamese delegation went home, Ho stayed on to conclude, on 14 September 1946, what Sainteny has called 'that pathetic *modus vivendi*' which gave France economic concessions and the promise of maintaining cultural connections in return for her co-operation in securing an armistice in the South. Again, it left the basic issues of independence and Cochinchina unresolved but perhaps, as Ho had said, it was better than nothing. For the moment it may have smoothed or at least covered the jagged edges between the two sides. Although it may have also been one of the last, desperate attempts to keep the road open to a negotiated settlement, Ho was being accused by the French, who compared the diplomatic assurances in Paris with continuing violence in Vietnam, of duplicity; and, ominously, by the intransigents in Hanoi, of treachery. Perhaps it was just procrastination. He may have believed, and was encouraged to think, that the Communist Party would win the coming election in France and form, or at least be made part of, a new government; and the Russian advice seems to have been to hold on and to wait for 'democratic France' and its 'progressive forces' to support the cause of colonial liberation.[60]

Alternatively, Ho may simply have been waiting for something to turn up, something that would tip the scales one way or the other in the situation that was neither peace nor war. It was also, one must remember, a situation of continuing revolution which had no more ended in August 1945 than the French revolution had in July 1789. Although compressed into less than 18 months there are certain similarities between the two revolutions, in their tactics as well as their phases, and although it is not explicit there is a remarkable comparison that may be inferred from Devillers' brilliant essay in which he describes a Vietminh, at the end of 1946, already losing momentum and because of that, driven to imprudent acts:

> The Vietminh had subjected the people to an extremely painful strain, practically a permanent mobilization, with its unending meetings, mass demonstrations, and the like, with its requisitions, with its control of thoughts and acts, with its atmosphere of suspicion and its informers, with the arrogance – and often the arbitrariness – of its officials, with its youth corps (the Tu Ve), and with the arrests, the abductions or assassination of its opponents and even of those considered lukewarm or suspect. If the Vietminh still seemed to be the only movement capable of achieving

the fulfilment of the people's aspiration to national independence and to social justice, it nevertheless ruled with the aid of physical terror and moral constraint. As under the old régime, the political police, now called Trinh Sat or Cong An, was the main buttress of the régime.[61]

FLASHPOINTS

Whether or not it was 'in their haste, their unwillingness to temporise, that the Vietminh leaders, with their fathomless vanity, had driven their country straight into conflict with France' – the reproach of Vietnamese intellectuals and non-marxist nationalists – it was a rather academic if not drawing-room argument that the Vietminh could easily have brought about national unanimity and created a national state rather than revolution and the party state. The Vietminh, like the original French Commune, were embedded in the events of a more or less national revolution, turning it in particular directions but by no means in complete control. The *enragés* and the Girondins had their counterparts in Vietnam and in some respects, for example asceticism and a belief in virtue, whether Confucian or revolutionary, one might even compare Ho with Robespierre. More important one should realize that attempts at accommodation between the two new Republics, French and Vietnamese, were taking place not between two sovereign states but between two political forces in the same country, each in the throes of revolution, each unwilling to concede sovereignty to the other. As both manoeuvred for position, whether it was cutting down trees and digging up streets in Hanoi or sending 'unauthorized' French battalions to various strategic points, the risk – and incidence – of clashes increased and both sides were at least preparing for war. Before he left Fontainebleau Ho had given instructions to be ready for any eventuality. A few weeks earlier, on 10 April 1946, a circular from General Valluy, at that time d'Argenlieu's deputy in Saigon, had raised the question of a purely military operation 'in the scenario of a *coup d'état*'; and for both sides there seemed to be obvious advantages in striking first.

The attempt by Frenchmen to seize a Chinese junk carrying what was considered to be a cargo of contraband fuel, and their ensuing capture by Vietminh militia, was an unlikely incident to trigger a war and falls, no doubt, into Aristotle's category of trivial occasions. The incident, trivial in itself, of 20 November 1946, culminated three days later in a terrible bombardment of Haiphong which was a prelude to pitched battles in Tonkin between the Vietminh forces and the French; and although the usually quoted figure of 6,000 Vietnamese dead in Haiphong may be too high, the ease with which casualties of this order could be inflicted, with a French cruiser joining in at close range, suggested misleadingly that when French forces were fully engaged it would be such a one-sided contest that the Vietminh would learn the appropriate lesson.[62] Such, indeed, seems on the French side, to have been the object of the exercise. When d'Argenlieu dispatched himself hastily to Paris a few days after the French elections and before the Haiphong incident, it was to lobby intensively for a policy of firmness; and his tactic, says Devillers, was simply to create fear.[63] Not only was this the only way, according to d'Argenlieu, to stop a Vietminh that was determined to oust the French but, in effect, it would be the only way to hold the French Union together. When the Inter-Ministerial Committee on Indochina met on 23 November 1946 and heard d'Argenlieu's report it resulted in what Devillers affirms was obviously the government's decision to face up to every infringement of the Franco–Vietminh agreement, if necessary by force. And these infringements, needless to say, could only come from the Vietminh.

Whether or not Bidault actually insisted '*Il faut tirer le canon*',[64] d'Argenlieu cabled his commander in Saigon, General Valluy, to this effect and, by-passing General Morlière in Hanoi, orders were sent direct to the 'irascible' Colonel Dèbes in Haiphong. Thus, after two days in which a negotiated settlement to the original squabble seemed possible, an ultimatum to the Vietminh to clear out of Haiphong in two hours led to a bombardment which must have killed at least 1,000 people, many if not most of whom would be described as innocent civilians. As a result, the Vietminh undoubtedly came, as General Valluy intended, to a better appreciation of the situation. There were fragments of evidence, however, to suggest that the final collision might have been avoided. In the last interview he gave to a French journalist before the war began, Ho, in envisaging the way in which 'at all costs war must be averted', seemed to accept independence within the French Union; although unless this was based on a total misunderstanding of the nature of the French Union, which also seems unlikely, this was probably more of a smoke-screen than a smoke-signal.[65] On the French side although the Communists failed to form a government and were thus not in a position to change French policy towards Vietnam – whether they would have wanted to do so is not quite so clear – the impasse between them and the MRP had resulted in a caretaker government under the veteran Socialist party leader, Léon Blum; and Blum, calling for an end to equivocation and an absolutely clear definition of policy, had urged not only confidence and friendship but 'sincere agreement' on the basis of Vietnamese independence.[66] Ho responded immediately to this newspaper article by proposing various measures which might lead to a return to normality and to the hopeful provisions of the *modus vivendi*, not least an end to the press and radio incitements from both sides, [67] but whether at this stage Ho and Blum were in the saddle or not, things were beginning to fall apart. For one thing it seems that Ho's reply, via Saigon, was held up deliberately by the French authorities so that it was not received in Paris until after the war had begun. For another, the 'war party' may already have taken over within the Vietminh: at least when Sainteny, attempting his last act of mediation, saw Ho for the last time before the war started, he complained about the moderate elements who had been eliminated from the government to the benefit of the notorious Francophobes; and as the war was on the point of beginning, and as attacks on French soldiers and civilians had not ceased, nor had French retaliation, Sainteny's exasperation was to be seen in his demand that culprits should be punished within 24 hours.

This was hardly a crucial ultimatum but, coming from a moderate, indeed sympathetic Frenchman, it suggests that the French, generally, were beyond the point of no return; while for the Vietminh, with assorted military forces estimated at 60,000, having already lost Haiphong as the point of entry for many of their weapons and in danger now of facing overwhelming French fire power in Hanoi, the temptations of a pre-emptive strike, even if it was an act of desperation, must have been irresistible. With d'Argenlieu returned to Saigon but no more amenable to close control from Paris than Paris seemed disposed to provide it, with the French forces understandably nervous and anxious at least to clear Hanoi of their opponents, one may feel that whether it was the French or the Vietminh who brought about the final rupture does not much matter.[68] In the event, and after at least a hint of treachery, shortly after eight o'clock on the night of 19 December 1946 the Vietminh blew up the power station in Hanoi and signalled the formal beginning of the Vietnam war.[69]

NOTES AND REFERENCES

1.   Virginia Thompson, *French Indochina* (London 1937), p. 249.
2.   Dennis J. Duncanson, *Government and Revolution in Vietnam* (London 1968), p. 99.
3.   Lancaster, *The Emancipation of French Indo-China* (London 1961), pp. 65–6.
4.   Duncanson, op. cit. p. 109.
5.   William J. Duiker, 'Hanoi Scrutinizes the Past: The Marxist Evaluation of Phan Boi Chau and Phan Chu Trinh', *Southeast Asia*, Summer 1971, Vol. 1 Part 3.
6.   For the development of Soviet policy see Charles B. McLane, *Soviet Strategies in South-East Asia* (Princeton 1966).
7.   The significant part of the text is given in Hélène Carrére d'Encausse and Stuart R. Schram, *Marxism and Asia* (London 1969).

8. Jean Lacouture, *Cinq Hommes Et La France* (Paris 1961), p. 12.
9. d'Encausse and Schram, op. cit. pp. 199–200.
10. William J. Duiker, *The Communist Road to Power in Vietnam* (Boulder 1981), p. 18.
11. I. Milton Sacks, 'Marxism in Vietnam' in Frank N. Traeger (ed.) *Marxism in South-East Asia* (Stanford 1959).
12. Sacks, op. cit.
13. James C. Scott, *The Moral Economy of the Peasant* (Yale 1976).
14. Duiker, op. cit. p. 43.
15. July 1 1931. Sacks, op. cit. p. 136.
16. McLane, op. cit. p. 217.
17. Douglas Pike, *Viet Cong* (MIT 1968), p. 24. Pike says that, according to reliable sources, the day war began someone delivered to Sûreté headquarters in Saigon the full Fourth International Party membership roster, listing names, aliases, addresses, and locations of every Trotskyist in the country. Within hours French police had rounded up virtually all leaders and dispatched them to the New Hebrides, New Caledonia, Madagascar, and other French colonies remote from Indochina. Years later, according to Pike, many Vietnamese historians and political scientists in Saigon asserted that only the ICP had the resources and the capability to accomplish such a feat of tactical intelligence. Pike, *History of Vietnamese Communism, 1925–1976* (Stanford 1978), p. 37.
18. Duiker, op. cit. p. 68.
19. Pike, *History of Vietnamese Communism 1925–1976* p. 47.
20. Bernard Fall, *Ho Chi Minh on Revolution* (New York 1967), p. 132, 134.
21. As Christine White suggests in her introduction to Truong Chinh and Vo Nguyen Giap *The Peasant Question (1937–1938)*, Cornell Data Paper no. 94, Ithaca January 1974.
22. Op. cit. p. 22.
23. Edward R. Drachman, *United States Policy Towards Vietnam, 1940–1945* (New Jersey 1970), p. 33.
24. British readers will scarcely need to be reminded that the Japanese torpedo bombers which sank the *Prince of Wales* and the *Repulse* had taken off from French airfields in Vietnam.
25. Christopher Thorne, *Allies of a Kind* (London 1979), p. 468. Churchill concluded his note to Eden by asking him if he really wanted to go and stir all this up at such a time as this, i.e. (as Thorne notes) on the eve of D-day. Roosevelt, too, is on record as telling a number of diplomatic representatives, Russian, Chinese and British included, that he 'had been working hard to prevent Indo-China being restored to France who, during the past hundred years, had done nothing for the Indo-Chinese people under their care' and advocating a UN trusteeship to prepare the territory for independence. Thorne, op. cit. p. 463.
26. Duiker, op. cit. p. 79.
27. According to Duiker the first unit was formed on 22 December 1944 and consisted of 34 men. Two days later, on Christmas Eve, it is supposed to have attacked and destroyed two French camps and captured a number of weapons. Duiker says that the unit then moved

north 'to consolidate the border area' although this was obviously a large task for such a small force.

28.   The controversy has continued for the last thirty years. After the war was over the US 14th Airforce Commander, General Chennault wrote that '. . . orders arrived from Theater Headquarters stating that no arms and ammunition would be provided to French troops under any circumstances.' Wedemeyer's orders not to aid the French says Chennault, came directly from the War Department. 'Apparently it was American policy then that French Indo-China would not be returned to the French.' Quoted in Bernard Fall *The Two Vietnams* (London 1963). Peter M. Dunn, in the course of compiling his book *The First Vietnam War* (London 1985) succeeded, where Fall had failed, in interviewing General Wedemeyer. Among his conclusions was that much of the disagreement between Wedemeyer and Mountbatten originated with Chiang Kai-Shek who 'told Mountbatten one thing and Wedemeyer the opposite'. It is hard to accept the proposition of Ronald H. Spector in his volume on the US Army in Vietnam *Advice and Support: The Early Years* (Washington 1983) that 'The view that the United States deliberately limited and delayed its help to the French during the Japanese takeover is thus incorrect' (p. 34) and the source of the delay and limitations to American assistance to the French in Vietnam was to be found in attitudes that went all the way up to, and policy directives that came down from, the highest levels of American Government. For months Roosevelt refused to discuss the matter with anyone except Churchill. Churchill was noticeably reticent to raise the issue himself until the Japanese coup precipitated operational decisions; and at the time that French forces were fighting their way out of Vietnam Roosevelt is on record that he had not changed his ideas: that French Indo-China and New Caledonia should be taken from France and be put under trusteeship. 'The President hesitated a moment and then said – Well, if we can get the proper pledge from France to assume for herself the obligations of a trustee, then I would agree to France retaining these colonies with a proviso that independence was the ultimate goal. I asked the President if he would settle for self-government. He said no. I asked him if he would settle for dominion status. He said no – it must be independence. He said that is to be the policy and you can quote me in the State Department'. This excerpt from *Foreign Relations of the United States, 1945* (FRUS) Vol. 1 p. 124 is contained in Allan W. Cameron, *Vietnam Crisis* (London 1971), p. 33. Equally revealing, in the same volume is Roosevelt's conversation with Stalin at Tehran in November 1943: 'He felt that many years of honest labour were necessary before France would be re-established. He said the first necessity for the French, not only for the government but the people as well, was to become honest citizens.' Cameron, op. cit. p. 10. For another account of the generally unsuccessful efforts of Force 136 in Indo-China, secret French missions, and some less than transparent honesty between allies see Charles Cruickshank, *SOE in the Far-East* (Oxford 1983), part 2 ch. 4. It is, incidentally, in the latter aspect of clandestine operations that Dunn makes the sensational claim that on

the night of 22 January 1945 two British four-engined 'Liberators' (American B 24s) flying to Tonkin were destroyed by American night fighters based in China, a loss which Dunn describes as a logical outcome of the Mountbatten–Wedemeyer dispute over activity in Indo-China. This would certainly have been possible – Dunn suggests that for a period at least the American P 61 night fighters destroyed more Allied than Japanese planes – and while the original information came from the British military representative in Chungking, and the results of a subsequent investigation were apparently not released or cannot be found in the Public Record Office, it is also possible and more likely that the aircraft ran out of fuel and crashed in Burma on its return flight. Dunn op. cit. pp. 87–8. Also author's correspondence with Ministry of Defence, Air Historical Branch, London; and Wing Commander Peter Farr. An authentic, evocative account of RAF support for clandestine operations in Southeast Asia has now been published by Terence O'Brien *The Moonlight War* (London 1987). See in particular pp. 106–8.

29.   FO 371 F63/11/6 Eden to Duff Cooper, 12 March 1945 Public Record Office, London.

30.   R.E.M. Irving, *The First Indo-China War* (London 1975), p. 4.

31.   Ibid.

32.   David Halberstam claims that there is considerable evidence that five thousand weapons were air-dropped to the Vietminh in the summer of 1945 by the Allies. Presumably this was mostly if not entirely by the United States. David Halberstam *Ho* (New York 1971), Ch. 4.

33.   Charles Fenn, *Ho Chi Minh* (London 1973), p. 82.

34.   Cited in Cameron op. cit. p. 27. See, also, Duncanson 'Ho Chi Minh And The August Revolution Of 1945 In Indochina' in *The Lugano Review*, May 1975.

35.   Brian Crozier, *De Gaulle: The Warrior* (London 1973), p. 364.

36.   Bao Dai, *Le Dragon D'Annam* (Paris 1980), p. 119.

37.   Rima Rathausky (ed.), *Documents of the August 1945 Revolution in Vietnam* (Canberra 1963), p.53.

38.   In an article 'The Vietnamese August Revolution Reinterpreted' Huynh Kim Khanh says that the ICP skills in revolutionary analysis, organization, propaganda, and leadership were undoubtedly superior to *all* save none, of Vietnamese political parties. The Japanese coup was equally important but by destroying French colonialism it merely provided the Vietnamese revolution with an opportunity, a chance for success. The rest was up to the Vietnamese revolutionaries themselves. *Journal of Asian Studies* Vol. xxx no. 4, August 1971.

39.   Duiker, op. cit. p. 91.

40.   Quoted in Bernard Fall, *The Two Vietnams*, (London 1963), p. 68. Patti's account is to be found in Archimedes L.A. Patti, *Why Vietnam?* (Berkeley 1980).

41.   Starting with the *a priori* assumption that the French should not have returned to Vietnam, Harold Isaacs, an American journalist in Saigon at the time, suggests that numbers of Vietnamese were killed in the September coup. This is denied by Dunn who provides a credible account of what was happening during the British occupation. Harold Isaacs, *No*

Peace for Asia (Cambridge, Mass. 1967) and Dunn, op. cit. The most recent and most reliable account, which has the added advantage of comparison with what was happening in Indonesia, is to be found in Peter Dennis, *Troubled Days of Peace* (Manchester 1987).

42. For years one of the armed factions of Vietnamese political life who paraded proudly under a voluminous banner which said 'Binh Xuyen Pirates'. See Lancaster, op. cit. p. 137.

43. Lancaster notes that, as part of the general turbulence in Vietnam at this time, another of the armed religious sects, the *Hoa Hoa*, some fifteen thousand or so, had attempted to set up their own 'kingdom' early in September but had been repulsed by the Vietminh and the Japanese. On the deadly rivalry between the Vietminh and the Trotskyists, Lancaster says that the Vietminh leader in the South, Tran Van Giau, was responsible for the mass arrests and executions of the Trotskyist leaders, ibid.

44. Dunn, op. cit. p. 196.

45. Ibid. p. 286, 293, 309.

46. Ibid. p. 263.

47. Ibid. p. 251.

48. D. Bruce Marshall, *The French Colonial Myth and Constitution-Making in the Fourth Republic* (New Haven 1973), p. 135.

49. See Alistair Horne, *A Savage War of Peace* (London 1977), Ch. 1.

50. See Marshall, op cit. Chs. 5, 6 and 7. Also Clark W. Garrett 'In Search of Grandeur: France in Vietnam 1940–1946', *The Review of Politics* Vol. 29 no. 3 July 1967.

51. Marshall, op. cit. pp. 103, 110.

52. Garrett, op. cit. p. 317.

53. Irving, who had access to the papers of Jean Letourneau, the MRP Minister of Overseas France, quotes from the Leclerc report of 30 April 1946, op. cit. p. 19.

54. Philippe Devillers *Histoire Du Viêt-Nam* (Paris 1952), gives one of his chapters the title 'La chevauchée cochinchinoise'. Rather than a cavalcade, however, the Provisional Government may be seen as a charade with very little power and doubtful popular support. See also Hammer, op. cit. and Lancaster, op. cit.

55. According to André's interview with Irving, op. cit. p. 27.

56. Hammer, op. cit. p. 167.

57. Duiker says, without comment, that 97 per cent of the electorate voted, op. cit. p. 117. This would have been a spectacularly high figure even allowing for the excitement of Vietnam's first general election. Hammer, op. cit. says: 'It was, in fact, impossible to talk of real fairness and accuracy in a country-wide election held in conditions of quasi-war and among people who had no knowledge of the techniques of democracy.' p. 143. Devillers gives a qualified answer to the question 'Can one speak of free elections?': 'Yes and no.' Be that as it may, he says, from now on the Vietminh had their democratic façade. op. cit. p. 201. Lancaster, op. cit. concludes that in spite of many irregularities the results 'were probably fairly indicative of the state of public opinion at that time'. p. 127.

58. 'Even before the armed conflict blanketed the entire country,

the Communists felt perfectly justified in equating opposition to the Vietminh with anti-state activity. Though the communists introduced radical democratic reforms, they had no compunction about imprisoning or even murdering those who tried to use these reforms to oppose them.' Joseph Buttinger, *Vietnam: A Political History* (New York 1968), p. 258.

59.   The Dutch, by coincidence, had just convened a similar meeting at Malino to contain and dilute the strength of the Indonesian Republic within a federal structure. But, having chosen the delegates, the Dutch were apparently surprised by their demands for genuine independence.

60.   'Until the outcome of the Communist struggle for power in France was known, a clear-cut policy in Indo-China was blocked. No Communist, respecting Stalin's interest in a Communist France, could urge the revolutionary course which the situation in Vietnam appeared to warrant.' McLane, op. cit. p. 271.

61.   Devillers, 'Vietnamese Nationalism and French Policies' in William L. Holland (ed.) *Asian Nationalism and the West* (London 1953).

62.   By contrast, when British and Republican forces had fought a comparable pitched battle in the Indonesian port of Surabaya a year earlier – a battle which may also have had essentially accidental origins – the violence of the encounter left no doubt, at least for the British, about the strength of Indonesian nationalism.

63.   Devillers, *Histoire Du Viêt-Nam* pp. 340–1.

64.   As Communist former Minister Charles Tillon told the National Assembly in 1949. Quoted by Irving, op. cit. p. 29.

65.   Devillers, op. cit. pp. 347–8.

66.   Ibid. pp. 342–3.

67.   Ibid.

68.   Irving, op.cit. p.29.

69.   The events that led up to the outbreak of war on 19 December are dealt with in two brilliant and fascinating pieces of historical reconstruction by the Norwegian historian, Stein Tønnesson: *The Outbreak of War in Indochina 1946*, International Peace Research Institute, Oslo 1982, and *1946: Déclenchement de la guerre d'Indochine, Les vêpres tonkinoises du 19 Décembre* (Paris 1987).

Chapter 2

ACHESON AND THE ENTANGLING ALLIANCE: 1946–1952

THE INCLINATION TO INTERVENE: HOPE OF A NEGOTIATED SETTLEMENT

As soon as the French war in Vietnam started the US began to think about forms of intervention. At first the ideas appeared as rumours and reports: that, although it had not yet been announced, the US had already taken steps to halt the fighting; that, in Washington, ambassador Bonnet had been called in and told that a settlement was imperative; that if the matter was brought up in the UN the US would not necessarily support France; that the US wished to ensure that no Lend-Lease weapons were being used 'to suppress Vietnam' – although it was suspected they were; and that the head of Southeast Asian Affairs at the State Department (Mr A.L. Moffat) was already in the area and would be glad to assist both sides.[1] According to the US consul in Saigon, three and a half of these four statements were completely false but, in fact, not only may Under-Secretary of State Dean Acheson have offered the 'good offices' of the US[2] (as they were to be offered in Indonesia) but there was also at the same time in effect a plea from Moffat, then in Singapore, that for various reasons the US should intervene. Third-party action, he said, was essential. There was a deep need for US moral leadership. The Vietminh record was no worse than that of the French. America's 'hands off' policy was based on European rather than on Asian considerations. The USSR was not directly active in Southeast Asia: there was, said Moffat sarcastically, no need because the democracies were performing most effectively on their behalf. And Moffat himself seemed hopeful of a political solution based on an independent Vietnam which was to be associated with or even part of the French Union.[3] At about the same time as the State Department was receiving this cable from their most senior man on the spot, Secretary of State Byrnes was cabling the Paris embassy that the French were planning to reconquer Tonkin and might set up a puppet government; while in Hanoi the French commander, General Morlière, was claiming that the US and Chinese consuls had denounced the 'criminal and bestial folly' of the Vietminh; although apparently they hadn't said a word one way or the other. Thus, by the very beginning of 1947, and well before 'containment', the Marshall plan and the Zhdanov doctrine drew the battle lines between Russia and the US in Europe and in general it may be seen that a framework of impressions, intentions, hopes and misunderstandings was being thrown up which would support US policy towards Vietnam for the next 20 years and under whose weight it would ultimately collapse. Specifically, there was the idea of intervention; historic doubts about and antipathy towards European colonialism; corresponding commitment to self-determination and, above all, an impressive self-confidence founded on US power, a resurgence of Wilsonian ideals, and a belief that the principles of the Atlantic Charter and those of the UN should at least inform if they did not determine the foreign policies of the US. At any rate at the beginning, there was a certain even-handedness towards France and the Vietminh coupled with resistance to France's manifest intention that the US could hardly help being involved, one way or another, even though they professed neutrality. This role may have been rather a disappointment to both sides, as General Gallagher said when he got back from Hanoi,[4] although by opposing the clearance of wartime US mines that had been laid in Haiphong harbour, thus preventing an early return of French troopships, Gallagher seems to have come down rather heavily on the Vietminh side.[5]

Once the war between France and the Vietminh had begun, the time had obviously passed when American operational decisions such as this would affect the fortunes of either side. For someone like Moffat, one of the professionals who was helping to mould US policy in Southeast Asia, there had been no doubt, at least before the event, that the liberation of Indo-China was going to depend upon the US defeat of Japan. Because the US was sacrificing blood and treasure to assure peace and stability in the Far East, the maintenance of which after the war would be largely a US responsibility, it would not have been unreasonable 'to insist that the French give adequate assurances as to the implementing of policies in Indo-China which we consider essential to assure peace and stability in the Far East'.[6]

Perhaps, as Moffat said, Americans could see the situation in Southeast Asia more objectively than the British, the French and the Dutch because 'they could analyse problems without the handicap of self-interest, prejudice, pride or domestic politics'.[7] When it came to actually making policy, however, and actually using 'the power we had to try to secure self-government in Indo-China', not only would the problems of intervention against US allies presumably have been more difficult than against her enemies, but there was always the risk as well that circumstances might prejudice ideal or even optimum solutions. For example, when the State Department's Far Eastern Office was trying, unsuccessfully, to put together a compromise paper that would be agreed with the European Office, one may applaud the objective of an Indo-China that was to be fully self-governed, autonomous, and democratic: but there was a world of difference between a 'national' and a 'federal' government which would become obvious as events unfolded and the qualification, which Moffat and his colleagues seemed to accept, to full self-government which was explicit in Indo-China's recommended partnership in the French Union, and was, by implication reserved to France as a matter of imperial concern, precisely the point, or at least the formality, which produced the irreparable break between France and Ho's infant Republic.[8]

Moffat's testimony although, obviously, personal would seem to uncover therefore not only the roots of US policy in Vietnam – a belief in trusteeship, and international organization generally, a distrust of France, a traditional antipathy to colonialism – but also an immanent if unconscious belief in US intervention that was necessary for the ordering of a more perfect world. At the same time he reflects the important belief that Ho Chi Minh was first and foremost a Vietnamese nationalist even though in his next sentence Moffat said 'He was also a communist and believed that communism offered the best hope for the Vietnamese people.' This may, of course, have been a retrospective opinion that was at least tinged with 25 years' subsequent experience and challenged, both before and after, the worldwide definitions of the late 1940s which seemed to require that the Vietminh should have been put into either one of two boxes, nationalist or communist, but not both. At the time, however, the question of Ho Chi Minh's communism and his connections with Moscow and with 'international communism' seemed somewhat academic and certainly no more important to begin with than the mounting suspicions of France's unreconstructed colonialism.[9]

When Secretary of State Marshall was cabling the Embassy in Paris that Ho Chi Minh had direct Communist connections – whether or not this was a fact depends upon what one means by 'connection' – he argued that it was also a fact that colonial empires, in the 19th-century sense, were rapidly becoming a thing of the past. Although the US, or at least the State Department, 'frankly [had] no solution of problem to suggest' it was obvious that the US was at this stage hoping for a negotiated settlement, a settlement in which their further hope was that France would find it possible to be more than generous.[10]

By this time it was becoming obvious that in spite of the fact that the French were conveying the impression of a limited operation 'to restore order' (which might be at least six months to a year) they were hoping for more moderate Vietnamese leaders to emerge and, in the meantime, they would not after all negotiate with Ho Chi Minh. Thus, although the US had been told by the French not only that there was no question of the 'reconquest' of Indo-China but that it was also doubtful that France had the military strength to accomplish it,[11] they were also invited to believe, by the French, that Ho was in direct contact with Moscow and was receiving advice and instructions from the Soviets. Acheson, as acting Secretary of State, may not have gone so far; although just before the war began, when it looked as if Moffat was going to meet Ho in Hanoi, Acheson asked him to 'keep in mind Ho's clear record as agent international communism, absence evidence recantation Moscow affiliations . . . and support Ho receiving [from] French Communist Party.'[12] (Incidentally, during the Fontainebleau conference Ho had called on the US Ambassador in Paris to assure him that he and his party aspired to independence in the French Union and that he was not a communist.)[13] Again, neither these comments nor what was described as the least desirable eventuality 'the establishment of a Communist-dominated, Moscow-oriented state in Indo-China', seem inaccurate or unreasonable: although it may be argued that the inherent fault was to assume that this represented the limit of Ho's power and appeal. In any case the State Department was uncertain about the nature of the Vietminh's communist connections – 'possibly in indirect touch with Moscow and direct touch with Yenan'[14] – and French influence was reckoned to be important not only as an antidote to Soviet influence but also to protect Vietnam and Southeast Asia from 'future Chinese imperialism'.[15]

THE FRENCH CONNECTION

Such hopes as there may have been – American, French, even Vietminh – of a cease-fire or negotiated settlement lingered on for several months but once the French had begun fighting they presented their case, modestly, that military operations were designed with no thought of reconquest but simply to persuade the Vietminh that they had no hope of victory. After all, of course, negotiations would be possible and already the French claimed that with an estimated eight to ten thousand dead, Vietminh resistance was weakening. In diplomatic exchanges, at least, the French accepted American reservations about unregenerate colonialism in Vietnam although, as the French pointed out, they could not be expected to assist in or condone the establishment of a government of Vietnam which would not follow democratic principles 'as these are understood in the West'. As they did not regard the existing 'Democratic Republic' as representative of the people of Annam and Tonkin (the question of Cochinchina tended not to be raised) this obviously ruled out serious negotation.[16]

At least, one may take this assumption from the terms which the French emissary Paul Mus, after an arduous journey, presented to Ho in May 1947 and which required what amounted to a conditional surrender; and in any case now that the Communist Party had been ousted from the French government there was no longer the same effective demand in France for a negotiated settlement. Nevertheless, with repeated French insinuations that they had neither the means nor the intention of reconquering Vietnam, it obviously came as a shock to the US to discover that this was exactly what France seemed to have in mind. As it happened, in spite of General Marshall's fears, France's colonial policy did not become a Congressional issue in 1947 nor did it, contrary to what Marshall feared, have much effect on public opinion in the US. In any event, in so far as Congress was interested in Asia, and had assumed many direct responsibilities, its concern was with military assistance and 99-year leases on bases in the Philippines and the dilemmas of policy that these signalled towards China. Although the US may never have been on the brink of intervention in China she had sent 50,000 marines to Northern China in 1945, followed by General Marshall acting as Truman's personal representative. His mission, in so far as it was to reconcile the Nationalists and Communists, was a failure and indeed could hardly have been expected to be otherwise. Events in Vietnam, in many ways comparable although obviously complicated by the factor of French colonialism, were of infinitely less interest and for the moment seemed to require only a definition of attitudes rather than acts of policy.

Nevertheless, Vietnam, as well as China, represented entanglements for US policy although, in one respect at least, the possibility that the US might be able to influence French policy and be able to exert sufficient influence on France to reach a negotiated settlement made the situation more hopeful. It was, moreover, a hope which the French encouraged from time to time although what was achieved seemed always to be less than what was promised. Perhaps Bidault, on a visit to the US, gave the best idea of French intentions when he said that Marshall Aid would make it possible for France 'to avoid the abandonment of French positions'[17] and even where there were the generous intentions that the US had hoped for, one way or another they always seemed to be frustrated. Thus, Bollaert, who had replaced d'Argenlieu as High Commissioner, apparently wanted France to take the initiative and to pronounce the word 'independence' in a major speech on 15 August 1947, the day on which India was to receive independence.[18] Even though it seems only to have been conditional independence the terms were so alarming to General Valluy that he flew back to Paris to warn the French Government and the outcome was a special cabinet meeting at which hardly anyone supported the Bollaert initiative. The result was that when Bollaert finally made his speech on 10 September it was obvious that, for all the rhetoric and for all the idealization of the French Union, if it was independence that France was offering, it was so heavily circumscribed as to make it obvious that France had, at most, transferred the Jacobin concept of 'the nation one and indivisible' to a French Union in which she would still be in a commanding position.[19]

Whether or not one regards this as a prime example of the way in which a political settlement was undercut by the optimism of those Frenchmen who believed in a military solution it should also be pointed out, as Irving does, that 'Any policy which might have been construed as the abandonment of Indo-China would have been rejected by the National Assembly in 1947, if not by an overwhelming majority, then at least by a decisive one'[20] but this, in turn, did nothing to resolve the US dilemma. As it was formulated by the US Consul at Saigon:

> Morally, end French believed have in view and tactics to achieve such end are to be condemned and US cannot be party to return pre-war status or even give such appearance without risking destroying large amount confidence natives still have in US. Practically, however, it is of paramount importance that Indo-China does not become prey to an imposed totalitarian régime by use recognized weapons of repression, reprisal and terrorism – natives are divided and majority unprepared for democratic freedom and in such division and unpreparedness the single-minded purpose of 80 to 100 real Communists could easily gain upper hand. No brief can be held for any solution that would put France and Western democracy influence out of Indo-China or leave natives believe US indifferent.[21]

Given these premises, then, and Moffat's distaste notwithstanding that it would imply 'democracies reduced resort monarchy as weapon against Communism',[22] one wonders what else, apart from outright rejection, the US might have done when the French turned towards ex-Emperor Bao Dai: at least as a rallying point for non-communist Vietnamese nationalists and, of course, as someone who might be expected to be more amenable to French influence than Ho Chi Minh.

Nevertheless there was a chance, perhaps, that a French government might have been so far-sighted or faint-hearted that it would have ordered a cease-fire, entered into serious negotiations, abandoned its insistence on membership of the French Union, accepted, at least by instalments, an independent, more or less communist state in a presumably close relationship with either the USSR or the Chinese Communist Party, or both, and been prepared to rely on Vietminh goodwill, such as it might be, for the preservation of whatever position they chose to accord France. It is just conceivable that something like this might have happened had there been a Communist government in France. It is inconceivable that it would have happened under any other party or coalition in the time that remained before the French decided on a military solution. It is also problematic what line the US would have taken if France had decided on such a negotiated settlement. On the one hand an opinion within the Southeast Asian Division of the State Department that 'the ardent leadership of the small Communist group will become less vital' and would be followed by the natural development of political parties. On the other the robust scepticism of the Western European Division:

> It may not be certain, as Ken Landon says, that Ho and Co will succeed in setting up a Communist State if they get rid of the French, but let me suggest that from the stand-point of the security of the US, it is one hell of a big chance to take.[23]

In the event the acceptance of an alternative Vietnamese state under Bao Dai was, from the beginning, recognized as almost as big a risk. Although the US was anxious (or at least willing) to approve the Bay of Along agreement which would have reincorporated Cochinchina with the other two parts of Vietnam and paved the way for the return of Bao Dai as the Emperor of a legally united Vietnam, the French government was hesitating to submit the agreement to the Assembly because Indo-China, as the US Ambassador in France described it, was a stick of dynamite or, to change the metaphor, the French government was like an overloaded ship incapable of accommodating one more passenger without capsizing: 'Indo-China is that passenger'.[24]

On 27 September 1948, the State Department's policy statement was in fact a re-statement of the US dilemma. In one sentence it was 'The objectives of US policy can only be attained by such French action that will satisfy the nationalist aspirations of the peoples of Indo-China'. French sovereignty, it was suggested, had been recognized over Indo-China; but the paper maintained that this did not imply any commitment on the part of the US to assist France to exert its authority over the Indo-Chinese people. 'Since VJ day, the majority people of the area, the Vietnamese, have stubbornly resisted the re-establishment of French authority, a struggle in which we have tried to maintain so far as possible the position of non-support of either party'. Thus, the US had declined to permit the export to the French in Indo-China of arms and munitions for the prosecution of the war against the Vietnamese. (Although, as the free export of arms to France had been permitted, the restrictions were more nominal than real.)

Since early in 1947 the French have employed about 115,000 troops in Indo-China, with little result, since the countryside except in Laos and Cambodia remains under the firm control of the Ho Chi Minh government. A series of French-established puppet governments has tended to enhance the prestige of Ho's government and to call in to question, on the part of the Vietnamese, the sincerity of French intentions to accord an independent status to Vietnam.

As the statement concluded, the objectives of US policy towards Indo-China had not been realized. Three years after the termination of war in 1945 a friendly nation, France, was fighting a desperate and apparently losing struggle in Indo-China. The solution by French military reconquest of Indo-China was not desirable. Neither, however, was complete withdrawal of the French from Indo-China for, as it was assumed that in all likelihood Indo-China would be taken over by the militant communist group, at best there might follow a transition period marked by chaos and terrorist activities, which would then create a political vacuum into which the Chinese inevitably would be drawn or pushed.[25]

It is interesting that, apart from generic communism, it was the power of China that was here identified as the principal threat to Indo-China. A couple of weeks later, on October 13 1948, the State Department's secret circular instruction 'Pattern of Soviet Policy in Far-East and South-East Asia' afforded a general conspectus which, apart from assuming boundless and malevolent Soviet intentions, also inferred a single goal 'to ensure Soviet control being as surely installed and predominate as in the satellite countries behind the Iron Curtain'.[26] If this was the overall assumption then, given that the communists were reckoned to have captured the nationalist movement in Vietnam, there could, logically, be no other course open to the US – France, naturally, would have her own reasons – than to resist. Later on, and particularly in 1950, one might wonder whether the particulars of US policy towards Vietnam had been swamped in the generalities of across-the-board resistance to communism; but even before some critics have discerned a militarization and globalization of US policy, and before the emotional climate of the US changed, one may see, as a piece of sober analysis, the beginning of a policy based on certain not altogether unfounded assumptions about communism, China, and the objectives of the Soviet Union. Implementation of that policy, in Indo-China however, would depend upon France; and after two years of war and in spite of some growing and ineffable optimism, the French were still looking for a purposeful Vietnam policy and had revealed not so much procrastination and missed opportunities as a sort of political paralysis. Nevertheless, and at least from the time the North Atlantic Pact was signed in April 1949, France had a certain entitlement as an ally. For Acheson, who became Secretary of State in January 1949, as for most of the Administration, Congress and probably most of the American people, and as a straight and simple choice, France was more important than Vietnam or Indo-China and more valuable than a party aspiring to be government which, in spite of impeccable anti-colonial credentials and its ability to present itself as all things to all men, was beginning to look more and more like an affiliated communist state.

Already, then, it might be seen that the French were digging the pit into which the US would eventually fall. Already, too, one may see the start of a symbiotic relationship in which France would increasingly depend upon American resources to achieve purposes which, left to herself, would be beyond her, while American objectives, although they did not entirely coincide with the French and for all the power which they would ultimately deploy, had to include France as a frail but, for the moment, indispensable means by which they might be attained. From time to time however there were vivid flashes of US policy-making which suggested that Indo-China was regarded as a means to an end, rather than an end in itself; and those of a philosophical disposition may see this as the flaw which turned idealism into tragedy.

In his study of Dean Acheson, Professor Gaddis Smith devotes a chapter to 'The Reversal of Policy toward Indo-China' a reversal over which he says, Acheson presided, which he encouraged, and in part, initiated. In Gaddis Smith's account this is something which happened in 1950 and there was, as will be seen, a cluster of commitments round about April and May of that year from which it would be difficult to turn back; although another of Acheson's biographers has argued that, contrary to what revisionist historians say, Acheson's Indo-China policy did not make future American military involvement inevitable.[27] Acheson's ideas on Indo-China and South-East Asia, says Gaddis Smith, were vague and sometimes shifted depending on the person to whom he was talking. Even as Acheson pondered the problem Smith argues that the US was already moving toward support of the French although it might not have been so much a matter of whose hand was on the tiller as how the compass was being set.[28]

DIVISION IN THE STATE DEPARTMENT?

Within the State Department it has been argued that two competing strategies – one 'Asian-oriented' and the other 'Europe-oriented' – had emerged and that the critical question was whether the US should have insisted on French concessions to Vietnamese nationalism as a condition of US support.[29] Alternatively, it may be suggested that the question was *how much* the French should have been asked to concede; and even if the critical time, (according to Edmund Gullion,) was 'right after the Elysée agreements of March 1949'[30] and for all the complaint that 'South-East Asia's policy has been junked',[31] and dismay at Acheson's 'French captivity', a closer inspection suggests that there may not in fact have been all that much difference in the assumptions upon which different parts of the State Department were operating. The reference to a French captivity was the occasion when Walton Butterworth, the Department's Director of Far Eastern Affairs, had, in Acheson's absence, attempted something in the nature of a diplomatic coup. Under the *imprimatur* of the Acting Secretary of State, Butterworth had sent the Embassy in Paris what purported to be the Department's views on the Elysée agreement with the request that the memorandum should be presented to the French government. In brief, it was a recommendation that France should recognize the equality and acknowledge the sovereignty of Vietnam and that Vietnam's participation in the French Union should, at most, be voluntary. As it happened Acheson was in Paris when the cable arrived; the Embassy replied with the unanimous opinion that it would be a serious mistake to deliver the memorandum; and Acheson, having seen the correspondence, agreed that it would be inappropriate at the time.

The 'Far Eastern' memorandum was a superb and elegant paper even though, in its abstract idealizations of how colonialism should have come to an end, it sounded rather like a secular Sermon on the Mount. Nevertheless one should ask, even on the basis of this lecture, whether there really was a dichotomy between Western Europe and the Far East divisions in the State Department. Certainly Ambassador Bruce's reporting from Paris appears to have been impartial; while the Far Eastern memorandum took for granted first that those in command of the so-called Vietnamese Democratic Republic were men trained in the methods and doctrines of international communism; secondly, that should they succeed, a pattern of foreign totalitarianism would be clamped upon Vietnam under which all liberties, national and personal, would be lost and thirdly, that the paramount question in Indo-China was whether the country was to be saved from communist control: all other issues were irrelevant. It was, in fact, because of Vietnam's importance that the French should be compelled to concede independence.[32] In any event the 'Far East' solution depended, with rather specious simplicity, on the ability to separate communist sheep from nationalist goats and even though the distinction was recognized as the *sine qua non* of a solution, it assumed that those who would not support genuine independence, once it was granted by the French, would identify themselves as communists: and would thereby distinguish themselves from the rest of the 'nationalist elements' who comprised the major part of the resistance forces. An even more extraordinary paper originated in the State Department: described as a 'possible method of solving the Indo-China problem' which would 'once and for all smoke out Ho Chi Minh and determine whether he is primarily a nationalist or a communist'. Assuming that a common position could be reached between the US, France, Britain, India and the Philippines, either one of the last two countries would convene a conference; France would be induced to grant Vietnam full independence; and an international commission would be established that was to remain in place for several years. Ho, as well as Bao Dai, was to be consulted and it would be put to him that if he was the real nationalist which he professed to be he would 'accept loyally the decisions and mandates of the government and the subsequent constituent assembly, etc. and bind himself unequivocally not to . . . subvert the true nationalism of his people or a government that might emerge from the multilateral effort'. It could even be suggested to him that he leave Vietnam and 'take up once more the philosophical studies to which he had devoted a great deal of his previous life', and it might also be suggested that 'there would be pension adequate to support him in those studies'.[33]

Apart from understandable concern with the French side of the triangular relationship with Vietnam, US policy makers were under two further constraints had they wished to take a more free-wheeling course. Both of them were self-imposed. In 1972, when he chaired the Hearings before the Senate Foreign Relations Committee which were given the imposing title 'Causes, Origins, and Lessons of the Vietnam War', a rather dyspeptic Senator Fulbright sought to put much of the blame for American involvement on Dean Acheson, on his European orientations and on his close war-time connections with the British. As Fulbright presented it, in what amounted to a proclamation of American innocence and British guilt, the US had been 'had' by her allies; and while this may not appear to be entirely convincing, Fulbright had picked up the importance of what Acheson had described as the danger of Ho Chi Minh's 'direct communist connection' – and might, indeed, have gone further. The issue was not whether Ho was a communist but whether there was, in principle, any possibility of voluntary, autonomous communism. By a sort of transposed assumption based on post-war experience Acheson had told the National War College in December 1947 that for Greeks, Italians and others it had not been a free choice whether they accepted or rejected communism: because they were being coerced either by an internal organization financed by other countries or by external pressure to adopt a system of government which had the inescapable consequence of inclusion in the system of Russian power. And this, in turn, would seem to justify Professor Gaddis's conclusion that the assumption was that such governments, whether in Western Europe or Japan, and whether or not they came to power by legal or illegal means, could only be regarded as instruments of the Kremlin and hence not truly independent.[34]

A priori then, it would seem that Ho Chi Minh and his government were only to be regarded as an extension of Soviet power; an assumption that was to be reinforced by the second constraint which originated in the Department of State. It was that Southeast Asia was 'the target of a co-ordinated offensive plainly directed by the Kremlin'. This was the conclusion of the Policy Planning Staff which, when it began work in February 1949, certainly had enough circumstantial evidence to prompt such a conclusion. In March 1948 a communist insurrection had broken out in Burma. In Malaya, the government and the communist party stumbled into action against each other in June. In the Philippines, Taruc resumed his struggle against the government and announced that he was a communist while in Indonesia, whatever triggered it off, communists at Madiun in September 1948 attempted to stage a revolution within the revolution. Added to this there was the alarming, although on closer inspection ambiguous, evidence of concerted communist plans for Asia as a whole that were discussed at the World Federation of Democratic Youth Conference in Calcutta in February 1948.[35]

In the end, however, and in spite of Acheson's approval the Policy Planning Staff paper (PPS 51) remained, as Robert Blum puts it, a non-policy paper: for information rather than for action. But it was sent to the National Security Council and in the meantime Secretary of Defense Johnson, according to the internal 'History of the Indo-China Incident' prepared for and by the Joint Chiefs of Staff, had called upon the NSC to determine exactly how US security was threatened by the current situation in the Far East and to formulate tentative courses of action which were to be co-ordinated for the whole region and were to outline specific objectives to be attained. Thus, the NSC had before it the State Department's political assessment that the area was, to repeat, 'the target of a co-ordinated offensive plainly directed by the Kremlin'. And the following month, July 1949, Acheson apparently issued instructions that it was a 'fundamental decision of American policy that the United States does not intend to permit any further communist domination on the continent of Asia or in South-east Asia'.[36]

A COMMUNIST OFFENSIVE IN SOUTH-EAST ASIA?

One could argue, then, that by July 1949 the battle lines had been drawn in Southeast Asia, and even that they had been drawn unilaterally, by the US. A threat was perceived: a co-ordinated, Kremlin-directed offensive. And the Secretary of State had declared what might otherwise be regarded as a powerful if not irresistible force would be met by the immovable object of US resolution. The Policy Planning Staff opinion on Kremlin-directed strategy went word for word into the NSC report *The Position of the United States with respect to Asia* (NSC 48/1) whose conclusions were approved by the US President on 30 December 1949 (NSC 48/2), although in the NSC paper it was an expression that was qualified by the proposition that it was the colonial–nationalist conflict which had provided a fertile field for subversive communist activities. By the end of February 1950 the 'threat of communist aggression against Indo-China' had become 'only one phase of anticipated communist plans to seize all of South-East Asia' and a week later the Department of Defense was told by Assistant Secretary of State Dean Rusk that Southeast Asia was in grave danger of communist domination: now identified 'as a consequence of aggression from communist China' as well as 'internal subversive activities'.

With Senator McCarthy's campaign against treason in the State Department having just got under way this may hardly have been the best time for dispassionate analysis although, if it is not too academic a point, one cannot help comparing these propositions with an earlier assessment (13 October 1948). This set out a *Pattern of Soviet Policy in Far East and South East Asia* in terms of a Soviet policy which sought to weaken the ties between the colonies and the colonial powers through the encouragement of nationalism and by capitalizing on the discontent caused by long periods of 'colonial oppression' and by disrupting the colonial economies either by armed action or by labour disorders so that the metropolitan powers would be deprived of revenue and resources. Thus the USSR would be able to fish profitably in the troubled waters of economic chaos.[37]

At the time when this paper on basic factors in Soviet Far Eastern policy was being composed, the late summer of 1948, the major points of difference within the State Department were whether or not the Russians would actively support the Chinese communists in the civil war if there was a danger that they might deviate along the path recently chosen by Yugoslavia and whether, for the same reason, the Soviets might be reluctant to foster the expansion of Chinese communist influence in Southeast Asia. A year later, autumn 1949, the communist victory in the Chinese civil war was no longer in doubt and even though other factors, not least intellectual preconceptions, should be taken into account, one must accept Robert Blum's general proposition that 'The American containment policy in South-East Asia arose from the ashes of its failed policy in China'.[38]

THE CHINESE CONNECTION

If it is obvious that US policy towards Indo-China could not be considered in isolation from its policy towards the rest of Asia, it is even more obvious that the integration of US policy for Vietnam came about at the same time as the disintegration of its policy towards China: the most traumatic episode in US power-war policies in Asia, at least until the outbreak of the Korean war. China, or at least the Nationalist government, like a great ship going down, had taken many hopes and illusions with it. One of Acheson's biographers has argued that Americans, having never understood the realities of the Chinese situation, were wholly unprepared for the deluge of hate and vituperation which descended on them from Peking once the Chinese People's Republic had been established.[39] As an extension of Acheson's ideas about communism it was likewise impossible for Americans to think of the Chinese embracing communism of their own volition and rejecting the US in such a humiliating fashion.[40] Some of the last-gasp attempts to save the Nationalist governments that were considered in Washington – with the wilder arpeggios such as encouraging the fragmentation of China or even, apparently, a series of punitive air strikes against the Chinese communists (not to mention the sheer fantasy of creating ten new Chinese armies in six months) – originated in the Far Eastern division of the State Department, and in fact the Administration, says Blum, had come close to re-intervention in the Chinese civil war on the mainland, but backed away at the last minute when it discovered that there was no viable force left to support.[41]

It is, therefore, with a sense of mounting horror that one listens to Acheson sounding the knell of US policy in China in the letter which accompanied what is usually known as the China White Paper, oblivious to the possibility that the bell was tolling for the same policy that was being reborn in Vietnam. Not of course that the comparisons seemed in any way apposite at the time. For example, 'Its leaders had proved incapable of meeting the crisis confronting them, its troops had lost the will to fight, and its Government had lost popular support'. And the conclusions: 'a realistic appraisal of conditions . . . leads to the conclusion that the only alternative open to the US was full-scale intervention on behalf of a Government which had lost the confidence of its own troops and its own people. Intervention of such a scope and magnitude would have been resented by the mass of the . . . people, would have diametrically reversed our historic policy, and would have been condemned by the American people. The unfortunate but inescapable fact is that the ominous result of the civil war . . . was beyond the control of the Government of the United States.' In each of these examples Acheson was, of course, referring to China but so much of what he said here (or to which he gave his name) now seems to be an epitaph for the experiences of Vietnam. But at the time, as one American policy was ending and another beginning, Vietnam seemed to be exempt from similar considerations.[42]

Looking at it a different way, having decided not to attempt to save China by its efforts, there was only a faint hope that the US could save Vietnam by its example – as a successful democracy. It was being drawn in to Vietnam by the necessity of responding to developments there, in France, and in China, as well as on account of its own perceptions and its formulation of a general policy of containment. So, as the internal JCS (Joint Chiefs of Staff) history suggests, the decision to help France combat the Vietminh may have been the logical outgrowth of a reassessment of US interests in Asia as a whole; and yet the particular origins of the US aid programme suggest something less systematic. Like much policy making, it was rooted in domestic considerations.

President Truman's Democratic Administration existed side by side with a Congress in which there was a Republican majority. A bi-partisan approach to foreign policy could be maintained in the most momentous ever commitment in US foreign policy, the North Atlantic Pact, but it had broken down on the issue of China even if 'the attack of the primitives', as Acheson put it, had as much to do with Truman's unexpected victory in the presidential election in 1948 and the consequent fury and frustration of the Republican Party. When, therefore, on 9 December 1949, an amendment to the Military Aid Program bill proposed by the combined Senate Committees on Foreign Relations and Armed Services sought to earmark the sum of $75 m. for what was eventually described as the 'general area of China', in voting to cut the appropriation for the Military Assistance Program in half the House of Representatives may, as Acheson said, have been in one of its berserk moods; but in order to save the Program, and its underpinning of the fledgling North Atlantic Alliance, Acheson was prepared to accept the amendment and, as he presents it, it seems to have been one of the easiest passages in that summer of difficult decisions. Symbolically, at least, a formal connection had been made in which the success of US policy in strengthening Western Europe had been linked to what was in effect Congressional interest in policies which would 'contain' communism in Asia. There was also the effect that the existence of this $75 m. fund, to be spent at the discretion of the President, would have not only on departments of the US administration but on foreign governments as well.

In January 1949 the French had suggested that the US might consider extending Marshall Plan assistance to Vietnam: the rapid economic rehabilitation of Vietnam, they said, could be the key to Bao Dai's success.[43] A year later (in his celebrated address to the National

Press Club) Acheson raised the question whether American military assistance to Southeast Asia might provide 'the missing component in a problem which might otherwise be unsolved'.[44] Now, with the approximate end of the Dutch-Indonesian conflict, the foremost of US political and strategic concerns in Southeast Asia, and given the conceptual underpinnings of US policy and the operational commitment to the success of the Bao Dai experiment, Vietnam was the obvious place to begin.

In its internal history for the Joint Chiefs of Staff, their secretariat give them the credit (or blame) for taking the first step in shifting the battle for Asia from China to Southeast Asia. This, they suggest, was done on 17 December 1949 when the JCS proposed that the $75 m. fund should include French Indo-China, as well as Burma and Thailand, and this provided the means for an early programme of assistance in the French struggle against Ho Chi Minh.[45] In point of fact the JCS had been pressing for consistent applications of containment ever since 1947, had identified US security interests with Nationalist success in China and had declared that, if the Chinese Nationalists were to fall, the US must be prepared to accept eventual Soviet hegemony over Asia.[46] In point of time, however, one can find the specific civilian proposition from the US Ambassador in Paris a week earlier, on 11 December, not only to extend aid to Vietnam from the President's special $75 m. fund but also recommending direct 'Marshall Plan' financing for Indo-China: which the French had tentatively asked for at the beginning of 1949.

For France, it was a time of economic and even incipient military crisis. To finance the French war effort in 1949 had cost them, in US terms, $500 m. – which was greater than the estimated French budgetary deficit for the year – and had eaten up over two-thirds of the annual total of US aid to France. France was maintaining an army of 150,000 men in Indo-China, of whom, by the end of 1949, 16,000 were killed or missing. They were already in some difficulty in northern Tonkin, where they had abandoned some of their isolated posts, so that, once again, it was the presence of China – shadow, perhaps, rather than substance – which was helping to transform the appreciations and perception of the struggle. Already, in effect, US military commanders – in this case, the commander of US naval forces in the Western Pacific – were testifying to the domino effect: if Chinese communists were not stopped in South China, Indo-China, Burma, and perhaps Malaya, would then fall, either from internal subversion or external attack.[47] Appearing before a Senate committee that was pondering 'the general area' of China and its implications, an official of the State Department said of the fund: 'It might be used in other areas of the Far East which are affected by the developments in China. That would include such areas as Burma, the northern part of Indo-China, if it became desirable to suppress communism in that country.'[48] As the same study of the executive and legislative roles in the Vietnam war points out, another of the provisions of the 1949 Mutual Defense Assistance Act – approved with almost no debate – authorized the President to send US armed forces as non-combatant military advisers to any 'agency or nation' in the world. For the moment, however, it was not military advisers that the French wanted, but other types of military assistance, some of it symbolic but spectacular. Thus, French High Commissioner Pignon was hoping for American assistance in replacing and repairing military equipment; said he was prepared for US military aid to go direct to the Vietnam government; but also, in order to deter a Chinese invasion of Tonkin, was trying to talk the US into sending warships, particularly aircraft-carriers, into Indo-Chinese waters. Above all, however, the French had two objectives. First, to secure recognition of the Bao Dai 'government' by as many countries as possible. Second, to obtain recognition, as French Foreign Minister Schuman put it in tripartite talks with the Americans and the British in September, 1949, that the French were the hard core of resistance to communist attempts to take over, initially, Indo-China and ultimately all of Southeast Asia and that as France was fighting the battle of all the democratic powers she would need help.[49]

NO ALTERNATIVE: THE BAO DAI SOLUTION

The recognition of Bao Dai's government was a problem not only for the French. For the US or Britain to have been the first to recognize Bao Dai would, said Acheson, have been to give him the kiss of death. The British opinion, for what it was worth, was that by no stretch of the imagination was Bao Dai's régime in *de facto* control (they also warned the Americans that Schuman would claim that the French had gone as far as they could in Vietnam without creating trouble in French North Africa). In spite of these hesitations, with no one anxious to recognize Bao Dai first, not least because the French themselves had not even ratified the Elysée agreement, the US hoped, or wished to persuade itself, that full Vietnamese sovereignty would emerge from the chrysalis of the Bao Dai solution and as Acheson defined the US position on 23 December 1949: 'There is no apparent alternative to Bao Dai régime other than Commie domination Indo-China'.[50]

The fact that China and the USSR recognized Ho Chi Minh before the US recognized Bao Dai is sometimes taken as cause and effect; but on closer inspection the sequence does not seem to bear that much significance. Acheson, at least, had practically made up his mind as soon as the French had promised to ratify the Elysée agreements; and in setting out the arguments to the US Embassy in Bangkok no alternative to recognition was in fact suggested.[51] The Southeast Asian states themselves were reported as having their doubts about Bao Dai's recognition and, eventually, the Thai Foreign Minister, Pote Sarasin, made it the issue on which he resigned. The fact that the US was canvassing support from other Asian states would very likely have been known to the Russians and Chinese; and it is at least conceivable that this fact influenced their own decision. In the event, one feels, recognition of Ho Chi Minh's alternative government by the communist bloc was an additional argument for the US to recognize Bao Dai; but it hardly seems to have been a sufficient cause.

AID TO INDO-CHINA

A State Department working party had concluded on 1 February 1950 that the US, together with France, was already committed in Indo-China, i.e., failure of the Bao Dai experiment would mean the communisation of Indo-China. Failure to support French policy in Indo-China would have the effect of contributing to the defeat of US aims in Europe and, applying the practical test of probability of success, 'the US would be backing a determined protagonist in this venture . . . French military leaders soberly confident'.[52] To prevent failures of this order, even if success was not absolutely assured, might, other things being equal, have seemed to be within the scope of US policy at the time. Certainly in the matter of military aid, as the working party concluded, the US (without sending troops) was in a position to make a unique contribution: but even more positive results might have been expected from economic assistance. Memories were fresh of what it may be fair to call 'America's failure in China'. As Charles Wolf[53] points out there had been mounting Congressional criticism of the Administration's alleged neglect of Asia and although the strength of Republican feeling had been resisted in the matter of China it was at the cost of a critical concession in Southeast Asia generally – Vietnam in particular – which accorded, nevertheless, with the sentiments and announced global purposes of US policy: to resist communism, to encourage free peoples throughout the world, and to strengthen democratic nations against aggression.[54] Aid to Indo-China meant accepting French assurances that Vietnam would become a free state but if doubts occurred, in Congress for example, there was the sheet anchor of general resistance to communism and, in the case of China, and as the influential Congressman Walter Judd explained, a belief that China was the original domino and that Malaya, Indonesia, the Philippines and even India would not be able to resist communist pressure for long. In any case fear of the spread of communism reinforced the belief that Asia, too, could benefit from the treasure that was being poured into Europe by way of Marshall Aid and, as Wolf concludes: 'It is fair to say that the desire to avoid "another China" no less than the desire of the Administration to avoid further Congressional attacks on its Asian policy, determined the timing of US aid to Southern Asia.'[55] There was also a personal connection. When, in March 1950 the State Department, under strong Congressional urging, had sent its aid survey mission to Southeast Asia it was headed by Mr R. Allen Griffin, a Californian newspaper publisher and editor, who had been deputy chief of the US Aid Mission to China. As he told Wolf he saw the mission's task 'as one of formulating a constructive program of aid to help prevent in Southeast Asia a repetition of the circumstances leading to the fall of China'.[56] The conclusion of the Griffin mission was, first, that US aid would help France and Vietnam to checkmate Chinese communist invasion, if it came; and second, it was assumed that it would somehow 'sterilise areas of Vietminh infection'. As subsequently printed, the purpose of aid programmes in Southeast Asia was 'to demonstrate that the local national governments are able to bring benefits to their own people and thereby build political support, especially among the rural population',[57] or in the words of the Country Report prepared for the director of the Mutual Defense Assistance Program: 'to ensure the existence of governments . . . which represent the legitimate nationalist aspirations of those Indo-Chinese people who do not desire to see communist-orientated governments in Indo-China'.

Aid, therefore, in a sense, appeared to be a substitute for analysis: certainly for the sort of analysis that might have suggested the hazards attending US policy objectives in Vietnam. Doubts were expressed in Washington[58]; but in spite of Griffin's assertion that the wave of communist risings in Indo-China were not economic, social or ideological, rather they were predominantly nationalistic, he concluded that it was because the Bao Dai government was itself so intensely nationalist that it was worth supporting. On 4 May 1950, three days after Truman had approved programmes of military assistance to Indo-China (and to Indonesia) with $13 m. worth of funds which Acheson himself was to approve, Griffin was raising his sights. It was doubtful, he said, whether the Vietnamese government could succeed without the most generous, if not passionate, French assistance; and yet how France's partners within the French Union could evolve had never been defined: indeed no one knew what the French Union meant. The Bao Dai government's first need was public respect – which Griffin thought could be created – but, in what had undertones of a Humpty Dumpty argument, Griffin said

'If Bao Dai once starts slipping it will be impossible to restore him.' It was obviously an extremely fragile position: and this was an extremely fragile argument: but it was also one which would seem to require an unlimited US commitment. In any event, Acheson had realized that the US bargaining position with the French disappeared 'the moment we agree to give them aid'[59] and, as if to confirm this predicament, a couple of days after Truman's cabinet had decided unanimously in favour of recognition, the French were letting it be known that, although their intentions were indeed evolutionary, they could not 'afford to kindle unrealistic national appetites'. So, once again, having committed itself to support the fictional or, at most, 'evolutionary' independence of Vietnam, the US was just as dependent as ever on France to make this vision a reality. Of course, if it were true, as the State Department and eventually the National Security Council professed to believe, that the threat of communist aggression against Indo-China was only one phase of anticipated plans to seize all of Southeast Asia, then this was an unthinkable alternative. Perhaps by this time the general had submerged the particular. For example, the Vietminh were now identified as 'forces of communist aggression' and for Dean Rusk, Deputy Under Secretary of State, the danger of communist domination of Southeast Asia was a consequence of 'aggression' (whatever that meant) from communist China. Rusk, who appeared to be setting the pace, had asked the Pentagon to prepare military plans as a matter of the greatest urgency; and when NSC 64 was endorsed by the President on 24 April 1950 the US was committed, by all practical measures, to prevent the expansion of communist aggression in Southeast Asia in spite of the fact that less than a third of Vietnam was reckoned to be controlled by the legal government. So, when on 8 May Acheson announced that the US would send economic and military aid to the French in Indo-China (for Gaddis Smith, the turning point – 'the scales had swayed for three months and then came down hard on the side of France')[60] the French position was at least potentially desperate and one cannot help asking whether there were any countries receiving military aid under the Mutual Defense Assistance Program, other than Vietnam, in which there were such powerful revolutionary forces and where a revolutionary war was already in progress. Henceforth, of course, there would be a need to promote Vietnam to the position of an established, legitimate and more or less popular state deserving of US assistance.

Whether or not it was realized, then, how exposed the French position was in Vietnam, the universal scope of US foreign policy had just been restated in its most monumental form. In response to the President's request for a re-examination of US objectives 'in peace and war' and their effect on strategic plans, and with the background of the development of thermo-nuclear weapons, the Secretaries of State and

Defense had produced a paper which was approved by the National Security Council: NSC 68. In it was set down the 'The Fundamental Purpose Of The United States' and 'The Fundamental Design Of The Kremlin' together with their 'Underlying Conflict In The Realm Of Ideas And Values'. Attacked by its critics as a sort of institutional megalomania in which a defeat of free institutions anywhere was a defeat everywhere it was a supercharged containment policy in which, in defence of the perimeter, all points seemed to be of equal importance.[61] As Robert Lovett, former Under Secretary of State, told the drafting committee, there was practically nothing that the US could not do if it wanted to. He also advised that the paper's conclusion should be stated 'simply, clearly, in Hemingway sentences'[62] and amongst these conclusions was the contingency that, within the next four or five years, the USSR would be able to deliver a surprise atomic attack against the US. In the midst of a world crisis of such magnitude and given the 'dangerous potentialities' of the USSR for weakening the relative world position of the US, 'sufficient resistance' that was required from the US and other non-communist countries might be presumed to extend to Indo-China. More particularly, and because Vietnam had already been accorded the key position in Southeast Asia, 'Soviet domination of the potential power of Eurasia, whether achieved by armed aggression or by political and subversive means, would be strategically and politically unacceptable to the US'.[63] Indeed, Indo-China had already been identified, together with Korea, Berlin and Austria, as a primary area of Soviet interest.[64] As a simple response one might expect that the US could try to frustrate this Soviet purpose. In principle, therefore, there was now a global US policy even if, in Vietnam, it depended upon a French surrogate, and when Acheson and Schuman met face to face, after apparently unrecorded or at least so far undisclosed conversation, Acheson wanted to establish a close and immediate connection between the problem of Southeast Asia and the defence of the West.[65] The most obvious connection was, of course, France itself and on most occasions which presented themselves the French told the Americans of their difficulties and requirements in Indo-China, how many of their troops were there and, usually, how many they had lost. In this instance Schuman described Vietnam in terms of financial and military haemorrhage, a burden that France could not be expected to carry indefinitely and one which threatened her ability to meet European defence commitments. France, as he put it, was not fighting for selfish interests but was defending a vital area against communist infiltration and control and, to underline the point, Schuman emphasized that, since the Second World War, France had definitely abandoned colonialism; although what the new policy of the French Union amounted to remained to be seen – and understood.

If Acheson had any doubts, he kept them to himself. The official line[66] was that 'true character of French concessions to Indo-Chinese nationalism and ultimate intentions are clear to Department' and it was for this reason that no further substantive concessions involving parliamentary action in France were called for at that time. Although the French may have persuaded themselves that they were moving as fast as they could towards the 'perfection' of Vietnamese independence, it was perhaps indulgent of Acheson to have allowed himself to be persuaded as well. Even if the US kept up the pressure, would public statements from France about her intentions be enough? Particularly in view of what they had told the US so far? Could the French have moved faster? Did they want to? Were they able to? Perhaps there was a glimmer of hope in 1949 when someone of the stature (rather than the disposition) of de Gaulle might have seized the burning brand; and four years later Mendès France could face the unacceptable although by then there was practically no alternative. Before the Americans were irrevocably committed, however, and before the French positions on the Chinese frontier were overrun, they could conceivably have strengthened non-communist national forces in Vietnam to the point where they had a better chance of competing with the Vietminh or even, biting on the bullet, the French could have tried to negotiate a settlement, no matter what alarm that prospect might have caused their American allies.

Given the importance of the French holding their part of the line in Southeast Asia the threat of a settlement was itself sufficient to elicit renewed US support. If it wasn't exactly political pessimism of the order of 'mourir pour Danzig' it must have been alarming for Americans to hear from High Commissioner Pignon's diplomatic adviser of the feeling that French interests were not important enough to die for because the country was being given over to the Vietnamese and when the war was over French influence would have disappeared. According to this argument French troops had to see that they were fighting for something and, moreover, they needed the feeling that their actions were approved.[67] For the French, who declared that old-style exploitation of colonies was a thing of the past, all that they said was necessary were economic and social programmes to dissipate 'the racial hatred that was drummed up by immature political leaders'.[68] It was not an argument that one could apply to Vietnam without swallowing hard. And it was hardly one which appealed to Emperor Bao Dai, no matter what one may have thought of his political maturity. When the American chargé at Saigon (Edmund Gullion) called on him in June he said he had returned to Vietnam because of French assurances that seemed to promise independence. 'But', apparently on the verge of tears, he asked, 'this independence, what is it? Where is it? Do you see it?

Is a government independent without a budget? When it has to beg 20 m. piastres a month for its existence?' He no longer thought the French had any intention of leaving Vietnam.

Years later, Acheson agreed in an interview that the French had blackmailed the US in Vietnam.[69] It was the expression which Bao Dai had used in June 1950 although, as the Americans reported 'He understood our delicate position since France was our friend in Europe'. But if the French had threatened to withdraw their troops it was, said Bao Dai, pure blackmail; and the Americans had fallen for it. On the other hand, as Acheson said in his memoirs, there are limits on the extent to which one may successfully coerce an ally.[70] When US assistance for the French in Vietnam was announced on the same day as the 'Schuman Plan' that was to merge coal and steel production in France and Germany 'and thus make war between the two countries not only unthinkable but materially impossible', it was the prospect of strengthening France, and Germany, in the defence of Western Europe that filled Acheson's political landscape.

THE MELBY–ERSKINE MISSION

The fact that the US announced its continuing if not open-ended assistance for the French in Vietnam on the same day as the Schuman plan began Germany's rehabilitation in Europe was, obviously, a coincidence in spite of any gratitude which the US might have felt for this imaginative and, at the same time, practical French gesture. Six weeks later when the Korean War erupted the focus of Acheson's attention turned to the other side of the world but the concept of all-round defence meant that, for the US, strengthening France and Germany was now even more important in a Europe which, if strong enough, might deter communist aggression and in Asia where the aggression had already begun. Up to this point the US had been binding itself to Vietnam with conceptual associations, policy objectives, and some material considerations. The purposes were essentially prophylactic, contingent, and, in spite of official exaggeration, somewhat confused by the absence of what could clearly be identified as 'communist aggression'. All this was removed by the Korean War. There is no real reason to believe that the civil-military mission which the US sent to Vietnam would, in any event, have come to substantially different conclusions but the fact remains that their report was made under the impact of the Korean War and as one of its leaders said of the other his thoughts seemed largely to be with 'his' division in Korea. Wherever they were General Erskine's thoughts were certainly not in accord with the French in Vietnam. Why, he asked, listen to a bunch of second-raters who hadn't won a war since Napoleon?

The Melby–Erskine mission had been sent to Vietnam to consider the feasibility of a US economic and military aid programme. The first problem, which obviously reflected the Korean events, was defence of the frontier against external aggression. The second was the problem of internal security. Its agreed conclusions were a curious mixture and although, no doubt, reflecting the position as they found it, hardly provided the foundation for an unequivocal policy. Thus, a military solution was seen as a primary requisite for solving the overall Indo-China problem; but one that in no sense could be decisive without what the report called 'the application of political and economic techniques'. In general terms, it was nicely balanced. There was a mutual absence of good faith on the part of the French and the Vietnamese; nevertheless, they had to be persuaded to rise above their parochial interests. After the event Melby was far more pessimistic: 'the sickening feeling that this was China all over again' and if, as he allowed, that in Indo-China French colonial policy was as intransigent as ever it may well have been reciprocated as High Commissioner Pignon and General Carpentier both admitted to Melby 'privately and with great reluctance that hatred of the French outweighed all other considerations in the thinking of all Vietnamese, whatever their political persuasions'. If it did, and even allowing for Melby's overwhelming dilemma, it is a little surprising to read his conclusion that, if the French were really serious about decolonization and that if military force was properly applied, they could at least hold the lid on the Indo-Chinese kettle for the predictable if only relatively limited future. Beyond that his proposals were extraordinary even if they were conditional.

I would propose the following: a French undertaking for Vietnamese independence within a specified period of five, ten, twenty, or thirty years . . . A Vietnam national army would be rapidly created to assume responsibility for the internal situation and as this progressed French forces would withdraw to border areas or where unnecessary depart. Civil administration would be increasingly a Vietnamese responsibility. All such agreements would have a US guarantee and such supervision as necessary. Assumably the US would pay most of the bills . . .

What is perhaps most surprising about this prescription is the assumed validity of the Bao Dai government. It was matched, operationally, by General Erskine's conviction that the Chinese border could be made impregnable and the coastline sealed off to prevent external aid reaching the Vietminh; although it was admitted this could not be done with existing forces on the border.

Erskine therefore forwarded what he described as a local suggestion that Japanese troops 'experienced in warfare in this kind of terrain' might be used. Then, 'once border sealed Vietminh problem would be immeasurably simpler with proper combination of military and political activity.'[71] Commenting on Melby's 'pessimistic but valuable appraisal' the US Minister at Saigon (Heath) felt it necessary to balance it with local French military opinion that, barring Chinese intervention or a massive increase in their aid to the Vietminh, guerrilla and terrorist activities could be reduced to a policing problem within two years. This, in the event, was wildly optimistic: but it was, by contrast with Melby's extraordinary projection, what the State Department's Policy Planning Staff considered as the maximum period which France would have to grant independence if it were to satisfy 'genuine nationalism' in Indo-China.[72] Capitalizing on the Melby report they suggested that Paris should pass a large measure of responsibility for the Indo-Chinese problem to the UN: thus enlisting wider support from free Asian countries and perhaps even inhibiting Chinese communist support for Ho Chi Minh. Their memorandum on US policy towards Indo-China recognized the possibility that without what it called 'a bolder political approach' the French – and the US – might well be heading into a débâcle which neither could afford; but the drastic political measures which were reckoned to be necessary would have to be a matter for voluntary decision by the French government. Direct Chinese intervention at this time, mid-August 1950, did not loom large and, in any event, there was a cryptic reference (or perhaps unexamined idea) to 'international surveillance of the border'. When Melby had suggested special compensations for the French in the course of their anticipated decolonization these had, curiously, been linked to their undertaking 'to guarantee inviolability of Indo-China border'. Such a guarantee, had it even been considered, would almost certainly have been worthless and, as the events which were unfolding were to prove, was totally beyond the abilities of the French command in Indo-China. For whatever reason, the French failed either to withdraw their forces from what were intended as border strongholds or to reinforce them sufficiently to be able to withstand attacks from Vietminh forces which could now be launched at divisional strength trained and commensurately equipped by the Chinese communist armies which had reached the frontier the year before. After disaster at Dongkhe, and the horrors of the Cocxa gorge, the French fortresses at Caobang, Langson and Laokay were abandoned but, in their retreat, the French had lost 6,000 men in what has been called their greatest colonial defeat since Montcalm had died at Quebec.[73] They had also lost an estimated 11,000 tons of munitions at Langson; and it was said that almost everything that the Vietminh fired at the French in after years came from that remarkable prize.[74]

THE CHINESE SHADOW

The French had obviously suffered a débâcle but, in itself, the opening up of the frontier with China might only have been a prelude to Chinese invasion and ensuing catastrophe. The shadow of Chinese intervention now darkened French and US assessments, even before Chinese intervention became a reality in Korea. France was in enough trouble already with her Vietminh opponents: to the point where her second most senior General, de Lattre de Tassigny, wartime commander of the French First Army, was detached from his command of French and other allied forces in Europe and arrived in Vietnam in December 1950 to assume the dual function of High Commissioner and Commander-in-Chief with the immediate responsibility of saving Hanoi.

The war had been transformed. It would not be long before de Lattre faced the divisions of Giap's new model army in the set-piece battles which the Vietminh were prepared to risk in a premature general offensive; and it was in more conventional war of this kind where US assistance and particularly US munitions would apparently tip the scale. For example, when faced with the large-scale Vietminh attacks of early 1951 the personal intervention of the chief US military adviser on Vietnam with General MacArthur in Japan secured the delivery of American napalm, which in turn allowed de Lattre to claim his victory.[75] On a less spectacular level French defence minister Moch had admitted, or attempted to persuade his opposite number, General Marshall, and Acheson, that with the bulk of French battalions on garrison duties in the pacified areas in Vietnam, they were left with an effective mobile force of only five or six battalions. And this, as he put it, to face, in addition to guerrillas, 50 fully equipped enemy infantry battalions equipped with liberal amounts of artillery and mortars. Although the French would send out another five battalions plus 1,100 French officers and NCOs as cadres and instructors for new Vietnamese units – almost inevitably Moch emphasized the possible effects on the military programme for metropolitan France – General Marshall pointed out that all the material for Indo-China was in fact coming from what the US was supplying to France itself.

ONE WAR?

There was now therefore a *de facto* alliance between France and the US in Vietnam. It was becoming obvious that the French by themselves were quite incapable of making the economic and military effort to fight a decisive war even if, at this stage, such a thing had been possible. Politically, too, it is worth remembering that, as the American Embassy in Paris reported, the Pleven cabinet faced a dozen problems, any one of which was capable in normal times of causing the downfall of two or three French governments.[76] The outbreak of the Korean War and, even more, the intervention of Chinese armies would allow France to persuade the US that Vietnam really was part of one allied operation. Not only must the battle for Southeast Asia be fought in Tonkin, as General Juin told the Americans in Saigon, but as de Lattre was to present his case in Washington, it was not *his* war but *our* war.

For the US the problem was more complicated. First of all they were becoming involved, also *de facto*, in the process of French decolonization which, like any successful retreat, was more difficult than an advance. Limited, *de jure*, to an aid programme, it was to assist something that was not yet there: an independent Vietnamese nation state. In practice, at least in South-East Asia, it made all the difference whether aid was given before or after independence. The Dutch, for example, had what at least from their own point of view were admirable and generous plans for what might have turned out to be an independent Indonesia; but, like the French, had failed to persuade their Republican adversaries that their ultimate freedom was assured in European hands. They had on two occasions tried to pre-empt the issue and had, in so doing, lost not only the confidence but the indispensable economic assistance of the US. Now, however, the French, no matter what they might have thought of American rhetoric, could at least pretend that they took it seriously and that their actions were being taken in defence of 'the free world'. Faced, therefore, with the apparent metamorphosis of a colonial war and continuing French sacrifices for what were now declared to be American purposes, the US had succeeded in trapping itself. France was neither oblivious of nor indifferent to the outcome of the war which *she* was fighting and for which, as the US kept saying, *she* was primarily responsible; but to have had a chance of winning at that stage it would probably have had to be a French rather than a Vietnamese war. Although, if it *was* a French war, might it also be assumed that the Vietnamese, whose tendency to sit on the fence was the subject of American as well as French complaint, would want to join in with the same enthusiasm that they would give to a national cause? If not, did the Vietnamese have that much chance of winning as a national army? When would the French be able to hand over to them? Indeed, given the fact that they were in the middle of a war the balance of which they were afraid might tip disastrously against them, would they really have opted out other than by a deliberate political decision which would not be taken until well into the future?

This was a decision that would be taken after a climactic battlefield disaster but in the meantime two alternatives were to hand. Either the US could allow themselves to be convinced that they were fighting one war, in Vietnam and Korea; that with practically unlimited US military and economic assistance the French could defeat the main Vietminh forces in Tonkin; and that revolution or insurgency could be contained in the rest of the country. Or, the US could try to overcome the political disability of association with what was at least a latent French colonial enterprise; as midwife help to bring the independent state of Vietnam into existence; and, as godfather, protect and support it in a cruel world.

Either of these looked like a possibility and both were tried: but whichever course was being followed seemed to lead to closer and closer involvement. For example, relations with the Emperor Bao Dai, who was to be told on Acheson's instructions, when he arrived back in Saigon in October 1950, that many people including a great number of Americans, had been unable to understand the reasons for his 'prolonged holiday' on the French Riviera and had indeed misinterpreted it as an indication of lack of patriotic attachment to his role of Chief of State.[77] Specifically, it was to be suggested that he should embark upon an immediate programme of visits to all parts of Vietnam making numerous speeches and public appearances in the process. Or, as it was being discussed in Washington at the time, it was a matter of holding Bao Dai's feet to the fire. It seems to have been assumed, however, that His Majesty would have acquiesced in a suggestion that he should invite the US to train the Vietnamese army and although the suggestion, like Acheson's message, was not carried through because of political sensitivity the US was becoming involved in the war one way and another. In Saigon, for example, the US Minister was urging that his country's influence must be felt 'not only through the gravitational pull of our aid program but in actual participation in certain controls and in accelerating certain French concessions'. Not only was US advice on war plans to be sought and heeded but 'we should give our views on organization and training of army and advancement of senior Viet officers' and there should also be some Franco-American rather than Vietnamese control over the 'dilatory fiscal collections' of Vietnam.[78]

An apparent opportunity for, or at least inclination to, US participation in Vietnamese national affairs as suggested in Saigon was soon to become a recognized imperative in Washington: and when the French ministers arrived in October 1950 to ask how much could be expected from the US to avoid financial disaster it was the drain of resources in Vietnam as much as the problems of French rearmament in Europe which prompted a close examination of French budgetary as well as military plans. The French were in fact asking for 270 billion francs and it was hard to see how the distinction could be made between helping to improve the French position in Europe and the position in Vietnam. France was an ally of the US and it was as such that she was to receive the greater part of the half a billion dollars in military assistance for the Far East which had been appropriated by Congress. When it was announced by the State Department on 17 October that military equipment, including light bombers, was being supplied for the armed forces both of France and of the Associated States, it was a distinction without a difference because in practice it was the French who were in control: even if Bao Dai was insistent that the French officers who were to train the soldiers of the Vietnamese national army should be responsible directly to him rather than to the French High Command. The divergence and even the incompatibility of purposes between France and the US had certainly occurred to various officers of the State Department and prompted sarcastic comment. But the dilemma remained and had left the US with the choice of two ghastly courses of action. 'Either we wash our hands of the country and allow the Communists to overrun it; or to continue to pour treasure (and perhaps eventually lives) into a hopeless cause . . . at a cost of alienating vital segments of Asian public opinion.' It was, obviously, a monstrous dilemma and although Ogburn in the State Department was concerned that the Congressional Foreign Relations Committees should not be misled, his suggestion of periodic cocktail parties with non-communist Asians seemed to offer only slight relief.[79] In any event, at the higher level Rusk announced that the independence of the Associated States of Indo-China within the framework of the French Union was now assured,[80] even if this did mean squaring the circle or at least begging the question. A similar attempt to draw attention to an approaching commitment that was so deep that it might even lead to direct US intervention was made by the Deputy Director of the Mutual Defense Assistance Program, John Ohly, in a long and thoughtful paper which he submitted through Rusk to Acheson. Ohly, without being absolutely sure, thought that US foreign policy was wrong and was at least in need of urgent re-examination. Substantial aid to Indo-China might, without achieving its intended purpose, make impossible the fulfilment of US mutual defence objectives elsewhere in the world. To continue without a far more searching analysis than had so far been made would have been the height of folly. The US, because of limitations in resources, could no longer simultaneously pursue all of its objectives in all parts of the world. Certain objectives might have to be abandoned if others of even greater value and importance were to be attained. As it was, however, the US was slowly, and not too slowly, getting itself into a position where its responsibilities tended to supplant rather than complement those of the French: and this was something which at least had to be offset against all the delays that would ensue in European rearmament.

As with the Ogburn paper it was a matter of incisive and impeccable analysis rather than recommendation. Ohly's proposal was for an assessment by a special task force before any further substantial commitments were made in Indo-China but, coming as it did, a month after the US had made its half-a-billion-dollar commitment, it was probably too late. In any case although Acheson in his memoirs acknowledged the 'perceptive warning of an able colleague' and admitted that these fears were eventually borne out by events, at the time he decided nonetheless 'that having put our hand to the plough we would not look back' and added his own to what would be hundreds of similarly hopeful assessments. 'Moreover, the immediate situation appeared to take a turn for the better'.[81] What Acheson had in mind, principally, was the agreement to create a Vietnamese National Army; a hopeful assessment of the agreement that had been reached after the long-drawn-out negotiations at Pau to turn local administration over to the Vietnamese early in 1951 (although, as Acheson notes, the transfer date kept being postponed) and de Lattre's appointment to Indo-China. There were, however, other and less hopeful signs that the French were not in fact going to make any substantial concessions. According to Letourneau, the Vietnamese looked on concessions as weakness and would only ask for more. According to de Lattre, France had spent too much blood and treasure for the Vietnamese to expect the sort of independence that was to be found in the British Commonwealth. And there was still the absurd question of protocol involved in who should occupy the Presidential Palace in Saigon which was turning into a long-running farce and one that was unlikely to be resolved in Bao Dai's favour as long as de Lattre was High Commissioner.

In the meantime, the US Joint Chiefs of Staff were giving their professional opinion how the French were to win the war and what the US would and would not do. The JCS were already on record that the US should assume 'positive and proper leadership' among the Western powers in Southeast Asia in order, as they put it, with no excessive modesty, 'to retrieve the losses resulting from previous mistakes on the part of the British and the French, as well as to preclude such mistakes in the future.'[82] Their recommendations to the Secretary of Defense, General Marshall, in November 1950 were yet more overweening and ingenuous, even if the imperative form was unintentional. Having decided for themselves that the problem lay in the lack of will and determination on the part of the Indo-Chinese to join whole-heartedly with the French in resisting communism, the US had to obtain assurances from the French that a programme of French government *will* be developed; national armies *will* be organized; France *will* despatch sufficient additional armed forces to Indo-China to insure that the restoration of peace and internal security *will* be accomplished in accordance with the timetable of the overall military plan for Indo-China (which made it sound more like a military parade than a war) and that the French *will* eliminate their policy of colonialism. The emphasis is added here; but even more emphatic was the JCS opinion that, in the event of an overt attack by organized Chinese communist forces in Indo-China, the US should not permit itself to become engaged in a general war with communist China although assistance short of the actual employment of US military forces should be provided.[83] In this event the American military assistance programme was to be expanded appropriately but, presumably in the meantime, neighbouring states were to be induced to commit their armed forces. (Chiang Kai-shek was not specifically mentioned but it is hard to think of other forces that might have been available.) All this, one may presume further, was supposed to supply the missing will and determination of the indigenous people and just in case the French might be feeling a little faint-hearted at the prospect, the US should immediately reconsider its policy at the first sign that the French were planning to give up or even if they planned to take the problem to the UN.

As 1950 ended the National Intelligence Estimate prepared by the Central Intelligence Agency presented a sombre picture of what it was the US had underwritten in Vietnam. On their own, it was reckoned that the Vietminh in Tonkin, who now outnumbered the French regular forces, could probably drive the French out in six to nine months and there were many indications also of impending Chinese communist intervention.[84] As 1951 began these indications had become an 'unavoidable assumption' on the part of the US minister in Saigon (Heath) who reported that 'sooner or later and probably soon' Chinese communists will invade Indo-China with organized units,[85] and near panic conditions were reported from the North. Whether or not, as Heath reported, the Vietnamese were turning increasingly to the US for advice and assistance in a situation where the Governor of Annam wasn't speaking to the Prime Minister – who was being kept on for fear that he would start a separatist movement in the south – there was some point to his suggestions that Bao Dai should be better advertised; that he should have an American adviser and that American technicians should give the Vietnamese government a 'new look'.

Six months later, in June 1951, after de Lattre had halted the Vietminh offensive in Tonkin and with the immediate threat removed, Heath reported from Saigon that the current phase in Indo-China was now to be seen as a holding operation.[86] This opinion was shared by Robert Blum in his capacity as chief of the American economic mission in Saigon (he was apparently also a CIA officer). 'Perhaps the best we can hope for is to conduct here a kind of uneasy holding operation until something else happens in another place'[87] – but in most other respects, certainly in conclusions and prescription, they diverged to the point of confrontation. For Heath it was a partnership in Indo-China between France and the US, whose interests required loyal and ungrudging although not uncritical support from the US. It was childish, he said, to think of ousting the French from Indo-China and stemming communism with the means then at hand and, considering the size of the military and economic aid programmes that were available, the pro-American movement could not be built overnight. Blum, on the other hand, was looking to a more distant future when the French might have to withdraw entirely and in order to maintain the position of influence in the future he believed that the only firm foundation was a break with the past. In practice this appeared to mean a break with the French and, like many Americans engaged in day-to-day dealings in Vietnam, Blum's frustration had reached the point where he would recommend withdrawing US assistance altogether rather than endlessly humouring the French. The irritation, if not exasperation, was mutual. Apart from calling Blum 'the most dangerous man in Indo-China' de Lattre complained of all the 'missionary young men' the US was sending to Vietnam, of the way in which they undermined the idea of the French Union and, as he obviously had time to read the reports as soon as they were sent, he objected strenuously and in person to US correspondents who did not share his more exalted view of France's mission in Indo-China. Presumably acting on de Lattre's orders, and certainly in keeping with his ideas, French censors altered the more exuberant and less sensitive American publicity releases and, in an extraordinary outburst, at the last moment de Lattre refused to allow the government of Vietnam to sign its economic agreement with the US. France, he said, must insist on exact compliance with consultation provisions and 'if the Vietnamese were to be allowed from the start to negotiate and sign international treaties without full prior consultation and approval the foundation and future of the French Union would be in peril.'[88] This was the first separate treaty to be negotiated and signed by the government of Vietnam and de Lattre's refusal was described as a slap in the face in the report which had caused de Lattre to explode and to consider expelling the American reporter. Perhaps not surprisingly for some Americans, as Heath reported, it was not the Vietminh who were seen as the enemy but the French.

DE LATTRE'S COMET

At the same time, as de Lattre was to repeat constantly to mostly more important Americans, France was an ally and an ally, moreover, that was not far off the point of victory in Vietnam. In

Paris in March, 1951 he assured Eisenhower, then Supreme Allied Commander in Western Europe, that with 12 extra infantry battalions plus the Vietnamese army which he was organizing and training, he would repel the anticipated Vietminh mass attack in September and go on to deal them a decisive blow. That in itself would win the support of a substantial group of Vietnamese fence sitters, and would unite all Vietnamese in solid opposition to Ho Chi Minh; and the Chinese communists, practical people, when they saw their aid resulting in no real accomplishment, would be less ready to see it frittered away.[89] De Lattre, it seems, had himself in mind as a Supreme Allied Commander for Southeast Asia and his proposals for a joint intelligence operation together with a strategic reserve of six or eight divisions would, if it had come to anything, have meant not only an American but a British commitment to French fortunes in Indo-China. As it was, de Lattre constantly held out the prospect of Chinese intervention, apparently believing it himself and certainly capitalizing on it in the US. There was a widespread feeling in 1951 that at any moment the Chinese, who had already identified themselves in US eyes as aggressors in Korea, might extend their intervention to Vietnam. Thus, a major paper on US military assistance to Southeast Asia to which Rusk gave his name early in 1951 was predicated on 'the imminence of a communist invasion of that area'. On closer inspection there was quite a muddle between 'Chinese imperialism' and 'Vietminh military operations', but it seems to have been an elementary mistake to base the assessment entirely on capability rather than intention, which the paper admitted, and was an extraordinary foundation for Rusk's conclusion which was that: 'Above all, we cannot afford to jeopardise the considerable measure of success our policy has already had in Indo-China by neglecting to provide the proper maintenance for our investment.'[90]

Reports and assumptions such as this continued, off and on, throughout the year and reached a climax in December 1951 in a memorandum from the acting Assistant Secretary of State (Allison) to Acheson which reported that from various sources and for various reasons, not least the fact that some 200,000 Chinese communist troops in Kwangsi Province were prepared to move on Indo-China as 'volunteers', a large-scale attack against French Union and Vietnamese forces in Tonkin must be expected on or about 28 December.[91] This was remarkably precise and remarkably misleading and seems once again to have been based essentially on Chinese communist capability.

When de Lattre had visited Washington in September 1951 it was this theme, 'the ability of communist China to invade Indo-China and South-East Asia' that the State Department had chosen to stress in their briefing for President Truman and their up-beat assessment of the General who had transformed 'an army beset with defeatism into a force which has since won every major engagement against the communist forces'. Truman was reminded that it was an agreed military estimate that if Indo-China falls, 'very likely all of South-East Asia may come under communist domination' and, although it might not have seemed a very credible danger, it was pointed out that the Philippines were less than 800 miles from Indo-China.[92] It does not appear in Heath's brief memorandum of de Lattre's meeting with Truman but de Lattre subsequently claimed to have been very reassured by the President's statement: 'We would not let Indo-China fall into enemy hands.' What is certainly on record, however, is de Lattre's ineffable assurance to Acheson that 'If it were made possible to carry out his present military plans and if there were no Chinese military intervention the Vietminh could be eliminated as a fighting force in a period of between one and two years.' In regard to his relations with the Vietnamese de Lattre claimed that Bao Dai was the ablest statesman in Vietnam; but perhaps rather spoilt things by adding that there had been several recent instances when Bao Dai 'had showed the proper co-operative spirit and, in some cases, even initiative'.[93]

The gist of de Lattre's message in Washington was that if the US would give him the tools, he would finish the job. Brushing aside the major political problem of French colonialism, ('there was no reason to discuss the question further') the real problem for de Lattre was guaranteeing priorities on the delivery of equipment. Putting the question point blank he said 'Did the US admit that Indo-China was the key-stone in South-East Asia? If the answer was no, nothing more could be accomplished; if yes, the US must provide the weapons to make continued resistance possible.' As de Lattre presented his case, his plan to construct 1200 bunkers of the Siegfried Line-type (one wonders why its French counterpart was not mentioned instead) was to provide against future Chinese attacks but, on the assumption that the Chinese might be deterred, French success seemed to be simply a matter of US munitions and confidence and, although it might have been misleading as a performance indicator, at the end of his visit to the Pentagon de Lattre was rewarded with Defense Secretary Lovett's assertion that General de Lattre was regarded as a comrade in arms and that the US would do everything they could for him that was within their capabilities.[95]

On his return to Vietnam de Lattre was even more euphoric. Morale in the Vietminh forces was dropping, Ho's prestige and popularity were waning. Providing there was no direct Chinese communist intervention he was utterly confident that in one year not only would he have secured the Tonkin Delta but would have completely eradicated the Vietminh from South Vietnam so that, by the spring of 1953, the Vietminh revolt would have been stamped out.[96] It was, of course, one thing to talk up such confidence, either in Saigon or in Washington, but quite another whether it would be believed. While a few professional eyebrows were raised, nevertheless, when the US Army Chief of Staff, General Collins, visited Vietnam he was not only impressed by de Lattre's 'Siegfried Line' but told the Joint Chiefs of Staff that unless the Chinese intervened the French and Vietnamese forces should be able to hold Indo-China indefinitely. In the meantime, he said, the French were making genuine progress in building up native forces although it would be some years before the Vietnamese would be competent to defend themselves. There was, however, a warning. This, said Collins, is largely a General de Lattre show. If anything should happen to him, there could well be a collapse in Indo-China and it was for this reason that Collins recommended that the US should continue to extend military and economic aid 'in order to check the spread of communism in South-East Asia' – but only as long as de Lattre was in Indo-China.

Two months later de Lattre was dead. He had blazed like a comet across Vietnam and the light did as much as anything in 1951 to dazzle the US and to persuade them that their assessments were right, that it was the right war and that, on certain conditions, it might also be a winnable war. But 1951 was also the year in which the climax had not happened because the Chinese did not arrive and all the plans for increasing US assistance, in which this was a contingent but major factor, would in the end go to help the French reinforce their position in Indo-China or, at most, help them to decide the time when they might depart. As a policy that might have succeeded it suffered from impossible political equivocation. At the same time as the US sought to stiffen French resolve, at least to continue the war, it had to persuade France in effect to let go because, at the very least, it had recognized that the forces of what was nominally 'the French Union' in Indo-China in reality needed men: and these men would have to be found for and fight in the National Army of Vietnam. The costs for the US would be enormous, indeed the requirement of the French was that the US would pay the entire cost, but money and munitions could be regarded as the essential calipers which might allow the rickety infant to walk; and as long as it had an American account it would grow up and would be able to buy everything that was needed for a new nation state.

Apart from this it was probably true to say that the Truman Administration, well before it came to an end, had run out of ideas on Vietnam; and it is probably true also that at the end of 1951 the weight of the French problem was beginning to shift: not so much how the US could get France out but how to keep her in. In the meantime, whether or not Acheson's alleged insensitivity to the nationalism of China's leaders could be reckoned to extend southwards to Vietnam[97] and whether or not the evidence suggests European rather than Asian priorities, Truman's momentous post-war Democratic Administration, and his partnership with Acheson, had taken the US into the tiger's cage. For the moment, however, it was France who was riding the tiger and it would be her problem how to dismount. Whether the US would help her or would decide to take her place were the questions which the next Administration would have to decide.

NOTES AND REFERENCES

1. *Newsweek*, 6 January 1947.
2. At least the French professed to believe he had. See *FRUS* 1947 Vol. VI p. 58; cf. the account cabled to the US Embassy in Paris, on Christmas Eve. *FRUS* 1946 Vol. VIII. In any case Lacoste, Minister in the French Embassy in Washington, had been horrified when someone in the State Department mentioned 'good offices': either a third party or the UN. No French government, he said, would ever consider it. *FRUS* 1946 Vol. VII p. 71.
3. *FRUS* 1947 Vol. VI The Far East, pp. 54–5.
4. *FRUS* 1946 Vol. VIII The Far East, p. 19.
5. R.H. Spector, *United States Army in Vietnam. Advice and Support; The Early Years 1941–1960* (Washington 1983) p. 69 says this would possibly have led to war between the French and the Vietnamese: which is why neither General Gallagher nor General Lu Han wanted the harbour cleared.
6. *Causes, Origins and Lessons of the Vietnam War*, Hearings before the Committee on Foreign Relations. United States Senate, 9, 10, and 11 May 1972. Washington, 1973 pp. 175–6.
7. Ibid p. 169.
8. Ibid p. 167.
9. Probably the first report on the political complexion of the Vietminh to reach the American Secretary of State came from the Director of the OSS on 22 August 1945 which it described, unambiguously, as 'A 100% Communist party'. *United States–Vietnam Relations, 1945–1967*, (Washington 1971), Book 8, p. 46.
10. *FRUS* 1947, Vol. VI, p. 68 (3 February 1947).
11. *FRUS* 1946, Vol. VIII, p. 65 (3 December 1946). Professor Robert J. O'Neill points out that the French, in their offensive of 1947, with a force of 15,000 men, had to find and defeat an army of 60,000 in an area of 7,500 square miles. A reasonable task, he says, would have been to defeat a force of 3000 guerrillas within an area of 400 square miles. *General Giap* (Washington 1969).
12. Ibid. p. 67.
13. Ibid. p. 58 (11 September 1946).
14. Ibid. pp. 72–3 (17 December).
15. Ibid.

16. According to the French monitoring service, Radio Vietnam on 26 March broadcast a statement from the new Minister of Foreign Affairs, 'We accept independence of Vietnam in the framework of the French Union'. And even more remarkable were Ho's remarks on the death of Colonel Dèbes, the bombarder of Haiphong, in an air crash: which were either astonishingly generous, or gross dissimulation. *FRUS*, 1947 Vol. VI, pp. 83–6.

17. Irving, *The First Indochina War* (London 1975), p. 49.

18. According to Irving, op. cit. p. 48, who had interviewed Bollaert.

19. An English text of the speech may be found in Allan B. Cole, *Conflict in Indo-China and International Repercussions* (Cornell 1956), pp. 62–6.

20. Irving, op. cit. p. 49.

21. *FRUS* 1947 Vol. VI pp. 141–2.

22. A telegram to the US Embassy in Paris which went out above Marshall's name on 13 May 1947 but which was apparently composed by Moffat's South-East Asia Division, *FRUS*, 1947 Vol. VI p. 97; *Causes, Origins and Lessons of the Vietnam War*, pp. 170–1.

23. Quoted in Gary R. Hess, 'The First American Commitment in Indo-China: The Acceptance of the "Bao Dai Solution 1950". *Diplomatic History* 1978 Vol. 2 Fall.

24. *FRUS* 1948, Vol. VI pp. 32–3.

25. Ibid.

26. *FRUS* 1948 Vol. I part 2 p. 643.

27. David S. McClellan *Dean Acheson: the State Department Years* (New York 1976), ch. 21.

28. Gaddis Smith, *Dean Acheson* (New York 1972), ch. 12.

29. Gary R. Hess, op. cit.

30. *The Pentagon Papers* (Gravel 1971) Vol. I p. 74.

31. Charlton Ogburn's complaint from within that Division, that it was 'the culmination of three years of consistent effort on the part of Western Europe to set aside all considerations of our position in Asia and to keep a free hand of the French'. Hess, op. cit. p. 342.

32. *FRUS* 1949 Vol. VII pp. 39–45.

33. The details of this plan, and the even simpler proposal of Harold Isaacs, the foreign correspondent, 'Contact Ho Chi Minh, find out what he wanted, and then accept his terms', are given in Robert M. Blum's important account, *Drawing the Line* (New York 1982), ch. 7.

34. J.L. Gaddis, *Strategies of Containment* (New York 1982), pp. 63–4.

35. At Calcutta what was virtually the keynote speech was given by a Vietnamese delegate. See Ruth D. McVey, *The Calcutta Conference and the South-East Asia Uprisings* (Cornell 1958). On Malaya see Short, *The Communist Insurrection in Malaya, 1948–1960* (London 1975).

36. 'History of the Indo-China Incident, 1940–1954' Historical Division Joint Secretariat Joint Chiefs of Staff August 1971. The Acheson memo was dated 18 July 1949. There are references to it in Philip C. Jessup *The Birth of Nations* (New York 1974), p. 29; and in *Hearings*, Senate Foreign Relations Committee 81st Congress, 2nd Session 'Nomination of Jessup' p. 603.

37. *FRUS* 1948 Vol. I Part 2, p. 643.

38. Blum, op. cit. p. 214.
39. McClellan, op. cit. p. 193.
40. During the war, the widely respected columnist Walter Lippmann had sought to explain 'The mystery of our China policy' to the American people, why and how the US, rather than assent to the conquest of China, chose to accept the Japanese challenge, and he concluded that the US decision to become the champion of China was, second only to Monroe's commitment to defend the Latin-American republics, the most momentous event in America's foreign relations. Americans, said Lippmann, being incapable by the nature of their own society of sustained imperialism, were the opponents of imperialism wherever they encountered it. 'They have believed profoundly that their own principles of liberty were founded upon the laws of nature and of nature's god, and that at last they would prevail everywhere.' Lippmann believed that the history of US relations with East Asia had proved that these convictions were the mainspring of the foreign relations of the US. Walter Lippmann, *'US War Aims'*, 1944, reprinted in Robert A. Goldwin, *Readings in American Foreign Policy* (New York 1971).
41. Blum, op. cit. p. 102.
42. 'United States Relations with China' in Goldwin, op. cit. pp. 290–301. Also Acheson, *Present at the Creation* (New York 1969), Ch. 39.
43. Spector, op. cit. p. 97.
44. Quoted in Spector, op. cit. p. 101.
45. JCS, *History* p. 149.
46. Ibid. p. 41. The influential Congressman Walter Judd had already identified China as the original Asian domino. Quoted in Charles Wolf Jr, *Foreign Aid: Theory and Practice on Southern Asia* (Princeton 1960), p. 26.
47. *The US Government And The Vietnam War Executive and Legislative Roles and Relationships Part 1 1945–1961.* Prepared for the Committee on Foreign Relations United States Senate by the Congressional Research Service, Library of Congress (Dr William Conrad Gibbons) (Washington 1984), p. 58. Hereinafter cited as 'Gibbons'.
48. Gibbons, op. cit. p. 61.
49. *FRUS* 1949 Vol. VII p. 86.
50. Ibid. p. 113.
51. Ibid.
52. *FRUS* 1950 Vol. VI p. 711.
53. Wolf, op. cit.
54. See, for example, President Truman's 'State Of The Union' Message: 5 January 1949.
55. Wolf, op. cit. p. 40.
56. Ibid. pp. 80–1.
57. Ninth Report of Economic Co-operation Administration, pp. 99–100. Quoted in Wolf, op. cit. p. 82.
58. For example by Charlton Ogburn, Policy Information Officer, Bureau of Far Eastern Affairs, who said: 'The trouble is that none of us knows enough about Indo-China.'
59. *FRUS* 1950 Vol. VI 733.

60. Gaddis Smith op. cit. p. 315.
61. The paper may be found in *FRUS* 1950 Vol. I, pp. 235–92. It is criticized in J.L. Gaddis, *Strategies of Containment*, Ch. 4; by Samuel F. Wells in *International Security*, Fall 1979; and again by Gaddis in *International Security*, where there is also a reply by Paul Nitze, one of the principal authors of the paper.
62. *Strategies of Containment*, p. 94; p. 107.
63. *FRUS* 1950 Vol. I p. 288.
64. Wells, op. cit. p. 125.
65. *FRUS* 1950 Vol. III p. 1007.
66. Acheson's telegram to the US Embassy in Paris, 29 March, *FRUS* 1950 Vol. III p. 769.
67. Ibid. p. 939.
68. As the French explained to a sub-committee on colonial questions at the preparatory talks for the Foreign Ministers' meeting in May 1950, *FRUS*, Vol. III p. 949.
69. McClellan, op. cit. p. 383.
70. Acheson, *Present at the Creation*, p. 673.
71. Accounts of the Melby–Erskine Report can be found in *FRUS* Vol. VI pp. 840–8; Spector, op. cit. pp. 111–15; and Melby's own memoir 'Vietnam – 1950', *Diplomatic History*, Vol. VI no. 1 Winter 1982, pp. 97–109.
72. *FRUS*, 1950 Vol. VI p. 858.
73. Bernard Fall, *Street Without Joy* (London 1963), p. 30.
74. Lucien Bodard, *The Quicksand War* (London 1967).
75. But the political impact of this appalling weapon had also to be weighed. In the words of the editor of an ultra-nationalist Hanoi Catholic paper: 'Americans are too anti-communist and therefore neglect other considerations. They give napalm to the French and are surprised by the reactions shown by the Vietnamese against its use on innocent villagers.' *FRUS* 1951 Vol. VI p. 444.
76. *FRUS* 1950 Vol. III p. 1416.
77. *United States-Vietnam Relations 1946–1967*, Book 8 p. 389.
78. *FRUS* 1950 Vol. VI pp. 865–7.
79. Ibid. pp. 862–4 (18 August 1950).
80. 27 November 1950, *FRUS* 1950 Vol. VI p. 938.
81. Acheson, op. cit. p. 674.
82. *United States-Vietnam Relations 1946–1967*, Book 8 p. 318 (2 May 1950).
83. *FRUS* 1950 Vol. VI, p. 947 (28 November).
84. Ibid. pp. 958–63.
85. *FRUS* 1951 Vol. VI p. 332.
86. *FRUS* 1951 Vol. VI p. 438.
87. Ibid. p. 451.
88. Ibid. p. 439–41.
89. Ibid. p. 401.
90. Ibid. p. 21.
91. Ibid. p. 562.
92. Ibid. p. 497.
93. Ibid. p. 502.
94. Ibid. p. 508.

95. Ibid. p. 521.
96. Ibid. pp. 540–2 (10 November).
97. As David McLean asserts in 'American Nationalism, the China Myth, and the Truman Doctrine: The Question of Accommodation with Peking, 1949–1950' *Diplomatic History* Vol. X no. 1, winter 1986, p. 40.

Chapter 3

DULLES AT THE BRINK: 1952–1954

Nineteen fifty-two, the year in which General Eisenhower announced that he was a Republican and returned to the US in triumph to secure his nomination and election as the first Republican President for 20 years, was also the year in which the US almost postponed its most important decision on whether or not it would commit its own men for the defence of an area which it had decided was vital for its security.

REPLACING THE FRENCH

It is generally understood that administrations which are nearing the end of their life, whether in America or Britain, will seldom embark voluntarily on a new and dangerous course, particularly if it is an avoidable choice, in foreign policy. Indo-China in 1952 was to be recognized in the State Department as a critical area for decision making, even more important than Korea, and under the threat or at least the impression of imminent Chinese intervention in Tonkin the Administration decided to define its position. The result was the National Security Council paper 124/2: the strongest position that the US had adopted so far towards Southeast Asia, but a paper which had taken six months to prepare.

From one point of view a six-months debate on a problem which had already existed for more than 18 months may seem something of a luxury even on the part of a government that may have been in no hurry to take a major decision but, from another, it may be seen as masking an agonizing choice: were there circumstances in which the US would have to intervene in Indo-China even if this meant war with China and, conceivably, the USSR as well? The immediate contingency had been Chinese intervention; but to this was added further uncertainty in what was, conversely, the first unmistakable sign that the French were, after all, and in spite of vociferous denials, preparing to pull out. On 6 January 1952, French Foreign Minister Schuman had told his party at a meeting of the MRP in Toulouse that 'If an armistice can be concluded under honourable conditions France will not hesitate to make peace'.[1]

At about the same time tri-partite military conversations on the defence of Southeast Asia which had been convened through direct negotiation between the American, French and British Chiefs of Staff, opened in Washington and it was only at the last moment that a single representative of each foreign ministry was permitted to be present as an observer. There was probably nothing particularly sinister in this, even if, in principle it might have cut out any countervailing 'civilian' opinion, but the presentation of General Vandenberg, the US Air Force Chief of Staff, left no doubt that he saw Indo-China as part of a bigger picture. 'Eventually we military people must face the fact that in many fringe areas around the globe our nationals are being killed in battles with satellites, and the whole thing is directed by the Soviet Union.'[2] The meeting coincided with the visit of the new British government, in the shape of Churchill and Eden, to Washington and for a moment, an impression was created of allied solidarity. Eden, for example, in a speech which he gave at Columbia University and to which he referred several times afterwards, spoke of the conflicts in Indo-China and Malaya and said 'These positions must be held'. However, when military discussions were continued in an *ad hoc* committee which included Australia and New Zealand and the participants were confronted with what could have been regarded as a logical implication of Eden's statement, agreement dissolved. Instead of insubstantial generalities, and even though these were contingent on Chinese intervention, they were confronted with plans for naval blockade and air attacks on China and what the British, at least, feared were possible attempts to overthrow the Chinese People's Republic as well as the dangers of activating the Sino-Soviet pact.

They, or again, at least the British, would probably have been even more alarmed had they known of the discussions that had been going on in Washington between the State Department and the Department of Defense. The cases that were being discussed by the military experts may, indeed, only have been hypothetical, and one can understand that they and practically everyone else were searching for an underlying political purpose, but it is hard to avoid the impression that, if only hypothetically, the US was preparing for war. Or perhaps one should say, was clearing its conceptual decks for war with China. For example, at one of the weekly meetings between State and the Pentagon, General Vandenberg wanted to know whether the British and French 'would go the whole hog politically' and whether the US was prepared to switch to a war economy. General Collins, the Army Chief of Staff, wanted to know whether he could count on the use of Chinese Nationalist forces and raised the rather delicate question of whether the US would be able to bomb the outskirts of Kowloon. He pointed out that the necessary course of action would undoubtedly result in the British loss of Hong Kong; to which Mr Nitze of the Policy Planning staff replied that: 'while we cannot sell them a complete change of western strategy, we might be able to sell them on the idea that a serious risk of the loss of Hong Kong ought to be accepted, along with a spreading of the war to China, because of the importance of defending South-East Asia.'[3]

From these meetings it would seem to emerge that the civilians more than the soldiers were prepared for war and, moreover, were prepared to blur the distinction between plans which were contingent on Chinese intervention and those which were not. Logically, perhaps, this was impeccable. If the loss of Southeast Asia was unacceptable and, as Bohlen put it 'If we lose South-East Asia we have, in my judgement, lost the Cold War' (and in that case we would be headed for war with the Soviet Union sooner or later)' then it did not seem to matter very much whether the objective was to prevent a Chinese invasion or a Vietminh victory. In comparing Southeast Asia with Greece, Bohlen continued 'Was not South-East Asia equally worth the risk of general war?' To which General Collins gave the forthright answer 'I doubt it'.[4]

The alternative to a unilateral declaration of intervention on the part of the US was, of course, agreement on some sort of 'allied' intervention: something that could be presented as a technical decision on military grounds or else a concerted response to a commonly perceived threat. At neither level was it successful. Whether or not the *ad hoc* military committee only succeeded in producing parallel courses – American, French and British – which never met, Acheson eventually blamed the British for reservations which he said made their report useless whereas, for him, the answer to the problem lay in unrestricted military talks. Certainly at the political level Eden had been back-pedalling hard. Where Acheson favoured a joint warning to China – public or private – Eden reserved his position; and where the US had already announced that French efforts in Indo-China were an integral part of the free world fight against communist aggression, Eden said he was not now in a position to associate the UK with that statement. Very likely, as Admiral Radford, who was then US C.-in-C. in the Pacific told the ANZUS Council (from which Britain was excluded) the US, France and Britain were not working together politically. But it was most unlikely that, even in Britain's absence, the Australian and New Zealand delegates would have subscribed to Radford's proposition. In response to a question about the dangers of all-out war he said, 'We are already engaged in such a war with communist China but are limited to a single theatre.'[5]

In the absence, then, of allied agreement on common dangers and common policies, what chance was there, that by continuing doggedly along the furrow which it had already started (in the recommendation of the new Assistant Secretary of State, that they should 'keep on keeping on') the US might by some means achieve success? Which meant, as he put it, that 'the Vietminh was liquidated and therefore no longer an effective instrument of the Kremlin and Peiping.'[6] Practically everything, it was now suggested, turned on 'the formation and commitment to battle of the Indo-Chinese national armies': as much, it seems, for political as for military reasons.

> In Indo-China, as in other oriental countries, political stability as a practical matter, often results from the maintenance of a strong national army. In Indo-China the national armies will represent the only attribute of sovereignty and independence which captures the imagination of the indigenous population. Finally, only through the commitment to battle of Indo-Chinese troops can the problem of the shortage of French man-power in Indo-China be solved.[7]

In this particular paper it had been argued that over the previous two years US assistance had been remarkably successful and relatively cheap; but these rather comfortable assumptions were almost immediately challenged head-on in a remarkable memorandum from the Secretaries of the Army, Navy and Air Force who disapproved of 'the sit-tight philosophy', 'the uninspired program of wait and see' and who argued instead that it should be the US who trained and equipped the national armies and that 'the out-phasing of French influence is essential'. Even they did not quite manage to square the circle. In spite of an unequivocal, finite, declaration of withdrawal, the French had to continue fighting and supporting the American programme, but they did succeed in presenting what was apparently an agreed inter-service position[8] and it was from here that the Department of Defense took off on its inductive leap: that the US should be prepared to make as great an effort to prevent the loss of Southeast Asia in the Cold War as to counter overt aggression in that area.[9]

This recommendation, part of 'A Cold War Program to Save South-East Asia For The Free World' offered a detailed programme as well for 'Removal of the bugbear of Western colonialism' and concluded naturally enough that the Indo-China States should be free to choose whether or not they wanted to remain in the French Union. The possibilities of UN intervention were considered but the conclusion once more brought up the question of defence against Chinese aggression. The Joint Chiefs of Staff, who submitted a separate paper, were hesitant about committing US ground forces in Indo-China – because it might 'occasion overt Communist Chinese intervention' – thought naval and air forces could be used without running that risk and asserted that, presumably for psychological reasons, 'the presence of US naval forces could have an important effect as a deterrent to the international spread of communism'.[10] Even more important as far as the direction and character of US policy was concerned was the assertion that 'In any event the JCS consider it may become necessary in the security interests of the US to take a calculated risk with respect to Communist China'[11]: but this, in the opinion of the State Department, was just the sort of advice which would, for various reasons 'result in the very situation which our past and present actions have been designed to avoid – an immediate choice between allowing Indo-China, and possibly all of South-East Asia, to fall into communist hands or attempting to defend it ourselves with little or no assurances of outside help'.[12]

Acheson, perhaps thinking about the unthinkable, had, as he put it, been hoping for 'progress without commitment' and although he suggested a thorough-going study of priorities – the importance of Indo-China compared specifically to NATO – it looked as though he himself did not yet have the answer to his question of what the US was really prepared to do to keep the French in Indo-China. Even if he was unable to assemble them into the structure of an obvious answer, the fragments of evidence and probabilities were depressing. For example, Ambassador Heath in Saigon, whose optimism had been so resilient, was reporting on what was now evidently a tremendous struggle, evenly matched (something like 11 m. people on either side) where, in spite of 'numerical, material and financial superiority', the bulk of the French Union troops were still hemmed in the Tonkin perimeter; and where the enemy, in spite of tremendous privations, had kept on fighting and were indeed apparently more efficient, more dedicated, more disciplined and more hard-working than the legal government. Perhaps they were also more ruthless; but another fragment, remarkable in that it came from the head of that legal government, was Bao Dai's comment to Heath on the 'sad fact' that Vietnamese troops entirely under French command were now committing the same excesses as did African soldiers.[13]

By this time, Acheson, who probably never had many illusions about Bao Dai, had completely lost patience with his inactivity and pretensions,[14] but even at a lower level there were few signs of the vitality in the Vietnamese political struggle which would give hope of an acceptable, i.e. non-communist, political solution. Among other things it was reported that four of the Vietnamese cabinet members had French wives; and while this may have impugned their nationalist credentials Acheson faced far more embarrassing questions when he went to Paris for the tripartite Foreign Ministers' meeting at the end of May. Were the French, asked Defence Minister Pleven, fighting for themselves in Indo-China or was it in the allied interest? It would, of course, as Pleven pointed out, be extremely difficult for his government to defend the European Defence Community Treaty which had been signed the day before if there was not a rapid and generous increase in US assistance for the national armies in Indo-China. In case Acheson had not got the point, Robert Schuman articulated France's major fear of European disequilibrium: that Germany would receive US aid without having to apply it to Indo-China.[15]

Having heavily, if not quite inextricably, involved itself with French fortunes in Europe as well as in Southeast Asia, having a two-year-old commitment in Vietnam and having a number of other actual or potential allies in the area who were watching it closely, it was perhaps time for the Truman Administration in its last months to have made an unequivocal statement of policy on Southeast Asia; and, at first sight, this is probably what its statement of objectives and courses of action seemed to be in the final draft of its position paper, NSC 124/2, which the President approved on 25 June 1952.[16]

IDENTIFYING THE TARGET

The objective was clearly stated: to prevent the countries of Southeast Asia from passing into the communist orbit. But instead of the initial premise, Chinese intervention, it was now communist domination, by whatever means, of Southeast Asia which would endanger, seriously in the short term and critically in the longer term, the security interests of the US. In a statement of the domino effect two years in advance of President Eisenhower's better-known version, it said that the loss of any single country in Southeast Asia would probably lead to relatively swift submission to, or an alignment with, communism by the remaining countries of the group – and it did not stop there. Communist alignment of India and most of the Middle East would in all probability follow eventually – and it would be extremely difficult to prevent Japan's eventual accommodation to communism as well. Ultimately, however, one may say the trail of causes and consequences led back to China, which was where France's problem arose and America's dilemma began. In the event of overt intervention in the Indo-China conflict by Chinese communist forces, including volunteers, the responses envisaged by the NSC were comparatively clear-cut even though the fact of intervention had to be determined in consultation with the French: an appeal for immediate action by the UN, failing which maximum international support for the minimum courses of military action. The US would provide naval and air forces for the 'resolute defence' of Indo-China and they would expect to provide the major forces for 'Interdiction of Chinese communist communication lines including those in China'.

In addition, subject to French and UK agreement, there would be a naval blockade and intensified operations in and against communist China to disrupt lines of communication and military supply areas. At the same time as Chinese Nationalists were being sent in, the US would help, if required, in bringing the French and the British out of Tonkin and Hong Kong.

In retrospect, at least, this may be seen as a schedule for rather a risky operation but it may also be seen as a measured response. If it did not work, or, as the paper put it, if 'the US determined jointly with the UK and France that expanded military action against communist China is rendered necessary by the situation' then

> the US should take air and naval action in conjunction with at least France and the UK against all suitable military targets in China, avoiding insofar as practicable those targets in areas near the boundaries of the USSR in order not to increase the risk of direct Soviet involvement.

> In the event the concurrence of the UK and France to expand military action against Communist China is not obtained, the US should consider taking unilateral action.

All this, it will be remembered, was to be in the event of open Chinese military intervention in Indo-China. What, however, was to be done if this did not happen? There was in para. 10 of NSC 124/2 an extraordinary qualifying clause: everything that was to be done in the event of open intervention could also apparently be undertaken if Chinese communist forces were 'covertly participating to such an extent as to jeopardise retention of the Tonking Delta area by French Union forces.' What was to be understood by Chinese 'participation'? And was this the major premise? Or was it 'retention of the Tonking Delta'? The first had not yet been established. Once it was, it offered a drastic way out of the American dilemma, what to do about Vietnam, on the assumption that China could be safely blockaded and bombed into compliance and that this might be achieved without the support of America's apprehensive British ally – or the intervention of the USSR. It was however, instrumental, a means to an end, so that the Vietminh 'rebellion' could then presumably be reduced to manageable proportions but, in the event, the NSC at this point had *not* decided to light the fuse. The decision was postponed but the dilemma remained: if the Tonkin Delta and Vietnam had to be retained, was there any other way to do it than by that course which led inexorably to China? When the first Indo-China war reached its climax in 1954 and the US approached the brink of intervention and war with China, in the latter respect at least the arguments had been rehearsed two years before. It was not as if Dulles had stood US policy on its head: simply that he was following that earlier argument to its logical conclusion.

In the meantime, as the French position in Vietnam showed little sign of improvement, the US was looking for a more flexible definition of 'Chinese aggression'.[18] Military representatives of the ANZUS countries, plus Britain and France, meeting in Washington in October 1952 'to consider the defence of South-East Asia in the event of Chinese aggression' decided that nothing much could be expected of a naval blockade but were also assuming that 'The retention of South-East Asia within the allied sphere is considered vital'; while the State Department Director of Philippine and South-East Asian Affairs (Bonsal) asserted in November that 'a defeat of the present communist forces affords the only prospect for the constitution of a really viable and dependable non-communist government in Vietnam'. More French forces were needed, said Bonsal ('although SHAPE would probably yell its head off') and he took a hopeful view of the military prospects, more particularly if as few as two French divisions could be 'seconded' for even a limited period.[19]

As far as the military aspects of revolutionary war were concerned this last was essentially an amateur opinion. Again, a serious re-examination of the military situation and prospects was recommended: but now it was time also for 'the incoming President to make a statement as soon as possible regarding the importance of the Indo-China struggle'. As it happened, on the date this recommendation was made, 18 November 1952, Truman and Acheson were briefing the newly elected President Eisenhower on Indo-China. France, they said, lacked a militarily aggressive attitude and the Vietnamese were sitting on the fence. The US was bearing up to half the cost of the war but many Frenchmen thought it was a lost cause. Five-power military discussions had failed to devise agreed military solutions in the event of overt Chinese intervention and it was, said Truman, an urgent matter on which the new Administration must be prepared to act.[20]

Thus, in the last year of their Administration, Truman and Acheson had been told by the Army (General Collins) that the French were going to be driven out unless the US did something soon to prevent the Chinese Communists from getting supplies down into Indo-China; but they had rejected the Air Force proposal (General Vandenberg) 'to really go in to clean the thing up' – in this case meaning China. Almost to the end they had resisted the commitment of US forces but in the Truman Administration's dying days, fortified perhaps by a North Atlantic Council resolution that the campaign waged by the French Union forces in Indo-China deserved continuous support from the NATO governments, the first insignificant decision was taken which would put US servicemen in to Vietnam. On 22 December 1952 Assistant Secretary of State Allison's telegram to Saigon and Paris read:

'Department concurs in US participation maintenance C-47's by 25–30 USAF personnel at Nha Trang on temporary loan basis. Defense notified and has taken similar position.'[21]

VISIONS OF VICTORY

As with nearly all new Administrations, the Republican Presidency of General Eisenhower promised to get American foreign policy moving again. As a soldier, Eisenhower had promised to end the great military stalemate of the outgoing Democrats with the offer that he would go to Korea. So unpopular had that war become in the US that it seems likely that it was this issue above all that ensured Eisenhower's election. While there were those who looked forward to an apocalyptic ending in which the forces of evil would be destroyed, most Americans probably trusted Eisenhower's military experience and insight to provide a less dramatic finale. Stressing the heavy casualties that had been suffered, Eisenhower talked about 'the job of finding an intelligent and honorable way to end the tragic toll' and, having seen for himself the nature of the struggle, observed 'small attacks on small hills would not end this war'. That, of course, was Korea, those were US casualties, and, along with the promise of peace, there was to be the threat of war. But, if the US was preparing in whatever circumstances to negotiate with the communist enemies in Korea, what were the prima facie objections to the French, who had been fighting almost three times as long, drawing the same conclusions and looking for the same result?

In the first place, perhaps, was the fact that, for the French and the Vietnamese they were supporting, although the war had not been won it had certainly not been lost and, given the weight of American assistance and a sufficiently prudent approach, it seemed unlikely that the Vietminh on their own could defeat the French in the foreseeable future. By contrast, at least in the French presentation, it still appeared as if a French victory was just around the corner and even if it were not, the 'situation mondiale' might change, something might turn up, but in the meantime there were enormous reserves of Vietnamese manpower to be tapped, as well perhaps, as an inexhaustible flow of American assistance. Even if the French had by now little reason to want to hold onto Indo-China in itself – in one of his first recorded opinions as Secretary of State on the matter Dulles said they did so because of the French position in North Africa – and in spite of their determination to present their struggle in terms of an allied cause they had even less reason to accept the more exalted premises on which the Republicans had based their presidential campaign.

Before he became Secretary of State John Foster Dulles was probably most widely known for his rather sensational article 'A Policy of Boldness' which had appeared in *Life* the previous May. This essay in liberation theology had enlivened the Republican attack on post-war US foreign policy – 'the negative, futile and immoral policy of containment' – and Dulles' stress on a 'liberation policy' which would create hope and resistance inside the Soviet Empire held out the promise of an eventful foreign policy when, after some apparent hesitation, he was chosen by Eisenhower to be his Secretary of State.[22] Eventually the Republican campaign rhetoric was inscribed in national policy; and in its statement of basic national security policy (NSC 162) approved by the President on 30 October 1953 one could clearly see the reflected image of liberation and the ideological context within which specific policies were made. If, in general, the American purpose was 'to reduce the strength of Communist Parties and other pro-Soviet elements' and if, in order to counter any threat of 'a party or individuals directly or indirectly responsive to Soviet control' achieving dominant power in a free-world country, the US would take 'all feasible diplomatic, political, economic and covert measures' to prevent this happening, it was unlikely that the Vietminh and their associates in Indo-China would be given the benefit of any doubt about their communist credentials.[23]

To begin with, however, even though he had attacked the basic premises, Dulles did not really need to do much more than continue the previous Administration's policy towards the French in Indo-China although, as he discovered on his first ministerial trip to Europe, there was a further complication in the relationship in the shape of the European Defence Community within which alone the French were reluctantly prepared to accept the idea and the fact of a rearmed Germany. The US would before long link their assistance in Vietnam with the French ratification of EDC – hence the contribution of German forces to the defence of Europe – but with over 70,000 French troops in Indo-China, including 5,500 officers and men engaged in training the new Vietnamese army, and the possibility that more rather than less would be needed if there was to be much hope of military success, it would be difficult to say who at this point was able to put more pressure on whom. However, with 25 per cent of France's regular army officers and almost 40 per cent of her regular NCOs serving in Indo-China and with an increasingly apparent need for them in Western Europe where they would balance the German contingents in a European army, at least psychologically, it was also increasingly obvious that there was a basic problem here of limited means and competing ends.

It was not, however, reckoned to be an insoluble problem and although, at least in retrospect, there was little evidence deriving from contemporary operational performance of the French Union and Vietminh forces, from French intentions, or from popular support that would bolster such optimism, 1953 was the year in which French and Americans exchanged visions of victory. On the US side, certainly in Admiral Radford, the Pacific Commander-in-Chief who was soon to become the new Chairman of the Joint Chiefs of Staff, they sometimes suggested irrepressible confidence and some mistaken ideas about the nature of the conflict. In the critical Tonkin Delta for example Radford reported that two good American divisions with the normal American aggressive spirit (a spirit, incidentally, which the French were usually reckoned to lack) could clean up the situation in ten months.[24] A subsequent, even less balanced opinion, suggested that 10,000 African troops might wind up the war within six months.[25] In the State Department there was still the same expressed necessity to defeat and destroy Communist aggression in Indo-China and while, in Washington, this went with the caveat 'if at all possible', in Saigon Ambassador Heath said the US was entitled to receive, in forthcoming talks with the French, a plan of offensive operations calculated to break the Vietminh resistance in so many months or so many years.[26]

As far as the duration of operations was concerned this, of course, was again in the nature of an amateur opinion but the prospect of victory – defined as breaking the back of the Vietminh – within a matter of months now had a military hallmark as well. If French Union forces were to be increased by the new units which were under consideration, Brigadier-General Trapnell, who was heading the American Military Assistance Advisory Group in Vietnam, reckoned the job could be done within about 18 months.

While success in Indo-China would not be achieved *solely* through military means, Trapnell said that military success was the prerequisite for political progress: something which he reaffirmed when the reverse order was suggested.[27] Could it really be achieved in a definite time and at a definite cost? Just before the members of a new French government led by Prime Minister Mayer arrived in Washington at the end of March 1953 Dulles had told the NSC that it was beyond French capabilities simultaneously to meet their commitments in Europe and in Southeast Asia and that he was going to explore with them a programme which within a year or 18 months would substantially reduce the strain.[28] No more details seem to have been given but in a telegram to the Paris Embassy to prepare the ground with the French Dulles had called for considerable increased effort on their part and the liquidation of the principal regular armed forces of the Vietminh was suggested 'within a period of, say, 24 months'.[29]

When the French and Americans began their cruise on the Presidential yacht on 26 March Eisenhower opened their meeting by recognizing the Indo-China war as part of the general struggle against communism, not merely a French colonial affair, and is then recorded as saying, engagingly but perhaps rather disingenuously, that the US was most interested in hearing of any French programme for the solution of the Indo-China question. There followed the usual explanations and assurances – one new item was Mayer's suggestion that the axis of the communist offensive now seemed to be aimed at India across Laos and Siam – but in regard to Indo-China the obvious purpose of the French visit, greater US aid for the Indo-China war, was now tied up specifically by Eisenhower to America's need to know what the French plans were, both political and military, for the conduct of the war.[30] Although it is not recorded in the *FRUS* documents, according to the notes made by the Assistant Secretary of Defense, Mr Nash, the President apparently told Mayer 'in a very pointed manner' that before the US could consider providing any additional aid, the French would have to produce a plan which 'if it did not lead to complete victory, would, at least, give hope of an ultimate solution'.[31] The result, says the official US Army historian, was that 'American insistence engendered the so-called Letourneau plan; a clever piece of improvisation produced by Letourneau and his staff on the spot in Washington'. Whether or not it was quite so impromptu, what is of considerable interest in another respect is that, having called for defeat of the Vietminh in 24 months, the US now received the perfect echo: while he could not promise complete victory Letourneau said that the French plans – to create 54 new 'light' battalions of the Vietnamese army – would break the back of the Vietminh in 24 months.[32] Even this, in the circumstances, splendid offer was described by Eisenhower as rather disappointing and while it may, in general, have been because it did not seem to be much of a plan it was, in particular, because of the 'slowness of its time-table'.[33]

Re-reading the discussions and exchanges in the first year of the Eisenhower administration it becomes increasingly evident that they wished to believe and then largely persuaded themselves that something like victory in Vietnam was attainable in a period of between one and two years; and that two years was rather too long to wait. Over the longer period, however, as it emerged from Letourneau's 'strategic concept', the US would be expected to pay for the training, arming, and equipping of 135,000 additional Vietnamese troops. In a war which seemed to be evenly balanced in numbers this was a dazzling prospect. Together with other Franco-Vietnamese units they would somehow 'clean up' the enemy centres of resistance in south and central Vietnam, the more heavily armed Franco-Vietnamese regular units would then take on their Vietminh counterparts in the north and 'it is estimated that these latter forces will be brought to a decisive battle during the first half of 1955'.[34] It was also, at least in retrospect, wildly optimistic not least in its assumption that these 'light' battalions, starting from scratch, would be able to take on even the regional forces of the Vietminh, many of whom had been fighting for years. Hopeful signs, of course, could always be found. Day by day, Letourneau said in Washington (he left out the 'in every way' part of M. Coué's popular pre-war psychotherapy) things were getting better. In some respects, however, they seemed to be getting worse. The French performance in the 1952–53 fighting season had been a great disappointment – at least to the Americans. When General Mark Clark had visited Vietnam General Salan told him of the Vietminh's 'surprising capability' of mobilizing three regular and one heavy division for an attack on a French position (Na San) the previous autumn against which the French could only oppose eight battalions; and Salan was already anticipating a Vietminh offensive with four divisions against northern Laos. At the political level Bao Dai told the visiting Adlai Stevenson that the Vietnamese National Assembly would be fairly useless since half of his country was in enemy hands[35], but after wide-ranging discussions in the State Department on everything from exchange rates and taxation down to on-the-job training for Vietnamese civil servants and subsidized imports of raw silk, it must have seemed that instrumentalities such as these held out sufficient hope; and on 9 April 1953 a new Assistant Secretary of State, Walter Robertson, in a memorandum evaluating the French plan authorized the opinion 'If Defense finds the French concept militarily acceptable, the Department (of State) supports it from the political point of view'.[36]

Was the concept acceptable? Was the plan workable? Were these, in fact questions to which there were military answers? The French, said General Trapnell, were too conservative and overly cautious in their operations – but otherwise the plan appeared to be sound and, barring unforeseen developments, would probably succeed. General Collins was sceptical about the French plan, as he was about their 'totally negative attitude' to training procedures which the US had found to be successful in Korea, and about what he called the spurious reasons the French gave for not creating units larger than battalions. But when Dulles, after pointing out 'the implications of the fall of Indo-China to the whole South-East Asian picture', asked him whether the US should be prepared to stop all aid to Indo-China he replied 'No, but we should use maximum effort and persuasion to get them to adopt a more sensible program'.[37]

There seemed therefore to be the possibility that the play might develop with an alternative script. One, suggested by Collins, was that the French should construct their defence line across, and thus presumably interdict, the Vietminh's supply lines from China. Another suggestion from Saigon was for increased American control and leadership in the aid programme: a new look at the Indo-China war and every right to demand that new conditions be met.[38] The Joint Chiefs of Staff thought the French were not sufficiently aggressive and, again, wanted big unit operations, something that would cut the enemy's supply lines in northern Indo-China. Overall, however, although the French plan could be improved, they thought it was workable; but when asked (by Nitze, of the Policy Planning Staff) what that meant, the optimism began to evaporate. General Vandenberg, for example, said that if the French did a lot of other things there might be some slight chance of success and among them seemed to be something like a NATO solution: sending an additional two French divisions to Indo-China even though this meant, as General Collins said, that the French would have to change their conscription law.[39]

There was, then, at this time what looks like an increasing and self-induced American conviction that something was almost within their grasp which would change the course of the Indo-China war: and change it comparatively soon. It would have to be achieved comparatively quickly and for two reasons. The first, as Dulles told the French in Paris in April, was that there 'would have to be a program where we could in effect say to Congress: this program has enough chance of success that if you invest a certain amount for a certain time it will largely clear up the situation' although by this he meant not actual victory but reducing the dimensions of the war to those of Malaya or the Philippines.[40] Second, the French were becoming tired, restless and, in spite of official optimism, by no means altogether convinced that victory was possible. Particularly as it was becoming clear that the US, having been unable to achieve its enlarged objectives in Korea, was about to settle for a compromise peace which, after three years of war, had left the country divided at approximately the same line as it was in 1950. 'The conclusion of an honourable armistice, the immediate cessation of hostilities and the prompt initiation of political discussion leading to the holding of free elections' were the particulars of what Eisenhower called 'the last chance for peace' in a speech he made on 16 April 1953: but these were the conditions for peace in Korea. In Indo-China, however, as far as the US was concerned there were no acceptable conditions for a negotiated settlement, bar one. In a reasonable anticipation of the Vietminh terms the Western European desk in the State Department said that the withdrawal of foreign forces would be a precondition for a plebiscite and 'a plebiscite under present conditions could with certainty be predicted as giving a thumping majority to the Vietminh'. If there were two Vietnams, that 'state of affairs could not be expected long to endure what with greater dynamics of the Communist elements in Vietnam coupled with the half-heartedness of Bao Dai and his government'. However, two Vietnams were a possibility *provided* most of the French forces in Indo-China stayed in south Vietnam for a long time. 'There should be no illusion that anything much better would be possible in negotiation without hitherto unimaginable military success.'[41]

The unimaginable had now to be imagined and, moreover, it was to be what another level of the State Department described as 'the necessary basis of any settlement which our side could honorably accept'.

> The key to the problem remains prompt and vigorous military action by our side with US material support leading, in as short a time as possible, to a serious curtailment if not an elimination of the military potential of Ho's regular divisions.[42]

By now, the US was involved in another part of Indo-China with the crisis that developed in Laos as Vietminh forces threatened the royal capital of Luang Prabang and the US responded, as it had on a previous occasion, by sending more transport aircraft, this time with civilian American pilots to fly what for the French was an unfamiliar model. The Laotian crisis seems to have taken Eisenhower by surprise and his reaction was to press for more vigorous French leadership. He described most of the French generals who had been sent to Indo-China as 'a poor lot' and had apparently already tried to secure the appointment of General Guillaume as French Commander there. That evidently having failed Eisenhower now recommended General Valluy, presumably also on military rather than political grounds but, having ordered the bombardment of Haiphong in 1946, to appoint Valluy would have been rather like proposing General Dyer as Commander-in-Chief, India, after the Amritsar massacre. In the event, the French decided to send Marshall Juin's NATO Chief of Staff, General Henri Navarre.

After the débâcle at Dien Bien Phu which effectively terminated his brief career in Vietnam, Navarre maintained that he was never given a clear political brief in Paris; but even before he had arrived in Saigon the combined civil and military opinion in the US embassy was that the test of French sincerity would be whether or not Navarre adopted 'a more positive attitude' towards the war.[43] When Ambassador Heath returned to Vietnam he had no doubts on this score but attributed what he called Navarre's 'sharpened attitude' and 'acceptable plans' to the arrival of General O'Daniel, Commander of the US Army in the Pacific, and to the presence of the US Military Assistance Advisory Group. O'Daniel had apparently been sent out to do far more than a survey of French military requirements and Dr Spector, the US Army historian, says it was at O'Daniel's urging and with his assistance that Navarre prepared an aggressive new concept for the conduct of operations in Indo-China, soon to become known as the Navarre Plan.[44] Whoever should be given the credit (or blame), one may wonder whether it was O'Daniel who persuaded Navarre that he could succeed, and then reported to the Joint Chiefs of Staff on Navarre's 'full co-operation', his 'new and aggressive concept' that would emphasize larger formations and initiate a three-division offensive by mid-September.[45] If Navarre was given political support O'Daniel said he would do much to bring the war to a successful conclusion; but as one examines the details of O'Daniel's report, one may suspect that this was as much as anything because the war was beginning to look more like a Franco-American joint enterprise.

It was also, after France had been more than a month without a government, and after a brief caretaker administration, looking as if the Laniel government offered the last chance of a victorious conclusion to the Vietnam War; although this was to be measured in political determination rather than enhanced military capabilities. After him it was assumed, in a revealing State Department memo, that there would be 'out and out negotiations with the Communists' which would lead to a French evacuation but it must already have been becoming clear, from what the French made no attempt to deny, that they would be hard put to maintain their existing military effort. Navarre's requests – and O'Daniel's expectations – of another two French divisions were, said Defence Minister Pleven, out of the question.[46] For all the continuing, egregious, and perhaps by now exasperating optimism radiating from Ambassador Heath in Saigon – 'persuading the French of the possibility, I would say certainty, of French victory' – the State Department position paper in July 1953 was fairly depressing and its most hopeful word was 'persevere'. At one of their regular joint meetings with the JCS General Collins, somewhat surprisingly, suggested that the French already had enough troops to do the job, if they would use them properly, but when he was asked 'If we were faced with the loss of Indo-China to the communists what would your advice be from a military point of view?' he answered, rather lamely, 'I think we would just have to sit down with our political leaders and talk the things over'.[47]

This was another meeting in which the basic contradiction lay near the surface. Was Southeast Asia essential to the US from a military point of view? Yes. Was the US willing to commit two American divisions? No, that was something that was up to France and the Associated States. But, as General Collins put it, it would not just be a question of putting in one division. 'If we go to Indo-China with American forces, we will be there for the long pull. Militarily and politically we would be in up to our necks.'[48] When Foreign Minister Bidault came to Washington a few days later to ask for another 20 billion francs he was already pessimistic about the Navarre plan even though he said it was being speeded up. Dulles, on the other hand, sought to persuade him – or perhaps convince himself – that 'with the necessary strength and spirit of initiative' the destruction of substantial organized enemy forces seemed possible; and it was this belief which he nurtured until he was able to secure formal assent in the early autumn.

There could now be little doubt, however, that the US was engaged in a race against time; or at least was moving fast to the point where they would have to decide whether or not they would augment or even replace the French. Peace, said Bidault, linking Korea and Indo-China, was indivisible. If there were no prospects for peace the French government would be in an absolutely impossible situation; and while Dulles held to the Navarre plan as the only way to bring the war to an end – and seemed to be hinting a propos the ending of the Korean war, at some sort of comparable and 'massive' retaliation – Bidault was already envisaging a negotiated peace on the basis of free elections under UN supervision. For Dulles, evidently, there could be no negotiation except from a position of strength and although he denied that the US wanted to keep the war going 'except for the purpose of protecting interests vital to all concerned' he described negotiations 'where our side would have no alternative' as bankrupt, ending only in disaster.

There can be equally little doubt that, for Dulles, there was no alternative to victory and that this was something that the French could have if the US paid. For the sake of argument one may even locate the approximate point at which the US took over the baton (or went into the lead) in its determination to win the war. At the same time (3 August 1953) as the French political adviser (Claude Cheysson, who eventually became French Foreign Minister) to Vietnamese President Tam told Ambassador Heath in Saigon that the French – 'Reynaud and others' – had no intention of continuing the present effort over any protracted period and were hoping for 'sufficient victories' to make some sort of deal with the Chinese or Vietminh – 'and thus allow France to withdraw troops and reduce expenditure without apparent loss of face or honour',[49] the State Department (5 Aug) recommended that the National Security Council agree to a further increase of $400m in US aid provided only that, in the opinion of the JCS, 'the French plan holds the promise of military success'.[50]

CONGRESSIONAL INTERESTS

So, a week after it had decided that Korea was an unwinnable war, the American administration had chosen to persuade itself that in Indo-China, on the contrary, and in spite of discouraging evidence, there was likely to be the promise of military success. In spite of subsequent rather nervous qualification by the JCS there was no official dissent, but readers of this presentation of US foreign policy may reasonably complain that it is more appropriate to the late-18th or early-19th centuries when it was argued that its conduct was executive, altogether, than to the middle of the 20th century when Congress, if not the Judiciary, had been admitted to equal partnership. Nevertheless the US entanglement in Vietnam was altogether executive. There was, as yet, no surge of public emotion, there was little public interest even, no part or process of American life or business that could be identified in or with Vietnam. But, at least in Congress, one could say it was beginning. In May 1953, on the day Senator John F. Kennedy addressed a list of 47 questions on Indo-China to the Secretary of State, he and Senator Mansfield had lunched with Mr Ngo Dinh Diem. The lunch had been arranged at the Supreme Court Building by Mr Justice Douglas; Diem was identified as a Catholic Vietnamese Nationalist leader; and Gullion, of the State Department, filed the report.[51] Kennedy's interest in Vietnam went back to a trip he had made there in November 1951 when he had succeeded in annoying General de Lattre. The annoyance was obviously mutual and at the end of June 1953, when the bill to provide another $400m in military aid reached the floor of the Senate (there had been very little discussion in Committee), Kennedy was highly critical of the French performance in Vietnam. Using Diem's words Kennedy said that the concessions to Vietnamese independence had been 'too little and too late' to win the Vietnamese over from a position of sullen neutrality and he wanted all the US Mutual Security funds to be spent and administered in such a way as to encourage freedom and independence. This, as Dr Gibbons and his staff point out in their study of the executive and legislative roles in relationship in the Vietnam War,[52] was the first serious debate to have been held since the war had begun and it was also perhaps the last occasion before the climax at Dien Bien Phu when the Executive might have had to take account of Congressional restraint. In the event, and somewhat ironically, Senator Kennedy's criticism was accepted as part of an amendment to the US aid bill that had been proposed by the conservative Republican, Senator Goldwater, which required the French to give a fixed date for complete independence in Indo-China. In the event, also, the amendment was heavily defeated and it seemed as if most of the Senators accepted the proposition that it was the President rather than Congress who should be making foreign policy 'when a war is now actually in progress'. Perhaps it is rather sentimental to feel moved by Goldwater's quotations from the Declaration of Independence and when he asked if, perhaps, they did not apply to Indo-China; but whether one considers it naive or not it was, ultimately, an instrumental argument. Unless the French conceded real and proper independence and freedom it would end up with American boys in the jungles of South-East Asia. Or, as Kennedy put it to the Secretary of State: 'The American people want in exchange for their assistance the establishment of conditions that will make success a prospect and not defeat inevitable.'[53]

As far as the Eisenhower administration was concerned the

irrevocable commitment to a French victory in Indo-China was made in the National Security Council on 9 September 1953: ironically, in Eisenhower's absence. Two points stand out from this momentous meeting. The first was that if, as Dr Spector suggests, the new Joint Chiefs had been even more cautious about predicting success and had, in effect, withdrawn the earlier endorsement of the Navarre Plan, there was no sign of caution or disapproval on the part of their Chairman, Admiral Radford, or of the Secretary of Defense. Indeed, although Radford entered a caveat about the skill and effectiveness with which the plan was carried out, he stated the Joint Chiefs' firm belief that it ought to be supported and, speaking personally, observed that for the first time the political climate had actually improved to a point where military success could be achieved. There was, perhaps unfortunately, little ambiguity about this statement and even less about Radford's prediction that, with aggressive prosecution, the war could be reduced to mere guerrilla operations in the course of a single fighting season – certainly in two.[54] The second is the way in which Dulles presented his case as if only the formality of approval was necessary. The President, he said, had already indicated his general approval of how to assist the French – although the NSC was free to discuss the details. Perhaps, on the reasonable assumption that the Secretary of State enjoyed the President's full confidence, no one was going to challenge Dulles when he reduced the issue to what he said was essentially a financial problem. A month before, the chances that the State Department, the Foreign Operations Administration and all the Services, as represented by the Joint Chiefs of Staff, would agree on the feasibility of the Navarre Plan seemed somewhat remote. Now, instead of any one of them saying 'It isn't going to work' everyone agreed it might work – and the brakes were taken off. Again, more as a formality than a necessity, it was agreed that Congress would be informed; and at the other end of the contingency scale, France, it was also agreed that it would be a mistake to attempt to secure written assurances from the French government that, in return for this assistance, it would press for ratification of the EDC treaties. Any such written assurances, it was said, would be certain to leak out.

It is, of course, more than conceivable that the decisions would have been the same even if Eisenhower had been present and it may be suggested that, having just received news of the successful CIA coup against Mossadegh in Iran, the President in particular and the foreign policy establishment in general were in a buoyant and optimistic mood. They were also in the final stages of putting the US into a fundamentally different defence posture, the 'New Look', in which its capacity for massive retaliation would be the principal US contribution to the defence of its allies and other parts of what it called 'the free world', but where the underlying theme was not so much the idea of retaliation *per se*, but that of seizing the initiative.[55] After the unwelcome sensation caused by the explosion of the first Russian hydrogen bomb in August 1953, the Navarre plan certainly looked as if it would regain the initiative in what was designated as an area that was vital to US security. If, that is, it worked. Inside the National Security Council doubts were stifled. Outside, there was at least one muted protest in the Senate: 'pouring money down a rat hole', 'it was going to be one of the worst things this country ever got into', but the President had decided and so Democratic Senator Russell would keep his mouth shut. However, as the Republican chairman of the Armed Services Committee, Senator Saltonstall, pointed out, Congress now had to underwrite the President's open-ended commitment to the Navarre plan. And, one might add, to Vietnam.

Virtually from this point on one could argue that events were in train. The French had had some tactical success in Vietnam – the ability to destroy large quantities of Vietminh munitions and, more to the point, the ability to extricate their forces either by land (Lang Son) or by air (Na San) from such operations without significant loss. For those who were impressed by France's solemn declarations there had been yet another, on 3 July 1953, which would perfect the independence and sovereignty of the Associated States; but while they had avoided and, indeed, in the early stages of the Navarre plan intended to avoid, large-scale encounters with the danger of defeat, the French suffered almost irreparable political damage when, in the effusion of a Vietnamese national congress – in lieu, that is, of anything like a national assembly – they were told that the French Union should not endure, at least as far as Vietnam was concerned, and was in fact quite contrary to the sovereignty of an independent nation. This meant that for many Frenchmen, such as Bidault, there really was not much left to fight for even though, in circumstances which are still not fully explained, the French Union forces were about to launch an operation which would indeed be one of the decisive battles of the 20th century. So much has been written about Dien Bien Phu, yet not enough to account for such a dreadful mistake.[56] Had it worked, had its purpose been kept clearly in mind and its chances of success constantly evaluated, and had French resources been large enough to allow it to have been mounted on a sufficiently large scale, it could conceivably have met the American criteria for operations that would have cut or at least disrupted the Vietminh's supply lines as well as give them, the Vietminh, some anxiety about political or prestige attacks to which the French would be bound to respond in Laos. To begin with, when the parachute battalions dropped on 20 November 1953 and even after signs that the Vietminh were responding to the challenge, the French saw no cause for alarm and were, it seems, genuinely looking forward to a

Vietminh attack and the chance of a decisive engagement. Thirty years later General O'Daniel wondered whether Navarre might have been influenced by the sort of operation in Korea which drew the enemy into the range of US artillery but concluded, as did Eisenhower after the event, that it was an absurd place to choose.

As Navarre himself presented it, Dien Bien Phu was not a major scheduled operation, indeed his purpose was to avoid a battle on such a scale so early in his plan. But, as it developed, it became the focus of the entire Vietnam war as well as drawing in men and munitions from the other scheduled operations which Navarre had in mind. Perhaps when he revealed to his influential visitor, Senator Knowland, in mid-September, that he only had three divisions in his 'corps de bataille' whereas the Vietminh had approximately seven, the alarm bells should have started ringing in Washington; although it is easy to see, the decision to support Navarre having just been taken, why they did not.[57] When General O'Daniel went out to Vietnam for the second time, in November 1953, it was to try to persuade Navarre that he should seal off the Red River delta; but as Navarre pointed out he could hardly do that as well as build up his own divisional forces. In spite of the Vietnamese light battalions, which had had one or two unhappy experiences at the hands of their more experienced Vietminh opponents, the war was having to be fought on two levels by the French Union forces; and, as the map in Navarre's memoirs shows quite clearly, the Red River delta was already riddled with villages under Vietminh control. The French, therefore, were not very receptive to US advice on how to conduct the war, at least at this level, and the disparity between the way in which they were fighting and the advice which, based on their Korean experiences, the US gave them on how they should fight was never really overcome. Towards the end of 1953, then, apart from the question 'how', one should ask who was fighting for what in Vietnam. On one side an emperor who represented French hopes and at least their political investment but, as far as Vietnamese were concerned, little more than a non-communist alternative future; and that only as long as his government was supported by French Union troops and US money. There was no pretence of democratic government or parliamentary assembly to lend credibility to a ramshackle régime but at least for Vietnamese there were few of the exactions of a totalitarian system nor was there any compulsion to defend it. For the French, who were there in fact rather than in name, what happened in Vietnam was perhaps more a matter of consequence elsewhere. If the French Union were to hold, more especially in North Africa, it would have to hold in Vietnam. And if numbers of Vietnamese in whose name the French were fighting had no intention of remaining within the French Union, and furthermore, were likely to be in a position of power once the French had left, then, from a French point of view, the continuation of the war was futile. But not as America saw it. Rather, it was an enterprise deserving of allied support for the transcendent purpose of defending her allies, her friends and herself but one to which the US had not yet decided, and perhaps might never need, to commit more than material support. On the other side, whatever it was that kept them fighting, was associated with, if not deserving to be, branded as communism; not least because of the support that was given by the Chinese Peoples' Republic and the USSR. Without their help the war conceivably would not have lasted as long as it had. With their help it was very likely going to last a lot longer. Yet this might have been the wrong perspective from which to view an event that, rather than war, could equally well be presented, from the beginning, as revolution.

While, historically, one might argue that America had ambivalent feelings towards revolution, the record of the Eisenhower administration, like the attitude of its predecessor, was unequivocal towards what it regarded as communist revolution. In Guatemala, in Cuba and even in Iran when Mossadegh had been unfortunate enough to have the Iranian communist party rioting in the streets on his behalf, Eisenhower and Dulles, with the invariable assistance of John Foster Dulles' brother Allen as Director of the Central Intelligence Agency, had been prepared to intervene and in two countries out of three succeeded by their intervention in overthrowing men who they regarded as their political enemies.[58]

In Vietnam, however, the US was dealing with a much more intractable problem and one which, if it was to be solved, would call for a far greater commitment. The French, obviously, were unable, and unwilling, to fight the war on their own. For example, with so many isolated positions they relied heavily on American-made transport aircraft. By the end of 1953 the US had already lent a small aircraft carrier and were about to lend another. Most of the strike aircraft which the French were using were American also, as was their artillery. Large numbers of French Union forces came from North and West Africa and from the Foreign Legion; and the US was paying for the Vietnamese 'light' battalions. None of this had so far been enough although it always seemed possible to hold out the prospect if not the promise of success.

In December 1953, America's European allies, Britain and France, came to a summit meeting in Bermuda; and from Bidault they heard once again that things in Indo-China were going well, Vietminh forces were 'facing a stagnation in strength' while the French Union forces were creating 'a force of manoeuvre of considerable size' and from Churchill they heard of his great admiration for French exertions in Indo-China. The admiration was somewhat retrospective, for Mr Churchill, who seemed rather out of step, was making a favourable comparison of the French in Indo-China and the way in which the

British had left India – 'a colossal disaster' – although he did refer to the splendid work that France was doing in North Africa. Perhaps this was at least the semblance of allied unity from which more might be expected if the Vietnam war could be presented as a sort of extension of NATO interests; although it could equally well have been an occasion when, instead of Churchill's extravagant comments, French prospects in Indo-China might realistically have been examined. As it happened, however, and although this is not a definitive sequence, Dulles presented Communist China as the promoter of aggression in Indo-China. He was obviously convinced that by sending atomic weapons to Korea, and making sure the Chinese knew, the armistice there had been achieved from a position of strength[59] and as soon as the allies had gone he told the National Security Council on 10 December 1953 that he had encountered very stubborn resistance from the British and French 'to any idea of the automatic use of atomic weapons' and what Dulles described as 'our suggestions with regard to normalising' their use. The specific point of reference here was in the case of a communist renewal of hostilities in Korea but it was something that had implications for Indo-China as well. In the event of 'an actual US military commitment' the CIA, together with the intelligence organizations of the Services, the Joint Staff and the Department of State, concluded that: 'The chances are probably better than even that the Communists would accept the risk involved and that the Chinese Communists would intervene openly and in force in an effort to save the Communist position in Indo-China.'[60]

WAR PLANS

At about the same time as the Intelligence Advisory Committee was concurring in this estimate in mid-December 1953, and the noose was beginning to tighten around Dien Bien Phu, the Joint Strategic and Logistic Plans Committees of the Chiefs of Staff were drawing up their paper on whether or not to commit US forces in Indo-China. For the first time one might say that the US was facing up to the full implications of its declared policy on Indo-China. More like a Seventh Cavalry than a Seventh Fleet solution, the French were to hold on until the US and its allies rode to the rescue. In addition to the usual litany, of varying resonance – warning to China, UN action on the Korean model and a regional effort to include, surprisingly, Burma as well as, possibly, Nationalist China – there were similar fantasies of development for indigenous forces: if necessary by means of US-supervised training. Setting out a number of options its recommendation was for Alternative A: which was to support and intensify the development of indigenous forces and deploy US and allied forces (ground, sea, and air) to Indo-China to undertake operations with the objective of reducing Communist activity to the status of scattered guerrilla bands. This, the most positive recommendation, would offer the greatest assurance of success while the others ranged in estimated probability from 'some chance for success' to 'the very likely result of military defeat'. It would, however, present several problems. Specifically, that it would require seven US divisions; but only five were 'readily available'. Concomitant disadvantages included 'an increased calculated risk adversely affecting war plans', major alterations in fiscal and budgetary policies and programmes, major increases in military production and mobilization schedules, and a reversal of policy planning to reduce the size of the US Armed Forces. However, whether Alternative A, B, or C was initially adopted, if US forces engaged in combat in Indo-China, the US must be prepared to commit whatever forces were necessary to 'insure' [sic] military success.[61]

This, in its recommended action, was now very much more than a contingency plan. Indeed, it was so sensational, 'the substance of the Special Annex was so controversial, and the questions it discussed so sensitive' that, as Gibbons points out, it was thought prudent not to have it in circulation. However: 'contingencies referred to in the Special Annex would henceforth be discussed only orally, and all copies of the Annex would be recalled for destruction'.[62]

Given its premises, that the retention of Indo-China, Tonkin in particular, was vital to US security and that the French were in danger of losing it, these recommendations may have been logically impeccable but, given what was understood at the time to be US defence policy, they were both unlikely and, strictly speaking, politically irresponsible. It was, after all, a proposal that the US should go to war in Vietnam six months after it had stopped the war in Korea and yet, given the supremacy of end over means, this was the case that was put to the National Security Council on 8 January 1954 at the beginning of the great governmental debate on US intervention. It was, that is, a case for a limited war but not, said Eisenhower, vehemently, one in which the US should contribute ground forces because, as he foresaw, it would become a war 'that would absorb our troops by divisions'. This, however, was not the only option and where Admiral Radford wondered hopefully whether a squadron of US planes over Dien Bien Phu for as little as one afternoon might save the situation, even Eisenhower said it was certainly going to be necessary to work out some way by which US planes could be used even if 'we could not just fly them into combat off the carrier.'

From one point of view it looked as if Dulles had already begun to set the scene. On 6 January 1954 he had apparently reassured Democratic Senator Walter George of the Foreign Relations Committee that Congress would not be asked for its approval to send in American troops; but Dulles' memorandum of conversation adds 'We talked about possible sea and air activity, to which he did not seem seriously to object'.[63] On 7 January, speaking to the Foreign Relations Committee, Dulles had said 'There is no doubt whatever in the minds of our people that the thing can be licked' but this meant that, with qualifications, it could be achieved in another fighting season 'if the French will stick to it'. This was the doubtful element.[64]

Although it is not to be found in the official record of US foreign policy it would appear from another source, the Pentagon Papers, that Dulles at the meeting of the NSC on 8 January must have presented the State Department view: that the French position was so critical already as to 'force the US to decide now to utilise US forces in the fighting in South-East Asia'.[65] The Chief of Naval Operations had proposed a similar course to the Secretary of Defense; but, from another professional point of view, partial involvement, the use of naval and air units only, was a delusion and Vice-Admiral Davis wrote himself into the literature of the Vietnam War with his comment: 'One cannot go over Niagara Falls in a barrel only slightly.'[66]

At this point, however, the Joint Chiefs of Staff had still not been able to make up their minds on intervention and in the National Security Council as a whole the official record reveals the most intense opposition, both service and civilian, to Admiral Radford's proposals – for example supporting the French at Dien Bien Phu with a US aircraft carrier – and his assumption that the US was already in the war in a big way.[67] The strongest recorded opposition came from Treasury Secretary Humphrey who said he simply did not see how we could talk of sending people, as opposed to money, to bale the French out. Even the loss of Dien Bien Phu could not, he thought, be bad enough to involve the US in combat in Indo-China. What came out of this meeting therefore, instead of agreement on intervention, was a discussion of what the US might do by way of a *sub fusc* commitment, whether General Navarre could be persuaded to take several hundred US officers to train the Vietnamese forces, or, failing that, whether, as Eisenhower put it, they could find a little group of fine and adventurous pilots 'and then we should give them US planes without insignia and let them go'. The distinction between intervention and non-intervention was becoming dangerously thin. Admiral Radford was entitled to his complaint that once again the issue had been side-stepped, although the US was now at least one step nearer intervention.

The fundamental question, which it was perhaps indelicate to raise at this point, was whether or not the US was going to war. The Assistant Secretary of State, Walter Robertson, had warned

Dulles that public opinion in America was not ready for a decision to send troops to Indo-China: but the caveat was unless it seemed necessary to save South-East Asia from communist domination.[68] On the other hand, when the question was put to him direct in the House Foreign Affairs Committee and he was asked whether all the force that was necessary to save Asia would be used, Dulles, unless he was greatly misunderstood, at least gave the impression that it would. There is, he said, a will to act, there are plans of action; and even though he may have reassured the Committee when he said 'We have in mind the Constitution which says only the Congress can declare war' it would take a very good lawyer to work out from the record what Dulles actually told them. In any event one needs to look elsewhere for clear-cut opinions as well as for the options that were being closed off. The most important of these related to the French and while it was the US position to continue to support the French without direct military intervention this was threatened from two sides, or, as it were, by two converging lines of advance. First, on the diplomatic front, the Foreign Ministers' conference which opened in Berlin on 25 January 1954 had, after considerable US resistance, agreed to put Indo-China on its agenda, thus opening the way to a negotiated settlement. Second, having decided to accept the challenge, the Vietminh divisions were themselves converging on Dien Bien Phu where the French forces were already surrounded and entirely dependent on air supply. So far the Vietminh had stayed outside the range of French artillery and until the battle actually began both French and Americans summoned up or gave way to gusts of rather foolish optimism. To begin with it did not seem to matter that much whether the opinions which were so confidently advanced by Radford, for example that the Vietminh were not really going to attack Dien Bien Phu after all, turned out to be so dreadfully mistaken nor his assurance that even if the Vietminh brought up anti-aircraft guns they could be knocked out by fighter attack. At the beginning of the year even Navarre was worried by these anti-aircraft guns which would prevent French planes knocking out Vietminh artillery and although Navarre conceded that the Vietminh might now take Dien Bien Phu he declared bravely that even the loss of as many as ten battalions would not prevent him moving on to eventual victory.[69]

Quite obviously, if only to judge from the list of requirements which he submitted (including a small observation balloon!) at the beginning of January 1954, the French were in very serious difficulties and largely unable to provide the equipment that was needed for their own war effort. But so far it was only an impending crisis even if, in Washington, the reaction of columnists and commentators was sometimes more realistic than that of the State Department. Nevertheless it was sufficiently critical for the creation of an extraordinary Special Committee on Indo-China which was set up in January headed by

General Bedell Smith, Eisenhower's wartime Chief of Staff, who was to fill roughly the same role with regard to Indo-China. It was this Special Committee which dealt with the French request for more aircraft and for American mechanics to keep them flying. In the event, the request for 400 mechanics was cut in half but as soon as this recommendation was agreed it was approved by the President and the men were dispatched. A year before, Acheson's recommendation in the dying days of the Truman administration led to the dispatch of a handful of mechanics. Now it was 200: plus an agreement to send civilian pilots hired by the CIA as well as Bedell Smith's firm and influential opinion that the importance of winning in Indo-China was so great that if the worse came to the worst he would favour intervention with air and naval forces.[70]

In the Senate it seemed that the Armed Services Committee had been very unhappy with this development, even though the Air Force technicians were only supposed to be on bases where they would be secure from capture and would not be exposed to conflict. But when asked by the President 'What is the alternative?' and as it was, after all, a commitment that was now limited in time as well as in numbers, reluctance did not amount to dissent. Senator Mansfield, for example, might warn of a swiftly developing crisis: but he was opposed to a negotiated peace and was still hoping for clear-cut victory. Mansfield still had every confidence in men like Navarre and Bao Dai; he was very glad that the government was spending $1200m in Indo-China; and he would vote for another billion or more next year. Senator Fulbright seemed to be closer to the mark when he said that the war would not be won by B-26s or anything else that the US could put in but he, too, suggested that if Bao Dai was no good, the US ought to get something else. From here, perhaps, one can see the ball beginning to roll that would take the US to the brink of intervention in 1954. For the moment, however, it seemed to be more a matter of helping Sisyphus to reach the top of the hill; but when the rock began to roll back the question was whether the French would be crushed and what the Americans could do to prevent this happening.

DIEN BIEN PHU AND THE QUESTION OF INTERVENTION

Whether and how the US would or could come to the assistance of France in her Indo-China war was, at the time, one of the most critical and most intensively argued issues in post-war American foreign policy; and it is a question which has never been closed. The debate began when it was realized that intervention might, first, be necessary to keep the French fighting; and then, when the scale of her difficulty at Dien Bien Phu became evident, it became equally obvious that she might have to be saved from a self-inflicted and unanticipated defeat. Once Indo-China had been placed on the Foreign Ministers' agenda and the challenge had been issued and accepted at Dien Bien Phu, there was a certain uneasy awareness that this was to be the critical battle. Images of 'a veritable jungle Verdun' notwithstanding it became clear that the critical factor was air power, both in supply and attack, in which the French were hopelessly under strength. For the moment, however, and although the French were surrounded in their unhappy compromise between a fortress and a launching pad, the Vietminh attack had not begun at Dien Bien Phu and the National Security Council in Washington could still afford the luxury of more relaxed debate in which the President, against a background of recorded and presumably good-tempered laughter, wanted to find a good Buddhist leader to whip up some real fervour in Vietnam. It was still a time of relative complacency and hope even if, on another reading, the situation was basically hopeless. Thus, in the same meeting where Eisenhower was looking for his militant Buddhist, Dulles said that the most disheartening feature of the news from Indo-China was the evidence that the majority of people in Vietnam supported the Vietminh rebels.[71] Overall, however, the good news prevailed. In Saigon there was the irrepressible Ambassador Heath, who could not understand French pessimism. Two or three divisions, he said, could turn the present stalemate into early victory. In Washington there was the impermeable Chairman of the Joint Chiefs of Staff, Admiral Radford, who unworthily attributed the pessimism of General Trapnell, who was on the spot in Vietnam, to the fact that he had been a Japanese POW. In between, as it were, was the Director of South-East Asian Affairs in the State Department (Philip Bonsal) who reckoned that optimism would be the major asset in the coming weeks, presumably wished to nurture it, and conversely, warned Ambassador Heath that when the American Consul in Hanoi returned to the US he should not 'highlight unduly' the more sensational and pessimistic aspects of the situation.

It was with similar determined and rather perverse optimism that Dulles was apparently waiting for the Geneva Conference to begin: even if the context of his remarks suggests he may have been misunderstood. Whether he was or not, he is reported as telling the National Security Council at the end of February 1954 that both he and Bidault were approaching the forthcoming conference 'with considerable equanimity'. Dulles did not believe that the French would push too hard for a negotiated settlement. When the fighting season ended in May, the heat, as he put it, would be off so if the French government could hold on for a couple of months or so, Dulles did not anticipate too much difficulty. But there was a condition, which was repeated: that there should be no real military disaster prior to or during the conference. Nothing specific was mentioned and the dominant chord was optimism: that there was at least the fair probability of securing both French membership in EDC and the continuation of the struggle in Indo-China. All the same, two further thoughts occur. First, that by fixing his gaze on Geneva Dulles had momentarily taken his eye off the ball, or, rather, off the match that was about to begin in Indo-China. Second, that such a consummate lawyer as Dulles would be bound to put in a caveat that would allow him to extricate himself when the major premise collapsed. More to the point, perhaps, was that no one in the National Security Council at this time wanted to expose the foundation of his argument and no one mentioned Dien Bien Phu. Two weeks later, on 13 March 1954, the battle began with a Vietminh artillery bombardment of unimagined intensity, the French immediately lost their first outposts, and the US government reacted as if it, too, had been precipitated into a hitherto unforeseen political crisis.

A week after the attack began the French Chief of Staff, General Ely, arrived in Washington at the invitation of Admiral Radford. Air power was now the only way of saving Dien Bien Phu; which meant it would have to be American; and the requests would be made for it in all shapes and sizes. – More B-26 medium bombers, for example: but the French did not have enough air crews for those which they had. Ten or twenty B-29s, with French crews who scarcely knew how to fly them, operating from US bases in the Philippines whose government might not have been willing to give their permission. – A US airlift of two parachute battalions from North Africa was requested although in the event the French battalions were not yet ready to go. The wide-screen version, as it was projected by American enthusiasts such as Admiral Radford, eventually featured squadrons of B-29s, flying by day or by night, with fighter and fighter-bomber squadrons from US aircraft carriers, up to a total of some 350 aircraft; but in the meantime the French wanted bigger bombs and the large C-119s, the 'flying box-cars', adapted to carry napalm. Ultimately, it seems, Dien Bien Phu was important enough to the US to justify apocalyptic risks. The innocuously titled Joint Advanced Study Committee of the Joint Chiefs of Staff apparently concluded that three tactical atomic weapons, properly employed, would be sufficient to smash the Vietminh effort at Dien Bien Phu – 'clean up' was the expression used – and Admiral Radford's special assistant had been sent over to the State Department to ask whether, in the event of an allied coalition being formed, the French were likely to give their approval for such a cataclysm.[72]

BLUFF?

For approximately three months, from the middle of March to the middle of June 1954, the US administration discussed, projected and negotiated the possibilities of intervention in Indo-China. From the fact that, in the end, nothing happened it is possible to infer that nothing was intended and that even though, for political reasons, Eisenhower and Dulles may have been forced to tack from time to time they were in fact steering a course of determined non-intervention. They were, that is to say, nowhere as near the coast of Vietnam as the presence of US aircraft carriers at the time would otherwise suggest and there were no circumstances other than Chinese intervention in which the US would have been involved. Thus, for example, when Eisenhower set conditions for intervention he made them deliberately impossible; when he sent Dulles and Radford to talk to Congressional leaders he was expecting, and had presumably intended, them to refuse support; and when Dulles spoke of united action, this was clearly an absurd idea. None of it, therefore should be taken too seriously.[73]

On the other hand, given the apparently immutable importance of Indo-China to American security, it would have been surprising if the French predicament at Dien Bien Phu had been ignored or their exertions in Indo-China written off as a bad job. In any case, a couple of days before the assault began, the Special Committee had come up with a programme for military victory because, to continue the Verdun metaphor, 'on ne passe pas', at least not in Indo-China, and if this could not be done with make-shift methods such as US volunteers then, if things got worse or the French were difficult, the US might wish to consider direct military action.[74] To do what? With the Geneva Conference due to begin on 26 April 1954 it could have been to permit the French to negotiate from that elusive 'position of strength' or, rather, so that they should not have to negotiate from the humiliation of defeat. In practice this meant that something had to be done to relieve the French at Dien Bien Phu if that were at all possible but it also meant, given the guidelines that had been drawn, that because the idea of a negotiated settlement was unacceptable, intervention would have been as much to dissuade the French from giving up as to defeat the Vietminh or deter the Chinese. Beyond this fairly clear if negative object there lay a great deal of uncertainty: in method, in consequences, and in record. When, for example, Ely came to Washington in March 1954 one does not know whether, with perhaps limited English, he misunderstood Admiral Radford's remarks to mean the offer of nuclear weapons nor does one know the mood or the message in his off-the-record talks with the President. Ely, in turn, when Radford took him to meet Dulles, may not have

known what to make of the Secretary of State's elliptical argument
that, if the French wanted open US participation, it might involve
a much closer partnership: although these, said Dulles, were simply
broad considerations of principle and one may assume, as a lawyer,
he intended them without prejudice. Ely, however, could have been
in no doubt of one thing: in the hypothetical case of US intervention
they would have to win: 'We could not afford thus to engage the
prestige of the US and suffer defeat which would have world-wide
repercussions'.[75]

Would it be necessary? And how was it to be done? On the
assumption that French power was collapsing in Indo-China the
further assumption which Dulles presented to the National Security
Council (25 March 1954) was that the US would have to fill the void
rather than China; and for Eisenhower the question was how far
the US should go in employing ground forces in saving Indo-China
from the communists. In view of the subsequent nervousness about
using anything except US naval and air power this was a significant
starting point, and after considering the prospects of UN approval
or assistance the discussion centred on what would be necessary to
obtain Congressional approval. If, for example, Vietnam were to
invite assistance from various countries and the invitations were
accompanied by treaties Eisenhower thought they could probably
get the necessary two-thirds majority vote in the Senate: and
Congressional approval was essential.[76]

The question of using ground forces would obviously have meant
a much more deliberate and long-term commitment than the sort of
single air strike which Dulles and Eisenhower had talked about the
previous day – Eisenhower said it would have to be decisive – but
either would have involved the sort of risks about which Dulles was
apparently talking: risks which, he said, would be less if taken then
rather than in several years' time.[77] It was as much as anything this
element of danger that created world-wide concern when Dulles gave
his highly publicized radio and TV broadcast speech on 29 March in
which he called for united action to meet what he implied was a
Chinese and Russian threat to the whole of Southeast Asia and
it was certainly commensurate with what Eisenhower had publicly
identified as an area of 'transcendent importance'. All the same, it
was a curious speech, not least for its warning to 'a potential aggressor'
where his aggression could lead him, and its emphasis on the Chinese
connection. The Vietminh, by contrast, were hardly mentioned and
where they were they were described as having been largely trained
and equipped in Communist China and supplied with artillery and
ammunition through the Soviet-Chinese Communist bloc.[78] Rather
as if he were an advocate addressing a jury Dulles managed to convey
far more than the qualifications would permit. Thus, the substantive
purpose of Red China and Russia was to dominate Southeast Asia;

and it would be more difficult to remember that it was, in fact, as Dulles said, only their propagandists who made this apparent. Apparent, again, this time probably from French sources, was the less than substantive basis for the number of 2,000 Chinese who, Dulles said, were functioning in key positions with the Vietminh; although, even if this figure was accurate, according to the French half of them were Chinese Army lorry drivers.

CHINA: THE SUFFICIENT CAUSE?

The most detailed as well as the most familiar accounts which deal with the question of US intervention in Vietnam in the spring of 1954 for the most part consider it in terms of these two factors: the US and Vietnam.[79] In Dulles' 'united action' speech there was, however, more than an echo of 'massive retaliation' which was the prescribed principle of uncertainty that was now supposed to underlie US foreign policy: the times and places would be chosen by the US rather than by her enemies. Where and how could the US retaliate against communist aggression in Vietnam? And if there were to be insurmountable difficulties in using US divisions what would be the target for US naval and air power? At this point it is probably necessary to make an inductive leap but the logical answer would seem to be 'China', even if the fragments of evidence are by no means conclusive. Perhaps it is significant that before his 'united action' speech Dulles was worried about what he called 'a landslide psychology in favor of appeasement of Communist China': and felt that something strong needed to be said publicly to check it[80] and his attitude at the time, as well as his record at Geneva, shows that he was quite incapable even of considering the sort of accommodation with China that might have produced a settlement in Vietnam. Where it may have been more difficult to work up any strength of feeling over Ho Chi Minh and the lesser enemy there was, in the Republican administration, among men such as Senator Knowland, Congressman Walter Judd, Assistant Secretary of State Walter Robertson and even Dulles himself, a passionate intensity of feeling directed against the communist régime in China. This would, simply because of the Sino-American experience over the previous five or ten years, account for the violence of their hostility and their willingness to make life as difficult for the Chinese régime as they could and might explain the comparative lack of restraint or caution which seemed to characterize their thinking about Chinese problems. Now, however, China was not just a problem in its own right but one that could be identified as the major cause of the Vietnamese problem as well.

American intervention in Vietnam can be seen, therefore, as something which not only involved China but, in the way in which the Administration presented the case, it gave enough indication that China was considered to be the sufficient cause of the Vietminh 'rebellion', which might therefore be dealt with at its source. Thus, in what is sometimes regarded as the critical meeting of Dulles and Admiral Radford with Congressional leaders on 3 April 1954 – 'The Day We Didn't Go To War' – the draft Joint Resolution which Dulles may have been carrying with him, but which he had certainly taken to the White House the day before for Eisenhower's approval, began 'Whereas the Chinese Communist régime and its agents in Indo-China are engaging in armed attack against Vietnam and the duly constituted and friendly government of that country', and went on to assert that they were committing aggression against the friendly states of Laos and Cambodia, threatened other friendly states, and had as their object the domination of all Southeast Asia.

If it had ever been presented to and approved by Congress, this was the resolution which would have given the President a blank cheque to intervene in Southeast Asia subject only, in effect, to three conditions: that the naval and air rather than ground forces of the US would be employed; that Congress would still have the authority to declare war; and that the President's executive powers would only last until the end of June 1955. Again, it is remarkable that the Vietminh are not identified as such, that is to say that they were not considered to be a power in their own right; and furthermore, they were only designated as the agents of Communist China who were engaged in an armed attack against Vietnam. In other words that it was China, once again, who was guilty of aggression. In the event it seems the draft resolution was never mentioned but the concept of aggression was something to which Dulles returned when, for example, he told the House Foreign Affairs Committee that what he claimed was Chinese participation in the Vietnam war came 'awfully close' to the type of overt aggression that he had referred to in earlier statements. The purpose of this statement, according to Dulles, was, amongst other things, to indicate to the Chinese communists that they were getting perilously close to the point of serious risk to themselves; but for all the implication that this would be a self-inflicted injury there was no doubt that, if it happened, the US would be the instrument of destruction.

The dangers of Chinese intervention were real enough, if only perhaps because of the Korean precedent, although once US forces were engaged in Vietnam they would pose less of a threat to China than they did when they arrived, briefly, on the banks of the Yalu in 1950; but while the US obviously wished to provide a deterrent against Chinese intervention it seems that, for Dulles at least, deterrence was an elastic-sided concept. That is to say, it might be stretched to include what the Chinese were already doing rather than what they might do in the future. The constant worry of the French, incidentally, was that the Chinese airforce would intervene and with their Soviet-supplied MIG fighters would simply shoot the French airforce, which had no jets, out of the sky. But so far, in any meaningful sense, or at least on the scale of Korea, the Chinese had *not* intervened although if Congress, the American people, or America's allies could perhaps be persuaded that they *had*, then this would prove to be a greater justification for whatever it was that the US was going to do.

And there was, perhaps, just a chance that the US would not have to do it. One of the ideas which, in print at least, one can see taking shape is that, if China was confronted with a *de facto* allied coalition in Vietnam, which included the US and its awesome nuclear threat, they would be induced to withdraw their support from the Vietminh. So, as Dulles told the British Ambassador, he had hoped that his 'united action' speech would have a deterrent effect on Chinese communists. If, Dulles said, they could be made to see that 'stepped up activities' on their part in Southeast Asia could lead to disastrous retaliation 'on our part' by sea and air, perhaps the Chinese could be persuaded to refrain from adventures in that area. If so, Southeast Asia could be saved from communism and probably a world-wide conflict avoided. But, in any case, said Dulles, they felt the risk was justified.[81]

Whether Dulles had in mind current or future Chinese adventures is by no means clear but whatever it was US policy was based on extraordinary optimism. As Dulles informed the US Embassies in Paris and London on 4 April the alternatives at Geneva could only be face-saving formulae to cover the surrender of one side or the other; 'whereas if we [presumably the US and its allies] were strong and resolute enough to make the Chinese communists see clearly that their conquest of Southeast Asia would not be permitted without the danger of extending the war, they might desist and accept alternative b): that is, the surrender of the Vietminh.'[82] In the letter which Dulles drafted for Eisenhower to send to Churchill, in what was designed to be 'another act of fellowship in the face of peril', the hope was that the Chinese could be brought to believe that their interests lay in the direction of a discreet disengagement[83] and talking to the Australian Ambassador on 10 April in support of the idea of a coalition Bedell Smith, the Under-Secretary of State, said it was intended not only to boost French morale but also to discourage Communist China: 'It is not inconceivable, given the proper circumstances, that the Communist Chinese might be impelled to pull the rug out from Ho Chi Minh.'[84]

So, on the less familiar but more ambitious reading, united action was intended to assist the French by threatening the Chinese: but what form would it take and what was it supposed to do? Frighten China into cutting off support from the Vietminh? In that case what would constitute an effective threat? How long would it take? If that did not work was the US prepared to go to war with China? On its own? Was it really intended as any more than a threat and in the meantime what was going to be done to help the French? In the recorded turmoil of discussions, conditions and alternatives, in an atmosphere of crisis which became far more intense than the climax of Senator McCarthy's contemporary domestic drama, there is too much evidence to permit the more comfortable conclusion that it was only intended for effect. The Special Annexe (supra) with its Doomsday minus 1 scenario resurfaced and was put into circulation for the first time. Even General Ridgway, the Army Chief of Staff who in other respects showed commendable restraint, reckoned that if the US decided that the loss of Indo-China and the rest of Southeast Asia would be intolerable, and if China did not stop sending military aid to the Vietminh, the US should announce its intention 'to destroy or to neutralise the sources of Vietminh military power'.[85] This reference could only have been to China: even though the memorandum itself is harder to evaluate. Should it be taken at face value, i.e. that the US should be prepared to go to war with China? Or was it designed principally to reinforce Ridgway's argument that the use of US armed forces in Indo-China, apart from any local successes they might achieve, would constitute a dangerous strategic diversion of limited military capabilities and would commit US armed forces 'in a non-decisive theatre to the attainment of non-decisive local objectives'? With the experience of war that had only just stopped in Korea, the emphasis in America's 'new look' defence policy which favoured the Air Force and Navy at the expense of the Army, and the simple fact that, even if nuclear weapons *had* been used, the Army still did not have enough available divisions to engage in war in Vietnam, it might, ironically, and certainly from an Army point of view, have been easier for the US to attack China with naval and air forces than it would have been for the Army to repeat the Korean nightmare in Vietnam. And it might also have been more popular although, having said that, it is difficult to make out a case that 'in certain circumstances' too, the US could not have been involved in some sort of military intervention in Vietnam in 1954. In any case, the argument turns on the conditions for intervention. These seemed to change from time to time – what could be done to relieve Dien Bien Phu, what should be done to bolster the French before and after the Geneva Conference moved to its Indo-China phase – but the essential conditions were set out by Dulles to the National Security Council on 6 April. They were, first, that US intervention must be part of a coalition to include other free nations of Southeast Asia, the Philippines, as well as British and Commonwealth nations. Second, France must agree to accelerate the independence programme for the Associated States so that there could be no question of US support for French colonialism. Third, France must agree not to pull her forces out of the war if the US put her forces in. There was also, as far as the Administration was concerned, a prior condition: there would have to be Congressional support. And even though, when Dulles and Radford were unsuccessful in what seems to have been their attempt to persuade Congressional leaders, notably on 3 April, that they should give their unconditional support to executive action should it be required, the conditions that were set were by no means unattainable and for all the difficulties that each of them may have presented it can be argued that Dulles' attempted triple jump came very close to success.

THE BRITISH OBSTACLE

From the moment these conditions were set out, it was recognized that the British position was the one that was crucially important and the State Department (MacArthur) had already tried to carry it by storm. A curious if not deliberately misleading account of Dulles' meeting with Congressional leaders had been given to the British Ambassador who was told that if there were really united action . . . the US would be able to play its full part but, on the other hand, in a remarkably open threat he was told that if Britain, together with Australia and New Zealand, 'simply sat on their hands' it would virtually call into question the whole concept of alliances and, more specifically, would have the 'most serious impact on support we were contributing to collective arrangements elsewhere'.[86] As a matter for internal discussion there was little doubt about the risks which Britain was expected to run if the US could get her to line up with them throughout Asia to resist communism. Although the NSC did not seem to be particularly well informed on what was happening in Malaya, and Vice-President Nixon in particular, on the basis of a recent visit to Southeast Asia, claimed that British colonialism was a mill-stone around America's neck, Dulles reckoned that it might still be possible to save Malaya if Britain was prepared to risk the loss of Hong Kong.[87] Whether this would have been the result of US attacks on China, or some sort of united action in Vietnam, was not made clear but to put these half-formed ideas, impetuous proposals and spasmodic reactions into some sort of sensible framework one can see that Dulles was attempting to produce an instant alliance. Having kicked off, publicly, with his 'united action' speech of 29 March 1954 he had given himself less than a month to go into the Geneva Conference 'strong and united, with a good hope that we would come out of the conference with the communists backing down'.[88] Dulles' historical reminiscence was that it was the British who had let the US down in 1932 when she wanted to slow down the Japanese in Manchuria; but this time he thought they might follow the US lead.

Given the fact that an alliance already existed in Western Europe where America's historic decision and massive commitment was linking the destiny of the allied nations in the face of a perceived Soviet threat it was, from Dulles' point of view, not unreasonable to extend that alliance to Southeast Asia where, in Indo-China, France was already fighting for its existence against communist opponents whose major advantage lay in proximity to communist China. The immediate problem therefore was to persuade the UK to take up a similar position. And for a moment it seemed as if Dulles had succeeded.

The essential difficulty lay in convincing the British that events in Indo-China constituted such a threat to the rest of Asia as to necessitate 'allied action' and justify the risk of war with China and, not inconceivably, the third world war. Dulles had not liked Eden's attitude from the start: it was, as Dulles described it, a problem between the US and France with the UK standing on the side-lines as an uninterested party: a situation which, according to Dulles, actively encouraged the French to seek a negotiated settlement.[89] Nevertheless, the same argument that Dulles used against the French might have to be applied to the British: it might be necessary to beat them into line. MacArthur's exchange with the British Ambassador (supra) seems to be evidence of this but in several conversations which Dulles had with Sir Roger Makins there was less threat and more persuasion. Incidentally, on one occasion, according to the British account, Dulles argued that the USSR would use their influence in persuading China to discontinue its aid to the Vietminh; but this point is not to be found in the US record.[90] However, with Eisenhower's message to Churchill on 5 April the scene was set for a monumental misunderstanding. When Dulles arrived in London a week later, intent upon alliance, it was with a draft declaration of policy which looked more like a multilateralized Monroe doctrine for Southeast Asia than the sort of organization which would have been comparable to that of the North Atlantic Treaty. Indeed, on an historical parallel, it was not that different from the Holy Alliance with its transposed fear of 'International Communism', whose forces were now said to be subjecting the Associated states of Indo-China to armed attack and invasion and whose domination of any part of Southeast Asia and the Western Pacific would be a threat to the peace and security of them all.[91] Eden's reaction was much the same as that of Castlereagh in 1820: 'We shall be found in our place when actual danger menaces the System of Europe but the Country cannot, and will not, act upon abstract and speculative Principles of Precaution.'[92]

As it was, Eden's familiar but unconscious endearments and Dulles' chronic halitosis would help to produce a notable non-congruence over the next few weeks when, as one observer recalls, they seemed simply to talk past each other but whereas, when the American draft was 'informally' produced, the Foreign Office (Dennis Allen) 'expressed great reserve' because 'definitive action before the conference began might foreclose the possibility of successful negotiation',[93] Dulles emerged from this encounter without the draft declaration but with Eden's signature on what could be argued was a contract: a joint statement which said, 'We are ready to take part, with the other countries principally concerned in an examination of the possibility of establishing a system of collective defence . . .'[94] As Dulles, overlooking the setback to his draft declaration, told the French it was a communiqué which fully satisfied the purposes he had in mind in coming to Britain.

Certainly it might be seen as the basis for some sort of united action. The only matters it had not settled were what, and more important, when. Taken in the context of what can be seen were British attitudes before the communiqué was issued (rather than after, when they could be regarded as excuses for escaping from unexpected or unwelcome commitments) it hardly looks as if Britain contemplated armed intervention of any kind before the Geneva Conference had had the opportunity of arriving at a diplomatic settlement. The communiqué could be understood to mean just that. It could equally well be understood to mean than an armed coalition would be formed before the conference began, so that the French would not only be supported but would even be able to call on power which they were manifestly unable to command on their own and from this position of strength negotiate a settlement which might be acceptable to the US. If, however, this proved for whatever reason to be impossible, their opponents would at least have to reckon with an alliance in being. Either course might have been tried; both were implied; but the US came away from their first British encounter believing, or claiming to believe, that they had secured UK approval for the creation, announcement and even deployment of the forces of an armed alliance.[95]

As soon as he returned to Washington Dulles once more set about the task of creating a framework for united action first, by putting the fear of God, or rather, Godless communism, into the Ambassadors of Australia and New Zealand and then announcing that talks would begin on 20 April 1954 with the Ambassadors of other participant states – Thailand, the Philippines, the Indo-China states – as well as France. Eden had apparently agreed that an informal working group should be set up in Washington to consider 'how best we might proceed in organizing united will to resist aggression in South-East Asia'[96] but seems to have thought that this action either jumped the gun or exceeded the limits of its agreed competence. The British, or at least Eden, understood that 'The whole question of membership was a matter for further consideration' and that it might involve India and Burma as well as Pakistan.[97] Eden, considerably irritated, told the British Ambassador in Washington not to attend and the meeting was hastily converted into a more innocuous briefing for foreign ambassadors on the eve of Dulles' second departure for Europe, this time via Paris *en route* to Geneva. On the same day as the briefing Dulles had another, unrecorded, meeting with Congressional leaders in an atmosphere of mounting crisis after Vice-President Nixon's unscheduled and unattributed comments had become headline news: that if the French pulled out of Indo-China the US might have to send in its own troops.

Whether or not then, as the Joint Chiefs of Staff internal history put it, Dulles had begun to prepare the American people and world opinion for possible US intervention in Indo-China and whether or not these were contingent plans the question was certainly wide open when Dulles arrived at Paris to be told that nothing could save the situation at Dien Bien Phu except perhaps massive US air-strikes. Bidault waved aside the idea of a defence coalition: the French would regard it simply as a device to keep them fighting whereas, if Dien Bien Phu fell, France would want to get out altogether.[98]

As the agony of Dien Bien Phu reached its peak so did France's desperate hopes of US intervention. On 23 April, General Ely said if the US would intervene with 200–300 carrier aircraft he was convinced Dien Bien Phu could be saved: but hours were of the utmost importance and in three or four days such intervention would be meaningless. That afternoon, in the middle of a meeting of the North Atlantic Council, Bidault gave Dulles Navarre's signal to Laniel. The situation at Dien Bien Phu was desperate. The only alternatives were *Operation Vulture* – a massive attack by B29s – or a request for a ceasefire.[99] Dulles described Bidault as a man close to breaking point, particularly in the afternoon session of the Council, and this may account for Bidault's somewhat offhand assertion that Dulles had asked him whether they would like the US to give them two atomic bombs.[100]

Dulles reported to Washington that night Eden's 'grave doubts' whether Britain would co-operate in any active fighting to save Indo-China and his fear that US intervention might initiate world war three.[101] On 24 April, intervention seemed that much nearer. In the morning Dulles and Robertson, plus Ambassador Heath from Saigon, saw Emperor Bao Dai and received his assurances that, even if the French stopped fighting, Vietnam would fight on, provided their 'friends' would help them. On the matter of independence Dulles understood that Vietnam and France had practically reached agreement and so once again, if it was still Congressional approval that was required, the last remaining condition was UK participation. That afternoon Dulles and Admiral Radford, who had now arrived in Paris, did their best to persuade Eden. There appeared, said Dulles, to be no chance of keeping the French fighting in Indo-China unless they knew that the UK and the US were going to be in there with them. Under existing circumstances constitutional restraints made it impossible for the US to respond to the French request for massive air intervention at Dien Bien Phu. However, (and whichever way one looks at it, it was an unequivocal statement):

> If the British would go along with us the President was then prepared to seek Congressional approval for intervention by the US with its Armed Forces in Indo-China, but that an essential element in securing such approval would be the fact that it was firmly based on joint action.[102]

Eden asked exactly what it was they had in mind that the British should do. Radford replied: some prompt military contribution. And when Eden asked if this meant troops Radford's response was RAF squadrons from Malaya or Hong Kong where at the moment he understood, and Eden confirmed, there was a British aircraft carrier.

A few minutes later, when they were joined by Bidault, Eden said he wanted to make it quite clear that the UK was not committed by the London communiqué to action in Indo-China: a point on which, according to the UK account, he was supported by Bidault: and Mr Dulles did not dissent. The UK account continued:

> Mr Dulles also produced the draft of a letter which he proposed to address to M. Bidault, if it would be thought helpful. The substance of it was that the US government would be prepared, if the French government and their Allies wished, to take the necessary steps to obtain special powers from the President to move armed forces into Indo-China and thus to internationalise the struggle against communism in Indo-China and protect South-East Asia as a whole. There was no reference in this letter to the UK, although Mr Dulles had said more than once in our earlier conversations that if the UK was not prepared to take part he didn't think a majority would be found in Congress to give the President his special powers.
> M. Bidault, after some hesitation, finally said that he was prepared for Mr Dulles to address the letter to him.[103]

It had by then, as Eden said, become very clear that Her Majesty's Government would have to take a decision of the utmost importance. That night Dulles told Laniel that, on two conditions, the US would seek Congressional approval for direct acts of belligerency. First, that the UK would agree to join in the military defence of Indo-China. Second, that the Associated States had achieved real and complete independence: and he added that from what he had heard since he had been in Paris the second condition seemed to have been substantially met and should present no difficulty. As for the UK, he could not foretell their attitude but he was prepared to do everything in his power to make them see the seriousness of the situation and the necessity of joining in the defence of Indo-China. Dulles said he realized the effect the fall of Dien Bien Phu would have on French and Vietnamese morale, but he hoped it could be countered 'by the formation of an alliance that would bring to France's aid within the next few weeks the military forces of the US and the UK'. France would have to hold firm and in the meantime Dulles implied that Eden, who said he was 'undetermined in his own mind', would respond if the French were to ask for UK help.[104]

The UK Cabinet met in emergency session on Sunday 25 April. At six o'clock that morning the US Embassy in Paris had received a message from Bidault which said that French military experts confirmed that a massive intervention of US aviation would still be able to save the garrison at Dien Bien Phu.

> It is also the opinion of our command that the Vietminh has effected for the attack of the fortress an exceptional concentration of forces and material engaging there the essential of his battle corps. This accumulation of means accomplished for the first time by the Vietminh provides an occasion which will likely not be found again to destroy by air action a large part of the enemy forces. Finally taking place when the rainy season begins, this action could interrupt the supply of the Vietminh under conditions that would put in danger the remainder of its forces. It is not excluded that the situation presently difficult be thus transformed into perhaps a decisive blow against the Vietminh.[105]

This message, with its desperate hope of victory at the eleventh hour, was matched in London by another, equally urgent, which the French Ambassador handed to Eden at the end of the first of the day's emergency Cabinet meetings. It was, mysteriously, based on a verbal and unattributed message on behalf of the US government to the French Ambassador in Washington suggesting an immediate declaration of common will on the part of the US, UK, France, Philippines and the Associated States, the eventual use of military means, and on an all-out effort on the part of the French government to persuade the British government to join in.

> They (the French government) had been informed that, once he was assured that the UK government would associate themselves with such a declaration, President Eisenhower would be prepared to seek Congressional approval for military intervention in Indo-China, and that it was possible that US naval aircraft might be able to launch an attack by 28 April on the forces now besieging Dien Bien Phu. M. Massigli had strongly urged that the UK government should at once indicate their willingness to join in making a declaration on the lines proposed.[106]

This alarming message precipitated a second emergency Cabinet meeting in London at the end of which 'The Prime Minister said that what we were being asked to do was in effect aid in misleading Congress into approving a military operation which would itself be ineffective and might well bring the world to the verge of a major war. He had no doubt that this request must be rejected'.[107] Flying that afternoon to Geneva for the beginning of the conference Eden was unexpectedly met at Orly airport by Bidault who said he thought Dien Bien Phu could be held for a little while longer if help were in prospect: which was why the French government were asking for an air strike that Admiral Radford had told them would be of the order of 450 tons per sortie.[108] When Eden arrived at Geneva Dulles produced what may have been the source of Massigli's mysterious reference the day before. It was a telegram of Bedell Smith's conversation with Bonnet in Washington. It said 'The President could obtain authority to take action in Indo-China only on the basis of a joint Allied declaration. He [Bedell Smith?] hoped that a declaration could be obtained'. But now it was obvious, at least in the UK record, that there was an almost hopeless divergence in UK and US assessments and attitudes. According to Eden the US Government thought there was no reason why the Vietnamese, with proper training and support, could not effectively match the Vietminh.[109] And Dulles apparently made it quite clear at an off-the-record press conference that the US would intervene in the Indo-China fighting if HMG would do the same, to which message Eden added: 'I am beginning to think Americans are quite ready to supplant French and see themselves in the role of liberators of Vietnamese patriotism and expulsors or redeemers of communist insurgence in Indo-China. If so, they are in for a painful awakening.'[110]

As the Indo-China part of the Geneva Conference was about to begin another major effort was made by the US to secure UK approval for military intervention. This time it was Admiral Radford, Chairman of the Joint Chiefs of Staff, who did his best to convince his UK opposite numbers and, eventually, the Prime Minister himself. Radford's authority, as well as his position, is sometimes called in question – the impression of a rather punch-drunk Admiral who came out fighting whenever he heard the bell, not even representing the Joint Chiefs over intervention in Indo-China, someone who really should not be taken too seriously. In which case what should one make of his London proposals – and the authority he had to make them? From the account Radford gave of his meeting with the UK Chiefs of Staff on 26 April he seems to have found them very narrow-minded, both in regard to UK interests in the Far East as well as in Europe, minimizing 'our collective strength' while maximizing the risks and potential requirements. According to the UK record he asked for immediate intervention coupled with rapid formation of a coalition as the only way to prevent complete French collapse; and while he agreed intervention would involve not only air support but the build up of substantial land forces he said he did not see that the latter would be provided by the US. Instead, the greater part would come from Asian countries 'who had plenty of manpower'. He did not think there was much chance of active Chinese intervention but in any case, as he thought the USSR and the communist bloc were going to get relatively stronger, 'it was in our interests to take a risk now'.[111]

That night, at dinner with Churchill, Radford returned to the attack and portrayed the awful consequences of the fall of Dien Bien Phu and the failure of the US and the UK to take appropriate action.

> This was the critical moment at which to make a stand against China and he did not think that the Russians, who were frightened of war, would go openly to the aid of the Chinese. The situation would however be much worse in five years and indeed every day that passed meant a proportionate gain for the communist powers at our expense. He said that if we co-operated over this the US would be willing to help us in other spheres and that he thought that there would be no difficulty in revoking the present American policy of aloofness with regard to our difficulties in Egypt.[112]

Churchill's response was to contrast the difficulty in influencing the British people by what happened in the distant jungles of Southeast Asia with the knowledge that there was a powerful US airbase in East Anglia and that war with China, who would invoke the Sino-Russian pact, might mean an assault by hydrogen bombs on these islands. According to Radford 'the Prime Minister repeatedly referred to the loss of India to the Empire . . . since the British people were willing to let India go, they would not be interested in holding Indo-China for France'. We could not, said Churchill, commit ourselves at this moment, when all these matters were about to be discussed at Geneva, to a policy which might lead by slow stages to catastrophe. No doubt, as far as Radford was concerned, it was a faint-hearted reply but on the British side one can understand how Radford gave the impression that the time had come for a showdown with China. Presumably this was not part of his remit. At the same time, his was not exactly a free-fall descent on Churchill and the UK Chiefs of Staff. It was, in fact, Eisenhower himself who had told Radford to stop over in Britain 'to consult with the British Staff and to ask them baldly why they would prefer to fight after they have lost two hundred thousand French'.[113] This might, of course, have been an academic question, and Radford might have been too enthusiastic in the way in which he put his case, but unless it was intended as a masterpiece of deception one must assume that intervention was still a live issue and that Britain had not yet managed to kill it off.

THE CASE FOR INTERVENTION

The issue was still very much alive in the National Security Council, too, even if, after the event, one may judge from the respective weight of the principal opponents that it was a no-contest. In a long and furious meeting on 29 April the unlikely challenge to US policy, which so far had meant, in effect (and because of executive conditions) non-intervention, was mounted by the Director of the Foreign Operations Administration, Harold Stassen.

Opening the meeting the CIA Director, Allen Dulles, said that everyone was getting a little panicky about Dien Bien Phu and what might happen when it fell; and with the understanding with the British having come unstuck Bedell Smith told the NSC that the US had gone to Geneva with less of an agreed position and common understanding with its allies than it had entered any previous international conference. Most of the blame was put on the UK. Dulles, reporting from Geneva, described their attitude as one of increasing weakness, badly frightened by the fear of atomic attack, while Nixon, unwilling, as he put it, to let Britain have a veto on America's freedom of action, described the close tie-up with them as a painful liability. Presumably it was a similar lack of moral fibre which had caused Australia and New Zealand to have second thoughts about Dulles' united action scheme – Eisenhower talked about an Australian 'collapse' – and if one may see this as the last hope of 'respectable' intervention it might indeed, as Stassen said, have been the moment for the Council to make its ultimate decision. If the French folded, he said, and even if the British refused to go along with us, the US should intervene alone in what he called the southern areas of Indo-China. It was the time and the place to take our stand.

There followed a remarkable debate.[114] Confronting the President in effect with the implications of Republican policy in particular and ideas of containment in general Stassen said that if he made clear that direct intervention was needed to save Southeast Asia from communism, Congress and the US people would support the Commander-in-Chief. This, of course, is something that one can never know but what one can see is that where united action foundered on the rock (or was perhaps wrecked on the shifting sands) of UK objection so the momentum that might have carried America in alone failed to carry the President with it. In themselves, some of the close-quarter arguments were finely balanced. There was a danger, said Eisenhower, of replacing French with US colonialism. No, said Stassen, the obvious fact that the Vietnamese did not trust the French was no reason to argue that they did not trust us. If the US went in alone, said Eisenhower, it would mean a general war with China and perhaps with the USSR. Not if the US held the southern areas said Stassen, and did not attempt to roll back the Vietminh too far (he said 'beyond' but presumably meant up to the Chinese border). Ultimately, it seems to have been the weight of Eisenhower's experience and his all-round perception that carried the day against unilateral intervention. Presenting communism as if it were some global guerrilla movement that was trying everywhere to involve the US in indecisive engagements which would ultimately sap its strength, Eisenhower said that he was frightened to death of the prospect of US divisions scattered all over the world and now it was suggested that they should put six more into Indo-China. If that happened there would have to be general mobilization and, extending his argument, instead of becoming involved in brushfire wars 'in Burma, Afghanistan and God knows where' Eisenhower asked whether the right decision was not to launch a world war instead.

The apocalyptic choice was obviously unthinkable and so also, it seems, was the requirement of general mobilization to sustain intervention with US ground forces. It was precisely this term that had to be avoided. People, said Eisenhower, were frightened, and if they and Congress were to be won over to an understanding of their stake in Southeast Asia there should be no talk of ground forces. Which, presumably, left the possibilities of air and naval intervention open and here again, in spite of Nixon's support for the idea of US air-strikes because of the effect 'on the climate of free-world public opinion' and Bedell Smith's, who thought they would help the French to continue fighting, what is remarkable is that it seems to be on Eisenhower's authority that action was deferred.

As a professional soldier and former Supreme Allied Commander, the President obviously carried the heaviest guns in any dispute over intervention. For whatever reason Admiral Radford apparently chose not to speak in this debate so the interventionist case on this occasion rested on Stassen, Nixon and Bedell Smith. From earlier debates the Treasury and, variably, the Department of Defense emerged as critics of unilateral intervention and although it appeared, on 25 April, that Dulles was absolutely opposed, too, the representation of his views in the NSC meeting suggested that he had swung round to a more equivocal position while below him in the State Department, Bedell Smith, Robertson, Gullion and Bonsal, Ambassador Heath in Saigon and Ambassador Dillon in Paris, were all in favour of some sort of intervention. Had he, then, given the lead before Dien Bien Phu fell, one feels there was hardly anyone in the NSC who would not have followed Eisenhower over the precipice. As it was the US avoided all intervention because it looked as if the minor commitment (air and naval support) was likely to entail a major (US troops) and because the US was reluctant to join a war from which the French might decide to withdraw. For both countries war was an option but it remained an individual rather than an allied option and while 'victory' might have served the interests of both it would have been almost as difficult to define as to achieve. Intervention at that time, before the first Vietnam war was over, would therefore have involved the US in an entangling and uncertain alliance with France. It might still be necessary to strengthen French resolve so that she did not compromise vital interests at Geneva but as the US had chosen to define the retention of all Indo-China as vital to her interests, and as this was unlikely to be achieved at Geneva, it remained to be seen whether the commitment would lead to a different form of intervention or whether the definition itself would be changed.

For the moment, the US committed itself to continue its efforts to organize a regional grouping to defend Southeast Asia without waiting for the UK or for any developments at Geneva. When it was agreed that this meant communist efforts 'by any means' to gain control of countries in the area it was, if anything, expanding the range of circumstances in which it would be involved. Nor can there be much doubt that the US meant what it said about its vital interest in Southeast Asia and that it was also prepared to use any means to defend it even if, at this stage, it was apparently not prepared to tell 'proposed associates in regional grouping' that it might decide to use 'new weapons' on intervention for fear that it would frighten them off. Certainly this question was raised at the NSC Planning Board – the meeting which also considered lending the French an atomic bomb or two – and according to Vice-President Nixon 'I said that whatever was decided about using the bomb, I did not think it was necessary to mention it to our allies before we got them to agree on united action.'[115]

NO ACCEPTABLE SETTLEMENT

With time running out at Dien Bien Phu, and after what Eden described as a 'prolonged, and at moments somewhat heated, onslaught upon our attitude' by the US delegation at Geneva on 1 May 1954, Dulles went home just before the fall of Dien Bien Phu provided a stunning overture to the beginning of the Indo-China discussions at Geneva. On 7 May, after appalling casualties on both sides and with equally appalling casualties among their POWs yet to come, the last French defenders were overwhelmed and the battle was ended. Even if one only takes them as a back bearing, US fury and contempt for Britain reveal the depth of frustration. From Geneva the US delegation had reported that Britain was weak, scared, timid, badly frightened.[116] Dulles, reporting to the President, said the British, and particularly Churchill, were scared to death by what Dulles called the spectre of nuclear bombs in the hands of the USSR and although Eden had never said a word in defence of the US at Geneva he had had the gall to come to the airport to say good-bye.[117] With the fall of Dien Bien Phu the prospect of united action had faded, if only for the time being, and the French had now to be persuaded not to make a settlement of which the US disapproved. As there was, prima facie, no settlement in view which would not mean some loss of territory to communist control there was, by the same token, no possibility of an acceptable settlement. Thus, even though the US would be present at the negotiations, it would be essentially in the role of an associated power with no responsibility for upholding an agreement nor even for securing one in the first place. United action had so far failed on both levels, operational and prophylactic, and this would have enormous consequences for the diplomatic settlement. It had meant that the US was not accepted in the role of ally, in which it had offered itself, and that because there had been no engagement of her fighting forces to activate even a *de facto* alliance, there was thus no necessity on France's part or that of the other possible ally, Britain, to accept US objectives either. As much as anything it was the rift between America and Britain which helps to explain the disarray at Geneva. Dulles had, in effect, needed someone to sign his shotgun permit; and Eden had refused. Whether or not Dulles intended to use the gun, the fact that he had a permit, which could then be used as a threat, *might* have secured a better arrangement at Geneva but the question that would still have had to be answered was whether the arrangement would have stood by itself or whether it would need to be guaranteed and, if so, by whom. In spite of some further alarms and sombre contingency plans, Vietnam itself was moving into a situation of neither war nor peace; and, as the circumstances seemed somewhat less propitious for intervention, the indicator of US policy flickered for the moment towards that end of the Clausewitz continuum where peace was a continuation of policy with rather less of the other means.

REFERENCES AND NOTES

1. US Ambassador Heath in Saigon was immediately on guard against 'possible Asian attempts to produce Asian Munich' and said that 'for obvious reasons' the government-owned news service in Saigon had excised that item from its daily bulletin. *FRUS*, 1952–4, Vol. XIII, p. 13.

2. *FRUS*, 1952–4, Vol. XII. p. 9.

3. Ibid. p. 65.

4. Ibid. p. 62.
5. Ibid. p. 192.
6. *FRUS*, Vol. XIII, p. 32.
7. Ibid.
8. Ibid. p. 119.
9. Ibid. p. 123.
10. Ibid. p. 114.
11. Ibid. p. 116.
12. Ibid. p. 129.
13. Ibid. p. 167.
14. The French in Indo-China said (and were reported to Washington) that Bao Dai must be about the wealthiest man in the world. $4½ m. a year from government plus $¾ m. per month as rake-off from Cholon gambling. Vietnamese President Tam offered a charmingly ingenuous excuse for his Emperor: his hunting and fishing expeditions were an attempt to forget the 'moral distress' he must feel over his extravagant way of life. *FRUS*. Vol. XIII, p. 281.
15. *FRUS*, Vol. XIII, p. 157.
16. *FRUS*, Vol. XII, p. 127–34. It is preceded by a note of the deliberations which produced it.
17. Ibid. Vol. XII, p. 132.
18. See Nitze's idea of 'An Interpretive Minute'. Department of State–Joint Chiefs of Staff meeting, 16 July. *FRUS*, Vol. XII, p. 150.
19. *FRUS*, Vol. XIII, p. 287–98.
20. Harry S. Truman, *Years of Trial and Hope*, p. 519 quoted in *FRUS*, Vol. XIII, pp. 298–9.
21. *FRUS*, Vol. XIII, p. 316.
22. Steven E. Ambrose, *Eisenhower*, Vol. II *The President* (New York 1984), Chapter 9.
23. *Pentagon Papers* (Gravel) (Boston 1971), Vol. I, p. 427.
24. *FRUS*, Vol. XIII, p. 385.
25. Ibid. p. 516.
26. Ibid. p. 403.
27. Ibid. p. 382.
28. Ibid. p. 427.
29. Ibid. p. 417.
30. Ibid. p. 430.
31. Spector, op. cit. p. 170.
32. *FRUS*, Vol. XIII, p. 433.
33. Ibid. p. 435.
34. Ibid. p. 456.
35. He also claimed that Ho Chi Minh was 'now not an important figure and it made little practical difference whether he was alive or dead'. *FRUS*, Vol. XIII, p. 458.
36. *FRUS*, Vol. XIII, p. 458.
37. Ibid. p. 474.
38. Ibid. p. 480.
39. Ibid. p. 502.
40. Ibid. p. 485.
41. Ibid. p. 544.

42. Ibid. p. 557.
43. Navarre got off to a rather unfortunate start by telling McClintock, the American chargé, that the only parallels in military history for Vietnam which came to mind were the French campaign in Mexico and Napoleon's Peninsular wars. McClintock noted 'General refrained however, from drawing historical inferences'. (*FRUS*, Vol. XIII, p. 604).
44. Spector, op. cit. p. 175. Irvine also describes the Navarre Plan as 'American-inspired', op. cit. p. 106. Navarre himself does not. Henri Navarre, *Agonie de L'Indochine* (Paris 1956).
45. *United States – Vietnam Relations*, Book 9, p. 69.
46. *FRUS*, Vol. XIII, p. 643. Pleven added: 'We hope you can help me for after me comes Mendès France.'
47. Ibid. p. 649.
48. Ibid. p. 650.
49. Ibid. pp. 712–13.
50. Ibid. pp. 714–17.
51. Ibid. p. 553.
52. *The US Government and the Vietnam War*, prepared for the Committee on Foreign Relations, United States Senate by the Congressional Research Service. Library of Congress (Washington 1984). Hereinafter cited as Gibbons.
53. *FRUS*, Vol. XIII, p. 553 (footnote).
54. Ibid. p. 785.
55. This is the persuasive argument advanced by Glenn H. Snyder 'The "New Look" of 1953' who points out that for planning purposes in the New Look anything larger than small brush fire wars or border incidents were to be considered 'nuclear'. W. R. Schilling, *et al. Strategy, Politics and Defense Budgets* (New York 1962).
56. For example Navarre's own account, op. cit. Bernard Fall, *Hell In A Very Small Place* (London 1967), and Jules Roy, *The Battle of Dien Bien Phu*, (London 1965).
57. *FRUS*, Vol. XIII, p. 801.
58. There are some interesting comparisons in Steven Ambrose, *Ike's Spies* (Garden City 1981).
59. An account of the Bermuda conference is given in *FRUS*, 1953, Vol. V.
60. *FRUS*, Vol. XIII, p. 929.
61. Ibid. pp. 1183–6.
62. Gibbons, op. cit. p. 150.
63. *FRUS*, Vol. XIII, p. 939–40.
64. *Executive Sessions of the Senate Foreign Relations Committee*, Vol. VI, p. 22. Speaking of Indo-China Dulles allowed himself a surprisingly imperialist sentiment. He was a great believer in the general idea of giving independence but 'I am not sure that these people are qualified to be fully independent'. And he thought it had yet to be proven whether independence given prematurely to Indonesia was the proper thing. p. 23.
65. *Pentagon Papers* (Gravel), p. 89.
66. Ibid.
67. *FRUS*, Vol. XIII, p. 951.

68. Ibid. pp. 944–5.
69. Ibid. p. 937.
70. Gibbons, op. cit. pp. 157–8.
71. *FRUS*, Vol. XIII, p. 1014.
72. For this last point see *FRUS*, Vol. XIII, p. 1271. Another possibility was that an atomic bomb could be 'loaned' to France to drop on Vietminh troop concentrations in reserve behind Dien Bien Phu although this prompted further questions in the NSC Planning Board whether the French were capable of doing it, operationally or politically. 'Loan' was a curious expression to use – one wonders how it would have been repaid – and as part of the domestication process one notes that the Planning Board ignored the Confucian precept about the naming of names and the string of misfortunes that would follow 'if terms be incorrect'.
73. These examples, from the 'Non-intervention' thesis, are taken from Professor Stephen E. Ambrose's biography of *Eisenhower*, Vol. II, *The President*, Ch. 7.
74. Gibbons, op. cit. p. 168.
75. *FRUS*, Vol. XIII, p. 1141.
76. Ibid. p. 1167.
77. Ibid. p. 1150.
78. Excerpts from this speech may be found in Cameron, op. cit. pp. 1231–6.
79. I was particularly indebted to Professor George Herring for a rough draft of the article which subsequently appeared as George C. Herring and Richard H. Immerman: 'Eisenhower, Dulles, and Dien Bien Phu: "The Day We Didn't Go To War" Revisited'. *Journal of American History*, Vol. 71, no. 2, Sept. 1984. There is another detailed account of the crisis in Gibbons, op. cit. Chs 3 and 4 as well as acerbic observations in Townsend Hoopes, *The Devil and John Foster Dulles* (Boston 1973).
80. John Foster Dulles papers. White House memoranda. Meetings with the President, 1954, (4). Eisenhower Library, Abilene, Kansas.
81. *FRUS*, Vol. XIII, p. 1217.
82. Ibid. p. 1226.
83. Ibid. p. 1239.
84. Ibid. p. 1305.
85. Ibid. p. 1270.
86. Ibid. p. 1244.
87. Ibid. p. 1256.
88. Ibid.
89   Ibid. p. 1202. Whereas, according to Dulles, 'We clearly understood from Bidault at Berlin that our agreement to discuss Indo-China at Geneva was on condition France would not agree to any arrangement which would directly or indirectly result turn over area to communists'. Assuming this to be true it is hard to see what the basis of any negotiation would have been.
90. FO 371 112049 1071/121 Makins to FO April 3, 1954, *Public Record Office*, cf. *FRUS*.
91. *FRUS*, Vol. XIII, p. 1314.
92. The State Paper of 5 May 1820 contained another appropriate

observation: 'In this Alliance as in all other human Arrangements, nothing is more likely to impair or even to destroy its real utility, than any attempt to push its duties and obligations beyond the Sphere which its Conception and understood Principles will warrant'.

93.   *FRUS*, Vol. XIII, p. 1311.
94.   Ibid. p. 1321.
95.   The French Ambassador in London had told the Foreign Office, according to the US Ambassador, that when Dulles had dinner with Churchill and Eden assurances had been given that Britain was willing to join in a military contribution in Indo-China. Eden denied that either he or the Prime Minister had said anything of the kind. FO 371 1071/302. Memo FO 15 April.
96.   *FRUS*, Vol. XVI, p. 514.
97.   Eden, *Full Circle*, p. 98.
98.   *FRUS*, Vol. XIII, pp. 1361–2.
99.   Ibid. p. 1374.
100. Georges Bidault, *Resistance* (London 1967), p. 196. In subsequent attempts to discover whether or not this offer was ever made, de Margerie who, to begin with, had seemed quite convinced that it had thereupon backed down almost completely and said it was obvious there had been a complete misunderstanding on Bidault's part. Dulles' implicit disavowal may be regarded as absolute honesty or a certain economy of truth. He did admit, however, that in the restricted NATO meeting that day he said American policy on the use of atomic weapons was that 'Such weapons must now be treated as in fact having become conventional'. *FRUS*, Vol. XIII, pp. 1927–34.
101. *FRUS*, Vol. XIII, p. 75.
102. *FRUS*, Vol. XIII, p. 1387.
103. CAB 129/68 pp. 164–74. Eden took the unusual step of enclosing a ten-page narrative 'Discussions on the situation in South-East Asia – March 29 to May 22, 1954' in the Cabinet Minutes.
104. *FRUS*, Vol. XIII, p. 1395.
105. *FRUS*, Vol. XIII, p. 1401.
106. CAB 129/68 C(54) 155, 27 April 1954, p. 5.
107. Ibid.
108. FO 371 112055, p. 308.
109. Ibid. p. 309.
110. Ibid. p. 319.
111. Ibid. p. 344.
112. FO 371 112057, p. 350. Sir John Colville's elegant memorandum of the conversation.
113. *FRUS*, Vol. XIII, p. 1382.
114. The memorandum of this NSC discussion is in *FRUS* Vol. XIII, pp. 1431–45.
115. The minute of the Planning Board discussion on 29 April is given in Vol. XIII, pp. 1446–8. Vice-President Nixon's account of the meeting is in his *Memoirs* (London 1978), p. 154.
116. *FRUS*, 1952–4, Vol. XVI, p. 619.
117. *FRUS*, Vol. XIII, pp. 1467–8. The fact that Eden was photographed with him seemed to have annoyed Dulles even more.

Chapter 4

THE ASHES OF GENEVA: 1954

It is a commonplace observation that wars tend to arise out of preceding peace settlement. Nowhere can this have been more obvious than in respect to the Geneva Conference of 1954. Even before it began it was clear that the Conference itself was going to be unusual. In the first place, rather than providing the possibility of a political settlement, one may, indeed, from a different position, suggest that Dulles and the US negotiators saw it as a dangerous distraction from a policy which would somehow have contained communism in South-East Asia. On the assumption that, in the absence of victory, negotiation usually involves some concession, the prospect of a negotiated settlement at Geneva as far as the US was concerned seemed to have disappeared the moment Dulles set foot in Geneva. 'We hope', he said, 'to find that the aggressors [North Korean as well as Vietminh] come here in a mood to purge themselves of their aggression'. The public posture coincided with the private instructions. Before he left Washington Dulles had told the Australian and New Zealand Ambassadors that partition, coalition, and elections must all be rejected; and in his message to Bedell Smith, head of the US delegation, the basic instructions, 'approved by the President', suggested that there was to be very little negotiation at all. The Vietminh and the Chinese Communist régimes could be dealt with on a *de facto* basis ('in order to end aggression, or the threat of aggression, and to obtain peace') but the US was not prepared 'to give its express or implied approval to any cease-fire, armistice, or other settlement which would have the effect of subverting lawful govern- ments (of the three Associated States) or of permanently impairing their territorial integrity'. Moreover, the US was described as being 'neither a belligerent nor a principal in the negotiation' but, simply, as 'an interested nation' which was there to assist in the establishment of 'territorial integrity and political independence under stable and free governments'.[1]

On the level, therefore, of formal negotiation, with the US

negotiating position set at auto-destruct, it is hardly surprising that the Conference turned into a sort of surrealist boxing match in which contestants, seconds, trainers and spectators were all mixed in together and from which no decision could have been expected even if, surprisingly, a number of points were agreed simply in order to call the match to an end. Not that, for many of the participants, there were unrealizable objectives. For France, it was simply a matter of how to end a colonial war, in which she was well on the way to defeat and, if possible, how to retain some interests and presence in Indo-China. For the Vietminh, the objective was to take over as much of the country as they might be allowed and to which they felt they were entitled, not least by their victory at Dien Bien Phu. For China, the purpose was to secure peace in Indo-China and to keep the US out. For Britain, it was a matter of limiting the advance of communism as far as possible but, more important, it was to prevent a wider war. The objective for the USSR was probably to reach a settlement that would provoke neither the Chinese nor the US. But for the US it was an unfamiliar experience in that it was to be a negotiated rather than a dictated peace; in that she was not the leader of a victorious alliance; and in that, while there was certainly no victory on which to build, her status as ally was also in question.

What was, of course, even more in question was the status of 'Vietnam' itself, its government, its sovereignty, and its existence; but in the conspicuous absence of the Emperor Bao Dai it was sometimes easy to forget that there was a Vietnamese delegation at Geneva at all. Whatever its status was reckoned to be when the conference ended, or to have become in the course of the negotiations, when it began, at least, Vietnam was promised its integrity by the French. There was, said Bidault, to be no partition; but in the circumstances, his proposals were both ambitious and absurd. As a purely military solution the French plan was to be based on a cease-fire and a regroupment of regular military forces but as the political solution was to be left to the government of Vietnam, i.e. that of Bao Dai to decide, this obviously had a limited appeal. The Vietminh alternative, as proposed by Pham Van Dong, was also based on a cease-fire but envisaged the departure of French troops, free elections, and some rather limited supervision by a mixed commission. In the opening stages Bidault had refused to negotiate directly with the Vietminh but on 12 May the French government survived a vote of confidence by only two votes: which was a reminder that Bidault's terms might not be the ones which were finally agreed.

On what terms then, if any, would a settlement be made at Geneva? When the agreement was finally reached by Bidault's successor, Pierre Mendès France, he described it as the end of a nightmare for France. Before that particular settlement was made which allowed France to end the war it could equally well be said that, at least for the US Secretary of State, the nightmare was just beginning and although, as a sort of legal document, the Geneva settlement was to open up almost undreamt of possibilities for avoidance if not evasion, the Geneva experience for the US was something to be endured rather than approved and evoked the same kind of bitterness that might attend a hopelessly deformed birth. In the end it was perhaps this US attitude of suspicion and hostility to practically whatever the Geneva Conference produced which ensured that, as one distinguished Canadian observer described it, 'Of all the important peace-making documents of our time none was so badly drafted and curiously drawn as the so-called "Geneva Settlement" of 1954'[2] and which led, in the words of two French authors, to the situation where the US 'could neither accept nor openly reject the Geneva Settlement'.[3]

Much the same, of course, could also be said of the other dissatisfied party at Geneva, the Vietminh, although in their case restraint was the price they had to pay when they found their own objectives overlain by the purposes of their powerful communist allies. Indeed, another of the curiosities of Geneva was how the great powers negotiated among themselves the fate of a country on whose behalf they were variously committed, and how, having to a greater or lesser extent satisfied their own needs, they managed both to postpone the political settlement that was required if the 'agreement' was to be very much more than a cease-fire and, at the same time, avoid any responsibility for seeing that their terms were ever carried out. Measured against the standards of good statesmanship one may argue that it was irresponsible of them not to have produced an acceptable solution for what, at least on one level, may be seen in retrospect as a manageable problem – the end of a colonial war – which was in itself no more and perhaps rather less difficult than negotiating an end to France's Algerian war. The fact that so many great powers were involved at the end of France's Vietnam war, at the same time as complicating the issue, could also at least in principle have enhanced the quality of the agreement had they been prepared and able to offer some kind of guarantee. But this at once begs the question whether, in respect to Vietnam, the Vietminh could have been reconciled to the prospect of permanent partition or whether the US would have accepted the prospect of a communist victory even if it was achieved politically and postponed for two years.

Neither of these two questions was even considered by either party when the Conference began and both the Vietminh and the US took up positions of impregnable rectitude. The attitudes can be explained by a belief, perhaps, on the Vietminh side that the war was practically over while for the US there was a determination that the war had not been and should not be lost. Indeed, in one sense, that it had hardly begun. The gap was, of course, unbridgeable but the positions, for all the manifest intransigence, were not as secure as they might have seemed.

Although they sometimes gave the impression that the Vietminh were allowed to make the running, the Russians and the Chinese at Geneva left little doubt that the substantive negotiations would not be left to their Vietnamese ally and Molotov, after an argument with Bedell Smith on what percentage of Vietnamese supported Ho Chi Minh, said 'Perhaps the Vietminh deserve more than we were going to give them'. Perhaps, he said, they were entitled to more than 50 per cent of the spoils of war: as much as 75 per cent; a claim that was 'strongly contested'.[4] Molotov was described in this US report as 'courteous, friendly, in excellent humor and absolutely immovable' and while he is credited with last-minute intervention and improvisations to 'save' the conference, he might in fact have produced the winning formula quite early on, even if hardly anyone was prepared to accept it at the time. If one adds partition and elections, and subtracts the international guarantee, the outline of the final settlement can be seen in Molotov's 5-point proposal of 21 May. Essentially, it was that a military arrangement had to come first: which meant that the success of the Vietminh depended on the nature of the political settlement which followed.

For the US it was a question of whether to allow France to make peace on the best terms that could be got or whether it should again face up to the costs and implications of intervention. The two were not entirely and mutually exclusive and it is possible that some of the plans for intervention may have been designed to encourage the French and to dishearten their opponents. Even if the French hand was not as poor as Bidault suggested – the two of clubs and the three of diamonds – there was not much, practically, that France could do on her own to influence the negotiations. Quite a lot of the US war preparations may indeed have been intended as 'distant thunder' or 'noises off', as they were variously described by Eden and others, and, being designed to bolster the French, they can be considered as a means primarily to that end. But the French were themselves intent on making peace and, for all Bidault's original obstinacy, whatever settlement eventuated it could hardly be based on the US principle of 'no surrender'. Unless the US was prepared to deploy its own forces, and this was by no means out of the question, its own implacable objective of containment was bound to be compromised by the conditions which would be necessary for the French to make peace.

Acting on the pessimistic assumption that, if there were an armistice, it would only be one which paved the way for a communist take-over of the whole of Indo-China it is perhaps not surprising that, if anything, the fall of Dien Bien Phu seems to have induced even greater turmoil and confusion among US decision makers about which of the twin tracks to follow at Geneva: war or peace. For example, whether or not to 'bust up' the Conference; whether to put four US divisions into the Tonkin Delta in order to 'ginger up' the French and the Vietnamese; whether, if this resulted in Chinese intervention, the US should pull out of Indo-China 'and clobber the Chinese at the heart of their power, wherever that might be, and in spite of the consequences'[5]; and whether, *in extremis* the USSR would provide the Chinese with nuclear weapons and the technical personnel required for their use.[6]

The irrepressible Radford would soon be offering Korean divisions to General Ely but there were other, more substantial, offers which must have been made to the French: probably in response to their request for a limited commitment of US ground forces. That particular telegram, from the US Ambassador in Paris, (17 May) is missing from the State Department files but contained some reference to US Marines.[7] When Dulles and Eisenhower met on 19 May 'the President said he would not necessarily exclude sending some marines if we went in'[8] and in a telephone conversation with Dulles on the following day MacArthur, the State Department Counsellor, said 'What they [the French] want is a commitment of ground forces, and not what we offered' and one may infer that the offer was something to do with US naval and air forces.[9] Whatever it was, as Dulles told Nixon in the National Security Council meeting that day (20 May), seems to have been made in Ambassador Dillon's negotiations with Laniel and Schuman which were 'Strictly on an oral basis. Nothing in writing passed either way.'[10]

INTERVENTION STILL AN OPTION

Believing that there could be no serious negotiations with the communists at Geneva and certainly not prepared themselves to offer any compromise it was obvious that almost as soon as the Indo-China Conference opened the US was once again keeping its intervention option open as well. The French, however, could hardly be trusted not to give their position away: which meant that the preconditions were still critically important. There had to be a formal request from France and the three Associated States. France (as always) would have to guarantee complete independence, including the unqualified option to withdraw from the French Union at any time. But, conversely, France would undertake not to withdraw its forces from Indo-China during the period of united action so that US forces – it was Eisenhower who had stipulated 'principally air and sea' – and those of any other participating states would be supplementary and not in substitution and that agreement was reached on the training of native troops and on a command structure for united action. In the strictest confidence Ambassador Dillon in Paris was told that Admiral Radford contemplated a French Supreme Command and a US Air Command. All these conditions would have to be accepted by the French cabinet and authorized or endorsed by the French National Assembly so that, as Dulles put it, the US, having fully committed itself once it agreed to intervene, would be able to rely on the adherence to conditions by any successor French government.[11]

These proposals might indeed be seen as providing the US with a water-tight contract so far as France was concerned, even though the current French political crisis meant that the US initiative was postponed, and in Washington Dulles had gone so far as to draft a congressional resolution which he showed to Eisenhower on 19 May.

> The President is authorised to employ Naval and Air forces of the
> US to assist friendly governments of Asia to maintain their authority
> as against subversive and revolutionary efforts fomented by Communist
> régimes, provided such aid is requested by the governments concerned.
> This shall not be deemed to be a declaration of war and the authority
> hereby given shall be terminated on June 30, 1955, unless extended.[12]

Perhaps to Dulles' surprise, when he discussed the draft resolution with Senator Knowland, an ardent anti-communist and supporter of Chiang Kai-shek, he encountered strong opposition. It would, said Knowland, amount to giving the President a blank cheque to commit the country to war. Knowland was also a vociferous critic of those who hesitated to halt the march of communist aggression in Asia and it is interesting to note that his accusations that the British were promoting an Asian Munich were also shared by Eisenhower, who apparently told Dulles that it was incomprehensible that the British should be acting as they were. It is even more interesting to find that Dulles and Eisenhower now agreed that active UK participation was no longer a necessary condition for intervention, although that of Australia, New Zealand, the Philippines, Thailand and of course, the Associated States, was. Having discarded one condition, UK participation, Dulles and Eisenhower now seemed to be faced with another problem: their Congressional and, more particularly, Republican support might be fading away and one may speculate that it might have been Knowland's opposition to the draft Congressional resolution on 17 May which knocked out the linchpin for active US intervention. The previous night, as the author of the Congressional research monograph records: 'Secretary Dulles had held a very high level secret dinner meeting at his home to discuss the situation and to plan US strategy.'[13] In attendance were CIA Director Allen Dulles, the State Department's MacArthur, Vice-President Nixon, who was flown back specially from West Virginia and, as the only 'outsider', Dean Rusk, former Assistant Secretary of State for the Far East and at that time president of the Rockefeller Foundation.

THE UNITED STATES v. CHINA

As Dr Gibbons notes there is no information available with respect to what was discussed and in an interview (with the author) Mr Rusk himself declined to comment on the discussion. From the memorandum of a telephone call in which Rusk was invited to the meeting, Dulles said that critical decisions would have to be made in relation to Britain and France. Should the US go in alone or allow itself to be bogged down?[14] A few days later, Dulles having lunched with Admiral Radford, one may deduce that they had been talking about some sort of action involving the Paracel Islands, close to Vietnam, and occupied by the Chinese Nationalists more or less continuously since 1950. Radford was still the principal advocate of the cataclysmic solution to the Indo-China war – 'The only military solution was to go to the source of communist power in the Far East, i.e. China, and destroy that power' – and even in private conversation it seems that Dulles and Radford talked about the 'international Communist conspiracy' and agreed that the true source of its power lay in Russia. Radford reckoned that in three or four years' time, when they had a sufficient stockpile of nuclear weapons, the USSR would have the necessary capability to initiate and carry on general war on favourable terms and at no point in the future would the US be confronted with as clear-cut a basis for taking measures directly against China as was the case then in Indo-China.[15] On this occasion perhaps it was to counter the sheer belligerence of the JCS Chairman that Dulles somewhat surprisingly suggested there was much to be said for the UK point of view that if you drew a line in advance you gave the enemy an opportunity to retreat, an option that was not open if the war was already under way. Radford was unimpressed but he was not the only one at this time, mid-May, who was presenting a case for intervention in apocalyptic terms. Harold Stassen, Director of the Foreign Operations Administration, who had previously argued passionately with Eisenhower in favour of US intervention, had again discussed the issue with Dulles and followed this up with a suggested Presidential address to a joint session of Congress and a Senate resolution based on the premise that while they wanted the Geneva negotiations to succeed the Conference would have a better chance of success if the US was, at the same time, prepared for its failure. Which presumably meant that, if they wanted peace, they must prepare for war. And for Stassen, Southeast Asia, 'an area of high strategic significance', simply must not fall. 'If it does it would make a Third World War almost inevitable.'[16]

There were a few unexamined propositions in Stassen's premise – 'The manner of preventing the fall of South-East Asia is to act in time, to act with others, to act in keeping with a very successful experience with the Atlantic Community' – but the idea of some kind of collective security arrangement seemed to be taking hold now as something which could be put into effect more or less independently of the outcome at Geneva. It was obviously far more congenial to the US to be able to set its own conditions, rather than have to comply with terms that might be agreed by others in Geneva, and if Thailand and the Philippines, as well as Australia and New Zealand, could be brought to subscribe to common purposes one could at least pretend that there was some sort of incipient free-world community whose interests might properly be defended. It is not easy to decide whether this line of argument ran parallel to the purposes of the Geneva Conference, which were presumably to make peace, or directly against them. Whatever position one takes in the continuing historical controversy about the Seven Last Conditions For American Intervention – whether they were intended as a prelude for action or as an excuse for inaction – it is hard to disagree with Dr Gibbons' conclusion 'It seems clear that the alternative of US military intervention in Indo-China was more of a consideration than it had been earlier, and that, in this sense, the response to Laniel was genuine and straightforward' in that there was, indeed, 'further preparation for the contingency of intervening with force'.[17]

All this, it will be remembered, was at a time when the Geneva Conference on Indo-China had already begun; and even though Eden, for example, was given no hint of US activities, at least by the Americans, and although Bedell Smith went out of his way, whether deliberately or not, to play down reports that were appearing in the papers, continuing US policy towards Vietnam was characterized at this stage at least as much by the mailed fist as it was by the velvet glove. The plenary sessions, reported as fully as national positions demanded, or as the stamina of reporters allowed, were for striking attitudes and scoring debating points and with some speeches lasting two hours or more were both tedious and uncompromising. There were, in addition, smaller, unreported, and restricted sessions which might have been expected to produce a little more movement and, eventually, highly secret conversations between French and Vietminh military representatives once the point had been conceded that a cease-fire would precede a political settlement. One such highly secret occasion was when Molotov gave a dinner for the US delegation on 22 May and, in an atmosphere of some cordiality, it seemed that both Molotov and Bedell Smith were prepared for some kind of settlement. Twice, perhaps with the implication that they were impatient or new at the diplomatic game, Molotov described China as a young country; and the other inference was that at Geneva at least there was something less than a united communist front. On the face of it Bedell Smith's outline of an armistice, a withdrawal of regular contingents to specified areas and what he said would probably be prolonged discussions leading towards a political settlement, all under supervision of some genuinely neutral authority, was equally frank as was his admission to Molotov that he doubted whether there could be any meaningful negotiations at all with the Chinese.[18]

As a point of practical comparison the US had the recent experience of over two years' negotiation with the Chinese and North Koreans at Panmunjon, during which time the fighting had continued practically unabated in Korea, and was determined to avoid a similar experience over Indo-China. Eisenhower for one seemed to have serious doubts about Geneva generally and was particularly disturbed by what he thought was the heavy reliance which the UK placed on the value of negotiating with the Communists.[19] Dulles was convinced that the Communists would be negotiating in bad faith while others, such as Robertson or Judd, thought the Chinese were unappeasable and Bedell Smith told Dulles: 'I know that China has been after the Red River Valley and the Delta for years, and it seems to me that they now intend to have it, or at least the greater part.'[20] Whether or not these were realistic assessments – and the Chinese seen in their first international conference since the revolution at times seemed remarkably obdurate – Eden reckoned 'that the Americans were unwise in thinking this the moment to challenge China. The Chinese were in no mood to be browbeaten'. Conversely, he told the Cabinet on 24 May, that while an agreement might be possible it would depend among other things on dissuading the US from military intervention, from organizing their own Southeast Asia security organization, and from appealing (in the shape of a complaint from the Thai government) to the UN.[21] From this position, therefore, it would appear as if the Chinese and the Americans were the principal adversaries at Geneva even though the immediate issues had to be resolved by the French and the Vietnamese. The French, well before the Conference had begun, had identified the problem in terms of outside support for the communists in the Greek civil war and were said to be overwhelmingly in favour of the 'Markos hypothesis': that the war could only be ended as the result of some form of international negotiation in the course of which the Chinese would be persuaded to drop their support of Ho Chi Minh.[22] At that time the French Foreign Office thought that a settlement based on partition was a non-starter but a couple of days later the USSR told the Foreign Office in London, that having provided a Korean solution, this might also be a suitable arrangement for Indo-China.

Indo-China, they said – and they repeated it twice – was a question on which China was particularly sensitive and it must therefore have come as a pleasant surprise to the French at Geneva when they were told, on 18 May, by Wang Ping-nan: 'We are not here to uphold the Vietminh point of view but to make every effort to re-establish peace.'[23] In subsequent negotiations with Zhou En-lai, according to Joyaux, Mendès France was convinced that China was clearly in favour of the prolonged existence of two Vietnams[24]; and Zhou had, apparently, told him pointedly: 'If France would give way a little the Vietminh would give way a lot.'[25]

Before this could happen, however, it would first be necessary for both Chinese and Russians to limit the scope of their ideas of partition. Whether the Russian *démarche* in London meant Indo-China or Vietnam it took some time for them and the Chinese at Geneva to realize that the situation and revolutionary potential in Laos, and even more in Cambodia, was very different from Vietnam. In a free-scoring attack in the fifth plenary session on 8 June Molotov ridiculed claims of the Associated States to independence and objected that half of Laos, for example, was not under government control; but on 16 June Zhou En-lai conceded that the situation was not the same in all the states of Indo-China and when he subsequently developed his ideas to Eden the latter concluded:

> It really looks as if the Chinese may want a settlement in Laos
> and Cambodia: Zhou went so far as to say that the Vietminh would
> respect the unity and independence of Laos and Cambodia and that
> the Chinese would recognize the Royal Governments, who might be
> members of the French Union, provided they could be left as free
> countries without American or other bases.[26]

The breakthrough in Geneva at this time was practically simultaneous with what may be regarded as the breakthrough in France itself. On 9 June, the day after Molotov's verbal attack at Geneva and in spite of Bidault's defence in the National Assembly debate, the Laniel government was defeated and on 12 June, by a narrow majority and after continuing debate on Indo-China, it fell. More than a month before it happened Dulles had told the Senate Foreign Relations Committee that if the Laniel government fell it would probably be succeeded by a left-wing defeatist government which would accept almost any terms at Geneva.[27] What happened in the event was not what Dulles and others had predicted but in the interval between the fall of Laniel and the arrival of Mendès France, and fearing the worst, Dulles told Bedell Smith 'Final adjournment of Conference is in our best interest': provided that could be done without creating the impression that, at the critical moment, France had been deserted by the US and, he added, the UK.

Both from the explicit instructions and the tone of this telegram it was obvious that Dulles saw no reason to continue the conference, let alone negotiations, and before the communist concessions became known he derived a certain grim satisfaction from thinking that it would be obvious even to the British that diplomacy was getting nowhere; so there could be no excuse for any further delays in 'collective talks on SEA defence'.[28] Perhaps that was what was uppermost in Dulles' mind all the time, the collective defence of Southeast Asia, but as the matter of Indo-China, particularly Vietnam, had still to be resolved, ideas, not to mention the contingency plans, that surfaced in Washington suggested that the US was still not very far from the knife-edge of intervention. In Geneva, speaking, as he said, as a soldier, Bedell Smith was under the impression that the Franco-Vietnamese forces had a two-to-one superiority in numbers, and a great superiority in armament which, he told the leader of the Vietnamese delegation, Prince Buu Loc, should be enough to defeat the Vietminh even under a second-class general, provided of course, there was the right political situation and leadership.[29] It was obvious however, that Bedell Smith's optimism notwithstanding, hopes of a decisive outcome still rested on the possibility of US intervention and although, in the end or at least in the dying days of the Laniel government, Dulles had been unable to discover whether the French were prepared to internationalize the war or not, the US Administration had prepared a most elaborate and far-reaching scenario, NSC 5421 'Possible US Action Regarding Indo-China' 1 June 1954, which involved separate studies by the Department of State, the Department of Justice, the CIA, Defense, the Office of Defense Mobilisation, the Foreign Operations Administration, and the Bureau of Budget.[30] This suggested that it was rather more than an intellectual exercise.

MENDÈS FRANCE ARRIVES

Preparing itself, fitfully, for war it may seem as if the US was largely unprepared for peace or at least for negotiations that might lead to an acceptable peace settlement; and although it had only allowed itself a minor part on stage at Geneva it now found itself caught up in a drama which began in Paris on 17 June in the sensational, in some ways obvious, but equally fraught announcement by the incoming French premier, Pierre Mendès France, that he had given himself one month in which to make peace in Indo-China. If by that time he had not succeeded his government would resign. When the offer, or the wager, was made the draughtsmanship for the contract was by no means clear although there were signs that for France at least peace was possible. Her principal hope lay not so much with her military and political opponents, the Vietminh, but in their supporters, China and the USSR; but with the US maintaining a position of impregnable inertia France depended heavily on UK initiative and negotiating skills. The British, in turn, were at least aware of if not directly responsive to Indian sensitivities, as well as those of the Colombo powers and Asia generally, and in spite of bouts of almost morbid pessimism Eden for one acted as if a successful outcome to the Geneva negotiations was possible. Successful, of course, begs the definition of success but for the French, the British, and perhaps the Russians and the Chinese, this was identified in the first place as a cease-fire, to be followed by a political settlement which reflected the realities of time and place. In spite of last-minute complications the settlement that was agreed for Cambodia and Laos might, other things being equal, have been workable but proposals made on behalf of the Bao Dai government – in effect an amnesty for surrendered Vietminh rebels and the reincorporation of their troops within the forces of the French Union – while they may have had a certain naive simplicity could hardly have appealed to anyone else. In any event the French felt themselves entitled, as the architects of the French Union and at least co-ordinator of its forces, to decide not only how and with whom negotiations should be conducted but also whether there was any need to accord anything other than a supernumerary role to representatives of the Vietnamese 'state' whose future turned on negotiations with her actual and potential enemies.

The greatest uncertainty soon attached itself to the exact status of Bao Dai's government and whether the Treaty of Independence of the State of Vietnam that was initialled in Paris on 4 June, 1954, but never signed or ratified either by France or Vietnam, meant that Vietnam was a sovereign state or not.[31] Effectively at any rate it was not. It was not until a week or so before agreement was reached that either the Vietnamese delegation in Geneva or the government in Saigon seemed to have been told what was going on. What the US thought was going on, however, was enough to make Dulles withdraw Bedell Smith's basic instructions on 25 June and by this time any semblance of common purpose seemed to have dissolved when the French were told that if, in the course of their negotiations, they surrendered even a minimum enclave north of Haiphong, the US would disown the settlement. In reply they were told that as no French parliament would approve the conditions which the US had laid down for intervention, France had no choice but to make the best deal she could. Even though by this time he realized that the US could hardly count on unwavering UK support, it must nevertheless have been disappointing for Eisenhower to find Churchill endorsing this French opinion a couple of days later and on the eve of Churchill's arrival with Eden in Washington the US took stock of its position.

A SALVAGE OPERATION

Conceptually, at least, Dulles had little to offer as long as there seemed to be a tacit alignment with France and there was the possibility that the US might be asked to underwrite a settlement of which it profoundly disapproved. As he told the National Security Council on 17 June, the day Mendès France was invested as Prime Minister and the day after it had finally become clear that France was not prepared as a condition of American intervention to go on fighting, it might be best to let the French get out of Indo-China altogether – then try to rebuild from the foundations.[32] A week later Dulles was doing his best to sell the idea to Congress, or at least a group of 30 Congressmen and Senators, who heard him present the optimistic alternative after Bedell Smith had come back from Geneva with the bad news. Instead of partitioning Vietnam, handing over at least a third of Laos to communist control and, said Bedell Smith, giving Zhou En-lai what he really wanted – a guarantee by the Geneva powers of three little buffer states south of the Tonkin Delta – Dulles, without being very specific, said it was presumably possible to salvage something from an Indo-China that would be free of the taint of French colonialism. Whatever it was, he suggested, would have the support of Burma and other Asian states as well as the benevolent neutrality of India 'and this something could be guaranteed by a regional grouping which would include the US'. The latter, obviously, referred to the still unformed SEATO but what was of equal interest, not least because Dulles said that in losing Tonkin the US had not lost valuable assets, was a suggestion that territory might be lost, at least for the time being, and that what was left could be put under what would be largely US protection.

In retrospect one may see or at least argue that this could have been the beginning of a Two Vietnams policy which, other things being equal, might have enlisted enough support to have got it going. Burmese acquiescence and Indian benevolence may have been rather too much to expect but for the plan to have worked would have required some prospect of support from at least one of the major communist powers. This in turn would almost certainly have meant some agreement with them, particularly China, that while there could well be 'a build-up of indigenous military strength' it would not be an opportunity to replace French with US forces or bases. To reach that agreement would almost certainly have meant a US signature on a treaty of guarantee and it was on the rock of American refusal that such a settlement foundered. Perhaps in any event the negotiations would have been too delicate and the prospect was too remote but, ultimately, for Dulles and for what may be called the attentive US public, it was apparently a matter of principle.

Assume that the Soviet will want the eventual settlement to be 'guaranteed' in some way by the principal powers, including the US. This guarantee would presumably be designed to preclude any efforts on the part of the US at the liberation of the peoples who were subject to captivity. This, on a small scale, would be what we have refused on many occasions to do in relation to Europe, where we have said we would never make a statement which would give the stamp of approval to the captivity of Eastern European peoples. We believe that a 'guarantee' which committed the US to sustain Communist domination of the peoples of Vietnam, Laos and Cambodia, or at least many of them, would be unacceptable as cutting across our basic principles for dealing with the Communist world. We believe also it would be deeply resented by the American people and the Congress.[33]

Dulles did not exaggerate: as Eden for one discovered when he arrived in Washington, even though he seems to have wondered what it was he had said to bring the roof down on his head. The day before Churchill and Eden had left London, Eden had told the House of Commons that he hoped there would be an international guarantee of any settlement that might emerge at Geneva and, more specifically, he mentioned a reciprocal arrangement in which both sides would take part 'such as Locarno'. The thought behind Locarno, according to Eden, was that of 'a reciprocal defensive arrangement in which each member gives guarantees' and if the settlement was broken the guarantors could act without waiting for unanimity.[34] As a procedure this might have been commendable but while the reference to the Locarno Agreements of 1925 may have been intended to suggest a spirit of conciliation, to the US it suggested first, a guarantee of the 'fruits of aggression' and second, as Locarno had led to Germany's admission to the League of Nations, the entry of the Chinese Peoples' Republic into the UN.[35] Whether or not they appreciated the historical nuances 11 members of the House Foreign Affairs Committee wrote to the President as soon as they had heard of Eden's statement – 'He advocates that the free world not only accepts Communist conquests and gains, but in fact guarantee them' – and warned Eisenhower that unless this was repudiated the whole Mutual Security concept and programme would have to be re-examined. When the House debated the Mutual Security Bill a few days later Representative Vorys moved an amendment which provided that none of the funds for the Far East could be used 'on behalf of governments which are committed by treaty to maintain Communist rule over any defined territory of Asia'. That it should have been passed by the House 389–0 was almost incredible, but it was nevertheless accepted by the Senate and enacted into US law.[36] Another historical comparison that was being made in Washington was 'a Far Eastern Munich' although, as Bedell Smith pointed out to Senator Knowland, 'in Korea nobody gave away one damned inch while in Indo-China we haven't given up anything that wasn't first occupied by force of arms which cannot now be retaken'.[37] At the time, however, with Bedell Smith suggesting that the Reds might not take Hanoi and Haiphong, Dulles' emphatic statement that the US was not going to be a party to giving away anything that belongs to someone else, Bedell-Smith's assertion 'We are going to draw a line somewhere', but no one responding to the question 'If there should be a partition, would the free world guarantee the free side of the line?' it was not easy to see this or any other line that the US would draw or follow at Geneva.[38] In Vietnam, however, a line was already being drawn, one that had its origins in operational rather than diplomatic considerations, and one which might be defended at either the military or the diplomatic level. With the French anticipating a major defeat in the Delta in September unless they were heavily reinforced, and convinced that the loss of Dien Bien Phu had rapidly altered the military balance in favour of the Vietminh, Admiral Carney reported to the National Security Council on 17 June that it was now a matter of considering a new defence line 'at the narrow waist of Annam'.[39] This, at any rate, was the conclusion drawn at the Five Power Staff conversations in Washington and it depended on whether or not sufficient French forces could be extricated from the Delta. If the attempt was made to provide the French forces from southern Indo-China it was reckoned that security there would collapse but the implication, of course, was that northern Indo-China would have to be abandoned. Carney himself didn't think that even such a restricted defence line could be held for long but the opportunity was seized by Dulles and what may at first have seemed to be little more than a straw was soon to become a plank. As Dulles first saw it there was the opportunity to man such a defence line by forces representative of 'the coalition', in which case he thought it was unlikely to suffer a frontal attack. It was, he admitted, problematic whether real military strength could be built up south of the line, because political factors would play such an important role, but apart from the uncertainty of knowing what to do, there was a growing conviction in the State Department in favour of intervention and at the beginning of July it seemed 'that all the people below the Secretary and Under-Secretary are unanimous that we should intervene or rather make up our mind to intervene now with or without the French'.[40]

SEVEN CONDITIONS FOR A SETTLEMENT

Among the more intervention-minded members of the State Department the point had been reached where they were prepared to tell the

French 'that Indo-China could only be saved if French troops were not doing the fighting'[41] but although Bowie, the head of the Policy Planning Staff, was in favour of offering four US divisions to hold a defence line at about the 17th parallel in Vietnam, and of dropping the pre-conditions for US intervention, this was apparently an option which Dulles did not forward to the President. For the moment, at least, and in spite of the gravest doubts whether the French would strive to secure or the Communists be prepared to concede, there was still a possibility of a not completely unacceptable settlement, the criteria for which seemed to have been established in the course of the Churchill–Eden visit to Washington and which would be confirmed a few days later by Mendès France. The terms on which the American and British governments 'would be willing to respect an agreement' were that it:

1. preserves the integrity and independence of Laos and Cambodia and assures the withdrawal of Vietminh forces therefrom;
2. preserves at least the southern half of Vietnam, and if possible an enclave in the Delta; in this connection we would be unwilling to see the line of division of responsibility drawn further south on a line running generally west from Dong Hoi;
3. does not impose on Laos, Cambodia or retained Vietnam any restrictions materially impairing their capacity to maintain stable non-Communist régimes; and especially restrictions impairing their right to maintain adequate forces for internal security, to import arms and to employ foreign advisers;
4. does not contain political provisions which would risk loss of the retained area to Communist control;
5. does not exclude the possibility of the ultimate unification of Vietnam by peaceful means;
6. provides for the peaceful and humane transfer, under international supervision, of those people desiring to be moved from one zone to another of Vietnam;
7. provides effective machinery for international supervision of the agreement.[42]

As Dulles subsequently told the National Security Council the US would continue to take a stiffer line than the UK: something which seemed to be epitomised in point 4: the settlement would not contain political provisions which ran the risk of losing the retained area to Communist control. Unless, however, it was to be assumed that any 'unification of Vietnam by peaceful means' in the foreseeable future would be effected under a non-Communist government the anomaly of points 4 and 5 could hardly be resolved. Nevertheless, it was a blueprint for a partitioned Vietnam and the semblance of a compromise if such a settlement could be obtained.

That a settlement could be made was in doubt almost up to the last moments of the Conference but in the meantime, and to some extent, at least the military negotiations between the French and the Vietminh reflected the realities of a war that was still going on. In the matter of the 'Dong Hoi line', referred to in point 2 of the desiderata that were agreed by the US, Britain and France, this was approximately 17½° north. The French were offering 18° but the Vietminh were demanding a line drawn at 13°, far to the south, which, in effect, would have left the French forces and the state of Vietnam in control of little more than Cochinchina. At this point the French were about to abandon a major part of Tonkin and they had just suffered at Ankhe, far down the coast of Annam, what was described as their third greatest defeat in Indo-China and by far the biggest reverse they had ever known in the south. It seemed unlikely therefore that the Vietminh had been exhausted by their efforts at Dien Bien Phu and even in terms of set-piece battles, and even if they were carefully chosen, they looked capable of inflicting further heavy losses on the French Expeditionary Corps. Left to themselves it seems unlikely that the Vietminh would have concluded an agreement which would have met the Mendès France deadline and almost certainly not on the approximate terms that had been agreed with the Americans. But by discounting the possibility that their Russian and Chinese allies might prevail upon the Vietminh to reduce their demands or to offer France what in effect would be extended credit terms the US not only excluded itself from the settlement but also from the negotiations that might conceivably have produced a more durable arrangement.

Durability, in the case of the Geneva Settlement, would have meant not only that there was, in fact, agreement among the negotiating powers but also enough residual common purpose to have produced some sort of guarantee. Dulles was certainly right in his assumption that the USSR wanted one, and he had explained in terms of current US politics and ideology how this would have offended US principles of dealing with the Communist world, but if one goes further it is easy to see how difficult it would have been in the form of a full-scale treaty to have enlisted the support of two-thirds of the US Senate. But it was not only the USSR which was looking for a guarantee. The French had proposed it, the UK was in favour (and had strong Australian support)[43] while it was only at the very last moment that the Chinese dropped their demand that the agreement should bear a US signature. As subjects of the settlement, the successor states of Indo-China would not be expected to contribute to the guarantee, and the US was already considering them as objects of a collective defence arrangement; but their individual agreement, and particularly that of Vietnam, was now brought forward by the US as an extra criterion for an acceptable settlement[44] and although, in spite of an extraordinary eleventh-hour drama involving Cambodia, which meant that the agreements were not concluded until the morning of 21 July, there was no express dissent on the part of either Laos or Cambodia.

Vietnam, which was the centre of the conflict and on behalf of whose government a political settlement was being prepared, announced its vehement and unalterable opposition.

NGO DINH DIEM

As a government that was recognized by more than 30 countries it was of course entitled to speak on behalf of the state even though it was obviously and actively opposed by large numbers of its citizens. It may or may not have represented national feelings but it certainly had nothing like a representative government and in so far as it was a sovereign state it depended upon French forces, US money and an absentee emperor. For the first time, it had as Prime Minister a passionate and uncompromising nationalist whose violent dislike of the French was exceeded only by the intensity of his opposition to communism and who, if one were to take his government's claim and the new US ground rules seriously, was now empowered to cast a veto on behalf of the US on whatever settlement that was reached which did not meet with his approval.

In just under ten years, up to his violent death in 1963, Ngo Dinh Diem and his family came to represent a war that could not be won. When, however, he was asked by Bao Dai to form a government in June 1954 and accepted, two days after Mendès France took office, Diem could present himself by virtue of his unusual but almost impeccable record of attachment to Vietnamese independence as a symbol of an alternative and in some respects purer nationalism than that represented by Ho Chi Minh. The fact that he was a Catholic, had spent most of the previous three years in American seminaries and had the support of such influential figures as Cardinal Spellman and Senator Kennedy did not immediately disqualify him. If anything and in so far as the US, too, was interested in genuine Vietnamese independence it was an advantage; and within days of his return to Vietnam he was making it perfectly plain, and with frequent reiteration, that the future of Vietnam depended on the US. Ngo Dinh Diem and his brother Ngo Dinh Nhu were described as being at an almost insane pitch of hatred against the French and while the US chargé in Saigon described Diem as 'a messiah without a message' nevertheless Diem was asking for immediate US assistance in every possible form which included not only refugee relief but the training of troops and armed US intervention as well.[45] Bao Dai's choice of Diem as Prime Minister provided the US with a more or less unexpected and fortuitous opportunity. With only six weeks to go before an agreement was reached at Geneva Diem was scarcely more unrealistic than his predecessors in government had been in his attachment to an undiminished Vietnamese sovereignty; but Diem was different in his almost mystical belief that Vietnam would be saved, through him, by a reassertion of its national integrity and its national, pre-colonial, traditions. In some of the earliest reports filed by the US embassy in Saigon on his position Diem was presented as quite obsessed with the loss of northern territory: to the point where he said he intended to attack the Vietminh in their heartland around Vinh (which, incidentally, was the birthplace of both Diem and Ho Chi Minh) even if the French did start withdrawing from the North; and convinced also that if the French gave up Hanoi it would be practically impossible to form a viable state from what was left even if it included Annam as well as Cochinchina. The Cochinchinese he said, ominously, were too easy-going either to become soldiers or to resist communist subversion.[46]

Given these opinions, and assuming that Diem went to no trouble to conceal them from the French, it is all the more surprising that when Mendès France confirmed with Dulles in Paris on 14 July that the seven points[47] could be obtained by negotiation and were acceptable to France, the French should say they were also believed to be acceptable to Vietnam as well. While the settlement was not to contain political provisions that would risk the loss of the *retained* area of Vietnam to communist control, and even, it will be remembered, would not exclude the possibility of ultimate reunification, nevertheless there could be no doubt that North Vietnam would be lost and that the French and the US and the UK agreed. Yet, if, as the US insisted, the settlement had to have the agreement of the Vietnamese government in Saigon, it was doomed from the start. Nor did the US take kindly to the idea of, and certainly not to the word, 'partition': a point that was not lost on the French who, as soon as they had established the possibility with the Chinese (at Mendès France's momentous meeting with Zhou En-lai in Bern on 23 June), seemed to go out of their way to help the US conceal its naked reality. As Chauvel, of the French Foreign Office, told the US Ambassador in Paris it could be made clear that the settlement was merely an armistice; Vietnam could continue to be considered as one country and it would eventually be reunited under one government after free elections at some indeterminate time in the future.[48] Among the great powers, whatever the settlement that was likely to be made, it was going to depend upon multilateral, hopeful, and ultimately rather disingenuous salesmanship. Of those principally concerned, the Chinese, while they might or might not have been prepared to wait indefinitely for reunification,[49] apparently did not press for early elections and even encouraged the French to think that a united Vietnam might remain within the French Union.[50] The French were selling the idea of an honourable end to their war in

Indo-China to the US and soft-pedalling the political arrangements. It remained for Dulles to sell the idea to Congress and the US people. Of the three, and in spite of the fact that he was selling the smallest and most basic model of a settlement, Dulles probably had the hardest job. Not the least of his difficulties lay in countering the charge that even the idea of negotiation was wrong and so Geneva was a mistake whatever settlement was produced.

This surprising, partisan and perhaps irresponsible criticism came not from the China lobby, someone such as Knowland or Judd, but from the influential Democratic Senator Mansfield who was probably evening the score for previous Republican criticisms of the Democrats and Korea; and Dulles had also to deal with those in his own party who were worried about the 'loss' of territory to Communism as well as any sort of guarantee. On 16 July, when the outline of the settlement was becoming clear, Dulles told Congressman Vorys 'we are free to work peacefully against it' and the next day he admitted to the publisher Henry Luce that it would be a partial surrender but insisted 'we can move in there and bolster their position'.[51] The position Dulles had in mind was presumably that of the non-communist Vietnamese but first the French had to be persuaded not to make last-minute concessions. Reluctant that either he or Bedell Smith should return to Geneva for fear of putting their heads into a noose Dulles was eventually persuaded (by Eisenhower, it seems, as much as anyone else) to see Mendès France and Eden in Paris and although, even at this stage, Mendès France was still unwilling to concede that Vietnam could withdraw from the French Union (nor did he seem to regard Vietnam as independent) Dulles was apparently impressed by Mendès France's timetable and preparations for continuing the war in the event that a decent peace could not be made by 20 July. He finally agreed that Bedell Smith might return to Geneva at least to create the impression of solidarity among the western allies but that, however, was about as far as he was prepared to go.

AN IMPOSED AGREEMENT

The day after the Geneva Conference ended Dulles told the National Security Council that, considering their actual capabilities, the communist demands had turned out to be relatively moderate: a statement which prompts two questions. First, why were they so moderate? Second, if this was the case, why did the US specifically dissociate itself from the final settlement to which the other great powers had agreed? The general answer in both cases would seem to be that, just as the involvement of China and the US had transformed a French colonial war, so a settlement in the various transcendental interests of what may be regarded as a consortium of great powers was imposed on what might otherwise have been a limited but finite proceeding.

In the case of the Vietminh, 15 years after Geneva when they had become established as the Democratic Republic of Vietnam and the country had been united, they let it be known that after Dien Bien Phu the Vietnamese people had been capable of liberating the entire country. The only thing that had stopped them – and prevented a total victory in Laos and Cambodia as well – was, they claim, China, whose leaders had betrayed them. By then, they had taken sides in the Sino-Soviet dispute and chosen to blame China for their earlier frustration but on at least one reading of the situation they would never have come to the Conference table at all had not a peaceful settlement of the Indo-China war been initiated by Moscow and the Cominform and at that time, almost as soon as Stalin died in March 1953, Moscow and Peking agreed 'there is no international dispute that cannot be settled through negotiations'.[52] Significantly, however, as Professor Chen points out, within days of his return from Stalin's funeral Zhou had proposed an immediate resumption of armistice talks on Korea and was endorsed by almost every communist country except Vietnam. It was not until the end of 1953 that Ho Chi Minh had held out the prospect of peace talks with France but, having brought off the marvellous victory at Dien Bien Phu, two months later, somewhere on the Chinese border, Zhou arrived from Geneva to present the big picture. In the 1979 White Paper the Vietnamese make no mention of the Ho-Zhou meeting although at the time a laconic communiqué announced that there had been a full exchange of views. Some idea of what went on between the Chinese and the Vietminh is to be found in the White Paper's assertions and brief documentation from which it seems that at one point and in one sense Zhou had proposed that the Vietminh should abandon Hanoi and Haiphong: the latter to be a free port and both to be part of a demilitarized zone.[53] For the Vietminh/Democratic Republic of Vietnam this evidence of what they called collusion between French and Chinese imperialism is what denied them total victory, particularly, they say, the pressure which the Chinese applied in the last ten days before Mendès France's deadline of 20 July. Instead of a temporary military demarcation line at the 13th parallel and elections within six months for national reunification the Vietminh were constantly urged to make concessions; and what the Chinese leaders advocated was a Korean-type solution, i.e. cessation of hostilities without any political solution.

At least it was not a political solution which the Vietminh accepted – a prolonged partition of Vietnam – even if, as they said, by sacrificing the interests of the Indo-China people China managed to secure its own security in the south. Although the Chinese evidently made use of the US threat of an expanded war to coerce the Vietminh, after the event, at least, they claimed flatly that the US had not been capable of direct military intervention in Indo-China. So, as far as the Vietminh were concerned and when, under duress, they accepted a settlement that was being made for them, Geneva for the moment represented a punctuation mark. Like other 'agreements' in the colonial territories of Southeast Asia after the war when the contending imperial and nationalist forces were manoeuvring for advantage it was more of a postponed disagreement[54] but it was nevertheless an arrangement that, other things being equal, might have worked. It might, for example from a western point of view, have provided a fig leaf of diplomatic respectability which would have concealed the starker realities of a French defeat and in any event would have postponed presently unbearable consequences for another two years. At any rate France had been rescued from war: she had been allowed to make peace and by the end of the conference, although it had come very close to the edge, the US had not committed itself to military intervention. Had it, conversely, committed itself to a peaceful solution of the Indo-China war? What was the nature and form of the settlement anyway?

CURIOSITIES OF THE FINAL DECLARATION

The Agreement on the Cessation of Hostilities in Vietnam bore only two signatures: that of a French Brigadier-General, on behalf of the C-in-C French Union Forces in Indo-China, and that of the Vice-Minister of Defence of the Democratic Republic of Vietnam. Although it was essentially an arrangement in which most of the details of the armistice were set out, and although it left major details of the political settlement blank, it made sense only in relation to what was agreed about the future political configuration of Vietnam. Nevertheless, even though it was a limited agreement certain provisions were unmistakably clear. There was, for example, no mention of partition: it was a provisional military demarcation line. On either side of the line civil administrations would be in the hands of whichever party's forces were being regrouped there (this seemed to beg the question which, in the south, was the competent political authority representing the French Union forces) but only until such time as general elections brought about the unification of Vietnam. In the meantime, civilians who wished to move from one zone to another were to be permitted and helped by respective authorities; there was to be no destruction or sabotage; no reprisals or discrimination against persons or organizations on account of their activities during the hostilities and their democratic liberties were to be guaranteed.

Chapter III of the Agreement was headed: 'Ban On The Introduction Of Fresh Troops, Military Personnel, Arms And Munitions, Military Bases.' No troop reinforcements or additional military personnel apart from rotation, replacement and temporary attachment were permitted and except for piece for piece replacement the same ban applied to arms and munitions, in particular to the heavier varieties such as combat aircraft and armoured vehicles. Both the French and the US knew of Chinese sensitivities about US bases in Vietnam[55] and in Article 19 it was agreed:

> No military base under the control of a foreign State may be established in the re-grouping zone of either party; the two parties shall ensure that the zones assigned to them do not adhere to any military alliance and are not used for the resumption of hostilities or to further an aggressive policy.

and, of equal importance both for China and the US, the establishment of new military bases was prohibited throughout Vietnam territory (Article 18).

As far as the implementation of the Agreement was concerned, and after the membership had eventually been decided as Poland and Canada with an Indian chairman, an International Commission would operate in Vietnam (as well as in Laos and Cambodia which had their own analogous agreements) by a majority vote concerning recommendations but unanimously in the matter of amendments and additions. In certain circumstances majority/minority reports would be submitted to Conference members – which might suggest that they had some sort of continuing entitlement or responsibility – but under Article 27 it was the signatories of the Agreement and their successors in their functions who were to be responsible for ensuring the observance and enforcement of the terms and provisions thereof.

These were the substantive agreements. Between the other countries that were present at Geneva nothing at all was agreed and signed although by listing them all as taking part, and speaking in the name of the Conference, the Final Declaration may convey the impression of an agreement and indeed had sufficient weight of numbers to suggest that in any event it would not be easily overturned. Taking note of the political implications of the cease-fire agreement in respect to foreign troops and bases and the declarations made by the Laotian and Cambodian governments regarding the elections, the Conference expressed its conviction that Vietnam, Laos and Cambodia would be fully independent and sovereign members of the peaceful community of nations; although in the case of Vietnam, where the military demarcation line was not in any way to be regarded as a political or territorial boundary, a political settlement was expected in the near future or, at least, the cease-fire arrangement plus the provisions of the Final Declaration were deemed to create the necessary basis for such an achievement. At this point the text lapsed into hopeful and alarming uncertainty. The settlement of Vietnamese political problems (effected on the basis of respect for the principles of independence, unity and territorial integrity) so the Conference declared, 'shall permit the Vietnamese people to enjoy the fundamental freedoms, guaranteed by democratic institutions' but these were to be established as a *result* (italics supplied) of free general elections by secret ballot.

ELECTIONS AND RESPONSIBILITIES

It could be, and it was, later, argued that this order should have been reversed: that to have free general elections democratic institutions should have been established in the first place but, again, in the next sentence, it was the general elections to be held in July 1956 which were to ensure that all the necessary conditions obtained for free expression of the national will as well as sufficient progress in the restoration of peace. The International Commission was to supervise the elections; and what were called the competent representative authorities of the two zones were to consult on the matter from 20 July 1955 onwards. Who these representative authorities would be, what they would do and how effective the understandings were likely to be were all affected by the last four paragraphs of the Declaration. It was noted that the French had announced they would withdraw their troops from the Indo-China states on request of their governments. France, and all the Conference members, undertook to respect their sovereignty, independence, unity and territorial integrity and to refrain from any interference in their internal affairs. Finally, to ensure that the agreements on the cessation of hostilities were respected, the Conference members agreed to consult each other on any question referred to them by the International Supervisory Commission and to study such measures as might prove necessary.

As a statement of intent the Final Declaration did seem to suggest at least the outline and some important detail of a political settlement in Vietnam but as a statement of fact it was vitiated if not invalidated by one major fault: it did not have the unconditional support of the US. Indeed, one may ponder America's own declaration and ask whether it amounted, rather, to a dissenting vote. Certainly and strictly speaking it was a *non sequitur* in that it was prepared in advance of the Final Declaration itself, rather than in response, at a time (16 July) when Dulles could only guess at the final shape of the agreements that might be reached but even if they conformed more or less to the Seven Points, Bedell Smith was only authorized to make the extraordinary statement that, in line with the general obligation of the UN charter, the US would not use force or the threat of force to disturb them.[56] The Declaration, Bedell Smith was told, was to be unilateral. In no circumstances would the US become co-signatory with the Communists.

Given America's political points of reference at the time this is understandable. Dulles had declared 'We could not get ourselves into the "Yalta business" of guaranteeing Soviet conquests'[57] and in his final instructions to Bedell Smith before the latter returned to Geneva Dulles had written:

> 7) You will avoid participation in the negotiations in any way which would imply, or give the Communists plausible case for contending, that the US was so responsible for the result that it is in honor bound to guarantee that result to the Communists. We apprehend that the Communists might offer to make certain concessions if the US would then guarantee the settlement so far as they were concerned. You should, so far as possible, avoid getting yourself into a position which would lend itself to such a Communist maneuver.[58]

The 'Communist maneuver' that was probably least expected, and to this day one cannot be sure whether or not it was a deception or whether it was to be taken seriously, was the possibility that the Chinese would take it on themselves to deny the Vietminh their anticipated and immediate triumph and the fact that it was a last-minute proposal hardly gave the US time to react even if Dulles, for example, had thrown caution to the winds.[59] There seems little doubt that the overriding Chinese objective at Geneva was the neutralization of the Indo-China states and the assurance, if not guarantee, that they would not be host to US bases or 'aggressive intentions'. The Chinese had already been assured by Eden that if the Indo-China states agreed not to join military alliances they would not become members of SEATO (they were not told, however, that they might be designated in the SEATO protocol: one reason why Zhou could subsequently claim that he had been duped)[60] but with two days to go before the Mendès France deadline they let it be known to the US delegation in Geneva that they were 'pressing for the stamp of American approval on the armistice agreement' (which, they said, was already agreed in principle by Britain and France) 'which would divide Vietnam between communist leader Ho Chi Minh's Vietminh and Bao Dai's pro-western regime'.[61] Made by the Chinese through the AP correspondent in Geneva it might, of course, have been a misunderstanding and of more immediate concern to the US at this point was the Chinese insistence that the US was obliged to subscribe to and guarantee any settlement. Nevertheless, even if one discounts the retrospective criticism of the Chinese from Hanoi there was the further supporting but circumstantial evidence of Zhou, in the presence of Pham Van Dong, at a dinner when the conference ended proposing the health of Bao Dai and suggesting to one of Diem's brothers, who was also a guest, that the State of Vietnam should open a legation in Peking.[62] Were, then, the Chinese prepared to see the indefinite partition of Vietnam into two separate and neutralized states if the arrangement had been guaranteed by the US and the other Geneva powers? Could they have persuaded the Vietminh that the balance of world forces and the needs of international socialism demanded such a sacrifice? Was this really what they were suggesting? Whatever the answers it seemed clear that the US at any rate was taking no chances. In any event they were more concerned that hints if not promises and inducements had not been made to the CPR by America's allies which might even involve displacing Chiang Kai Shek's representative at the UN in return for allowing Mendès France to meet his deadline. But in any event, too, Dulles was convinced that the Russians, the Chinese and the Vietminh between them would not let Mendès France win his wager even though he was, as he said, keeping his fingers crossed that there would be no last-minute under-the-table deals.

As Dulles described it the US had to play a war-of-nerves game: initially to arrive at an acceptable settlement and then to preserve it. Both stages involved the threat of war although when Dulles and Eisenhower discussed the matter on Sunday, 18 July, they agreed that Eisenhower should not, after all, go to Congress on the following Wednesday to ask for immediate war-time powers. As Dulles said, that would be too drastic and would scare everybody to death.[63] Nevertheless when the outcome at Geneva became known and it turned out to be less of a disaster than they had feared, Bedell Smith was able to issue the prepared declaration on behalf of his government whose second part came close to a 'guarantee' of what had been agreed. Any renewal of the aggression (which was one way of describing the revolutionary war that had just ended in Vietnam) in violation of the agreements would be viewed with grave concern and as a serious threat to international peace and security. What the US would do then was left to the imagination but it applied to only one side of the bargain. It should, of course, have provided some encouragement for the State of Vietnam who may or may not have been further heartened by another assertion that in the case of nations now divided against their will the US would continue to seek to achieve unity through free elections (supervised by the UN to ensure that they were conducted fairly). Much more important however was the reiterated statement of the traditional US position: that peoples are entitled to determine their own future and that the US would not join in an arrangement which would hinder this. If that did not make the position clear enough Bedell Smith added 'nothing in its declaration just made is intended to or does indicate any departure from this traditional position'. Unfortunately the position was ambiguous and the statement was equivocal. The entitlement of peoples to determine the future of Vietnam in 1954, if one were to take it seriously, would suggest something in the nature of a referendum. The entitlement of a government to determine what its people should be allowed to decide suggests something else. Obviously it was the intention of the Vietminh to have elections as soon as possible. Having been the first to raise the matter when the conference began, it was, apparently, the sticking point when the conference ended. At first they suggested six months, the French preferred something indefinite but, on the last day, they agreed on two years. It was of course a major concession but it seems to have been made in exchange for Vietminh agreement that the partition line might now be withdrawn to the 17th parallel.[64]

Obviously the prospect of elections, even though postponed for two years, carried with it a high probability of a communist victory. Eisenhower's often-quoted passage in his memoirs that 'Had elections been held as of the time of the fighting, possibly 80 per cent of the population would have voted for the communist Ho Chi Minh as their leader rather than Chief of State Bao Dai' can perhaps be regarded as the worst case but even after the fighting had stopped it was hard to envisage the circumstances in which the prestige of Ho and the Vietminh would have collapsed.[65] Hard, but not impossible. The advanced position of the US on elections seems quite reasonable: that they should only be held as long after the cease-fire arrangement as possible and in conditions free from intimidation to give democratic elements the best chance.[66] The role of the control commission was obviously going to be important to the US in this respect and although the presence of the Poles was alarming and that of the Indians somewhat suspect because of their inclination to what Dulles subsequently described as the immorality of neutralism, at least the Canadians would be there: even if they realized 'they have the delicate task of upholding an agreement to which the Americans were not prepared to give their support'.[67]

The most important as well as the most disputed feature of all that concerned the elections and, ultimately, the validity of the entire agreements was whether, if the state of the Vietnam was not a party to the arrangements, they should from the beginning have been considered null and void. When they eventually discovered that the ground had been negotiated away from under their feet the Vietnamese delegation lodged their formal objection to the principle of partition and the unhappy M. Tran Van Do, Foreign Minister in the new Diem government, rejected both the French and the Russian drafts for the final Conference resolution although he followed this up with a rather half-hearted and ambiguous statement that his government would not use force to resist the cease-fire.[68] In Saigon, where the French were anticipating some sort of popular backlash, there was no ambiguity. Flags flew at half-mast and Diem denounced the seizure by what he called Soviet-China – through its satellite the Vietminh – of over half the national territory. It was for that reason, he said, that they had not signed the agreement and had lodged the most solemn protest against the injustice.[69]

In the flurry of unilateral declarations that marked the end of the Geneva Conference on Indo-China one is sometimes overlooked: that of the Government of the French Republic, 21 July, 1954:

> For the settlement of all the problems connected with the re-establishment and consolidation of peace in Cambodia, Laos and Vietnam, the French Government will proceed from the principle of respect for the independence and sovereignty, the unity and territorial integrity of Cambodia, Laos and Vietnam.[70]

For Cambodia and Laos this was more or less reality but for Vietnam unity and territorial integrity were no more than a principle; sovereignty was divided, if only for the time being; while for that part of southern Vietnam which was territorially 'retained', independence was and has been called in question. For operational purposes it looked as if Dulles, for one, did not assume that the state of Vietnam was in fact independent. He told a news conference on 23 July that Mendès France had instructed French representatives in Vietnam to complete by 30 July 'precise projects for the transfers of authority which will give reality to the independence which France had promised' and if, as he said, by comparison, that independence was already a fact in Laos and Cambodia, then the completion of independence in Indo-China could only refer to Vietnam. Nevertheless if the French were ascribing sovereign independence to the state of Vietnam then the sovereign independent state of Vietnam had the legal entitlement, as well as a political disposition, *not* to be bound by either the cease-fire agreement or any of the implications of the Final Declaration, in particular the provision for elections. In practice, particularly as the state of Vietnam depended on French Union forces, there was an unacknowledged condominium in south Vietnam but the problems posed were far greater than deciding whether it was independent before 20 July or after 30 July. For example, in his exhaustive but still, in part, controversial treatment of Geneva Professor Randle says, of problems involving the law of state succession, that the facts are of such vital importance that it is almost impossible to make uncontroversial generalizations. As if to bear out this argument the relevant footnote continues for two pages; and in order to answer the question whether what he calls a provisional sovereign entity such as the Republic of Vietnam could refuse to consult for the purpose of planning elections he feels it would be necessary to elucidate the incidence and attributes of quasi-sovereignty and perhaps even to re-examine the whole concept of sovereignty and its place in international legal theory.

Apart from what at the time, and before more documentation became available, was the most comprehensive account of the Conference itself Randle takes as his legal premise (with, of course, enormous political implications) that whether sovereign in 1954, 1955 or 1956 the State of Vietnam government, and its successor, the Republic of Vietnam government, could refuse to be bound by the political provisions of the Final Declaration when it achieved sovereign status, and in so doing this violated no rules of customary international or treaty law.[71] Others, such as Professor Richard Falk, stress the context of international society within which the Geneva agreements were reached.[72] By contrast with the principle of textuality, i.e. that the *text* of an agreement must be taken as the only authentic expression of the intentions of the parties, the alternative thesis of 'contextuality' is adopted by Professor Hannon who attempts to determine whether a political settlement was an integral part of the Geneva Agreement or not.[73] This essentially political but persuasive argument is a recommendation 'to interpret the focal agreement according to the expectations shared by the parties during the course of their interaction, including both the making and performance of the agreement, as indicated by the context considered as a whole'; concludes that it was and, furthermore, that the major share of the responsibility for its failure must be shouldered by the US.[74]

State succession is, by all accounts,[75] one of the most confused areas of post-Second World War international legal practice and even when one examines, as Hannon does, comparable French treaties of independence for Tunisia and Morocco or the 'faculties of denunciation' which had been written into previous French treaties with the Associated States of Indo-China and by which the State of Vietnam might have absolved itself of responsibilities incurred by the French, it is tempting to cut the Gordian knot and say that the war did not begin again because of a failure to solve a problem of international law. Nor was there an obvious legal remedy, given the inconsistencies and anomalies of the Geneva Conference, its agreements and postponed disagreements, and the immense scope they provided for favourable but incompatible interpretations; so perhaps all one may do in the end is to agree with Professor Moore that they largely contained the seeds of their own destruction.[76] Before that happened, and whether or not it was expected to connive at its own destruction, the sovereign basis for and validity of the State of Vietnam had to be proved. Was it, in fact, a state or a temporary administration? Two forms which had mutually exclusive purposes but which were, perhaps, a true reflection of the contradictions of Geneva.

REFERENCES AND NOTES

1. *United States-Vietnam Relations*, Book 9, p. 458.
2. John W. Holmes, 'Geneva 1954' *International Journal*, 1967, Vol. XXII, summer.
3. Philippe Devillers and Jean Lacouture, *End of a War* (London 1969). A more recent French study is François Joyaux, *La Chine et le Règlement du Premier Conflit d'Indochine (Geneve 1954)* (Paris 1979). Sir James Cable's *The Geneva Conference of 1954 on Indo-China* (London 1986), is the most detailed and revealing study of Geneva based on Foreign Office documents and the author's own experience as a member of the British delegation.
4. *FRUS, 1952–4* Vol. XVI, *The Geneva Conference*, p. 1060.
5. *FRUS, 1952–4* Vol. XIII, Part 2, *Indochina*, p. 1694.
6. Ibid. p. 1708.
7. Ibid. p. 1580, footnote 2.
8. Ibid. p. 1583.
9. Ibid. p. 1593.
10. Ibid. p. 1589.
11. Ibid. p. 1535.
12. According to the Dulles memo Eisenhower's only response was to suggest that the resolution could be redrafted to define more closely the area of operations. *FRUS*, Vol. XIII, Part 2, pp. 1584–5.
13. *The US Government And The Vietnam War*, Executive and Legislative Roles and Relationships Part I, 1945–1961, US GPO (Washington 1984). p. 233. (hereinafter cited as 'Gibbons').
14. JFD, Telephone Memos, May 1–June 30, 1954 (3), (May 14, May 21), *Eisenhower Library*.
15. JFD Papers. Subject series. Box 8, May 9. *Eisenhower Library*.
16. JFD Papers. Subject series. Box 8, May 11. *Eisenhower Library*.
17. Gibbons, op. cit. p. 231.
18. *FRUS*, Vol. XVI, pp. 895–9.
19. Eisenhower, *Mandate For Change*, (Signet), pp. 41–2.
20. *FRUS*, Vol. XVI, p. 1055.
21. Cable, op. cit. pp. 88–9.
22. FO 371 1071/63, March 16. PRO.
23. Joyaux, op. cit. p. 183.
24. Ibid. pp. 322–3.
25. Ibid. p. 276–7.
26. Cable, op. cit. p. 97.
27. *Executive Sessions of the Senate Foreign Relations Committee (Historical Series), Vol. VI, 83rd Congress, 2nd session, 1954*, p. 269.
28. *FRUS*, Vol. XVI, p. 1147.
29. The British estimates, on the other hand, suggested that it was in fact the Vietminh who had a two-to-one advantage in their strike force of mobile battalions compared to the French Union forces – 132 opposed to 57 – while even in static battalions the French did not have that much of an advantage – 185 compared to 170 Vietminh. Cable, op. cit. p. 92.

30. *NSC Records,* National Archives, Washington. The Department of Justice had prepared a promising joint resolution which anathematised 'An illegal and rebellious combination known as the Vietminh League' supported by the 'International Communist Movement' and declared that the peace and safety of the US demanded that their insurrectionary and aggressive acts should be suppressed.

31. Translation of the treaty may be found in Allan W. Cameron (ed.), *Vietnam Crisis: a Documentary History, 1940–1956* (Ithaca N.Y. 1971), pp. 268–9.

32. *FRUS,* Vol. XIII, p. 1716.

33. Dulles to US Delegation at Geneva, 9 June 1954. *FRUS,* Vol. XVI, p. 1104.

34. Eden, *Full Circle,* pp. 132–3.

35. Cable's comment is that Locarno 'seems to have made an impression on Churchill and Eden that easily survived the failure of the Locarno system at its first test: Hitler's invasion of the Rhineland in 1936'. op. cit. p. 110. David Thompson, *Europe Since Napoleon,* offers a devastating critique of the treaties and their implications, pp. 636–7.

36. Gibbons, op. cit. pp. 249–50.

37. Whitman File Box 1, Memorandum for the record, June 23rd, 1954, *Eisenhower Library.*

38. Ibid.

39. *FRUS,* Vol. XIII, p. 1714.

40. *FRUS,* Vol. XVI, p. 1281. Gibbons has extracted the evidence and presents it op. cit. pp. 241–3.

41. Gibbons, op. cit. p. 242.

42. *FRUS,* Vol. XIII, p. 1758.

43. According to an Australian dispatch, which Eden circulated to the Cabinet on 15 June, Australian policy favoured an international guarantee, provision for enforcement, and the association of Asian countries, especially India. CAB 129/68. PRO.

44. *FRUS,* Vol. XIII, p. 1792, footnote 5.

45. Ibid. p. 1783.

46. Ibid. p. 1793.

47. *FRUS,* Vol. XIII, p. 1830.

48. *FRUS,* Vol. XVI, p. 1239.

49. According to Joyaux, Mendès France in his negotiation with Zhou was convinced that China was clearly in favour of the prolonged existence of two Vietnams. op. cit. pp. 322–3.

50. *FRUS,* Vol. XVI, p. 1240.

51. *FRUS,* Vol. XIII, pp. 1841–2.

52. King C. Chen *Vietnam and China 1938–1954* (Princeton 1969), p. 283.

53. The White Paper may be found in the *BBC Survey of World Broadcasts (Far East),* 6 October 1979.

54. For example between the Dutch and their Indonesian nationalist opponents at Linggadjati in November, 1946 or Ho's rather threadbare *modus vivendi* with the French in September of that year.

55. The AP correspondent in Geneva, whom the Chinese had used to establish their position with the Americans, provided some visual impressions as well. 'When Huang spoke of possibility of American bases in Indo-China or anti-Communist pact in South-East Asia, he

became very agitated, his hands shook, and his usually excellent English broke down, forcing him to work through interpreter.' *FRUS,* Vol. XVI, p. 1449.

56. *FRUS,* Vol. XVI, p. 1389.
57. To the NSC, 15 July. *FRUS,* Vol. XIII, p. 1835.
58. *FRUS,* Vol. XVI, p. 1390.
59. At the time the US seem to have been even more worried about the manoeuvres of its allies, e.g. in regard to SEATO.
60. Cable, op. cit. p. 118.
61. *FRUS,* Vol. XVI, p. 1428.
62. The point was initiated, innocently enough, by Diem's brother who said that in Hanoi war had destroyed part of the temples constructed on the Chinese model by the emperor Minh-Mang. Zhou said 'Come and see the originals in Peking' and Luyen asked under what title he should present himself. Apparently Zhou said 'Certainly Pham Van Dong is closer to us in ideology but that doesn't exclude representation of the South. After all, aren't you both Vietnamese and aren't we all Asians?' Joyaux op. cit. p. 297.
63. *FRUS,* Vol. XIII, p. 1852.
64. Franklin Weinstein's monograph *Vietnam's Unheld Elections,* East Asia Data Paper no. 60, Cornell University, 1966, cites Philippe Devillers as evidence. Cable says the two issues had to be settled together and concludes that the Vietminh price for their concessions 'was a definite date for the elections which would enable them to win politically that southern half of Vietnam which their allies had refused to help them conquer militarily'. Op. cit. p. 120. From Joyaux's account it seems that the date might have been fixed in bi-lateral Sino-French negotiations, op. cit. pp. 281–2 and, to confute the possibility that the Chinese were prepared for an indefinite postponement, prompted by a British comparison with the time it had taken to organize elections in India, Burma and even China itself, they said a specific date such as two or three years was the only way to make clear to the people of Vietman that the Conference was not fooling. *FRUS,* Vol. XVI, p. 1437.
65. *Mandate for Change* (Signet 1965), p. 449.
66. *FRUS,* Vol. XIII, pp. 1791–2.
67. Holmes, op. cit. p. 472. Holmes provides a first-hand Canadian account that is both sensitive and revealing.
68. Cmnd. 2834. *Documents Relating to British Involvement in the Indo-China Conflict 1945–1965,* p. 87.
69. Gareth Porter, *Vietnam: the Definitive Documentation of Human Decisions,* Vol. I, p. 656.
70. Cmnd. 2834, *Documents,* p. 83.
71. Robert F. Randle, *Geneva, 1954* (Princeton 1969), Ch. 23.
72. Falk takes as one of his starting points the implications of the Treaty of Westphalia which concluded the Thirty Years War in 1648 and argues that its legal political implications are too much orientated towards the status quo. Richard A. Falk, *The Six Legal Dimensions of the Vietnam War,* (Princeton 1968), pp. 25–9.
73. It derives, in part, from the study by McDougal, Lasswell and Miller *The Interpretation of Agreements and World Public Order,* (New Haven 1967).

74. John S. Hannon, Jr. 'Implications of the 1954 Geneva Conference' in Falk, *The Vietnam War and International Law* (Princeton 1969), Vol. 2.
75. Particularly Douglas A. Ross, *In the Interests of Peace: Canada and Vietnam, 1954–73* (Toronto 1984).
76. John Norton Moore, 'A Political Settlement for Vietnam: The 1954 Geneva Conference and the Covert Implications,' Falk, *The Vietnam War and International Law*, Vol. 2.

Chapter 5

DIEM AND THE NATIONAL LIBERATION FRONT: 1954–1960

The origins of the second Vietnam War – or what can be considered a resumption of the first – may, perversely, be thought of in analogy with events and concepts a hundred years earlier. Whether or not it merits the contemporary description of the only perfectly useless war of modern times, the decision of France and Britain to support the Ottoman Empire in its quarrel with Russia produced the Crimean War of 1854. In Lord Palmerston's view the war was fought to curb the aggressive ambitions of Russia – not so much to keep the Sultan in power as to keep the Russians out – but when the war ended and material circumstances for the moment forced the Russians to conclude what they regarded as a humiliating peace it was a settlement which 'came to rest, essentially, on the faithful observance of treaty obligations'. This, it has been suggested, proved to be a slender foundation.[1]

Palmerston, for one, thought that peace would only last a few years – ten at most – but even this required some guarantee and a fortnight after the Peace of Paris was signed in 1856 Britain, France and Austria engaged themselves in a Triple Treaty to defend the settlement. Comparisons with the Treaty that was signed at Manila in September 1954 to protect the Geneva settlement may seem far-fetched, although a quotation, in which they are implicit, is irresistible.

There is, as the fate of the Triple Treaty shows, little value in
diplomatic engagements not based on a lasting community of interests;
yet where such a community of interest exists, written agreements, as a
rule, would seem hardly necessary. The Triple Treaty designed to buttress
the Crimean settlement was shown in the event to have embodied the
permanent interests of not one of the three signatories. It was this which
spelt its doom. Unwanted, ignored, broken in the spirit if not the letter,
it dragged out its undistinguished existence. It did not achieve even
decent burial and consignment to the 'sepulchre of archives'. Unwept,
unhonoured and unsung, it had, in fact, ignominiously 'sneaked out of

existence' years before the British government posthumously proclaimed its demise. Like other carefully negotiated instruments both before and since, it had failed signally to achieve its object or, in fact, to serve any useful purpose whatever.[2]

As its death was comparatively recent, an attempt to extend this obituary to SEATO might seem unwise as well as spiteful but there can be little doubt that its principal purpose, which was an American purpose, was to guarantee the sovereign integrity of Laos and Cambodia and to legitimize the birth of South Vietnam. In a word it was to keep the communists out and the territory most at risk was that of South Vietnam. In 1856 it can be argued that the framers of the Triple Treaty were careless in their drafting – 'They should clearly have written into the Treaty a guarantee of the Ottoman Empire as valid only so long as Turkey was capable of defending herself single-handed'[3] – and even if one would not go so far as the unlikely event of an out and out attack upon South Vietnam by the Chinese People's Republic, nevertheless the ability of the South Vietnamese government to draw on substantial support in its own country was of major importance even if its legitimacy was not. If, in the aftermath of Geneva, the attainment of *de facto* and *de jure* independence as the French departed had coincided with a consolidation and integration of political purpose which to all intents and purposes would have been a demonstration of national sovereignty, a new and viable state could conceivably have been born. Comparisons, sometimes misleading, would often be made with West Germany and South Korea, neither of which had any absolute right to exist, and although it would have been hard to say right away that the régime that was being created by Ngo Dinh Diem lacked the essential qualities of national integrity, nevertheless, and to revert to another 19th-century concept, in retrospect at least it would seem over too long a period to have lacked that indispensable characteristic which Bismarck described as 'alliance-worthiness'.[4]

THE STATUS OF SOUTH VIETNAM

To begin with, in what Eisenhower called 'the miserable political situation' of South Vietnam, the frailty of what was still, nominally, the government of Vietnam was understandable and excusable and Diem himself was in an unenviable position. Whatever its status, the Final Declaration at Geneva had at least established a context and written a scenario for what might happen in the South. The government of Vietnam might have more claim to authority, by breadth of international recognition, than the DRVN in the North, but, rightly or wrongly, independence was more widely attributed to the efforts of the Vietminh than to the government of Emperor Bao Dai. In any case, the Cease Fire Agreement itself (the one that was signed) seemed to imply an equivalence of authority, with 'the conduct of civil administration' on either side recognized 'pending the general elections which would bring about the unification of Vietnam'. This carried the further implication that, as in the North, it was an interim authority, an arrangement and a government therefore that was liable to terminate in two years' time, and that Diem might be no more than the head of a caretaker administration. On this reading of the Final Declaration too, Diem's position might have been undermined by the International Commission for Supervision and Control which, if Geneva was an international settlement, then, like some conference of ambassadors, the Commission appeared to exist in order to carry it out. Only in this case none of the states represented on the Commission had had any part in the Geneva settlement itself; each gave separate instructions to its representatives; each had its own understanding of what had been agreed and what had to be done. The Indian chairman, for example, said that it should have been a Commission for supervision and conciliation, rather than control; of his colleague 'the Polish version of Machiavelli' the Canadian member added 'I doubt whether the Soviet Bloc could have had a more effective representative.'[5] The primary purpose of the International Commission was to control and supervise the application of the cease-fire agreement although it seems (Art. 28) that the primary responsibility for its execution lay with France and the DRVN. Apart from the regrouping of the combatant forces, the Commission's main concern was with Chapter III of the Agreement: 'Ban on the introduction of fresh troops, military personnel, arms and munitions, foreign bases' and what gave rise to even more disagreement under Article 14, how civilians were to be permitted and helped to move from one zone to the other and the prevention of reprisals or discrimination against those who remained.

Although it was to deploy hundreds of men in fixed and mobile teams, even if there had been no deliberate obstruction it would have required an army of observers to detect the import of illicit munitions in North or South Vietnam, particularly the North, and while the arrival of large, regular formations of foreign reinforcements would presumably have stood out, again, particularly in the North, smaller units or individuals who were 'rotating' did not. In the period before the second Vietnam War began (or the first one resumed) it is hard to say whether there was a significant change in the military balance and, although it was widely believed that the Chinese had effected a massive re-supply of the People's Army within a year or so of the armistice, it could be argued, to take just one category, that it was permissible replacement of artillery which had worn smooth and mortars that had practically burned out during the siege of Dien Bien Phu.[6] In so far as the International Commission was supposed to prevent a resumption of hostilities in the two-year period before the scheduled elections it succeeded; but in so far as war, to cite Hobbes, 'consisteth not in actual fighting but in the known disposition thereto' it was, and could hardly not have been, less successful. That is, if one assumes that its purpose was to maintain the unity of Vietnam rather than to assist as midwife at the birth of two Vietnams. Nevertheless, as one Canadian put it, 'The Commission reflected stalemate; it didn't create it'[7] and as far as the co-chairmen of the Geneva Conference, Britain and the USSR, were concerned, as long as the dogs were asleep, or at least quiet, they were content to let them lie. When Macmillan and Molotov met in New York in September 1955 no decisions were taken on reconvening the Geneva Conference (which might at this point have proved awkward for both powers) and extended Anglo-Russian conversations in London in April and May 1956 seemed to confirm, in the words of an Indian study, that the co-chairmen implicitly acquiesced in the virtual partition of Vietnam.[8]

If Britain and the USSR were anxious to absolve themselves of continuing responsibility for the settlement in Vietnam, France and the US were not. One, in spite of the disaster of Dien Bien Phu, wished to retrieve what it could and to retain what influence it might have even in a communist Vietnam. The other, having come so close to participation in the war at the time of Dien Bien Phu, was not yet ready to back off although the commitment was by no means confirmed, to begin with, by all branches of government nor was policy agreed at all levels. In the immediate aftermath of Geneva perhaps the commonest word in US analysis and memoranda was 'salvage' and for a moment, although one may wonder whether Dulles was ever serious when he talked about spending the money elsewhere, it seemed just possible that the US would not put all its weight behind a government in Saigon of doubtful worth. 'We feel' said the State Department a propos Diem a week after the Geneva Conference ended 'we must know whether his government is likely to last . . . we would not wish to give aid to government which did not enjoy support and confidence of Vietnamese people'.[9] But while these criteria had still to be met, and others were being proposed, the major evaluation of Geneva in terms of what was likely to happen in Indo-China suggested what the US might do in a sort of joint-stock venture to create a new Vietnam.

The National Intelligence Estimate of 3 August 1954 'Post-Geneva Outlook in Indo-China' was far more than a conventional intelligence assessment in that it had immense operational consequences as well as profound political implications.[10] In effect, while it was a most perceptive analysis and in almost all respects extremely accurate forecast, it put forward, at the highest level, a draft programme for US policy. The contrasts were vivid. In the North, Ho Chi Minh, who was regarded as the man who had liberated Tonkin from 70 years of French rule. In the South, where it was impossible to predict even the broad outlines of French policy, frustration, disillusionment, widespread uncertainty and the mutual jealousies of Vietnamese politicians. Rather than armed invasion, the communist offensive to control all Indo-China was expected to be political, psychological and para-military; and the course of future developments, it said, 'will be determined less by the Geneva agreements than by the relative capabilities and actions of the Communist and non-Communist entities in Indo-China', and it added, 'of interested outside powers'.

Retrospectively one might argue that while, in the then existing pattern, the fortunes of the South would depend heavily on what the French decided to do, the North was inherently stronger and more likely to be able to sustain itself at least over the short run if elections did take place in 1956, but the most potent if not the most interested outside power was, plainly, the US. Their inherent inexperience, immaturity and weakness notwithstanding, if they were given opportunity, guidance and material help in building nation states, the countries of Indo-China might be able to attain viability. 'We believe that the energy and resourcefulness necessary for the achievement will not arise spontaneously among the non-Communist Indo-Chinese but will have to be sponsored and nurtured from without.' Recommendations were hardly in order in an intelligence estimate but the inferences were inescapable. Energy and resourcefulness are recognized and obvious American characteristics. If they were applied to the requirements stipulated – an effective security force, local government organization and a long-range programme for economic and social reform – then the solution to a finite problem was there for the taking. The French, because of the traditional interests and emotions which governed their Indo-China policy, would be unlikely to arouse active loyalty and popular support for a South Vietnamese government and, in any event, it was expected that the Vietminh stay-behind units would become at least politically active within a year and might even be involved in open guerrilla fighting.[11]

SPONSORED OPPORTUNITY

For an administration in Washington that was still convinced that Indo-China was of vital importance to the US, that communists and particularly Chinese communists were poised to break out into Southeast Asia and beyond, and who had almost finished putting together the alliance that would stop them if there was open aggression, there might have seemed little doubt that it would respond to the clear invitation of the NIE (National Intelligence Estimate). Indeed, their military man on the spot in Saigon, General O'Daniel, was about to put forward his own ambitious proposals for comprehensive US assistance - alongside every key official and government agency in 'Free Vietnam' there should be one or more US specialists – that would include housing, schools, sanitation and hygiene. O'Daniel had already cabled his enthusiastic opinion that there was a great opportunity for the US to assist in pointing Vietnam in the right direction and, he said, the area was one that could be used as a testing ground to combat the warfare Communists would hope to employ elsewhere including, he added, mysteriously, the US.

Whether or not the US administration would take up the challenge, and on such a scale, there were practical matters that required their urgent attention as another massive exodus got under way in a familiar pattern of post-war partition. Most were coming from the North, whole villages at a time and, in the case of the predominantly Catholic refugees, led and organized by village priests.[12] Altogether something like 900,000 refugees, most of them Catholic, came south but when the number was still below 100,000 it was obvious that the government of Vietnam could not possibly cope and the US Ambassador was asking for enough tents to accommodate thousands. Moving that number was beyond French resources, too, and in the the end most of the refugees arrived in US ships. The spectacle and dimensions of this vast and often pitiful flow gave Americans an emotional as well as a practical involvement in those who were obviously fleeing from communism and a concern with what was to happen to them afterwards. There were some rather hopeful projections of political arithmetic which suggested that they might even turn the scales of an anti-communist vote if there were elections but, as long as the overall assessment of political prospects was unchanged, the possibility of elections and a communist victory was like an unexploded bomb which threatened to blow away whatever might be achieved.

From time to time over the next 18 months or so US officials gave the impression that elections were likely to take place and that US efforts were geared to putting the government of Vietnam into the best possible position so that they could take part and withstand the impact. That was certainly the French and, more or less, the British position as well but US instincts were different, even if it took time for operational policy to set hard. In the aftermath of Geneva and what it described as America's loss of prestige and increased Asian doubts about US leadership and capabilities to check further communist expansion, the National Security Council engaged in two massive debates in August 1954 as part of its general review of Far Eastern policy. For the most part they were in an aggressive mood but although it had been a Vietnamese disaster it was China, in effect, who was held responsible and who had to bear the brunt of America's cardinal as well as contingent reactions. In the agreed statement of policy (NSC 5429) South Vietnam was only mentioned once, the object of collective defence in a security treaty, but Southeast Asia generally was where there was to be a new initiative to protect the US position and to restore its prestige throughout the Far East. Limited military assistance and training missions would continue to be provided to the states of Southeast Asia (Vietnam, indirectly, had been far and away the largest recipient) so as to bolster their will to fight, to stabilize legal governments and to assist them in controlling subversion; but subversion, which was now identified as the nut that had to be cracked, was to receive the full sledgehammer treatment.

> If requested by a legitimate local government which requires assistance to defeat local Communist subversion or rebellion not constituting armed attack, the US should view such a situation so gravely that, in addition to giving all possible covert and overt support within Executive Branch authority the President should at once consider requesting Congressional authority to take appropriate action, which might if necessary and feasible include the use of US military forces either locally or against the external source of such subversion or rebellion (including Communist China if determined to be the source).[13]

The distinction that was made between 'legal' and 'legitimate' was probably unintentional and scarcely requires a philosophical disquisition; but a great deal would turn on whether South Vietnam, as well as being legal, was a legitimate government or not. Something, perhaps, which in certain circumstances might be decided by elections but, as Dulles told the NSC on 12 August, he had not believed that there was any way to bring about a non-communist victory in any all-Vietnam elections. So, instead, he 'thought our real objective should be to avoid having such elections'.[14] Defense Secretary Wilson, who was openly sceptical of Vietnam's vital importance to the US, was the only one to underline the Geneva agreements but in the absence of any other internal opposition or dissent US policy was now at least implicitly directed towards this end. The Government of South Vietnam was therefore to be seen as much as a means to this end as it was an end in itself, something that would help to ensure that the elections never took place but it was also a contingent government which from 21 July onwards depended upon a particular interpretation of the Geneva agreements and, from its inception, depended even more upon the massive support of the US. That, however, was not the same as absolute, immediate, and unconditional support as far as Ngo Dinh Diem was concerned and even though he would, before long, have the backing of a powerful lobby, the American Friends of Vietnam, he had first to show some capacity for government and his ability to take part in America's 'new initiative'. The principal attraction was that he was profoundly anti-French and the principal temptation was to assume that he could, if only for a limited period, maintain the integrity of South Vietnam without relying on French power. Economically, this was possible in that the US had been paying for most of the French war effort in Indo-China; but even if the structure of French colonial government could be rapidly dismantled without causing too much damage the same could not be said of the French Expeditionary Corps which was probably the most stable element in a compound which would not have taken much to dissolve or to explode. As long as French forces remained, so did French influence and so did the mutual fears and suspicions of Diem and the US concerning what it was the French were up to, either on their own, or with someone like General Hinh, Chief of Staff of the Vietnamese Army and other Vietnamese who still felt themselves aligned with the French rather than with Diem. This particular and personal confrontation between Diem and his Chief of Staff was beginning to paralyse Vietnamese government at a time when urgent decisions had to be taken on the matter of training the Vietnamese Army. When the cease-fire was signed the French still had some 5,000 officers and men engaged in training the Vietnamese Army. Diem's government now wanted the Americans to take over. Military assistance and training missions, the Americans agreed, would stabilize legal governments. Even the sober-sided Dulles, the morning after Geneva, had confessed he would almost rather see the French get out of the rest of Indo-China and allow the US to work directly with the native leadership. Now there was both opportunity and necessity and as the continuing turmoil of Vietnamese politics brought US assessments that Saigon was on the brink of an army coup so it also brought US mediation and personal commitment to Diem. For one thing Diem seemed to be so much more a Vietnamese nationalist. General Hinh would have been a better choice to impose the national discipline of a Praetorian Guard and would almost certainly have been more amenable to French purposes, but this in itself, in a Vietnam that was trying to assert its national independence, was as much a disqualification as Hinh's French citizenship and commission in the French Air Force.

SYMPATHY FOR DIEM

At least as far as the US was concerned, with a steady stream of telegrams from Ambassador Heath in Saigon, there was growing sympathy in Washington not only for the principle of civil supremacy but, personally, for Diem who was not only under threat from his French-trained military commanders but seemed to be subject to a fair amount of bullying from the French in Saigon who had told him to compromise with Hinh and had their own ideas as well who should be in Diem's cabinet. In fact both French and Americans were offering their advice on whom Diem should have and what he should do and although, as the French complained, he would play one off against the other, Diem was in close and frequent touch with various Americans and often used one as a go-between with another. Well before the Geneva Conference was into its stride the CIA in one disguise or another started arriving in Vietnam. According to French authors Lacouture and Devillers the successive arrivals in Saigon of Colonel Lansdale on 1 June 1954 and General Donovan, wartime head of the CIA's precursor, OSS, and currently Ambassador in Thailand, on 3 June were connected with a move by his brother Nhu to advance Diem to Prime Minister; and a month later the CIA major who, ironically, was heavily involved in the 1963 coup in which Diem and Nhu were murdered, arrived to join Lansdale and then to engage in some rather desultory sabotage around Hanoi.[15] Lansdale's account of himself as friend and confessor to Diem suggests a remarkably close relationship in which, even allowing for exaggeration, Diem is seen as a projection of US ideals and ambitions in Asia. As Lansdale put it, he was apparently trying to convince Diem that, like George Washington, he could become the father of his country. By this time, and although their ambassador had warned that a 'relief pitcher' might be necessary, the US was already a partner in an elaborate quadrille with Diem, the French and Emperor Bao Dai, not to mention the various sects, cabals and individuals who constituted Vietnamese political forces. None was quite so bizarre as either of the two religious sects, the Cao Dai or the Hoa Hao, on whose private armies the French had long relied and whose integration into the Vietnamese Army would provide Diem before long with his most serious challenge. Again, there was a US interest because it would be paying; and by an ironic coincidence the day before Heath had recommended the 'relief pitcher' Eisenhower had agreed that Diem should be reassured of US intentions to aid free Vietnam. Obviously it would have been difficult to tell Diem that the US was willing to send aid direct to his government and to train his army and, at the same time, to mention that they were thinking about his replacement and although in the event, the letter was not sent for another month, when it was finally delivered at the end of October it was a formal and personal commitment. Before that happened Dulles had gone one stage further in avoiding elections in Vietnam, telling the NSC that when the time came, as there was no possibility of fair elections in the north, 'we would have ample grounds for postponing or declining to hold them in the south.'[16]

DOUBTS AND COMMITMENT

There was no doubt about the seriousness in Dulles' mind concerning the US commitment to South Vietnam in the event of an overt attack from the North – US bombing of Tonkin and probably general war with China – although he explained: 'Our concept envisages a fight with nuclear weapons rather than the commitment of ground forces.' Within Vietnam, however, ground forces, that is to say a Vietnamese army, was what mattered and although he described grandiose plans originating from MAAG (Military Assistance Advisory Group) in Saigon for a ten-division army trained for an offensive mission at an annual cost of half a billion dollars as 'silly', it was obvious that an army was needed and Diem needed it most. By this time however the Secretary of State and the Secretary of Defense were notably at odds. Wilson told Dulles that it was hopeless to try to save Vietnam and further expenditures were a waste of money; and a week later, after another major decision had been taken, Wilson's words, if anyone remembered them – and they seem curiously little known – would have haunted US policy-makers over the next 20 years. The only sensible course, he said, was for the US to get out of Indo-China completely and as soon as possible. The situation there was utterly hopeless and these people should be left to stew in their own juice. There would be nothing but grief in store if we remained.

It was an emotional and prophetic statement and was, of course, contradicted by the logic of the situation as it was seen by others in Washington. On 22 October 1954 in Dulles' absence, the NSC was once again trying to work out how to save Indo-China and, again, policy seemed to be decided by operational necessities. In this case the premise was that time was running out, new and immediate US moves were necessary to break what was called a paralysing impasse and without them the Diem government would collapse.[17] The Operations Co-ordinating Board had already decided on a crash programme, the first stage of a limited training movement to sustain the Diem government and establish security in 'Free Vietnam' but the political implications were enormous. They amounted, as acting Secretary Hoover explained, to a mission of re-orienting the top officers of the Vietnam Army away from Hinh and towards Diem or, in the President's words: 'What we wanted was a Vietnamese force which would support Diem . . . the obvious thing to do was simply to authorise General O'Daniel to use up to X millions of dollars – say 5, 6 or 7 – to produce the maximum number of Vietnamese military units on which Prime Minister Diem could depend to sustain himself in power.'[18]

As a result of this meeting instructions were sent to Saigon that the Ambassador and Chief of MAAG were to collaborate in improving the loyalty and effectiveness of the Free Vietnamese forces in the hope that within a month or so Diem's government would be strong enough to decide on long-range programmes. The postscript, that the State Department would 'undertake to obtain appropriate understanding and means of augmentation', referred to the limit of 342 military personnel which the State Department thought could be on the strength of MAAG without breaching the terms of the Franco-Vietminh cease-fire but which, understandably, even if all of them were engaged in training, the Defense Department reckoned would be quite inadequate to build a new model army in Vietnam. The original condition that the JCS laid down for training the Vietnamese Army which, from their point of view, was absolutely essential, was that there should be a reasonably strong, stable civil government in control. It was hopeless, they said, to expect a US military training mission to achieve success unless the nation concerned was able to perform essential governmental functions effectively.[19] Now the sequence was to be reversed and US military assistance was to be given in order to produce a reasonably strong and stable civil government. Nevertheless, as a more or less formal contract, it could be argued that there were important conditions attached: as President Eisenhower's letter to President Diem revealed when it was released on 25 October. In return for 'an intelligent programme of American aid' given directly to Diem's government it must, in turn, be prepared to give assurances regarding the standards of performance it would be able to maintain and that it would undertake needed reforms. What these reforms were was not specified, but an independent Vietnam endowed with a strong government was expected to be 'so responsive to the nationalist aspirations of its people, so enlightened in purpose and effective in performance that it would be respected both at home and abroad'. At the same time it was to be a strong, viable state, capable of resisting attempted subversion or aggression through military means and although one may wonder, in retrospect, whether a comma may have been intended after 'subversion', if it was not then it may be argued that the US ended up with the state which its blueprint was intended to produce: one which would resist attempted subversion by military means.[20]

In the meantime, even as Eisenhower's letter of support was about to be delivered, the reports from Saigon became more alarming. 'Everyone in Embassy', said Heath, 'convinced that Diem cannot organise and administer strong government'.[21] Diem had hardly left the Presidential Palace where he had been working 18 hours a day; delegating responsibility would be counter to his fanatical sense of personal mission; it was doubtful that he would accept any limitation of his authority and, ultimately, 'We will probably have to use Bao Dai's thread of legitimate authority to compel Diem either to constitute effective government or, if he remains intractable and inept, to resign in favour of some person or persons capable of forming a government strong enough to keep free Vietnam from going Communist.'

THE COLLINS MISSION

Together with what was practically his valedictory a couple of weeks later – 'Diem may not be up to the job . . . a possible successor must be sought' – these reports would seem to confirm that Ambassador Heath had already lost confidence in Diem and, for that reason probably, Washington had lost confidence in Heath. On 3 November General J. Lawton Collins, currently US member of the NATO Standing Group and perhaps Eisenhower's best and most trusted corps commander from the Second World War, received the President's instruction that he was to go to Vietnam 'to assist in stabilising and strengthening the legal government of Vietnam under the premiership of Ngo Dinh Diem.'[22] He was told by Dulles that his chances of success were one in ten but whether these were the odds against better co-ordination of the US effort in Vietnam, improving internal security or engendering more support for Diem, is not clear. Nevertheless, according to Collins' own account: 'I made it clear that the US intended to support the government of Diem and a National Army as long as it was loyal to President Diem.'[23] Loyalty to Diem was obviously a cardinal issue; and, immediately involved in the Diem–Hinh feud, Collins told Hinh that if he attempted a coup it would mean the end of military aid to Vietnam. To which Hinh replied: 'The question was whether Vietnam was better off with Diem and US aid or without Diem and without US aid' but for the moment, and certainly as far as Collins was concerned, this was an academic question. Diem was there to be helped. The only question was how was it to be done. With a great deal of support from General Ely, Collins quickly produced the outline of US military support for the Vietnamese Army. General O'Daniel's MAAG would assume full responsibility for its development and training by January 1955 and it would be fully autonomous by the following July. The French, in effect, would be replaced in a matter of months.

There was, of course, far more to it than that and in General Collins, the US Special Representative in Vietnam, one may see the first of the American pro-consuls. That may equally well be an arguable proposition but his functions, both in his own and in the official account, went far beyond those of the normal ambassador. They were, as he reiterates in his memoirs, used to assist Diem and to strengthen his government, to the point where it could be said that Collins was himself taking on some of the normal functions of government even if, at this time, the result did not yet amount to the creation of a client state. As the US commitment deepened over the next ten years it went through the same progression as that for which the Dutch, ruefully, blamed themselves in their Indonesian policies: 'Let me show you how to do it. Let me help you do it. Let me do it for you.' It would have been for Americans anathema even to think that was what they were doing in Vietnam for the six months that Collins spent there but matters such as land reform, the selection and training of a national civil service, not to mention the creation of a National Assembly, are usually reckoned to be the prerogatives of an independent nation state rather than something to be delivered as part of a seven-point programme from a foreign ambassador, no matter how friendly or how benevolent the intentions.

As far as Diem himself was concerned it was not an unwavering US commitment, as his relations with Collins would show, and by mid-December 1954 it is probably not too far fetched to suggest that, for Collins, Diem represented the type of unsuccessful divisional commander who should be removed (and the sort who Collins had, in fact, removed during the war). The most striking feature, practically from the beginning, is that Diem's hold on power rested on US assent: and that the US should already have been in such a commanding position in Vietnam.

'A SYNTHETIC STRONG MAN'

Before he demitted office, and on an occasion when he was Acting Secretary of State, Bedell Smith identified the relationship, and the problem, quite clearly. Can we, he asked, make a synthetic strong man of Diem? And can we associate with him competent people who may compensate for his deficiencies in administrative abilities and governing capacity?[24] The trouble was that in answering the question Collins was not entirely consistent, allowing himself to be swayed by day-to-day developments, but if there were doubts whether Diem was playing the right tunes at least there was no question who was paying the piper. In the supplement to his report on Vietnam in January 1955 Collins estimated the Vietnam government's tax revenue for the year would be approximately $140 m., almost all of which would go on normal civilian expenditure. The small surplus, plus borrowing, would enable it to spend somewhat less than $70 m. on its military and refugee programme and the balance of almost $330 m. would have to be met by the US.[25]

DIEM ON THE ROCKS

Obviously, therefore, the government of South Vietnam was quite unable to meet the financial commitments of the political and economic programmes that were being devised for it; and in the absence of continuing French support it was at least in danger of becoming a minority shareholder in a joint-stock US–Vietnamese enterprise. Practically as soon as Diem's government took office it was recognized in Washington that it was incapable of standing on its own feet but as the months went by and, as Collins complained, one excuse for inaction followed another, the forecasts became gloomier and practically reached rock bottom in the National Intelligence Estimate of 23 November 1954. The authority of the South Vietnam state, it said, was nominal; it was 'largely ineffective in meeting vital tasks such as maintaining domestic order, performing the normal functions of civil administration, dealing with the extraordinary problems created by the armistice, and overcoming long-standing problems such as inefficiency and corruption'.[26] In Vietnamese political life expediency had in most cases substituted personal aggrandisement for integrity and devotion to public service. The Vietnamese National Army was described as an instrument of the French High Command, its General Staff was involved in political affairs to the exclusion of adequate internal security and the rest of the army were neglected, insubordinate and irresponsible.

Faced with this remarkably pessimistic and accurate forecast it may seem almost incredible that the US, on a reasonable calculation of the odds, could have hoped for successful intervention but there was a glimmer of light. According to the National Intelligence Estimate the Vietminh were unlikely to invade South Vietnam openly before July 1956 (on the assumption that the reunification elections had not been held by then) and as the US had already decided to build a strong anti-communist government in South Vietnam rather than allow one to develop that might seek accommodation with the North, there seemed to be a breathing space for the crash programme that would represent an act of will on America's part. The logical progression was something like this. The French, as the NIE recognized, held the key to political power in South Vietnam. The French were not reliable (because they sought accommodation with the North). Therefore the US must choose between the French solution, which would lead to a communist Vietnam; or replace them as the effective power in the South. As a crude approximation, get rid of the French, pour in dollars and 'expertise', and you might end up with an instant nation. After all, Diem, like Syngman Rhee in South Korea, was patriotic, anti-communist and, in Diem's case, seemed to deserve US support in mucking out the Augean stables.

He also represented a more rational and familiar style of government, at least by comparison with the garish anomalies of the religious sects and their mixture of mysticism and corruption, not to mention the Binh Xuyen gangsters and their even more shameful control of the national police that was sanctioned by Emperor Bao Dai for their mutual enrichment.

On existing trends, admittedly, South Vietnam would be lost but, paradoxically, the situation was so bad as to call for a policy of boldness. Whether or not the US could reverse the trend that, one way or another, would lose Vietnam, and in spite of some initial uncertainties and lack of commitment to Diem, when Mendès France came to Washington in November 1954 Dulles told him that Diem was 'our last and only hope'. Like Senator Mansfield, Dulles seemed to believe that there was no alternative to Diem and in spite of the possibility that Dulles was using Mansfield as a stalking horse for Administration policies what this meant was that neither was prepared to consider anyone else. It was an argument that the French had used to the point of exhaustion about Bao Dai and now, ironically, Collins would support the idea that Bao Dai, or some sort of 'imperial delegate', might have to replace Diem. The possibility that Prince Buu Loc, Bao Dai's cousin, a distinguished Vietnamese doctor associated in France with Joliot–Curie but, apparently, like him, sympathetic to communism and the Vietminh cause, might, presumably on French initiative, be sent by Bao Dai to replace Diem would have been doubly unacceptable to Dulles who, in any event, was deeply suspicious that the French had made their own deal with the Vietminh. To this day one hears echoes of the assertion that, in order to achieve peace in Indo-China, Mendès France had promised the Russians that the French would abort rather than deliver the European Defence Community and, at the time, French doubts about Diem could thus be dismissed in Washington on account of their probable duplicity. If there was duplicity it may not only have been on one side. When Mendès France had visited Washington in November he and Dulles had taken the unusual step of sending common instructions to French and US representatives in Indo-China, in effect that they should stop competing with each other, and stating categorically: 'It is not the purpose of the US to seek itself to supplant France in the Associated States.'[27] At the same time Dulles knew perfectly well, as he told Deputy Secretary of Defence Anderson, that Collins, with the strong backing of the JCS, was taking the position that, in effect, the French had to be phased out altogether from the standpoint of military forces and training. That, said Dulles, would be difficult to accomplish but perhaps it can be.[28] What worried Dulles was the question of US responsibility if they attempted to replace the French – who would, said Dulles, plaster us with the responsibility all over the world and try and sabotage the result – and the consequence that, if the US failed, 'It will be a tremendous blow to our prestige in that area'. So far, as Dulles said, 'We have been able to say the losses in that area have been French failures' and as he told Collins the same day: 'We do not wish to be saddled with full responsibility for what happens in Vietnam because prospective developments there are very dubious.[29]

There was, however, another facet to responsibility, as General Hinh, one of the 'alternative leaders' told Ambassador Heath when he was recalled to France by Emperor Bao Dai. Those, he said, who intervened to keep Diem in power are responsible for the future of Vietnam.[30] For a period of five or six months until the end of April 1955 US support for Diem rested on a knife edge. Conceivably, if Collins had stuck to his guns or if Dulles and the State Department had been less reluctant to part with Diem, the crisis would have come in early December 1954 when Collins reported that if Diem had not demonstrated by about 1 January 1955 that he was capable of governing, America and France would have to consider alternatives.[31] A week later Collins provided another gloomy forecast but he asked the State Department not to consider alternatives until he had communicated his 'final judgement'. In the meantime the Vietnamese Ambassador in Washington was trying hard to pull US policy in a different direction, putting most of the blame for Vietnamese government failures on the French, and asking why French commitments in Vietnam should be prolonged. Why not, he asked, in a naive but pointed question, replace advances from the French Treasury by advances direct from the US Treasury since in reality both came from the same US source? With a mixture of flattery and persuasion he sought to convince the US that it only needed to give aid, it did not need to fight, and that only America could save Vietnam: 'All the difficulties and defeats suffered in Vietnam stemmed from the fact that America tried to let someone else carry out a task which she alone could accomplish.'

The somewhat ostentatious way in which the State Department deferred to Senator Mansfield at this time, eliciting from him the opinion that Collins' ultimatum was 'political dynamite' and that the US should hold Vietnam as long as possible, even if it would cost a lot, suggests that they might have been succumbing to the temptation to regard themselves as the only people who could in fact save Vietnam and, furthermore, that Dulles had already gone firm on Diem. When Dulles came to Paris just before Christmas 1954 there might have been a last chance to establish a common Western policy towards Vietnam but he made no mention of Collins' inauspicious despatches and countered Eden's pessimism by saying that while he recognized Diem's deficiencies he had not heard of any acceptable substitute.[32] In tri-partite discussions on 18 December, however, Ely, who had returned to Paris, said, without apparent rejoinder from Dulles, that both he and Collins 'were virtually convinced that it was hopeless to expect anything of Diem', whom he described as a man in a dream. Rather optimistically Ely had told Radford that if it was established no later than January 1955 'a good strong government in Vietnam could win the elections in 1956' and from this it might seem that a last chance of a working partnership with France to get a more effective government in Vietnam had appeared; but only if the objectives coincided. The French at this stage wanted some sort of election in 1956. The US, and Diem, did not; even if Diem's role was never precisely defined either as an instrument of US policies to frustrate elections or as the sort of figure whose popularity might make it possible to win them.

It was, ultimately, to be an expensive and fateful ambivalence but, having decided, as Dulles put it, that even a slight chance of success was worth considerable investment and having put their money on Diem, the US was now embarked on a course not only that committed it to his government but which also required it to build a nation state that was capable of withstanding communism and the appeal of national reunification. Once they decided to get rid of the French, they would soon be on their own – apart, that is, from whatever support they might have from Diem. Positions were now practically reversed. Ultimately this meant that, for operational purposes, and as far as the US as principal shareholder was concerned, Diem might be dispensable. Diem's position depended therefore as much if not more on what happened in Washington as on what happened in Saigon. The two obviously influenced each other but in this period Diem seemed more secure in the US. Could any successor, asked Dulles in his Christmas Eve appraisal in 1954, make up for Diem's deficiencies without also lacking Diem's virtues? Could the US anticipate a stable process of succession and not worse confusion and weakness than there was already? Whether these were real or rhetorical questions Dulles answered the most important one himself. There was, he said, no successor in sight; and with this sort of predisposition in his favour it would have taken more than average misfortunes in Vietnam to unseat Diem. Another argument in his favour was that if he were replaced it would be seen as a French victory and as something that could lead to a North/South accommodation; and while Dulles would not prove to be entirely impervious to the evidence it is obvious that he was fighting a stubborn rearguard action to hold on to Diem.

A month after his outburst and apparent abandonment of Diem in December 1954 Collins had swung back in his favour – 'the best available Prime Minister to lead Vietnam in its struggle against Communism'[33] – and weeks later presented his assessments to the NSC. From a national army to a national assembly and taking in refugees and resettlement almost everything seemed to be within reach so there was, as Collins said, at least a fifty-fifty chance of saving South Vietnam from the communists. These were sporting odds, much better than a deeper analysis might suggest, but they were good enough to provide another few months in which to deepen US commitments. Collins, personally, did not get close enough to Diem to discuss major political issues, other than to record on one occasion 'his instinctive resistance to any political view contrary to his own'[34] and when Dulles arrived in Saigon on 1 March 1955 for a flying visit he did not get very far either. In a separate meeting with Foreign Minister Tran Van Do: 'The Secretary after an opening exchange of amenities, assured Mr Do of the complete support of the US government for the Diem government and of his satisfaction with the increasing position of strength in which the Diem government found itself.' But even this sort of reassurance which he also gave Diem – Dulles said that the President and he had great stake in him and that Congress and American public opinion had come to accept decisions of US support for Diem and Free Vietnam – did not tempt Diem to budge from a position of total if somewhat veiled intransigence.[35] In particular Diem had resisted Dulles' suggestion that, now that he was secure, he could afford to bring into his government men who might otherwise be his political opponents. Dulles, obviously, was hoping to strengthen Diem's national appeal. Diem, however, was more concerned with confronting his enemies in the Binh Xuyen and Hoa Hao and blamed the French not only for supporting but for encouraging them to move against his government. When the sects formed a nominally united front in March 1955 a government of national union was the object of their ultimatum and while transparently designed to improve their own fortunes it was also supported by the Foreign Minister whom Dulles had assured of total US support only a few days before. To Collins, in Saigon, it appeared that Diem was almost totally isolated and after a spate of resignations including Defence Minister Minh (Diem, characteristically, took over the portfolio himself) Collins reported that Diem was 'operating practically one-man government with his two brothers Luyen and Nhu as principal advisers'.[36] When fighting broke out between the Binh Xuyen and forces loyal to Diem, Collins was inclined to put at least part of the blame for the tension on Diem and was 'gravely disturbed' that he had not been consulted. In any case it was enough to provoke Collins into proposing once again that Diem must go – and suggesting alternatives.[37]

In Washington this seems to have taken both Dulles and Eisenhower by surprise. Collins, said Dulles, was apt to be hasty. While Eisenhower was not keen to have Dulles talk to him about Vietnamese affairs his advice to Collins was to play it by ear and not to give up on Diem 'until it is quite certain' because, as the President repeated, 'We bet pretty heavily on him'.[38] Obviously they were in a quandary. Having sent Collins to Vietnam to see for himself neither Eisenhower nor Dulles now wanted to take his advice. Dulles, in particular, could argue that it would be intolerable to treat Diem as inferior to rebellious sect leaders and was not the only one to think that the French were heavily involved in the affair; that the French were unreliable; and, at least by implication, that Collins was paying too much attention to what they thought. The French, incidentally, thought Diem was on the verge of megalomania, impervious to advice, but if they were right and the US agreed to his removal would this not be seen as a French victory and would not many Vietnamese conclude that the French were still the arbiters of political action in South Vietnam?

This at least was one of the arguments presented to Allen Dulles, Director of the CIA, by an assistant director together with a conclusion that if he was given full US and French backing Diem would be capable of dealing with the Saigon crisis and it was part of an emerging consensus in Washington that Collins was wrong. At the beginning of April 1955 the State Department may for a moment have been in two minds and Collins was certainly authorized to tell Diem that unless he could do better 'we may have to cease US support for Vietnam which would jeopardise not only himself but the whole country'. On the whole it seems to have been rather an empty threat which stands out as an anomaly against a background of support that was being mobilized on Diem's behalf both in Washington and in Saigon. Whether they were practical or moral considerations, the danger in getting rid of Diem, of going from frying pan into fire, or his obvious sense of personal outrage that the Saigon police should be in the hands of the Binh Xuyen who derived their income from gambling and prostitution, Dulles epitomized the State Department in its sympathy for Diem. Whether or not Dulles was drafting the cables himself there was at least a lively sense of Diem's predicament and sense of insecurity. Expressions of Congressional opinion, although limited to a few, were, in the person of Senator Mansfield or Congressman Judd outspoken in support of Diem and in their refusal to consider an alternative. Then there was Colonel Lansdale who, his rank notwithstanding, provided Dulles and the State Department with second opinions and an alternative news service. Lansdale was a genuine if romantic supporter of Diem and obviously in a position, directly or indirectly, to make his opinions known at the highest levels. Thus on an occasion when Dulles travelled to Augusta to brief the President he told him that Lansdale had much more confidence in Diem than Collins had: confidence which, by inference, Dulles appeared to share.[39] During the period of armed truce in Saigon between Diem and the Binh Xuyen another of Diem's US supporters and confidants, the remarkable young Professor Wesley Fishel who, like Lansdale, was now ensconced in Diem's presidential palace, journeyed to Washington to drum up support, notably from Senator Mansfield. Like Lansdale, Fishel blamed the

French and their influence on Collins: none of which may have been immensely significant in itself but taken together would have helped to undermine confidence in Collins' judgement.

Nevertheless Collins was a formidable opponent, both of Diem and of those who believed that he could be saved, and one can only assume that it was his return to Washington which, against the odds, finally persuaded the Administration that in certain circumstances Diem would have to be removed. Until then Dulles, notably, had stood fast in the face of Collins' repeated criticisms of Diem and his intransigence, whether it was changing Collins' 'authorization to acquiesce in plans for Diem's replacement' to 'discretion to acquiesce in the idea of replacement or in the search for "some intermediate solution"'.[40] Now that Collins was in Washington his message was that it would be a major error of judgement to continue to support a man who had demonstrated such a marked inability to understand the problems of Vietnam; that Diem simply could not get along with other capable men; that in five months he had not one original constructive suggestion, idea or plan; that compromise with Diem was impossible; and that other able men were available.

As the admiral who took notes on Collins' debriefing observed, the State Department was reluctant to face the fact that they must admit failure in US policy; and would therefore obviously attempt to retain Diem in some capacity.[41] Ignominious and shameful though it would be, it looked as if they would have to bring Bao Dai into play in order to get rid of Diem even though, almost until the last moment when the decision was taken, Dulles insisted it would be disastrous to destroy the morale and authority of Diem's government before they had any idea what would come next. One reason, perhaps, why Dulles and the State Department were about to change course was that they realized that Bao Dai, almost certainly with French support, was about to dismiss Diem: something that would have had very messy consequences as far as the US was concerned. Even then it was obvious from the first of three cables to Paris on 27 April how grudging was the admission that 'some change in political arrangements in Vietnam may be inevitable' and that until Vietnamese 'nationalist elements evolve another formula warranting continued US assistance and support' the US would continue to support the legal government under Prime Minister Diem. Assuming a managerial function in the second telegram the State Department said that, provided the French accepted certain conditions, Collins and Ely were jointly to inform Diem that, because of his inability to create a broadly based coalition government, and because of Vietnamese resistance to him, their governments were no longer in a position to attempt to prevent his removal from office. Do or Quat were to replace him; and even if, in practice, Collins and Ely would probably have to be the catalysts, every attempt should be made to keep the

Vietnamese label. In short, therefore, and *in extremis,* the US was prepared to take over the government of Vietnam.

A REPRIEVE

At this point, whether out of confidence or desperation, Diem launched his attack on the Binh Xuyen and their control of the Saigon police. Having been told by Collins before he left Saigon that it was unlikely he could be saved and that Bao Dai would probably remove him it seems to have been the obvious thing to do. At least, knowing that he was almost on the scaffold it was worth the chance, more particularly when he had US support at a lower but no less effective level. In the event, with the noose practically round his neck, it was a cable from Lansdale which secured Diem's reprieve and allowed the US to back away from the execution. Lansdale claimed, once the fighting started, that new facts were emerging and while he himself, and presumably the CIA, had been heavily engaged in the bribery and persuasion that was supposed to change the balance of political power in Saigon it was the limited but unmistakable victory of Vietnamese army units over the Binh Xuyen which allowed Diem to emerge as the local hero. The ordeal by battle which Dulles and Eisenhower had half anticipated was over and at the eleventh hour the instructions for Diem's replacement were cancelled. From this point onwards reservations were put on one side. Diem had succeeded. The gangsters had not won, after all, and even if there might be long-term risks for the moment, at least, Diem had saved the day: for himself and, it seemed, for the US as well.

From the non-agreements of Geneva and the promise of non-elections onwards, there had always looked like a connection between Diem as the anti-communist nationalist leader and Diem as the potential instrument of US policies. Now the connection had been fused, the commitment had been made and for the next seven years the Diem family government would represent itself as the epitome of South Vietnam's national interests and America, having allowed Diem to make the bed, would have to lie on it. From the beginning it was a connection which entirely transcended the alliance of one sovereign state with another. In the first place, South Vietnam, as an integral nation state, had still to be created; and while it would have denied the intention, and even the idea might not have occurred to it, the question which arose from the US assumption that the Vietnamese could not be left to themselves, was whether the US had the aptitude and capability for such a neo-colonial enterprise: here defined as the privilege and responsibility of running someone else's country. To begin with, however, and even though the US would be taking over from France, it seemed as if it could be quite a modest exercise: 'a real likelihood that training, technical assistance and moderate aid might be all that was required.' This, at least, was an opinion from the NSC Planning Board – a sort of low-risk, high-return investment – which 'would put us clearly in our traditional role of supporting the independence and legitimate aspirations of peoples'. If, however, the US really was going to be involved with peoples rather than their acknowledged governments, or what might dismissively be termed 'ruling cliques', it could be practically an open-ended commitment. It depended, of course, on what was identified as the need – and who identified it.

ADVISERS AND CRITICS

One of the most influential US advisers in Vietnam in the 'nation-building' exercise and period of the middle and late 1950s was Wolf Ladejinsky who brought comparable experience of land reform in Japan and Taiwan to his appointment as a personal adviser to Diem. Describing US advisers in general Gibbons says their role was central to the US programme: 'they provided access to, influence over and intelligence about Diem and his government that could not have been obtained in any other way.'[42] In the end none of them had enough influence to keep Diem on a course which the US approved but at the beginning it might reasonably have been argued that almost any government would have been overwhelmed by the size of the tasks which some Americans at least had perceived. Ladejinsky, for example, in a detailed and impressively honest account of one of his extended trips through the countryside of South Vietnam at a time when the national government might have been expected to be extending its authority reported on 'the lack of zeal and zest on the part of most officials encountered on this trip'. With few exceptions, he said, chiefs of provinces and district officers are disturbingly unconcerned.

> Even the exceptional official tends to engage in merely verbalising
> the need for the enforcement of the law rather than concentrating
> on what little he could do to gain the confidence of the farmers and
> persuade them to accept the national government as their government.
> The emphasis is on the word 'little', for, in justice to this better type
> of local administrator, he cannot do much until and unless the national
> government does its part in helping create a climate of 'acceptance'.
> The much vaster job of the national government lies beyond successful

trial of arms – it is to demonstrate its appreciation and understanding of the fundamental aspirations of the farmers. Of that there is only the merest beginnings. The people close to the grass roots must shift for themselves as best they know how, and the best is none too good. Unless the situation is radically improved, it will continue to benefit the anti-government forces.[43]

Ladejinsky took his stand on what he called the simple, unadorned truth that in Vietnam the peasant is the centre of the piece.

We cannot afford to forget that much of our economic and non-economic aid to Vietnam stands or falls in the degree to which the great majority of the people share or don't share in it.[47]

Concerned in particular with the peasantry who, he said, were more interested in land ownership than in rent reduction, he asserted that the greatest impediment to progress was the character of the national and local administrations.

This was in 1955. More recently, a study of South Vietnam between 1955 and 1975 – *Foreign aid, war, and economic development* – aggregates the experience of 20 years in its supporting assertion that 'this lack of interest in development by Vietnam's leaders goes far in explaining why it fell so far behind the others'.[48] The others, in this case, were Taiwan, South Korea and Israel and although the situation in Vietnam obviously was different it was taken for granted, says Professor Dacy, that the people would be provided for adequately by US aid. In spite of its prefaced political assertion ('If we learned anything, it was that troops, money, and advice by themselves cannot secure the loyalty of a people to its government and, in excess, abundance may even be counter-productive . . .') this was largely economic analysis after the event but it may be set alongside the experience of one of Diem's erstwhile supporters who was heavily involved with the South Vietnamese cause for many years. A refugee Austrian socialist with bitter memories of the struggle with communists as well as Nazis, Joseph Buttinger had helped in the autumn of 1955 to found the American Friends of Vietnam, an immensely powerful lobby and support group with which 'it is reasonable to assume that the US government was indirectly if not directly involved'.[46] History, says Buttinger, offered Diem a real chance but in the event he was unable to see that Vietnam's national revolution could be completed and the last vestiges of colonialism wiped out only through radical economic and social reform. Exploitation, says Buttinger, the dominant reality of a feudal land régime, was equated by the peasants with landlordism; the landlords, far from being eliminated were in fact more than any other group able to assert their interests under Diem.[47]

In the event, too, Buttinger argues that US aid became a substitute for political support while peasant dissatisfaction became the main theme of communist propaganda in the South and although he sounds at times like a disappointed suitor, and although liberal/socialist aspirations and critique were not widely shared in Republican Washington in the Eisenhower years, protection and support of the infant Vietnam was a cause that attracted all-party support. The future President Kennedy is often cited as an example of these generous feelings and in his speech to the American Friends of Vietnam in June 1956, with much the same rhetoric as his inaugural address, he described Vietnam in terms of US responsibility and determination and as a proving ground of democracy in Asia. If not the actual parents of 'little Vietnam' then, surely, said Kennedy, we are the god-parents.

> This is our offspring – we cannot abandon, we cannot ignore its needs. And if it falls victim to any of the perils that threaten its existence – Communism, political anarchy, poverty and the rest – then the United States, with some justification, will be held responsible; and our prestige in Asia will sink to a new low.[48]

With culminating hyperbole, he offered a non-communist revolution to a nation that was taking its first feeble steps towards the complexities of a republican form of government.

Three months later, if one were to have believed General O'Daniel, now chairman of the American Friends of Vietnam, that revolution had practically succeeded. O'Daniel, who had gone to Vietnam at Diem's invitation, reported to Walter Robertson, Assistant Secretary for Far Eastern Affairs, that 'Free Vietnam' was now entirely pacified and secure and that Diem's government was growing increasingly popular.[49] This was in September 1956, two months after elections might have taken place to re-unite Vietnam. According to what Diem and the US chose to regard as the optional schedule the consultations between the two parties, North and South, were to have taken place by July 1955 and it was an embarrassment to the US when Diem refused even to go through the motions of contacting the North. US strategy had been laid down in May 1955 in the NSC report on All-Vietnam Elections in which US policy was simply to prevent a communist victory. Instead of the Geneva protocol 'Free Vietnam' would have to be strong enough to win a free election limited to its own zone and held under its own auspices and control and US policy was to be directed to this end. By a sort of sleight of pen all the necessary conditions for the free expression of the national will – which at Geneva were supposed to come *after* the elections – were now neatly, reasonably and deceptively transposed to exist *before* all-Vietnam elections could take place. If the Government of Free Vietnam were to 'insist in the first instance on adequate guarantees of freedom, elections and adequate supervisory powers in a Supervisory Commission (eminently sensible but a revision of the Final Declaration nevertheless) it was fairly obvious, considering that the conditions included freedom of speech, press and radio, that there would have been enough excuses to invalidate elections in the North many times over.[50]

In the meantime elections, of a sort, had been held in South Vietnam which helped to compound the illusion, for those who wished to see it, that Diem's government was based on popular support. Dulles, for example, told Eisenhower that the elections had been 'healthy' but the first exercise had taken place in October 1955 when, after hurling anathemas at each other like rival Popes, Diem finally got rid of Bao Dai in a stage-managed referendum which produced the highly gratifying result of a 98.2 per cent vote in favour of the Emperor's deposition. In March 1956 elections for a constituent assembly produced a massive majority of members who were expected to support the government (more than 100 out of 123) with only three who could be said to be in genuine opposition. Although press censorship had been lifted temporarily during the election campaign publication of news or comment favouring 'communist or anti-national' activities were punishable by up to five years' imprisonment; ironically, the freedom of speech, press and radio which was demanded of the North was little more in evidence in the South. Indeed, aggregating the experience of elections in 1956, 1959 and 1961, one of the Michigan State University advisers, Robert Scigliano, wrote, shortly before Diem's death,

> even if elections were completely free in Vietnam, they would be ineffective channels of democratic expression. The control by the government of all political party life, of the press, of the Trade Union movement, and of most other organised activities make serious electoral competition a most difficult task.[51]

He concluded that for practical purposes South Vietnam had become a one-party state.

One may assume that in 1955 this had not been the result that was intended by the US. Rather, the purpose had been to rescue the people of South Vietnam from the clutches of a totalitarian state; that, as in Western Europe, they should be maintained as part of the free world; that there was an identity of basic interests, or at least congruence, between them and the US. If the last was not self-evident then it should and would become clear to them and as the US government had identified their country as of critical strategic importance, it, in turn, was prepared to make a major investment in order to accelerate South Vietnam's economic development and, if necessary, to help in remaking South Vietnamese society. With so many apparently similar or comparable examples to choose from, the preservation of the Philippines, military intervention in Korea, land reform in Taiwan – or Japan, as perhaps the greatest success of all – not to mention minor coups such as Iran or Guatemala,

South Vietnam in 1955 did not look like one of America's larger or more pressing problems. Retrospectively at least it could have been argued that five years of commitment and Cold War since 1950, while it might have been expensive, had in fact achieved more than half the territorial objective with the loss of hardly a single American life; with the departure of a dilettante emperor – and that of the French under way – there would, other things being equal, have been good reason to hope for a favourable outcome. Thus, the National Intelligence Estimate of July 1956 was able to offer what it called a moderately hopeful outlook for South Vietnam and good overall prospects for internal security. It was assumed that the South Vietnamese Army would probably be able to pacify and extend government authority into any areas of existing communist influence. Diem's 'success' in bypassing the July 1956 election date without evoking large-scale communist military reaction was given as the reason why many Vietnamese would be reassured and encouraged to co-operate with government programmes to expose and root out communists. This, in turn, was attributed to two factors. First, because the USSR had failed to press DRV demands that the UK and the USSR, as co-chairmen, should reopen the Geneva Conference, it was assumed that the Geneva Conference powers had tacitly accepted the partition of Vietnam for an indefinite period.[52] Second, because it assumed that the DRV was firmly committed to the Sino-Soviet bloc 'even to the extent of subordinating or postponing the pursuit of its local or regional objectives in the interests of overall bloc tactics and strategy'. As long as these factors obtained South Vietnam seemed reasonably safe and could get on with its own separate development and although the situation contained many elements of instability, progress would continue to depend on firm US support.

SOUTH VIETNAM AS AN AMERICAN DEPENDENCY

The firmness of US support, in fact, meant the difference between success and failure in Diem's retention of power; and although they should not be plucked from their context, remarks and questions such as 'We are concerned with lack of progress in agrarian reform' or 'In our long-range planning in Vietnam what should be the political targets in terms of political parties and political movements?' suggest something that bordered on corporate interest and managerial concern. In two out of three of its state functions, the economy and defence, South Vietnam was to be a case study in the practice (in advance of the theory) of dependency. Between 1955 and 1960 the US contributed, on average, 58 per cent of the South Vietnamese budget.[53] The French war had already cost the US about $2½ billion in what was primarily military expenditure. Now it was to start spending almost as much per annum in economic assistance alone using techniques such as the Commodity Import Program and counterpart funds which derived from the Marshall Plan and had helped to keep Western Europe alive after the war. South Vietnam was, however, becoming much more of a dependency, second only to South Korea among non-European beneficiaries, to the point where the entire cost of the military part of the South Vietnamese budget, which was itself half the total budget, was paid for by the US. By 1961 one of Diem's former tax advisers declared that after six years of large-scale US aid, Vietnam was becoming a permanent mendicant[54]; another of Diem's advisers says it was apparent that only the financing of the armed forces had succeeded (industrialization was unnaturally slow while consumer goods that were being imported stayed in the towns, whose middle-class tastes were being catered for) so that, regrettably, the US aid programmes must be reckoned to have failed[55]; and an economist 'simply speculates' that the availability of massive aid presented the Vietnamese government with little incentive to face up to their internal economic problem.[56] In effect, according to this last evaluation, the government used foreign aid to buy the support of the population – it was the easiest way to 'pacify' – but a further criticism is that at the same time as aid perpetuated Diem's dependence on the US 'it helped him towards independence of the people he was governing by making it less necessary to tax them'.[57] No doubt Vietnamese farmers in particular did not complain but it was one fewer point of contact between government and the people they were supposed to be governing. In practice nearly all tax revenue came from imports; another contribution which the US made to South Vietnam's economy.

Far and away the greatest contribution which the US made to the preservation of the Diem government was in equipping, training and paying for the Vietnamese Army. General O'Daniel and MAAG assumed responsibility for the organization and training of the South Vietnamese Army in February 1955 and straight away set about forming the divisions that were to be deployed in the event of a conventional invasion from the North. As US policy was directed to the prevention of all-Vietnam elections in 1956, perhaps it was only prudent to anticipate a violent reaction when the prospect of reunification was obliterated but by preparing for the major premise of invasion it neglected the minor premise of subversion and, eventually, armed insurrection. From the official history of the US Army in Vietnam it would seem that O'Daniel's successor as MAAG chief bears a heavy responsibility for turning the army of South Vietnam into the sort of force that might have done reasonably well if the Korean War had been refought in Vietnam but which was going to be of very little use, at least to begin with, in dealing with incipient revolution. General Williams, in spite of his appreciation of discipline in the US Army, was less successful with the Vietnamese; to the point where it may be argued that the RVN Army's reputation as oppressors rather than defenders of the people was the critical difference between it and the Vietminh. While he was not unaware of the guerrilla problem – communist guerrillas, he said, had been destroyed in Greece, Korea the Philippines and Iran and they could be destroyed in Vietnam, too – he did not seem to have the faintest idea about counter-insurgency or how to begin. The British concept of the army in support of civil power may have been too restricted and too sophisticated but Williams' plans called for aggressive action, seizing the initiative and applying relentless pressure: all of which may, in his experience, have worked in Korea but was the antithesis of successful counter-insurgency.[58]

Apparently obsessed with the importance of divisional training and field exercises Williams succeeded in creating an army of seven regular divisions, each with its own artillery battalions, which was a fair replica of US – or Korean – formations but which could hardly have been less appropriate to the situation they were soon to face. Apart from the fact that Williams, like many generals, did not like and did not understand small units and small wars, his command function with the American Military Assistance Advisory Group was largely independent of the structure of Vietnamese government: to the point where it was Williams, with or without the Ambassador, who told Diem what sort of army he needed – and what sort of army he was going to get. When it became evident that an insurrection was beginning the sort of army Diem had got was largely irrelevant to the task it faced and for all the assumptions that Diem simply wanted the Civil Guard and Self Defence Corps as his private auxiliary armies there are some recorded meetings which suggest that it may have been Diem rather than his US advisers, civil or military, who had the better, perhaps instinctive, sense of what security in the villages really meant.[59] Not that US civil and military ideas always coincided and apart from shouting matches between Williams and Ambassador Durbrow the co-ordination of US policy in Vietnam was made more difficult by the fact that it was being made by half a dozen agencies, including the US Embassy, each of which was doing its own thing. Ultimately President Eisenhower himself was responsible for the overall direction of policy but at a lower level the Operations Co-ordinating Board of the National Security Council was supposed to put the act together. Spector says its studies were vague and general – but in practice General Williams seemed every bit as important as Ambassadors Reinhardt or Durbrow, especially because of his access to and practically unwavering support of Diem.

Differences between the civil and the military approaches to Diem, or what might be called the Diem problem, were not that much in evidence in Saigon as long as US estimates agreed that he was doing well and as 1956, a year that seemed to catch both North Vietnam and Diem's opponents in the South by surprise, was almost a year of triumph, the differences were marginal. Everyone agreed that Diem needed help and no one appeared to challenge Admiral Radford's verdict (a propos the possibility that he was acting as his own Defence Minister) that, if this was so, his grasp of the problem was defective and would not be corrected unless it was through the medium of US advice. Like a great deal of US advice – well-meaning and much of it impeccable – it simply assumed that the US knew best or, at the very least, had far more experience over the whole range of government activities and institutions, from land reform and logistics to constitutions, police forces and propaganda. The trouble with Diem, however, was that while he enjoyed US support he was not amenable to US advice which impinged on the prerogatives he associated with a style of government that was somewhere between that of the mandarin and the paranoiac. Personally approving passport applications or four- and five-hour monologues could be described as idiosyncratic and his solicitude for his rather vicious family might have looked like misplaced loyalty but the political forms of, at best, the corporate state which may have seemed to be degenerating into one of the more obsessive tyrannies was probably only reaching its natural level. Described by supporters or friendly critics as 'democratic one-man rule' or 'patriarchy', others, in delineating his regime, used analogies with Divine Right and the Inquisition or else cited descriptions of 'Hitlerian gangsterism'. One of the characteristic political forms of the régime was the *Can Lao,* the Revolutionary Personalist Workers Party, a sort of sinister freemasonry, which, using the same cellular pattern as the communists, combined political support and political surveillance. It helped to create what has been called an anti-communist 'people's democracy' where, even if it did produce only a small number of 'verified unjudicial executions' nevertheless relied on detention without trial to the extent that, in the culminating crisis of the Eisenhower years, a civilian US adviser in Vietnam was reporting privately that the number of political arrests had risen to approximately 5,000 a month.

In a new state under threat, if not under siege, it was hardly surprising that it should pay so much attention to internal security. As long as it was self-sustaining it could, within limits, do as it pleased but the problem with and for Diem's increasingly despotic government was that it was not, that it had to rely on the US, and that it depended eventually upon its approval. For the US it raised a question whether a divided country in Vietnam's precarious position could afford a greater measure of representative government than that which the Diem régime was willing to permit. And whether, in US opinion, that was enough. Doubts about Diem and his resistance to US advice (significantly, perhaps, after the danger of non-election consequences had passed) began to surface in Washington towards the end of 1956 even in the minds of those like Kenneth Young, Director of South-East Asian Affairs in the State Department, who had been his most devoted supporters. But the response from the Saigon Embassy was that little could be done: the problem had existed since Diem, indeed it *was* Diem, 'and will', said Ambassador Reinhardt, 'likely be with us for some time'. It was also going to get worse. Having succeeded in inviting himself to Washington in 1957 Diem was preceded by his brother Nhu who made courtesy calls on Dulles and Eisenhower (the Acting Secretary of State reminded Eisenhower that Vietnam 'is our newest and one of our staunchest friends in Asia and we have great reason to be satisfied with President Diem's performance') and when he discussed more economic assistance for Vietnam he was assured by the Director of the International Co-operation Administration of the great admiration for such a fine man as Prime Minister Diem and of their pride in helping him to accomplish so much.[60] Not long after this Diem heard similar sentiments from Eisenhower directly and even more extravagant praise from Senator Mansfield 'for the man whom the Vietnamese admire and trust, a man in whom the US has unbounded confidence and great faith'. The saviour, in fact, of all Southeast Asia.[61]

Even allowing for US relief that the election deadline of 1956 had passed off quietly, the danger with commendations such as this was that Diem and his family would start to take them seriously. The US may have been indispensable to them but they, after all, were indispensable to the US. By the beginning of 1958, however, as the documentation of 'Divided Councils Amid Growing Insurgency' reveals,[62] the early doubts about Diem's worth were beginning to take root. From the US Consul in Hué there was an account of the beatings and torture that accompanied a communist denunciation campaign run by another of Diem's brothers, Ngo Dinh Can, and Can's instructions to tone things down so as not to upset the US; in May there was open, if temporary, disagreement between Defense and State Department representatives on the Operations Co-ordinating Board. Diem, the State Department insisted, had been heavy-handed over internal security and the authoritarian tendency was dangerous because it was creating opposition. Defense disagreed. *Their* reports were different; they preferred 'stern' to 'heavy handed'; in any case everyone agreed that because of America's substantial and successful investment in Vietnam further determined efforts would be justified. Like 'independence' under the French, political stability, economic progress and popular support were all being perfected.

'ADVERSE TRENDS'

In 1960, under the impact of an attempted coup in Saigon, all these
hopeful assumptions were shaken. As in the 1955 crisis, but after five
years' experience, Americans were still divided between those whose
advice was to loosen up and those who said batten down. Again,
the man on the spot, Ambassador Durbrow, was losing patience –
'all these resentments could only be met by assuring Diem that we
will back him at all times, under all circumstances and forever. This
we cannot do' – and once again Lansdale, from his position in the
Pentagon, was trying to play the role of king-maker, or at least grey
eminence, denouncing Durbrow and suggesting reasons to quash most
of his recommendations.[63]

By then, however, mounting concern in Washington as well
as Saigon showed itself in a Special National Intelligence Estimate
(23 August 1960) which said that the past six months indicated a
trend 'adverse to the stability and effectiveness of President Diem's
government . . . . These adverse trends are not irreversible, but if
they remain unchecked they will almost certainly in time cause the
collapse of Diem's regime.' The larger fear was that Hanoi had
probably been encouraged to take stronger action and behind Hanoi,
'supported and guided by the Chinese Communists', the CIA and its
associates discerned a probable Chinese objective of weakening the
American position in Southeast Asia at little cost or risk'.[64] Vietnam,
therefore, was again coming to the forefront of US considerations,
this time as an international problem, because, although it was still
only dimly perceived, the US was deeply if not irretrievably involved
in a revolution.

The genesis of that revolution, however, may still be regarded as
one of the most controversial origins of the Vietnam War. When the
authors of the Pentagon Papers sought the origins of the insurgency
– and by implication the origins of US involvement in the war – they
produced four principal questions:

1. Was the breakdown of the peace of 1954 the fault of the US,
   or of the ambiguities and loopholes of the Geneva Accords?
2. Was the insurgency in essence an indigenous rebellion against
   Ngo Dinh Diem's oppressive government, transformed by the
   intervention of first the US, and then the DRV?
3. Was it, rather, instigated, controlled and supported from its inception
   by Hanoi?
4. When did the US become aware of the Vietcong threat to South
   Vietnam's internal security, and did it attempt to counter it
   with its aid?

They decided, at that time at least, that they could provide no conclusive answers:

> Tentative answers are possible, and form a continuum: by 1956, peace in Vietnam was plainly less dependent upon the Geneva Settlement than upon the power relationships in South-East Asia – principally upon the role the US elected to play in unfolding events. In 1957 and 1958, a structured rebellion against the government and Ngo Dinh Diem began. While the North Vietnamese played an ill-defined part, most of those who took up arms were South Vietnamese, and the causes for which they fought were by no means contrived in North Vietnam. In 1958 and 1960, Hanoi's involvement in the developing strife became evident. Not until 1960, however, did the US perceive that Diem was in serious danger of being overthrown and devised a Counter-insurgency Plan.[65]

EMERGENCE OF THE NLF

Perhaps more questions, across the political spectrum, are in order. Was the National Liberation Front the response to Diem's repressive state? Was theirs the only course to take? Were peasants alienated by the lack of land reform? Did thousands of villages find it intolerable that their councils should now have appointed rather than elected heads? Was the Vietnamese Army trained to fight the wrong enemy (external rather than internal) and was that why they never managed to play a more positive role when the insurgency began? Was the resettlement programme so mismanaged as to create enemies rather than supporters of the government? Was the battle, in fact, lost before it began? On almost all these questions there is conflicting evidence but the fundamental question is whether the government of South Vietnam created its own insurrection by policies that were both vicious and inept. That is to say, did it eventually succeed in destroying itself? The answer: conceivably, although in the absence of the NLF it would probably have needed more time. Alternatively, in that time the Government of South Vietnam might have reformed or else destroyed its political opponents: either of which in the post-war perspective of divided nations would have helped its status as a sovereign state. Diem's régime, like scores of other repressive governments, would not necessarily have generated enough discontent among the organized but decimated groups and individuals who participated in the political system to have produced effective opposition. The pressure may have been there – and the occasional flashpoints – but for all the dislike and fear of his political methods there was no mobilizing factor or catalyst that was able or allowed to produce a democratic alternative. There was a communist party and apparatus that was for the time being dormant; when it either chose or was forced to reassert itself it found, rather as it had in the inter-war years, that the legal government had effectively disposed of its nationalist opponents and, in so doing, had practically cleared the field for its own team. To put it another way, in its determination to produce an antiseptic régime Diem and his US supporters had effectively destroyed the antibodies, too.

In the event it was touch and go whether the Communist Party in the south would survive; the fact that it emerged in December 1960 as the major constituent of the National Liberation Front conceals not only remarkable vicissitudes and hesitation but also what seems to have been a very close-run race. When the first Vietnam War ended in July 1954 probably well over 100,000 Vietminh soldiers and civilians went north. Of the Vietminh supporters and Party members who remained – some 50–60,000 – most were civilians who, by the agreed terms at Geneva, were entitled to amnesty in respect of their former association with the Vietminh and their resistance activities. What would happen to them, and what they would do, depended on what happened to the Geneva Agreements and how they were understood and this provided the first set of anomalies. Although most of the Vietminh fighting forces were regrouped in the north the greater part of their civilian support, indispensable for the guerrilla, remained in the south. Many of them were under the impression elections would be held in 1956 but in the meantime they were effectively at the mercy of the Diem government and whatever support would be forthcoming from the International Control Commission. Conversely, the Diem government knew that it could hardly rely on the support of the Communist Party and its adherents, even if some of them were initially impressed by Diem's patriotism and were waiting to see how he would turn out and what his government would do; and although General William's advice, that they should be exterminated like vermin, had yet to come there was the immediate and mutual problem of whether a Communist Party with what were ultimately revolutionary objectives could be reconciled with the purposes and existence of a non-Communist state.

If elections were going to take place in 1956 it was obviously only a temporary problem but in another sense, too, the problem might have been solved if the division was in fact to be perpetuated. Much would, equally obviously, depend on whether a credible and effective government emerged in the South but in the meantime, with the transfer of communist authority to the North, Ho and the Party were preparing for all eventualities. The most obvious, and the one that was ultimately most feared by those who stayed in the South, was the Stalinist option of socialism in one country. The signs that this was what was going to happen were there to be seen – and heard – from the middle of 1955 onwards when, in spite of sympathy for the South and the attempts to be even-handed – 'simultaneously to pay adequate regard to South Vietnam' – the Party Central Committee left no doubt that in order to win the struggle it was first necessary to consolidate the North.[66] As long as there was a chance that the reunification of Vietnam might be put to electoral choice in 1956 – and for quite some time it seems that the Party were expecting that the French would be able to insist that this happened – or that Diem's government would collapse or at least have to turn itself into a coalition, the strengthening of the new socialist fatherland was understandable[67]. When none of these events seemed likely, and the North was preoccupied with its own problems, it is equally understandable that many of the southern Party felt they had been abandoned if not betrayed.

Whether or not, as Pike argues, 'perhaps from the very start, unification passed from mere Party policy to holy crusade, from goal to obsession'[68], the Party in the North did not give way to romantic and Trotskyite visions of general revolution in 1954. Instead, by way of demonstrating their orthodoxy and their prominent position among the recipients of Soviet-bloc aid – Fall reckons that up to 1961, in terms of strictly economic aid, the North received about as much *per capita* as the South did from the US[69] – the Party invoked 'two important judgements' of the Twentieth Party Congress of the CPSU to strengthen its own position. First, that all existing world conflicts could be resolved by means of peaceful negotiations. Second, that the revolutionary movement in many countries could develop peacefully. Again, however, task number one was 'Firmly Consolidate the North' and although there might have been some ambiguity about the second task 'Strongly push the Southern Revolution Movement' and in spite of subsequent attempts to alter the incidence of advice, as Kahin has recently pointed out, nowhere in the document was there any reference to political struggle being supported by military activity.[70] The document in question was the first major analysis of the 'Southern problem' that was apparently prepared by Le Duan, later to be Secretary General of the Party and one of Kissinger's principal negotiating adversaries, entitled 'The Path of Revolution in the South'. Nevertheless, one might have at least inferred from it that the struggle had by no means been called off – 'There is no other path but Revolution' – but that would depend on what one meant by revolution and how it was to be achieved.

By 1956 it was becoming clear that if Christ and the Vietminh had gone South, Marx and Mao Tze Dong had gone in the opposite direction and there was, for many in the Party, the feeling that they had been left to get on with it even if one day, somehow, they might be rescued when things went wrong. For some, too, the revolutionary struggle had lost its intensity now that the French had gone and the South as well as the North had become independent but those who remained with and in support of the Party discovered that with their armed forces regrouped in the North they had lost their shield as well as their sword. Under orders to concentrate on the political campaign, first for reunification elections and then, when that had manifestly failed, to rebuild what was left of the Party machine 'The Path of Revolution in the South' was a message of hope but also an injunction to steer clear of premature propulsion. After the event, regional and provincial committees criticized the Party, or themselves, for 'rightist tendencies' and 'legalistic reformism' but if the figures which a senior and most articulate committee member (who subsequently defected) gave for his province are even only approximately correct for South Vietnam as a whole – 50 per cent of the Party cells smashed by the summer of 1955 and 90 per cent by the summer of 1956 – they were lucky that there were enough of them left for self-criticism or anything else.[71]

In spite of the Party's virtual annihilation in the South at the hands of an implacable government the situation was not without hope. Race, for example, has argued that of the province of Long An in 1956 it could not be said that *anyone* controlled it, politically or militarily. During the French war the Vietminh had succeeded in overthrowing the power of the local élite 'which the French had employed to carry out the functions of the central government in the countryside'; but even though the exiled village councils had returned in 1954 'the daily sight on village roads of those who had killed landlords' was a powerful reminder that the day of the village notables had gone forever.[72] Eventually, the vacuum of power in the villages would have to be filled. The peasant farmer of the South, left to himself, may have been unpromising material for a Communist revolution – believing, like Lenin, that the peasant was the greatest bourgeois of all, Party cadres were told never to mention collectivisation – but resentment, as long as it smouldered, could presumably be fanned into fire in the right circumstances and with enough time. Time, however, did not seem necessarily to be on the Party's side in spite of its assertions of inevitable victory. In 1956, in the North, it had encountered massive opposition which turned into revolt when its collectivization plans were revealed in Nghe-An province (coinciding with Suez and the Hungarian Revolution it was not widely reported or commented on at the time) and with its organization in the South very nearly in ruins, and in spite of the fortitude that was officially demanded, the Party went over to a limited offensive in 1957. Race describes it as a transitional year for the Party's armed forces in the South. Fall declared that in early 1957 the Second Indo-China War began by deliberate Communist design. Whether it did or not it was scarcely recognizable as such at the time but the activity to which both refer was the Party's campaign for 'the extermination of traitors'.

As Race's respondent explained, 'traitor' allowed for flexible definitions. In general it meant anyone who worked for the government, honest hamlet chiefs rather than corrupt ones, teachers who understood politics, were 'pure nationalists' or who might have become anti-Communist leaders. On one interpretation it might seem then that the revolution, if not the war, had now begun. By the end of the year several hundred government officials had been assassinated but still the signal had not been given, because of caution or uncertainty, to begin the armed struggle. Aware of the mounting pressure in the South to start, the Party in the North did its best to dampen the enthusiasm but even after another year had passed, while it was agonizing over 'rightist' and 'leftist' deviations, the message was still 'not yet'.[73] It was a message and a decision, or, rather, a postponed decision, which probably needs to be explained but even the decision to go, when it was taken by the Central Committee in January 1959, is still open to different explanations. Was it because the North was preoccupied with its own problems? Was it because the USSR was insisting that nothing should be done to rock the boat of peaceful co-existence? It is likely, says Race, that both factors entered into the Party's deliberations but in his interviews with Southern cadres neither of them was mentioned as an explanation for Hanoi's wish to postpone the phase of armed struggle. Instead, and although it may seem at first sight a metaphysical concept for professional revolutionaries, they believed that 'ripeness is all'.

> How does one create a 'ripe situation'? That is the purpose of political struggle. During that period Diem's terrorist policy was becoming more blatant day by day, and the alienation of the people from the government was becoming greater and greater. Thus the Party pushed the struggle movement, which increased the terrorism. But the more the people were terrorised, the more they reacted in opposition, yet the more they reacted, the more violently they were terrorised. Continue this until the situation is truly ripe, and it will explode, according to a saying of Mao Tse-tung: 'a fire-fly can set a whole field ablaze'. Yet for a fire-fly to set a whole field ablaze the fields must be extremely dry. 'To make the field dry' in this situation meant that we had to make the people suffer, suffer until they could no longer endure it. Only then would they carry out the Party's armed policy. That is why the Party waited till it did.[74]

DECISION IN HANOI

They had been waiting, that is, until indiscriminate repression in the South had become intolerable and in the meantime had been doing their best to help it in this direction. It had been touch and go because, at the same time, the Party and its supporters were being wiped out. There was a widespread belief that the cadres had suffered very heavy casualties – those who were killed as well as those who were in prison – and so it seems that apart from death, capture or surrender, the Party finally had no option but to activate its comparatively small armed units in the South, to begin sending Southerners back from the North and, in short, to start the armed struggle. These decisions were taken in January by the Fifteenth Plenum of the Central Committee and even if, subsequently, the operational instructions seemed to have been *sub rosa,* rather than a loud and unmistakable bugle call for all-out attack, there is no doubt that the Party, belatedly but unmistakably, had identified a revolutionary situation and that the decision had been taken in Hanoi.[75] When the Third National Congress of the Vietnamese Workers Party was eventually held in September 1960, after a lapse of almost ten years, the new policy was approved but even then it was not presented as armed struggle as such: rather a move from lower to higher and from legal to illegal forms of struggle.[76]

Internationally, it seems there may be two explanations for this *sotto voce* approach to revolution. The first was to avoid getting out of step with the world Communist movement. Even though the Chinese were pressing the Russians hard at this time to adopt a more revolutionary line, it needed another couple of months and presumably successful lobbying before the Moscow Conference of Communist and Workers Parties gave its cautious approval for continuing the revolutionary struggle against colonialism with, as Clausewitz might have put it, the admixture of other means. The second possibility was that the Party was preparing itself, and had now to persuade the people, to take on the US.

Whether war, in the case of South Vietnam, *was* the appropriate form of struggle for Vietnamese communists, was also subject to another qualification. A few days before the Geneva Conference and the first Vietnam War ended in July 1954, when he was preparing the Party for what he assured them was *not* partition but a temporary measure leading to reunification, Ho had told the Central Committee: 'US imperialism is the main enemy of world peace. Consequently we must concentrate our forces against it.' It was, at the time, an astonishingly prescient remark but over the next five years almost everything that happened in the South seemed to confirm what Ho had said. In part, perhaps, it was ultimately a self-fulfilling prophecy but it was not until 1960, when the National Liberation Front was created, that Ho, Hanoi, North Vietnam and the Party in the North as well as in the South were prepared to meet the challenge of the US.

REFERENCES AND NOTES

1.   W. E. Mosse, *The Rise & Fall of the Crimean System* (London 1963), p. 6.

2. Ibid. p. 201.
3. Ibid. p. 200.
4. My apologies to Dr Bruce Waller of Swansea, Dr Alasdair Stewart of Aberdeen and my former teacher, the late Professor W. N. Medlicott, in the likely event that I have misunderstood – or at least misapplied – the concept of 'bündnisfähig'!
5. Canadian delegation to ICSC Hanoi, to Secretary of State, Ext. Affairs, Ottawa. 14 February 1955, Sherwood Lett Papers, Department of External Affairs Library, Ottawa.
6. Western allegations were that the People's Army received enough military equipment to increase the number of their divisions from 12 to 20.
7. John W. Holmes, 'Geneva 1954', *International Journal,* 1967, Vol. XXII.
8. D. R. SarDesai, *Indian Foreign Policy in Cambodia, Laos and Vietnam, 1947–1964* (Berkeley 1968), p. 105.
9. *FRUS,* 1952–4, Vol. XIII, Indochina, p. 1889.
10. *FRUS,* Vol. XIII, pp. 1905–14.
11. 'Even if a stable government could be established, we estimate that the national elections scheduled for 1956 would almost certainly give the Vietminh control of South-Vietnam.' Subsequently amended 'If the Vietminh does not prejudice its political prospects.'
12. There is some argument about how much was spontaneous and how much was undertaken for political effect. The irrepressible and roving CIA agent, Colonel Lansdale, the model for Graham Greene's 'Quiet American', may or may not have been responsible for the slogan 'Christ and the Virgin Mary are going South'. It certainly seems to have his hallmark. Years later when he was working at the Pentagon he apparently sought to convince Cuban Catholics that Castro had lost God's confidence: 'Cuba was to be flooded with rumours that the Second Coming was imminent, Christ had picked Cuba for his arrival, and that He wanted the Cubans to get rid of Castro first. Then, on the night foretold, a US submarine would surface off the coast of Cuba and litter the sky with star shells, which would convince the Cubans that The Hour Was At Hand.' Thomas Powers, *The Man Who Kept the Secrets,* Pocket Books (New York 1981), p. 176.
13. *FRUS* 1952–4, Vol. XII, East Asia and the Pacific, p. 774.
14. Ibid. p. 730.
15. Lacouture and Devillers are cited in W. C. Gibbons, *The US Government and the Vietnam War* (Washington 1984), p. 264.
16. Ibid. p. 2122.
17. Ibid. p. 2159.
18. Ibid. p. 2154.
19. Ibid. p. 1938, (12 Aug).
20. The text of Eisenhower's letter (undated) which was delivered on 23 Oct. is given in *FRUS,* Vol. XIII, pp. 2166–7.
21. *FRUS,* Vol. XIII, p. 2151, (22 Oct.).
22. Op. cit. pp. 2205–6.
23. *Lightning Joe. An Autobiography* (New York 1979).
24. *FRUS,* Vol. XIII, p. 2085, (28 Sep. 1954).

25. *US-Vietnam Relations,* Book 10, p. 875 (not printed in *FRUS*).
26. *FRUS,* Vol. XIII, p. 2288.
27. Ibid. p. 2274, (20 Nov.).
28. Ibid. p. 2270, (19 Nov.).
29. Ibid. p. 2271.
30. Ibid. p. 2239.
31. Ibid. p. 2341, (6 Dec.).
32. Ibid. p. 2385, (16 Dec.).
33. *FRUS,* 1955–7, Vol. I, Vietnam, p. 53.
34. Ibid. p. 91.
35. Ibid. p. 102.
36. Ibid. p. 169.
37. Ibid. p. 170 (31 March 1955).
38. Ibid. p. 175–6 (1 April).
39. Ibid. p. 250 (16 April).
40. Ibid. p. 237 (11 April).
41. Ibid, p. 287.
42. Gibbons, op. cit. p. 311.
43. Louis J. Walinsky (ed.) *Agrarian Reform as Unfinished Business: The Selected Papers of Wolf Ladejinsky* (New York 1977), p. 244.
44. Op. cit. p. 267.
45. Douglas C. Dacy, op. cit. (Cambridge 1986).
46. Gibbons, op. cit. p. 301.
47. Accounts of the American Friends of Vietnam, and sundry ramifications, are given in Robert Scheer and Warren Hinckle 'The Vietnam Lobby', *Ramparts,* July 1965 and Robert Scheer, *How the United States Got Involved in Vietnam,* Center for the Study of Democratic Institutions, Santa Barbara, California, 1965.
48. Gibbons, op. cit. p. 304.
49. *FRUS,* 1955–7, Vol. I, Vietnam, p. 739.
50. Ibid. p. 412.
51. Robert Scigliano, *South Vietnam: Nation Under Stress* (Boston 1963), p. 91.
52. *United States – Vietnam Relations 1945–1967,* Book 10, p. 1080. When Gromyko and Lord Reading, as co-chairmen, met in London in May 1956 Britain committed itself publicly, and for the first time, to free nationwide elections for the re-establishment of the national unity of Vietnam and to the validity of the Final Declaration. Afterwards, the Foreign Office said that it had been 'the unavoidable price of Russian support for the cease-fire'. See Short, 'British Policy in South-East Asia: the Eisenhower Era' in Warren Cohen (ed.) *International Relations of East Asia in the Eisenhower Era* (New York 1989).
53. Dacy, op. cit. p. 225.
54. Professor Milton C. Taylor quoted in Fall, *The Two Vietnams* (London 1963), p. 290.
55. Dennis J. Duncanson, *Government and Revolution in Vietnam* (London 1968), p. 287.
56. Dacy, op. cit. p. 237.
57. Duncanson, op. cit. p. 285.
58. *FRUS,* 1955–7, p. 609.
59. One document which stands out (at least in my memory, having seen

it years ago in the US Army Center for Military History in Washington) is the memorandum of a conversation between Diem, Ambassador Reinhardt and Generals O'Daniel and Williams in November 1955. Diem wanted village defence units averaging ten men each for an estimated 6,000 villages. Williams asked why they had to be put on the government pay-roll. Diem replied that the villages were too poor to do otherwise and that they were needed 'to provide a strong nucleus around which to build morale and the will to self-defence in the villages'. The French, said Diem, had supported local defence units made up of local people who knew the community in which they lived and they had in fact been a more effective anti-communist instrument than the army itself. But they had been dissolved after Geneva. The document is now reprinted in *FRUS* 1955–7, Vol. I, pp. 582–4.

60.   *FRUS*, 1955–7, Vol. I, p. 773. In another conversation, in the State Department, Nhu seemed to be on the outer edge of reality. He had a secret plan which, within a few months, would provoke a massive exodus of up to 2 m. refugees from the North to the South (op. cit. p. 774). This was easily matched in its obsessional qualities by Diem. 'He, the President himself, frequently had to edit, to correct, to rewrite orders of service which had been prepared by lesser officials. This was true of almost every form he could think of, and he had himself created new forms for the civil servants because they did not seem to have any judgement of their own. His ministers did not know how to get the facts and he had to teach them. He had given them all the responsibility and all the authority they needed. He had delegated, and delegated, and delegated, but they had proved unworthy of the delegation of authority and responsibility time and again, and this was why he felt constrained to step into the breach which existed and bring order out of the chaos'. Op. cit. pp. 835–6.

61.   Gibbons, op. cit. pp. 332–3. In addition to a New York ticker-tape parade Diem was met at the airport by President Eisenhower, spoke to a joint session of Congress and to the National Press Club, was fêted in New York by the American Friends of Vietnam, attended a reception at the Council On Foreign Relations, had breakfast with Cardinal Spellman, and was given a private luncheon by John D. Rockefeller III.

62.   I am much indebted to Dr David W. Mabon, Office of the Historian, Department of State, for a copy of his paper with this title. As I am, also, to Dr Edward C. Keefer of the same Office for his paper 'The United States and the Consolidation of the Diem Government, 1955–1957'. They, of course, are not responsible for my selection and evaluation of the data.

63.   With his ad-man's adjectives Lansdale recommended 'thoughtful planning' on just how to introduce a National Assembly to a 'healthy, constructive role' and wanted Eisenhower to provide Diem with another endorsement. *FRUS*, 1958–60, Vol. I, Vietnam, p. 383. On another occasion, in August 1960, Lansdale, with a lot of insinuation, suggested that opposition to Diem was exaggerated if not actually produced by the communist enemy, questioned Embassy reporting and while he thought, on the whole, they had done rather well, hoped that the army and police in Vietnam 'will act in warm friendship with the

people'. Painting a rather idyllic picture of Diem's 'agrovilles' and grand resettlement programme Lansdale concluded with gratuitous and inimitable advice to the incoming chief of MAAG. 'Finally, I would like to pass along an operating rule which I have used personally as my 'passport' throughout Asia: remember to smile in a friendly way. It will make Asians want to do things your way. There is a responsiveness to a friendly smile in Asia which is a unique and wonderful thing – and you deserve this rich experience!' Altogether Lansdale seems to provide enough of the naivete and bland but sometimes sinister optimism to account for Graham Greene's portrait.

64. *FRUS,* 1958–60, Vol. I, Vietnam, pp. 536–41.
65. *Pentagon Papers* (Gravel) I, p. 242.
66. Gareth Porter, *Vietnam: The Definitive Documentation of Human Decisions* (London 1979), Vol. II, p. 8.
67. There is contrasting evidence about the Party's expectation of reunification elections. Higher-level Party cadres were apparently certain that general elections would never take place: although this was not discussed at lower levels so as to maintain morale. Jeffrey Race, *War Comes to Long An* (Berkeley 1972), p. 34. Carlyle Thayer says that in September 1954 the Political Bureau, on the other hand, expected that the terms of the Agreements would be honoured by the French and that unification would take place as planned. 'Southern Vietnamese revolutionary organisations and the Vietnam Workers Party: Continuity and Change, 1954–1974' 'In Joseph A. Zasloff and MacAlister Brown, *Communism in Indochina* (Lexington, Mass.), 1975. On 17 July 1955 Sherwood Lett, Head of the Canadian component of the International Control Commission recorded in his diary this conversation with Pham Van Dong: 'We are Communists. That is a fact. But I tell you that we will have elections for the unification of Vietnam. They will be free elections and we will give all the guarantees asked for, and those guarantees will be carried out. The form of election is immaterial to us as long as they are free and we will guarantee that they are free.'
68. Douglas Pike, *History of Vietnamese Communism, 1925–1976* (Stanford 1978), p. 115.
69. He also cites Tibor Mende's opinion that the Communist world was making a deliberate effort to transform North Vietnam into a show window for all of Southeast Asia: preparing for the day when the doors would be open to allow people of the area to marvel at the progress made by North Vietnam on the magic carpet of Communism. Bernard Fall, *The Two Vietnams* (London 1963), p. 178.
70. George McT. Kahin, *Intervention* (New York 1987), pp. 466–7.
71. Race, op. cit. pp. 375–362.
72. Race, op. cit. p. 40.
73. See, for example, Porter, op. cit. Vol. II, p. 36.
74. Race, op. cit. p. 112.
75. There are some interesting, and not altogether misleading, comparisons that may be made with the beginning of the communist insurrection in Malaya in 1948. See, for example, Short, *The Communist Insurrection in Malaya 1948–1960* (London 1975).
76. William J. Duiker, *The Communist Road to Power in Vietnam* (Boulder, Colorado), 1982, p. 193.

Chapter 6

KENNEDY'S FRONTIER: WARS OF NATIONAL LIBERATION: 1961–1963

LAOS

Among the many possibilities to be considered in the origins of the second Vietnam war is that it did not begin in either North or South Vietnam, but in Laos.[1] Whether it really wanted to or not, the US, like North Vietnam, was nevertheless prepared in 1960 to meet what it considered to be a major challenge: to the extent that it had allowed itself to become involved in a civil war which, in turn, at the end of the year brought the USSR into Southeast Asia. All of this took place, not in Vietnam, but in the neighbouring Kingdom of Laos, which at Geneva, in 1954, had been given the unlikely and unwanted role of shock absorber between China and Thailand.[2] It was, as Eden said, essential that the US should not attempt to establish a military influence there, for any attempt to do so was bound to provoke some counter move by China. At the same time it was obvious, not least to the US, that Laos had played an important and, in the prologue to the battle of Dien Bien Phu, even a critical part in the first Indo-China war and the fate of South Vietnam could no more be settled in isolation from Laos than it could from North Vietnam.

As in Vietnam, so in Laos, its peoples had fought with and against the French but, unlike Vietnam, and in spite of hopeful but rather preposterous claims that theirs was the only lawful government of Laos, the resistance forces of *Pathet Lao* were never, either in military strength or political support, in the same class as the Vietminh. Nevertheless they did have a regional foundation in the northern provinces of Phong Saly and Sam Neua which was recognized at Geneva in 1954; and after they in turn recognized the authority of the Royal Government in November 1954 it took another three years of negotiation, punctuated by sporadic skirmishes, government changes and incipient foreign intervention before authority in fact was transferred to the King of Laos in November 1957. On the following day, Prince Souvannaphouma formed his Government of National Union and included in it, as Minister of Planning and Reconstruction, his half-brother, Prince Souphanouvong, leader of *Pathet Lao*. Complexities such as this, not to mention what often looked like the Ruritanian character of Laotian politics, at one time suggested consideration in comic-opera terms but the unfolding tragedy of Laos, Vietnam and, above all, Cambodia also suggests that the origins of conflict should be sought in totally different comprehension of political purposes and values if not in almost total incomprehension of unfamiliar people and society.

Whether or not neutrality was possible Laos found itself in the same unhappy position as the island of Melos, as described by Thucydides, which wished only to maintain its neutrality in the war between Athens and Sparta. As the Melians were told when, in this classic account of *realpolitik*, they appealed to justice, that was something that was only to be found between parties who were equal in strength. Laos, with some 2½ m. people, was, as it had been historically, largely unable to deal with powerful and predatory neighbours and was now quite unequal to the power of those countries who thought of it as an extension of their own foreign policies rather than as an entity in itself: the US and North Vietnam. For the US it was convenient to pretend, to begin with, that Laos was an integrated nation state and it was expected to behave as such. But at best it was a nation state in the making and, whether or not neutrality would have worked, politics in Laos were never allowed to find their own level. Instead, from the US, it received reproduction furniture in the form of an army, support for a political grouping and controlled elections; massive and debauching economic aid; and the foreign policy role it was quite unable to fill. From the communist world it seemed at first sight to have received something more appropriate: an emphasis on national democratic revolution which looked as if it might be more useful in the Laotian context.

Thus *Pathet Lao*, the former army of the resistance, turned itself into *Neo Lao Hak Xat* (Lao Patriotic Front), a political party which, when, with its allied 'peace' party it challenged the existing but fragmented political parties in the 'supplementary' elections of 1958, won 13 out of 21 seats and Prince Souphanouvong got more votes than any other candidate. On one reading, 13 out of the 21 seats contested, it was a sensational result. As a proportion of the total seats in the assembly, 13 out of 59, it looked less impressive and less alarming. It depended on the inferences. The first, optimistic possibility, was that it was a genuine reformist vote, aimed at the corruption of the administrators and reflecting the alienation of the hill tribes.[3] The second, more sinister, was that in spite of his personal popularity and whether or not he could be said to be a communist, Prince Souphanouvong was the front man for a much smaller, hard-core communist party which took its orders from and relied heavily upon the Communist Party in North Vietnam. On the first interpretation, and if one may assume that the US was moving away from its objections to neutralism in principle, it might have taken a more relaxed and benevolent attitude towards an exercise in nation-building. On the second, and with its self-conscious and self-proclaimed fears of coalition with communist parties, whether in China or Czechoslovakia, it might have been expected to oppose these developments and, even, on the evidence and in the mood of 1958, to intervene.

Laos may have been incomparable but there were, at least in US perceptions, some striking resemblances with the Lebanon and, on the larger scale, between the problems of nationalism and communism in the Middle East and Southeast Asia. In both cases, at least on the evidence of Eisenhower's memoirs, it was a problem of communism and how to contain it. In 1957 Eisenhower had apparently come close to intervention in the Lebanon when President Chamoun appealed for help in dealing with pan-Arab agitation from Jordan.[4] In 1958, when Chamoun had provoked Muslim riots by attempting to amend the constitution so as to extend his term of office, his 'uneasiness', according to Eisenhower, was the result of 'one more communist provocation'. 'Behind everything', says Eisenhower, 'was our deep-seated conviction that the Communists were principally responsible for the trouble, and that President Chamoun was motivated only by a strong feeling of patriotism.'[5]

Whether Eisenhower's real fear was of radical Arab nationalism, rather than communism (much more obvious in the case of Britain's parallel intervention in Jordan) it was enough for him to send marine battalions on to the beaches of Beirut in an act of perhaps symbolic intervention. Their purpose, according to Eisenhower, was to encourage the Lebanese government in defence of its sovereignty and integrity which were deemed vital to the US national interest as well as to world peace; or, as he told the American people, it was essential to the welfare of the US.[6] The integrity of Lebanon was something that could, perhaps, have been taken for granted (in retrospect, the last 30 years suggest a different assessment) but the sovereign integrity of Laos and its preservation was another convenient argument for intervention in one form or another. Writing in his memoirs of King Saud's usefulness at this time as a potential bulwark against Communist expansion in the Middle East Eisenhower noted that, temporarily at least, it was at an end. In Laos, on the other hand, it seems as if Prince Souvannaphouma's usefulness had never begun. If it had, it disappeared at the moment when he took off on a visit to Peking and Hanoi in 1956[7] and agreement in 1957 for neutralization and coalition so infuriated Dulles, who, according to

George Ball, 'thought coalitions with Communists a halfway house to perdition', that:

> He made use of his own family ties by persuading his brother, CIA Chief, Allen W. Dulles, to force out Prince Souphanouvong and replace him with a politician bearing the more unlikely name of Phoui Sananikone.[8]

'Prince Souphanouvong' is, presumably, a mistaken reference to his half-brother, Prince Souvannaphouma. Ball has some fun with Laotian names in what he describes as 'a preposterous long-running serial' and his outspoken and invaluable memoirs are supplemented by another member of the Kennedy administration, Roger Hilsman, who says that on two occasions the US used its economic hold on Laos as a weapon 'to bring down the government of one Lao leader and to break the will of another'.[9] Whether the suspension of aid on this occasion was for political reasons, or whether it was a belated attempt to curb the rampant corruption in its distribution, there is little doubt both in general and particular that the clandestine activities of the CIA at this time had become a part of US foreign policy in general as well as in Laos. As a third of Kennedy's associates aver, two of the most senior members of the Board of Consultants on Foreign Intelligence Activities which Eisenhower himself had set up could discover no reliable system of control and reached the point where they begged Eisenhower once more to reconsider 'programs which found us involved overtly in the internal affairs of practically every country to which we have access'.[10]

Perhaps nowhere at this time was the US more heavily involved than in Laos although it was certainly not the CIA alone which was having such an impact on Laotian politics. Dulles and the State Department had called for an army of 25,000 men. The Defense Department demurred but when, eventually and illicitly, it became involved in training the Laotian army, and when the army turned to politics, the Americans inevitably had their favourites. The army as a whole could have been described as a foreign mercenary force in so far as it was paid for entirely by the US and, incidentally, was in aggregate the highest-paid army in Asia. Not that all the money reached the troops but in this respect, as with the overwhelming economic assistance, accounting procedures for a long time did not seem to matter too much. When, eventually, some sort of control was introduced so that, for example, TV sets were no longer imported for a country which had no television broadcasting, the Laotian economy had reached unbelievable dimensions.[11] In part, it was inflation in its various forms – the devaluation of money, swollen numbers in the army and in the bureaucracy – and the associated corruption which produced an extra-parliamentary reaction to the existing political élites. Before long the Committee For The Defense Of The National Interest, with its increasingly important army component, could be seen not only as a major influence in Laotian politics but as a major instrument of US policy as well.[12] Practically from the start it seems the CIA was involved. According to Hilsman, the CIA believed that sooner or later Laos would become a major battleground in a military sense between East and West and their programmes, which they conceived and pushed through in Washington, were based on this assumption. Commenting on their approach Hilsman says:

It was a policy, in a word, that had the weaknesses as well as the strengths of Allen Dulles' notion of fighting Communist fire with fire. In the first place, any organisation with the professed aims of the CDNI would be a natural magnet for political opportunists in any country, for men whose only principle would be their own driving ambitions. In the second place, there was a profound difference between an organisation espousing the goals of patriotism that is spontaneous and totally native and an organisation, which, while espousing such goals, still derived its impetus and its subsistence from interests, that are, inescapably, foreign.[13]

Under Souvannaphouma's successor, and a CDNI Foreign Minister, Laotian politics began to polarize and its foreign policy became that of 'co-existence with the Free World only'. One of two *Pathet Lao* battalions awaiting 'integration' was surrounded and disarmed; the other escaped. Prince Souphanouvong and *Pathet Lao* leaders were arrested as accomplices; they, too, escaped. A Nationalist China consulate opened in Vientiane, to the obvious anger of Peking. Skirmishes resumed between the Laotian Army and *Pathet Lao* forces and at the end of the year, after claims of massive intervention from North Vietnam, the arrival of a UN team and Secretary-General Hammarskjöld himself, the government admitted rather sheepishly that while their claims might not have been true they were designed to call attention to Laotian problems. They were, however, enough to step up US participation in the organization and training of the Laotian Army and in August 1960, after the CIA, with or without the Embassy's approval, had helped to rig an election, attention again focused on Laos when a diminutive paratroop captain, Kong Lé, staged a coup with his battalion in favour of Prince Souvannaphouma. Retrospectively, at least, Eisenhower described his motives as 'obscure' but had little doubt that Souvannaphouma was either an accomplice or a captive of Kong Lé who, himself, was an accomplice of the Communist *Pathet Lao*.[14] Closer observers, such as Hugh Toye, took a different view. It was a coup in favour of neutrality and against civil war. Kong Lé and his men knew from experience that there were no foreign communist invaders in Laos but on both sides foreigners were promoting the war between Laotians. Personally, Kong Lé liked Americans (there were ten of them attached to his battalion) but of course they were the foreigners on the one side as the Vietminh were on the other, and while their wish to help Laos was appreciated, they must not be allowed to fight their own battles in Laotian blood as the price of their aid.[15] Whether this amounted to any more than 'sincere nationalism', 'naive isolationism' or whatever, the US soon stepped up aid to their principal protégée, Souvannaphouma's rival, General Phoumi Nosavan, who had formed his own counter-coup committee and had taken up his position in the southern part of the country. From here, helped by a Thai blockade of his opponents as well as by US aid and advice, he eventually advanced upon the administrative capital, Vientiane.

A solution to the Laotian problem now seemed to be in the making. Having closed off what it regarded as unacceptable political options – Souvannaphouma, neutralism, national reconciliation – US purposes in Laos depended upon the military outcome with the overwhelming odds on the army which it paid for and the general it supported. If its opponents could be eliminated Laotian politics might again turn on a Lao–Thai axis and the link between northern Laos and North Vietnam would be broken, although the distance between Hanoi and the *Pathet Lao* stronghold of Sam Neua was only 120 miles. Even without intervention from North Vietnam, and making allowance for the fact that *Pathet Lao* would have found it difficult to survive without North Vietnamese support, it had been as difficult for the US to steer a course through the shoals of Laotian politics as it would have been to send a US battleship or indeed any kind of ship up the Mekong; the country simply did not lend itself to such adventures. Nevertheless, when the battle for Vientiane began in mid-December 1960 the odds were still very much on General Phoumi Nosavan's US-backed forces who, but for one miscalculation, might have won the day and put a military régime in power. A fusion between Kong Lé's forces and those of *Pathet Lao* might have been anticipated but when the Russians arrived in Vientiane that, one might say, was something else. Up to the moment when their planes started landing at Vientiane Russian intervention, while it may have been unthinkable, was quite logical. No petrol or food could cross the Mekong because of the Thai blockade. The US refused to help. Souvannaphouma turned to the USSR. As far as US calculations were concerned one must assume that the Russian airlift was both inadvertent and unexpected even though it might be regarded as a climax to Khrushchev's boisterous session at the UN that autumn when he was alternately praising Cuba and demanding colonial freedom and even if he made no mention at all of Laos. Conversely, when Eisenhower and Kennedy met just before Kennedy's inauguration in January 1961, Laos headed the list of foreign policy problems and the new US administration had to decide what to do about a civil war in which, no matter on how small a scale, it was already involved as one of the principal contestants.

If it did nothing else Soviet intervention in Laos suggested the need for American restraint unless they were prepared to challenge the USSR and to do in Laos what they were not, or not yet, prepared to do in Cuba. Even allowing for Khrushchev's adventurism it is unlikely that the USSR would have been prepared to withdraw there and then from a commitment that they had only just made even though this was itself a challenge to the US premise that *their* clients alone should control Laos. In Eisenhower's opinion the issue of communist control of Indo-China was so important as to justify, in the last resort, unilateral US intervention.[16] The question for Kennedy was whether Laos could conceivably be such a serious issue in itself even if it could soon be regarded as exemplar, catalyst and major influence in the formation of a new US foreign policy.

The atmosphere of excitement, the promise of major departures in foreign policy and the idea that the US stood on the threshold of a new age were all suggested or contained in Kennedy's inaugural address. It was devoted entirely to foreign affairs and, with its renewed sense of manifest destiny and its unlimited commitment to the survival and success of liberty, it was an unmistakable promise – or warning – that the US was about to take off on new and thrilling flights of foreign policy. Where Eisenhower, and Dulles before he died in 1959, had come to represent the old guard – faithful but rather tired and unimaginative defenders of the national interest – Kennedy was a young President and surrounded by many young, successful and supremely confident men who were convinced that they could get things done. It seems quite likely that by their nature and by the nature of the presidential campaign that had just ended they would in any event have given US foreign policy a much bolder profile but at the same time as they had to decide what to do about the physical confrontation with the USSR in Laos they felt they were confronted with a much more formidable ideological challenge and a contest for supreme influence in the under-developed world.

KHRUSHCHEV'S CHALLENGE?

The Moscow Conference of World Communist Parties that was held in November 1960 was, as Khrushchev said, principally concerned with questions of war and peace. In spite of his somewhat erratic behaviour there and the miscarriage of the Khrushchev/Eisenhower summit in Paris in May 1960, when the shooting down of the U-2 may have offered Khrushchev a convenient excuse to go home, it seemed to the Chinese that the Russians, both operationally and dialectically, were getting far too close to the US. In the aftermath of the Paris fiasco Khrushchev had said that he would seek agreement with the President who would be elected in November. To the Chinese, agreement of almost any kind with the US was anathema. What they wanted instead (as G. F. Hudson has argued) 'was an admission that American imperialism was incorrigible and that nothing more than a temporary truce with it was possible'.[17] Operationally, the Moscow Conference may be understood as an argument about *détente*. Ideologically, if not fundamentally, it was about the nature of peaceful co-existence and the inevitability of war with capitalist states and when the Conference was over Khrushchev set about squaring the circle: how to prevent war on the one hand and encourage it on the other. In retrospect, at least, Khrushchev's warning about the dangers of nuclear war may be seen to have been directed principally at the Chinese. A small imperialist war, Khrushchev told Russian party theorists in Moscow on 6 January 1961 in what was afterwards a widely disseminated speech, no matter which of the imperialists began it, might grow into a world thermo-nuclear and rocket war. All peace-loving forces, in the socialist camp and outside, had therefore to be mobilized to prevent aggressive wars; but their attitude to Khrushchev's third category of wars – 'liberation wars and popular risings' – should be entirely different. National liberation wars, of which the armed struggle of the Vietnamese people or the war of the Algerian people were the latest examples, were revolutionary wars and were not only admissible but inevitable. In Algeria it was a liberation war of a people for its independence, even, said Khrushchev, a holy war, which we recognize, we help and we will help. Communists fully supported such just wars and march in the front ranks of the people waging liberation struggles.

Obviously this was an outline of a global policy the significance of which went far beyond Southeast Asia but on the matter of Vietnam it was equivocal or, at least, historical.

> How was it that the US imperialists, while wanting to help the French colonialists in every way, nevertheless decided against direct intervention in the war in Vietnam? They did not intervene because they knew that if they helped France with armed forces Vietnam would get appropriate aid from China, the Soviet Union and other socialist countries, which could lead to a world war. The outcome of the war is known. North Vietnam was victorious.[18]

Khrushchev made no mention at all of South Vietnam but, on the evidence of his understanding of what had happened in the first Vietnam War, the role of the communist countries standing guard against US intervention seemed to apply with particular force to Laos: although that country was not mentioned by name either.

Having found itself locked into the rigidities of 'massive retaliation' and the comparative neglect of conventional forces it was hardly surprising that the new US administration should be looking at new or refurbished styles of warfare but, for all its ambiguities, it was the Khrushchev statement on the 'just wars' of national liberation which they understood as the announcement of a forthcoming communist offensive whose challenge they accepted. All members of his administration were apparently directed by Kennedy to read the Khrushchev speech and to consider what it portended.[19] At about the same time Lansdale's influence had reached its peak and after a visit to Vietnam his memorandum on the situation reached Kennedy.[20] It warned that 1961 was likely to be a fateful year; that the Vietcong were well on their way to winning but the situation could be reversed if it were possible to find an unusual American who, in Lansdale's characteristic prose, could work with 'real skill', 'great sensitivity' and 'a fine sense of the dangerous limits of Vietnamese national security in a time of emergency'. Too many Americans in Saigon, said Lansdale, believed in defeat. Ambassador Durbrow, for example, who was incapable of 'the warm friendships and affection which our close alliance deserves' should be removed immediately and 'if the next American official to talk to Diem would have the good sense to see him as a human being who has been through a lot of hell for years – and not as an opponent to be beaten to his knees – we would start regaining our influence with him in a healthy way'. In Lansdale's opinion Diem was still the only effective president to be seen but it may be significant that for all his approval Lansdale said that Diem would have to be supported until another strong executive could replace him legally. In the meantime he recommended, hopefully, ways in which the US could get the 'oppositionists' together and promote two-party government in South Vietnam.

Optimistic, or even naive, as these ideas and proposals may seem they at least recognized some of the political features of America's problems in South Vietnam. On the operational level, however, US plans for counter-insurgency, by contrast, were concerned to 'prevent the growth and possible final complete military success of VC (Vietcong) military action' while, as they put it, 'awaiting solution of the political "causes"'. This Counter-Insurgency Plan for South Vietnam, generated on the spot, which reached Washington just before President Kennedy took office bore, as the Pentagon Papers writer says, the impress of General McGarr, who had arrived in Vietnam in September 1960 as head of the MAAG (Military Assistance Advisory Group). By this time, even if there was not a clear-cut divergence between 'civilian' and 'military' opinions and solutions the latter tended to assume that the problems were essentially those of co-ordination or command structure. That if there was, as a Special National Intelligence Estimate put it in August 1960, evidence of increasing dissatisfaction with the Diem government this was because of its failure 'to communicate understandably with the population' and it was simply a series of 'psychological' tasks for all Americans in Vietnam (the 'Country Team') to attract the loyalty of the population to the Diem régime, to persuade people that the Saigon government was acting in its interests, and to foster a spirit of national unity and purpose among all elements of Vietnamese society.[21]

These last considerations, somewhat metaphysical and incidental to what, after all, was essentially a military plan were however the ones that were stressed by the President when the Counter-Insurgency Plan was discussed in Washington on 28 January 1961. Kennedy asked whether, in fact, increases in Vietnam's armed forces would allow them to go over to the offensive, which the plan purportedly would do, or 'whether the situation was not basically one of politics and morale'. Lansdale, who had been invited to the meeting, said that a maximum US effort in 1961 could thwart communist plans, enabling South Vietnam with US help to move over onto the offensive in 1962 and, according to a composite source, the Counter-Insurgency Plan was apparently accompanied by a memo which, if the Plan were put into effect, promised that the war could be won in 18 months.[22]

KENNEDY'S COMMITMENT

Kennedy was obviously much impressed by Lansdale although at the meeting on 28 January it appears that he had not yet read Lansdale's report. According to Walt Rostow, another admirer of Lansdale, he persuaded the President to read it, in full, on 2 February and on Kennedy's suggestion it was later published as an unattributed article in the Saturday Evening Post under the title 'The Report The President Wanted Published'. When it appeared it was, in a way, a rationalization of a decision that had already been taken. In spite of Ambassador Durbrow's reservations – which he withheld in view of the growing threat presented by the Soviet airlift in Laos – on 30 January President Kennedy approved the recommendation in the plan that the Vietnamese Army should be increased by 20,000 men to be paid for, like the increase of over 30,000 men in the Vietnamese Civil Guard, by the US. If it was seen, as the Pentagon Papers observed, as quite a routine action, it may also be regarded as part of the answer to Kennedy's question 'How do we get moving?' However one looks at it, ten days after his inauguration President Kennedy had signalled his commitment to Vietnam and had taken the first step towards the dual climax which, with his death and that of Diem, would find 17,000 US servicemen in Vietnam waiting for a more formal confirmation that another war had begun. Even so, spending another $40 m. to improve the defences of South Vietnam hardly looked like a major commitment in itself. It could be seen as the payment of another premium on the original containment policy which although it might not be entirely suited to new purposes would at least allow time for further enquiries. But the notes of the meeting where the Counter-Insurgency Plan was discussed on 28 January reveal a style of decision making on Vietnam which would characterize the Kennedy administration. The significant input, from Lansdale on this occasion, suggested a critical but manageable problem in terms – high morale, will to win, getting close to the Vietnamese – which must have appealed to Kennedy, as would anything that would persuade the Vietnamese 'to act with vigor and confidence'. Allen Dulles, as CIA Director, offered a non-specific, para-military solution to a para-military problem – build up counter-guerrilla forces first – and Kennedy, anxious to get moving, wanted to turn guerrillas loose in North Vietnam.[23] In all four contemporary crisis areas – Vietnam and Laos, Cuba and the Congo – we must, said the President, be better off in three months than we are now.

Of the four crises it was, arguably, Laos alone which would show any improvement over the next three months or so when a cease-fire was announced on 3 May 1961: but that was only after the US had been on the brink of massive military intervention and, having backed away, was itself prepared to change course. In Vietnam the problems were familiar, intractable, and open to no different assessment in Dean Rusk's State Department then they had been to his immediate, Republican, predecessors. Rusk, on the whole, was not an assertive Secretary of State. Some commentators, Sorensen for example, have suggested that Kennedy would have welcomed bolder, more explicit and more imaginative alternatives to Pentagon plans. At times Rusk 'seemed almost too eager to disprove charges of State Department softness by accepting Department of Defense toughness'.[24] Ultimately, and particularly under Johnson and in spite of Rusk's experience, this may have been so but in the early months of the Kennedy administration decisions on Vietnam seemed to have a presidential stamp. In any case it has been said that Kennedy was well enough qualified to have been his own Secretary of State and, moreover, had a genuine if somewhat superficial interest in Vietnam.[25] Rusk, too, had a long-standing interest in, as well as wartime experience of, Southeast Asia and although one could hardly distinguish his public position on resistance to Chinese communism from that of Dulles he was a steadfast supporter of collective security and the independence of small states.[26] For him this did not beg the question whether South Vietnam was a legitimate sovereign state or not. He took it as axiomatic that it existed in its own right and, furthermore, that the extension of SEATO'S protection to it, under the American-induced protocol, was itself part of 'the law of the land' for the US. That it might have been a tautology never seems to have occurred to him nor, as the Kennedy administration began to develop its own policy towards Southeast Asia, was there an occasion to stand back and re-appraise the Vietnam connection. Even if its peculiar and perplexing problems did not assume the dimensions of an absolute quandary, one which required the US to take on the role of unmoved mover in Vietnamese affairs, the State Department was not designed to function as a Colonial Office and, lacking such control or central point of contact, the management of Vietnamese affairs was, as it were, to be shared between a number of US government departments and agencies.

By January 1961 the armed struggle in South Vietnam had been going on for more than a year. As it grew in intensity so did the inclination to regard it as some kind of military problem, para-military perhaps, but one where the State Department had no particular expertise on offer. Indeed, in so far as persuasion and acceptability are two of the principal characteristics of the diplomat, the transmission of US policy in South Vietnam now suffered from the unacceptability of its Ambassador to an increasingly beleaguered and paranoid family government. Such was the intensity of US involvement in Vietnamese politics and its interest in a 'successful' outcome that, in the course of an unsuccessful paratroop coup against Diem in November 1960, for a while Ambassador Durbrow appeared as a mediator between Diem and the rebels, although the aftermath may well have been Diem's conviction that there were 'Americans in the Foreign Service who are very close to those who tried to kill him'.[27]

Intentionally or not Lansdale had been advertising himself as the ideal replacement to lead the American Embassy in Saigon if not to orchestrate US civil and military policy in South Vietnam. Whether it was because his unconventional views did not appeal to senior and regular officers or whether the State Department put its foot down, although Durbrow was removed he was replaced by another Foreign Service officer, albeit one with practically no Asian experience, who soon got close enough to Diem to identify with his fortunes if not to induce any visible change of course. However, even though it was not Lansdale in person who went to Saigon to inaugurate a new policy of what amounted, in effect, to 'Be nice to Diem', it sounded remarkably like the Lansdale script from which Ambassador Nolting was working and which had now become official US policy. 'Increasing the confidence of President Diem and his government in the US' was to be the starting point of a new US approach to Vietnam. It was one of the major points of the 'Politics' Annexe to what was described as 'A Program Of Action To Prevent Communist Domination of South Vietnam' which was devised and subsequently redrafted, principally by the State Department, for the Vietnam Task Force. This group, headed by Deputy Secretary of Defense Gilpatric, had been established on 20 April 1961 and given a week to produce its plan. Weighted, by membership, towards Defense, it included Lansdale, Nitze, Rostow as well as Alexis Johnson, the Deputy Under-Secretary of State, and representatives of the CIA and the JCS. Many years later, and knowing how it had all turned out, Gilpatric recorded what he felt was the group's basic lack of understanding of almost everything about the peoples of Indo-China or how the Vietnamese would react to US involvement and plans to make the Vietnamese more effective. 'We were', he said, 'kidding ourselves into thinking that we were making well-informed decisions'.[28]

Well-informed or not, and whether they were as brash and as bold as Gilpatric says they were, it was upon the Task Force's recommendations that US policy to strengthen South Vietnam was based. Not only, however, would the US seek to increase the confidence of President Diem and his government in the US. In the directive of the National Security Action Memorandum (52) of 11 May 1961 the US would also attempt to strengthen Diem's popular support within Vietnam by reappraisal and negotiation under the direction of Ambassador Nolting.[29] The US was therefore unmistakably locked into the internal politics of South Vietnam, as well as to its defence, and even if that was not his official designation, Ambassador Nolting, and his successors, were cast in the role of pro-consul. What this renewed, personal commitment to Diem also meant, the other side of the equation as it were, was that when it did not work, when the government and its people had not been made more effective, he would have to be removed. A situation, one might say, that was indistinguishable from a colonial relationship although not many Americans cared to recognize it as such at the time.

It was a situation that would also have been familiar to the French in their Indo-China war and in South Vietnam it was probably as bad as it had been during most of their struggle which, it will be remembered, had been mainly in the North. In April/May 1961 the Vietnam Task Force estimated there were already 12,000 guerrillas in the South (and the number was increasing rapidly), 650 violent incidents per month, 4,500 casualties (on both sides) in the first three months of the year, and 58 per cent of the country under some degree of communist control. This last figure in particular showed what a daunting task the US faced. Understandably, therefore, many if not most of President Kennedy's advisers throughout his first year urged him to send US forces of some kind to South Vietnam. What were they going to do when they got there? What exactly was the purpose? In the first instance, as the Task Force recommended, they would provide the training for another 12,000 Vietnamese troops. In the second instance, as part of the same plan, and taking their own declaration seriously –

'Come what may, the US intends to win this battle' – they had under consideration the deployment to South Vietnam of two US battle groups to be concentrated in two divisional battle training areas in the high plateau region plus an engineer battalion to build roads and airstrips. But if the situation got worse they suggested the deployment to Tourane (Danang) or Nha Trang of 'a tailored, composite joint task force specifically designed for carrying out a counter-guerrilla civic action/limited war mission.'

In the event this large and open-ended concept was only developed as a contingency plan. The actual deployment of forces was limited to 100 extra men for MAAG and then, a few days later, the President approved proposals for covert action: the dispatch of a 400-man Special Forces team was to be the first open US violation of the Geneva Agreements. That it was such a cautious enlargement of the US commitment, and one which it was thought could be reversed, may be seen in contrast to what were eventually the colossal numbers that were recommended for intervention in Laos but it is something which may first be explained by Kennedy's uncertainty and scepticism arising from another inherited plan of the Eisenhower era.

The US-sponsored invasion of Cuba at the Bay of Pigs in April 1961, for all the subsequent recriminations has been described as that rare event in history, a complete disaster. A modest US investment in the overthrow of communism in Cuba, it was liquidated in less than a week. They bombed on Saturday, landed on Monday, and surrendered on Wednesday. Eleven hundred prisoners of the Cuban Brigade were left on the beaches to face death or ransom. It was the plan which could not fail but it had come spectacularly unstuck. Nevertheless it served as a warning, at least to Kennedy, about the risks of similar adventures. 'All my life', he told Theodore Sorensen, 'I have known better than to depend on the experts. How could I have been so stupid, to let them go ahead?' In Sorensen's analysis, and its obvious implications for Vietnam:

> With hindsight it is clear that what in fact he had approved was diplomatically unwise and militarily doomed from the outset. What he thought he was approving appeared at the time to have diplomatic acceptability and little chance of outright failure. That so great a gap between concept and actuality should exist at so high a level on so dangerous a matter reflected a shocking number of errors in the whole decision-making process – errors which permitted bureaucratic momentum to govern instead of policy leadership.[30]

The immediate lessons to be drawn, however, were in Laos rather than in Vietnam. Again, as in Vietnam, Kennedy's civilian and military advisers – the JCS, Rostow and even Rusk – for different reasons and at different times declared that US troops had to be sent.

The numbers varied. According to Rostow, the State Department was trying to bring a SEATO force into being – the precedent for intervention, incidentally, was to be the Lebanon case – but if that did not work then a modified plan would use about 26,000 troops, something less than half of them American, to 'go in merely to hold certain key centers for diplomatic bargaining purposes'. Not, said Rostow, to conquer the country, although they would shoot if shot at.[31] Quite inadequate, said the JCS. If US troops went into Laos, or even into Thailand, and if North Vietnamese or Chinese troops moved into Laos as well, the US would need 60,000 men, plus air cover, and be prepared to use nuclear weapons against both countries. What the Russians, already involved in Laos, were expected to do in these circumstances and how the Americans, in turn, would respond is more difficult to discern. In fact, there is an almost complete blank in the Congressional Research Service Study but what, drawing as it does on other sources, is evident is, first, that Kennedy was considering a very limited force of four or five battalions to hold Vientiane and other key points and second, that every effort was to be made to get the USSR to agree to a cease-fire and a conference.

A month later after Kennedy had appeared on TV to draw attention to the seriousness of the problem, there was a real crisis in Laos produced, in part, by the rapid retreat of US-backed forces. On 26 April 1961 the US Ambassador in Laos asked for formal authority to call in air strikes against *Pathet Lao* to deprive them of key objectives.[32] The following day, said Robert Kennedy, everyone at a stormy National Security Council meeting was in favour of sending troops to Laos; the viable number, according to the JCS, had shot up to somewhere between 120–140,000 men, authorized to use nuclear weapons and, if there was serious opposition to an American air landing, the Chief of Naval Operations apparently made it perfectly plain that an atomic bomb should be dropped on Hanoi.[33] The crisis, such as it was, in Laos produced something like hysteria in Washington. Apart from Admiral Burke's drastic solution Robert Kennedy said the main question was whether the US would stand up and fight and Assistant Secretary of State Chester Bowles, perhaps the most 'liberal' of Kennedy's foreign policy team, declared that America was going to have to fight China anyway in 2, 3, 5, or 10 years' time and it was just a question of where, when and how (a remark which provided an unexpected opportunity for the belligerent Air Force General Curtis Lemay to suggest an early start. Within two years, he said, and before the Chinese acquired nuclear weapons.)[34]

With all this excitement going on about him Kennedy kept his head. Perhaps, with the Bay of Pigs fiasco only a week old he had more reason than anyone else to question the premises and assumptions of the advice which was being given on Laos; in many cases by the same men who had advised him so badly on the Cuban expedition. President Kennedy for one had drawn a lesson from the Bay of Pigs. 'I don't think there is any question', said Robert Kennedy, 'that if it hadn't been for Cuba, we would have sent troops to Laos. We probably would have had them destroyed.'[35] Instead, in Laos, the US went for a negotiated settlement but in return for its agreement on neutralization the President, according to Schlesinger, promised the national security establishment that he would do something for resistance in South Vietnam.[36] At least by comparison with Laos it looked like a better place for the US to take its stand. In any event, as Kennedy is supposed to have remarked, he couldn't take another defeat that year.

JOHNSON GOES TO VIETNAM

Nevertheless, at least to begin with, the problem of reaching a settlement in Laos served to restrain the US commitment to South Vietnam. On 5 May 1961, for example, Rusk argued that no combat forces could be sent to Vietnam before the Geneva Conference on Laos had begun, but the possibility that the US might have to settle for something that was less than satisfactory in Laos made South Vietnam, Diem in particular, understandably nervous. To a considerable extent it was becoming convenient for the US administration to attribute the insurgency in the South to the instigation of the North; the increasing number of insurgents to arrivals from the North; and to that part of Laos that was controlled by *Pathet Lao* and their North Vietnamese allies the certainty that this was the vital staging area for the North Vietnamese guerrillas who were going south. So far, however, the US had not been able or had not chosen to try to redress the balance of power in Laos and the danger, apparently, throughout Southeast Asia was that 'the public, or, more precisely, the political, reaction to Laos had drastically weakened the ability to maintain any strongly pro-US orientation'. This, at any rate, was the message Vice-President Lyndon Johnson brought back from Vietnam in May 1961.[37] He had been dispatched to increase Diem's confidence in the US and took with him a letter from Kennedy which must have been particularly gratifying. With its expression of great confidence in Vietnam's long-range political and economic future it was an offer of absolutely unconditional US support and one which implied that money was no object 'in our joint effort against the Communists'.[38]

Politically, too, it must have been gratifying for Diem to hear himself described by Johnson as the Winston Churchill of Southeast Asia and even more so had he realized that this was apparently a description suggested by the State Department rather than one of Johnson's flights of fancy.[39] Nevertheless, Johnson, as look-out man, had seen the shoals which lay ahead even though he had no doubt about the course to be followed. Described as his personal conclusion he reported: 'The battle against Communism must be joined in Southeast Asia; the struggle was far from lost; there was no alternative to US leadership; SEATO was not, and probably never would be, the answer.' In short, the time had come to make a basic decision; 'whether to help the countries of Southeast Asia to the best of our ability or throw in the towel and pull back our defences to San Francisco. If it was the latter', said Johnson, 'we would say to the world that we don't live up to our treaties and don't stand by our friends.' For Johnson there was no doubt that Diem was a friend. The country could be saved, if the US moved quickly and wisely, but they had to decide whether to support Diem – or let Vietnam fall. At that stage combat troop involvement was not only not required, it was not desirable. What was wanted, instead, was a fundamental decision: whether the US would meet the challenge of communist expansion in Southeast Asia.[40]

At that stage also one notes the nature of Johnson's commitment: Diem was Vietnam, there was no question of an alternative. To support him would cost another $50 m. in military and economic assistance; but at some point in the future, said Johnson, we may be faced with a further decision of whether to commit major US forces to the area. Johnson's recommendation was for 'a clear-cut and strong program of action' and without, on Johnson's assessment anyway, the necessity of sending US divisions – what he called 'the spectre of combat troop commitment' – it still did not look like an unmanageable affair. Rather, on the Dutch progression, the US had moved from 'Let me show you how to do it' to the next position 'Let me help you do it' although the joint responsibility that was to be assumed obviously required the massive injection of US resources into what they believed to be a nation-building programme. Thus, the economic mission headed by the Stanford economist, Dr Eugene Staley, went far beyond what might be expected of most financial groups. Understandably, considering South Vietnam's problems, its recommendation for 'a short-range economic impact program to strengthen popular support for the government' took priority over the one which, in the long term, was supposed to produce a self-sustaining economy but the report also recommended the establishment of parallel US-Vietnamese committees to improve the execution of military as well as economic programmes.[41]

If it had been possible to bolster South Vietnam economically and militarily, which meant at least that economic and military programmes would have been co-ordinated between South Vietnam and the US and the probability of a significant input of US political ideas as well, it is arguable that, by blunting the spearhead of guerrilla attacks and checking the erosion of government support in the villages, a commitment of substantial US forces could have been avoided. In so far as America's problems were with Diem and his government, as much as with the National Liberation Front, there were, however, few signs of progress. Diem claimed, characteristically, and by way of reply to Kennedy, that he had already anticipated reform. What he needed was more men and more money and, in the meantime, in response to Kennedy's suggestion that he should mend his fences with Cambodia, there was, he said, nothing to be gained from dealing with Sihanouk who was committed intellectually and morally to communism.[42]

A few days before Diem sent his reply to Kennedy, Kennedy was finding out for himself in Vienna what communism was itself committed to, or, at least, what points of contact and friction there were between him and Khrushchev. From all accounts it was a bruising encounter for Kennedy, with Khrushchev very much on the attack and leaving Kennedy in no doubt about USSR support for wars of national liberation.[43] For all that, it seems that Khrushchev had professed no great interest in Laos so that, in a remarkable joint statement, Kennedy and Khrushchev reaffirmed their support for a neutral and independent Laos under a government chosen by the Laotians themselves. In Geneva, where a 14-nation conference on Laos had begun, it was obvious from the beginning that the main confrontation was not between the US and the USSR but between the US and China (who, amongst other things, was demanding that SEATO be wound up) and with neither communist country showing that much interest in Vietnam it seemed as if the US might deal with the problems in the South without risking the sort of direct confrontation that had occured in Laos. That is, unless they chose to do so or unless the implications of their resistance *per se* to communist-supported wars of national liberation led them to consider an attack on what they presumed to be its source.

At the beginning of October 1961 a Special National Intelligence Estimate (October 5) put the number of armed, full-time Viet Cong in South Vietnam at about 16,000: an increase, despite substantial combat losses, of 12,000 since April 1960 and of 4,000 in the previous three months. Of the total strength, they reckoned that between 10 and 20 per cent consisted of cadres infiltrated from North Vietnam, mostly via mountain trails through southern Laos, and that most of them were drawn from the 90,000 or so Vietminh from southern and central Vietnam who had gone to the North after 1954. The Estimate was focused on what it called 'Bloc support' for the Communist effort against the government of Vietnam and although it assumed that most of the arms and equipment being used by the Viet Cong were of US and French origin it assumed further that the ability of the Viet Cong to maintain its expanded effort would to a large extent depend upon improved logistical support from outside. This was one of two critical premises. The other was that when the dry season began in November the Viet Cong would attempt to create a second 'liberated area' in the plateau region adjacent to Southern Laos (the first had been established for years in the Ca Mau peninsula at the southern tip of Vietnam) and that this would enable them to keep government forces divided and prevent their concentration against either guerrilla area.

Within the South perhaps the most ominous and obvious sign of guerrilla strength was their ability (when they chose to do so) to concentrate units of 500–1,000 men, and more, for attacks on government positions but concentrations of that size are tempting targets for regular forces particularly when they have the advantages of mobility and massive fire-power. In a sense this sort of reaction can be thought of as counter-insurgency and the opportunity which it might offer to US forces coincided with the apparent but growing necessity for 'saving' South Vietnam. It was also a matter of coincidence between the President's principal military and civilian advisers. The former, embodied first in the Joint Chiefs of Staff, were, however, about to propose a scheme of allied military intervention, a modified SEATO Plan 5, which would have had almost as many Commonwealth (4,400) as US (5,000) troops in a total force of more than 22,000. The primary purpose would be to allow South Vietnamese forces to conduct offensive operations elsewhere while the Field Force commander would also be free to join in operations to interdict the infiltration of men and materials from North Vietnam. Realistically, perhaps, it envisaged the possibility of a massive Chinese reaction in which case, as they put it, 'there would be issues whether to attack selected targets in South China with conventional weapons and whether to initiate use of nuclear weapons against targets in direct support of Chinese operations in Laos'. In this event also the SEATO force would have to increase to 278,000 men and would require a call up of appropriate forces to maintain the US strategic reserve.[44]

This, obviously, was Johnson's 'spectre' of US ground force deployment but the following day, 10 October, a rather more modest plan 'Concept For Intervention In Vietnam' was prepared which would have deployed a ground combat force of 11,000 men although it was conceded that 40,000 might eventually be needed to 'clean up the Viet Cong threat'. The difference between this plan and the somewhat apocalyptic proposals of the JCS was that it was an attempt to combine civil and military ideas and represented, in addition to the JCS and the State Department, another significant influence on US Vietnam policy: the White House staff in the persons of Dr Walt Rostow and General Maxwell Taylor. Part of what was described as a 'mini–State Department' their intention may not have been deliberately to by-pass the State Department itself but to the extent that the State Department proper was preoccupied with matters other than Vietnam, notably the crisis over the Berlin Wall, they made a major contribution to thinking about Vietnam, and, in Rostow's case, to the dissemination of ideas about counter-insurgency in general.[45]

It was not surprising therefore that, as the plans and the problems proliferated, Kennedy should have decided to send Taylor and Rostow to Vietnam to report on the feasibility of committing US forces. For one thing, the Vietnamese at this stage may have wanted them: although they might only have been an alternative to the alarming request from Diem for a bilateral defence treaty. For another, Taylor and Rostow represented a new, integrated approach to problems of limited war and the importance of its political dimension. Taylor had been retrieved from premature retirement after disagreement with the previous Administration's emphasis on nuclear deterrence while Rostow was widely quoted on the general problem of counter-insurgency. Whether they were sent by Kennedy in the expectation that they would report on the nonnecessity of sending US troops seems doubtful. On the other hand, if their visit was designed to produce a professional second opinion that troops were needed Kennedy went to extraordinary lengths to block the recommendation – as indeed he had to considering that when Taylor and Rostow came home in November he was almost the only senior member of the Administration who opposed it.

PRAGMATIC RESOLVE AND LIMITED PARTNERSHIP

The mood of Kennedy's Vietnam policy makers in the middle of November, 1961 was described by one of those most closely involved, William Bundy, as 'pragmatic resolve'. A month earlier he had told the President it was 'now or never' which meant that a 'hard-hitting' operation, if it were done soon enough, would have a 70 per cent chance of checking the decline and giving Diem a chance to do better. Having seen for themselves, the Taylor–Rostow team, which included Lansdale, had decided that although Diem should be kept in place (one State Department member considered and rejected the idea that the US might engineer a coup: 'not something we do well') his administration should be turned inside out. It would be part of the shift 'from advice to limited partnership' in which Vietnamese performance in every domain could be substantially improved if Americans were prepared to work side by side with the Vietnamese on key problems and it reflected the inevitable optimism of Lansdale: one year of devoted duty by Americans who were willing to stake all on the outcome would spark a complete psychological change in Vietnam and take the initiative away from the Communists. On a more mundane level, MAAG would have to become something like a wartime operational HQ and in the light of the Taylor–Rostow report it was subsequently suggested to Diem that he should establish a National Emergency Council which would include what sounded like a figure from Lansdale's cast: 'a mature hard-headed American'.

The difficulty with this and similar suggestions was that if he thought it meant losing power, Diem would not agree. As Ambassador Nolting reported from Saigon, Diem and most Vietnamese would interpret it as handing over his government to the US. Taylor, however, was confident that what the US could see needed to be done could be brought about by what he called persuasion at high levels, working with other Vietnamese who were prepared to collaborate and, by using the US presence, 'forcing the Vietnamese to get their house in order'. In short, a sort of benevolent administrative re-colonization which, in Rostow's view, would help the US to demonstrate its ability to cope with the example of a Khrushchev war of national liberation. By itself, however, it would not be enough and although the purpose was not altogether clear Taylor reported the unanimous opinion of US government officials in Vietnam that a US military commitment was needed as well. Whether or not it would function as the 'tough mobile striking force' which the CIA representative recommended, a force of 6–8,000 Americans, including combat troops, would obviously establish a US presence but this might not be sufficient to 'clean-up' the insurgency either. Ultimately, it was recognized 'there is no limit to our possible commitment' but the caveat which seemed to establish a terminal point was 'unless we attack the source in Hanoi'. Or, in the State Department's input to the Taylor report, which would be the foundation of policy for Kennedy's successors: 'If the combined US–GVN [Government of Vietnam] efforts are insufficient to reverse the trend we should then move to the 'Rostow Plan' of applying graduated punitive methods on the DRV [Democratic Republic of Vietnam] with weapons of our choosing.'

On the basis of this report the Secretary of Defense and the Joint Chiefs of Staff now prepared their recommendation to the President. South Vietnam would fall to communism unless there was a commitment of substantial US forces. The country would respond better to a firm initial position than to gradual commitment. The struggle might be prolonged but even if Hanoi and 'Peiping' intervened *their* (emphasis added) logistic difficulties would ensure that the US would not need to commit more than about 205,000 men. In spite of this finely calculated optimism in what might be thought of as something like a Doomsday enterprise the fact that success was seen to depend upon many factors, some of which were not under US control, introduced a final note of caution. It was, said William Bundy, who drafted the memorandum, sinking in how much a commitment depended upon South Vietnamese performance and it was for that reason that in the end they were only 'inclined to recommend' that the US commit itself to the clear objective of preventing the fall of Vietnam to communism and that this commitment be supported by the necessary military actions.

RUSK AND MCNAMARA AGREE

In the State Department there were even more doubts although, principally, they were about means rather than ends. When task forces were proliferating the State Department had set up its own, on Southeast Asia as a whole, which was in no doubt that the US had to resist communist encroachment 'by appropriate military means, if necessary, with or without unanimous SEATO support'. When it had reported in July it seemed concerned that the US 'should make the basic decision now'. In November this was still an outstanding issue but Rusk had begun to have doubts about Diem, 'attaching greatest possible importance to security in South-East Asia' but 'reluctant to see US major additional commitment American prestige to a losing horse'. Perhaps it was because he found the issue to be so finely balanced or perhaps, as Ball suggests, it was because he remembered what had happened in Truman's time when the Secretary of State and the Secretary of Defense weren't on speaking terms, but, whatever it was, ten days later Rusk had swallowed his doubts and had agreed with McNamara on a joint memorandum to be sent to the President. Both Secretaries had made concessions. At first sight Rusk seemed to have made more.

> The US should commit itself to the clear objective of preventing the fall of South Vietnam to Communism. The basic means for accomplishing this objective must be to put the government of South Vietnam into a position to win its own war against the guerillas.

> We shall be prepared to introduce US combat forces if that should become necessary for success. Dependent upon the circumstances, it may also be necessary for US forces to strike at the source of the aggression in North Vietnam.

Both agreed to the Taylor–Rostow proposal that individual US administrations and advisers should be provided 'for insertion into the Governmental machinery of South Vietnam', but when it came to a commitment of US forces they distinguished between small, specialized components such as helicopters or intelligence and 'larger organised units' and, for the latter, rediscovered Catch-22: if South Vietnam was strong enough they would not be needed. If it was not, US forces would not be much good 'in the midst of an apathetic or hostile population'. So, although contingency plans for operations that would go all the way up to dealing with 'organised communist military intervention' were to be made, the actual deployment would be limited to the small, specialist units.

Thus, on 11 November, anniversary of the end of America's first major war of the 20th century, the blue-print was submitted for what perhaps was to be the last. The President's principal Executive advisers simply wanted a recognition of the irrefutable objective. Once the end was agreed the means would follow even though it looked as if the war would not be limited to South Vietnam and even though the only war that was mentioned was the one which the government of South Vietnam must be allowed to win. It was a surprising compromise between the two principal Secretaries: instead of sending troops they should not do so yet but they should be prepared to send them rather than rule them out. It is also remarkable that they felt the need to ask for an irreversible commitment at all but perhaps it was because they felt that it was as much as they could get from a President who had more doubts than they had about where it would end and a far clearer view of what the arrival of US battalions in Vietnam would mean. Or, as William Bundy puts it in his account of a meeting that day when the memo was discussed: 'The thrust of the President's thinking was clear – sending organised forces was a step so grave that it should be avoided if this was humanly possible.'[46] Apart from the President's thinking there was also the Laos connection: what Rusk and McNamara recognized was the considerable risk of stimulating a communist breach of the cease-fire and the resumption of hostilities in Laos if US combat forces were introduced to Vietnam *before* a Laotian settlement. *After* a Laotian settlement, however, if there was one, it would be different: they would stabilise the position both in Vietnam and Laos because it would be seen that that was as far as the US would go and that communist influence would be allowed to develop no further. This would at least allow an immediate decision on combat troops to be postponed but the remaining issue was whether to accept the Rusk–McNamara proposal for categorical commitment to prevent the loss of South Vietnam.

At the meeting, again according to William Bundy's account, the President decided against the Rusk–McNamara proposal and in favour of George Ball's argument that a flat commitment without combat forces was the worst of both worlds. Ball was one of the few of the President's men with an acute and apocalyptic sense of what was impending. Remembering what had happened to the French he had warned Kennedy that once US forces were committed they would have 300,000 men in the paddy fields and jungles and never find them again. To which Kennedy replied, 'with an overtone of asperity': 'George, you're just crazier than hell. That just isn't going to happen.'[47] Kennedy had also been warned by General MacArthur against ever introducing any US troops into Southeast Asia under any circumstances[48] and although, at this stage of development, US policy may be seen as almost 'executive altogether' Congressional leaders such as Senator Mansfield had specifically urged the President not to send combat forces to Vietnam. But the dilemma remained. Five years before, Kennedy would have spoken for both himself and Mansfield when he described Vietnam as 'a test of American reliability and determination in Asia'[49] and what most of his advisers now proposed was in the logic of that conceptual commitment.

Before the meeting of 15 November when the critical decisions were made Kennedy received more recommendations that he should send troops. The whole world, said Rostow, with some exaggeration, was asking a simple question: what was the US going to do to stop North Vietnam supporting the war in the South? Rostow's fears that 'strong, decisive action' would not be taken and which, he said, would best avoid a war, might have been met if Kennedy had agreed there and then to send a division for military action in South Vietnam: when it was needed. This was the requested advice of his National Security adviser, McGeorge Bundy, who argued that, unlike Laos 'which was never really ours after 1954 . . . South Vietnam is and wants to be'. It was probably the underlying assumption of most of the National Security Council when it met to prepare its policy directive on 15 November and although they were considering a joint State Department–Defense memo that they should not send US divisions or even battalions into Vietnam at that stage one feels that, without the President, an emotional predisposition would nevertheless have become an operational commitment. McNamara, for example, seemed to think that the situation in Vietnam, which Kennedy, by contrast with Berlin, described as vague and the guerrillas as phantoms, would be clarified once US forces were involved and neither he nor Rusk excluded Hanoi, either, as an eventual target. Even if they were only involved in what Taylor called 'the guerilla-suppression program' McNamara warned, however, 'in all probability US troops, planes and resources would have to be supplied in additional quantities at a later date' which was in marked contrast to Rusk's more benign forecast that firmness 'might achieve desired results in Vietnam without resort to combat'.[50]

KENNEDY'S DOUBTS

Whatever the consequences of a major troop commitment would be it was the commitment itself against which Kennedy argued with considerable courage and skill. He disagreed with Rusk's attempted analogy with Berlin,[51] questioned Rusk's comparison with Korea, and said he could even make a rather strong case against intervening in an area 10,000 miles away against 16,000 guerrillas with a native army of 200,000 where millions of dollars had been spent for years with no success. All this notwithstanding, and in the absence of any conspicuous support for that proposition, Kennedy's role may really have been that of devil's advocate. Even though he was asking others to define their positions the action to be taken was more or less assured. In the President's mind at any rate, and according to William Bundy's analysis, there was the belief that the US seemed to be the single crucial, sustaining power against multiple communist threats. Standing firm on Berlin probably meant standing fairly firm at the same time on Vietnam, more particularly if concessions were going to be made over Laos; and if there really was a danger that South Vietnam was going to collapse, and if that could be avoided without a massive and sudden commitment of US forces, policy became self-evident. Like Eisenhower and Dulles before him, Kennedy also faced a problem of enlisting Congressional if not popular support and as the earlier crisis at Dien Bien Phu, while it had not led to unilateral US intervention, had at least created SEATO in the hope of dealing with situations like this, it might have been prudent to wait until the new crisis also became self-evident so that the US could engage in some genuine 'united action'. In the meantime, having come that far, the decisions would be taken that responded, even if they did not conform, to the advice that Kennedy had asked for from his White House advisers, Taylor and Rostow.[52] Theirs, in effect, were the assumptions that would bring Vietnam back to first principles. The Communists were pursuing a clear and systematic strategy in Southeast Asia which extended their power and influence in ways which by-passed US power as well as the conventional strength of indigenous forces in the area. International law and practice did not yet recognize the mounting of guerrilla war across borders as aggression justifying counter-attack at the source. But 'this new and dangerous Communist technique which by-passes our traditional political and military responses' led to Taylor's 'judgment and that of my colleagues that the US must decide how it will cope with Khrushchev's "wars of liberation" which are really para-wars of guerilla aggression'.[53]

The Taylor–Rostow mission produced a notable prognosis and some notable misconstructions. That South Vietnam was not an excessively unpleasant place for US troops to operate. That North Vietnam was extremely vulnerable to conventional bombing and, on one interpretation, that the risks of backing into a major Asian war by way of South Vietnam 'are present but are not impressive'. These assessments aside, the fact that they had gone to Vietnam in itself had been part of, as they put it, a sequence of expectations that had been set in motion by Vice-President Johnson's visit. Having found the atmosphere in South Vietnam to be, on balance, 'one of frustrated energy rather than passive acceptance of inevitable defeat' it remained for the US to harness this energy. If it did not, and unless there was a 'hard US commitment to the ground', they believed that morale in South Vietnam would crumble rapidly.

In the event it seems that neither Taylor nor Rostow was satisfied with the commitment that was made: increased airlift for the GVN forces, air reconnaissance, small craft and crews for naval operations, more training and equipment for the Civil Guard and for the Self Defence Corps, whatever was necessary to improve the military-political intelligence system, military assistance in operational collaboration with GVN and operational direction of US forces and, finally, the offer of individual administrators and advisers for the entire governmental machinery of South Vietnam and for joint operational surveys in every province of the country.[54] But at least of equal importance was the set of instructions that was sent to Ambassador Nolting in Saigon pointing out that Diem would soon be assigned an increased number of Americans for operational duties and that the new joint plan would involve them, not in the old advisory capacity, but in a much closer relationship. The US, in fact, would expect to share in the decision-making process in the political, economic and military fields as they affected the security situation.[55] Together with these instructions Nolting was given the *pro forma* of a reply from Diem although it was to be hoped that it would not be an exact copy.

When Taylor and Rostow had been in Saigon it seems from the record that they had given Diem little indication of what might be required of him in exchange for increased US help other than vague references to a loss of confidence on the part of the US and Rostow's comment that the 'secret of the turning point is offensive action'. Now, however, Diem would be expected to carry out thorough-going reforms to convince the American people, as well as world opinion, that they were not supporting an unpopular or ineffective régime and his understandable but unhelpful reaction to what his vice-president called great concessions in the realm of sovereignty in exchange for little additional help, was that Vietnam did not want to be a US protectorate. Nor, apparently, did a number of members in Kennedy's administration, not to mention Ambassador Nolting in Saigon, who responded to accusations in the government-controlled press that Vietnam was becoming a 'pawn of capitalism' by suggesting that the US concentrate on efficiency rather than on the 'particularly offensive' concept of political reforms. Two weeks after the US had demanded large-scale reforms as the price of its enhanced support, the situation was clarified. What the US really had in mind was a partnership that was 'so close that one party would not take decisions or actions affecting the other without full and frank prior consultation'.[56]

After more than five years of mutual assistance, during which time America had supported Diem and Diem had supported US purposes in Vietnam, the US now found itself at the end of Kennedy's first year in office in a common-law alliance with obligations that would be more onerous, and less reputable, than those towards states whose legitimacy was unchallenged. Even so, for any self-respecting government there must have been something rather demeaning about being rehearsed in the request it was to make for assistance. Conversely, while the US publicly reaffirmed that it would help the Republic of Vietnam to protect its people and to preserve its independence, it was doing rather less and rather more than responding to a request.[57] Either way it would have difficulty in treating the government of Vietnam as anything like an equal partner but South Vietnam could still be a show-piece of US resistance to what it regarded as a spurious war of national liberation. Nevertheless, and although it may have seemed insignificant at the time, once US armed forces were sent to Vietnam, once they started shooting and, unmistakably, once they were killed in combat, the US was engaged in acts of war. In attempting to conceal or deceive – for example, by having a Vietnamese on board US aircraft engaged in combat operations or attaching the prefix 'reconnaissance' to familiar Second World War medium bombers, in deference to the 1954 Geneva 'restrictions' – the US seemed to conceal from itself the fact that these were the first operations of its own war. The arrival of a 15,000-ton US aircraft ferry in the middle of Saigon on December 11, was a highly visible sign of the US commitment to Vietnam.[58] What was invisible, and might therefore be discounted, was the feeling of attachment and loyalty that had already developed, particularly between American Special Forces and their *montagnard* tribes, and a sense of an irrevocable commitment in the face of death. There were already several hundred American Special Forces in Vietnam and hundreds of US military advisers were about to arrive, many of whom would soon be engaged in combat. In these circumstances, and although it is perhaps sentimental, it is understandable that many of them felt that the personal and the national commitment had fused. It was now a matter of honour.

It may be equally sentimental but one should also, of course, consider the impact on those who encountered US power and might have been unable to understand its limited purpose. In Laos, for example, they would have derived little comfort from the fact that there had been no blanket authorization for the use of napalm by the nominally re-designated RB-26s: it was to be used only for particular targets.[59] Similarly, in Vietnam, where the appearance of Americans on field operations was supposed, by US law, to be in a non-combatant capacity both the Ambassador in Saigon and the President would have to lie to conceal the fact that US advisers had been in action and that the distinction between peace and war had become remarkably blurred.[60] However, as Rusk had told Nolting, they felt there had been no need for a decision which would, in effect, have shifted primary responsibility for the defence of South Vietnam to the US and, presumably, by this token, the US did not regard itself as a primary enemy as far as the Viet Cong were concerned. So far, in the first year of the Kennedy administration, the most important commitment to Vietnam had been conceptual. Although they may not have gone as far as McNamara, the JCS or even Rusk may have wanted they had committed themselves privately and publicly to Diem's government and, at the same time, by making the commitment visible, had attached the prestige of the US as well. Having set the compass the US course would now take it over the operational barrier represented by the Geneva limitation on the numbers of its military advisory group although this was at first done obliquely by denouncing the part played by North Vietnam in the reinforcement, supply and organization of the Southern insurgency.[61]

COUNTER-INSURGENCY

In this presentation South Vietnam, a sovereign state, was under attack from North Vietnam. What had until then been a US Military Assistance Advisory Group could now be transformed, on 8 February 1962, into a Military Assistance Command, Vietnam. Its commander, who would be responsible for all US military operations in Vietnam, would have authority to deal direct with Diem on military matters. According to an agreement reached between McNamara and Rusk, political and what were called 'basic policy matters', however, would be the responsibility of the US Ambassador and the only joint responsibility in Vietnam was that they should keep each other informed of their respective operations.[62] The stage was thereby set for a notable divergence of approach to a problem which had already been identified and to which the US was about to make a second conceptual commitment: counter-insurgency. On 18 January 1962, after various expressions of Presidential concern, the Special Group (Counter-Insurgency) was set up under the chairmanship of

General Maxwell Taylor which included, in addition to the Under Secretaries of State and Defense, the Chairman of the JCS and the Director of the CIA, and as a mark of Presidential concern, his brother Robert Kennedy, the Attorney-General. Its primary function was to 'insure' [*sic*] proper recognition throughout the US Government that subversive insurgency ('wars of liberation') was a major form of politico-military conflict equal in importance to conventional warfare but in designating South Vietnam, along with Laos and Thailand, as the area of special concern it left open the question of what the appropriate policies would be.[63] Again, perhaps, it was a matter of who deferred to whom although one may say that by having his own military adviser, General Taylor, as chairman Kennedy had put a presidential stamp on its proceedings.

In an earlier organizational stage of counter-insurgency deliberations in Washington, Kennedy had ensured that his own enthusiasm was transmitted through his brother's presence on the Counter-Insurgency Committee. In the end, according to Schlesinger, the failure of counter-insurgency was another phase in the education of Robert Kennedy, but from the beginning one can see in the scale of operations that was being recommended by another enthusiast, Robert Komer, a distinctively US approach which could create its own problems. 'What should we do? How about the President directing that all wraps are off in the counter-guerrilla operations etc. in South Vietnam. We will fund and pay for any crash measures however wasteful which will produce quick results.' The US would in fact do anything that was needed in sending arms and ammunition, and providing MAAG advisers in association with what were called socio-economic operations designed to win back the countryside. Instead of haggling with Diem over who should pay what proportion of the effort the US would regard this as a wartime situation in which the sky was the limit. In short, the US could not afford to go less than all out in cleaning up South Vietnam and the objective (this was written at the end of July 1961) was to achieve a major defeat of the Viet Cong before the end of the year.[64] Komer, as it happens, eventually became one of the most important and articulate proponents of, and participators in, far more sensitive pacification schemes but one can see how that sort of proposition and its embodiment in US policies in Vietnam could promote certain reflections on American character in general.[65] Towards the end of 1961 Americans in Saigon were somewhat annoyed by the interest being shown by the Vietnamese administration in the much smaller, more modest and more successful application of counter-insurgency which had, over 12 years, defeated a communist insurrection in Malaya. Ultimately, it may be argued, success in the Malayan experience, even in a colonial situation, had depended upon good government; and the last Secretary of Defence in the British administration in Malaya, Robert Thompson, arrived in Vietnam in October under US auspices to study the situation and to advise Diem on what might be done. The problems may or may not have been comparable and some of Sir Robert's subsequent premises about the moral imperatives of the war may be objectionable but he was, nevertheless, one of the outstanding analysts as well as one of the most successful practitioners of effective counter-insurgency *per se* and his proposals for a strictly limited application of a scheme that might have produced security in the Delta still suggest a fascinating alternative to what actually happened. What is also remarkable is what Thompson's subsequent experience in Vietnam, and his support for the US notwithstanding, led him to say about the defects of the US approach to counter-insurgency in Vietnam. As much as anything Thompson thought the problems were to be found in the American character. They were, he said, impatient, impulsive, aggressive and rich and, in a more professional assessment, 'influenced by the very worst interpretation of Clausewitz and the Prussian example of Moltke, so that the sole aim of most orthodox American military commanders had always been "the destruction of the enemy's main forces on the battlefield"'[66]

Perhaps, by 1962, the ability of the NLF (National Liberation Front) forces to launch attacks on a battalion scale, and larger, in any case made it imperative that numbers and fire-power should be assembled which would be sufficient to repel them. But the principal result in 1962, as far as the US Army and MACV (Military Assistance Command Vietnam) were concerned, was a concentration on fire-power and air mobility which, while it could inflict heavy casualties on identifiable targets, as long as they did not disperse, did not begin to tackle the long-range fundamental problem. 'If', as Thompson told Diem, 'the main emphasis is placed merely on killing terrorists there is a grave risk that more Communists will be created than are killed.' Any counter-insurgency plan must have as its overall aim 'winning the people' and this was something that everyone engaged in anti-terrorist operations, whether military of civilian, had to keep in the forefront of their minds.[67]

Thompson's detailed proposals and, even more, his suggestion for a complete governmental reorganization to deal with the guerrillas and his idea of an overall strategic plan for the entire country ran into immediate difficulties both in Washington and Saigon. Apart from the command problems it would pose, and how or whether the Vietnamese and US military efforts could be meshed, from a military point of view and using rather different criteria, it probably seemed unnecessary. On 1 January 1962 there were already 2,500 Americans in Vietnam and by the end of June the figure was due to increase to over 5,500. Almost 300 US aircraft, mostly helicopters, would give hitherto unimagined mobility to the Vietnamese Army as well as air-strike capabilities and by April 1962, General Harkins, the US

Commander in Vietnam, announced that the military defeat of the Viet Cong was at hand. There was, perhaps, some doubt as to what he meant by 'defeat' but when McNamara asked him in July 1962 at Hawaii how long it would take for the Viet Cong to be eliminated as a significant force he reckoned 'about one year from the time RVNAF (Republic of Vietnam Armed Forces) and other forces became fully operational and began to press the VC in all areas'.[68] McNamara, apparently more cautious, suggested that the end of 1965 would be a reasonable target date for the withdrawal of US forces.

In retrospect, at least, McNamara's assessment seems to have been founded not on caution, but on the wildest optimism. As the Pentagon Papers analyst puts it, describing the detailed projections for the simultaneous building up of GVN (Government of Vietnam) forces and the withdrawal of the US, all this planning began to take on a kind of absurd quality as the situation deteriorated drastically and visibly although it could be argued that until what he called the 'basic unrealities' were exposed there were enough people making more or less confident assessments to suggest that the US and the GVN might have been putting a successful act together. For example, in his self-confident and scathing report on Diem and his government in November 1961, Professor John Galbraith, Harvard economist, personal friend of President Kennedy and, at the time, US Ambassador to India had reported direct to the President: 'Given an even moderately effective government and putting the relative military power into perspective, I can't help thinking that the insurgency might very soon be settled.'[69] So, it might seem to have been just a matter of getting the factors in the right order, type and quantity; a finite problem with a finite solution. Certainly the statistical indicators appealed to McNamara – ratio of GVN to VC casualties, numbers of weapons lost and recovered, numbers of operations and 'contacts' initiated by government forces – and even if most of them were military and/or supplied from GVN sources the State Department's own Intelligence and Research report in June (from the cautious Roger Hilsman) while it warned against a premature judgement on ultimate success in the campaign against the Communist 'war of national liberation' in Vietnam, ended up by saying 'We do think that the chances are good, provided there is continuing progress by the Vietnamese Government along the lines of its present strategy'.[70]

The Vietnamese government and its strategy was the caveat, the critical factor and, ultimately, the excuse for what went wrong; but when McNamara was establishing a matrix for US policy whose objectives were to be accomplished in the finite period of three years there were other, hopeful, signs. First, there had been an extraordinary success on the night of 20 July when: 'In the largest helicopter attack so far in the war, day or night, government troops put down right smack on top of a Viet Cong battalion and killed 141 losing less than 30 of their own.'[71] Most important, was that agreement had been reached at Geneva three days later, on 23 July 1962 the same day as McNamara's Hawaii conference, on the neutralization of Laos. One of the inferences that was being drawn from this diplomatic settlement was that it was in fact a triumph of US resolution and proof that it had been US determination which had in large part brought about it. After another runabout battle in which General Phoumi's forces were again in headlong retreat from northern Laos to the Mekong in May, and after hurried consultation with Congressional leaders, 5,000 US troops had been sent to Thailand, units of the Seventh Fleet were in the Gulf of Siam and even Britain had contributed an RAF squadron from Malaya.[72] In Washington Dean Rusk had declared that the integrity and independence of Thailand were vital to US interests and, furthermore, that the US would honour its agreement to defend Thailand even if no other SEATO member was willing to do so. It appears that Kennedy, also, 'was thinking much more about intervening this time', even to the point of a Congressional resolution that would have approved US intervention, but in the event a cease-fire of sorts was resumed in Laos, the negotiations started again and the agreement was eventually signed in Geneva.[73] Ironically, as part of its confirmed neutrality, Laos declared that it would *not* recognize the protection of any alliance or military coalition, including SEATO, but whatever one thinks of the agreement, how it was reached, what, in the event, it was worth and why it collapsed, neutralization for Vietnam was an option that hardly received a second thought.

STRATEGIC HAMLETS

Instead, McNamara's divination led to the Comprehensive Plan for South Vietnam which was to direct US policy towards restoring the government of Vietnam in its normal functions, to the suppression of the insurgency and the expectation that all this would be accomplished within three years. Having imposed a semblance of order, purpose and, above all, time on US policy the Comprehensive Plan seemed to take on a life of its own and, whether or not it was a template of reality, it became an end in itself. As long as the correct sequences were observed, together with proper accounting, and the right figures kept rolling in it was possible to believe that the programme was on course and the US and the GVN were winning. Many of the military performance indicators were, indeed, improving but perhaps the most encouraging of all the performances and the one that was most important because it was what the GVN was doing itself, and because, for MACV, it took care of the awkward and unfamiliar requirement of 'pacification', was that of the Strategic Hamlet Programme.

Unlike the earlier and more modest attempts at rural resettlement which had only produced a score of so-called 'agrovilles' in a couple of years the Strategic Hamlet Programme that had got under way in January 1962 aimed at the total transformation of the South Vietnamese countryside. On 3 January 1962, as a sort of birthday treat for President Diem, it was announced that 14,000 strategic hamlets were to be constructed in 14 months. The scale and the time were unbelievable and so were the results that were announced. Placed in the hands of Ngo Dinh Nhu, Diem's daemonic brother, practically from the start the Strategic Hamlet Programme assumed a mystical purpose which, with a mixture of Confucian and Communist-style slogans, were supposed to turn them into vehicles of the Personalist Revolution. At times it took on a bizarre and almost certain counterproductive form. Nhu, for example, apparently told Duncanson, one of the British advisory mission in Saigon, that the defenders of the strategic hamlets would, at most, have weapons loaned but generally speaking they were expected to capture them from the Viet Cong. Equally hazardous, as McNamara discovered for himself, was the emergency drill to be followed when villages were under attack – they were expected to send a runner to the nearest military or para-military unit – and although this led to an accelerated supply of US radio sets in most other respects the strategic hamlets only provided the illusion of security and pacification. It is hard, for example, to see what purpose four- or five-strand barbed wire fences served even against guerrillas who had no wire cutters, and although traditional bamboo, either in hedges or as sharpened stakes, was often a better defence all that a province chief had to do was to say that every village had its fence, most of its people were living inside, and the province was formally declared to be 'pacified'. Even then, on this rudimentary basis, the GVN had something of a Red Queen approach to its own statistics. For example, on 1 October 1962 Diem announced that 7,267,517 people were sheltered in hamlets that had been completed or were in the process of completion. Ten days later in the report given by the Minister of the Interior, it seems the figure had gone down by almost 3 m. As the more objective US AID (Agency for International Development) noted later:

> From the very inception of the Strategic Hamlet Program it was apparent that many of these (provincial Vietnamese) officials did not fully understand the concept, and were so frightened by the pressures from the President (that is, Diem) and his brother that they would employ any measures from forced labour and confiscation to false reporting to achieve the quantitative goals set. Although these tendencies were at first restrained, the pressures for 'reporting' steadily

increased, while at the same time the influence of US advisors lessened, as a result of errors and misunderstandings on both sides.[74]

IRREDUCIBLE OPTIMISM

Errors and distortions notwithstanding, 1962 was announced as the Year of the Strategic Hamlets in South Vietnam. It was the centre-piece of Diem's 'pacification' programme and if, as the Pentagon Papers analyst suggests, it was an attempt to translate the newly articulated theory of counter-insurgency into operational reality it was nevertheless very difficult to make intermediate assessments of progress: 'one could not really be sure how one was doing until one was done'.[75] But even where specific indicators 'almost invariably pointed to shortcomings in GVN's execution of the program' they

> were treated as problems in efficient management and operation-al organisation; the ineluctability of increased control (of security) leading somehow to popular identification by a process akin to the economic assumption of 'flotation to stability through development' went unchallenged as a basic assumption. Critics pointed to needed improvements; the question of whether or not these could be accomplished, or why, almost never was raised.[76]

Simply to be able to report that a Strategic Hamlet had been completed thus became an end in itself. What happened then, apparently, seemed to be of less importance although it was certainly not likely to be what had happened in the analogous experience of the Chinese New Villages in Malaya which, after most of them really had been completed, provided, together with their approaches, the killing grounds during the insurrection. Chinese peasant farmers had provided the essential support for the guerrillas in Malaya. When they and their families were resettled or regrouped even within reasonably secure perimeter fences all that had been done was to make it more difficult for the guerrillas to get food. When New Villages began to enjoy some comfort and stability and, above all, some sense of identification with government – particularly when independence was clearly on the way – the next stage was reached. Finally, when New Villages showed that they were able to defend themselves successfully against guerrilla attack, and to provide the scraps of intelligence that allowed security forces to lay equally successful ambushes, the guerrilla's days were numbered. Whether, by analogy, 'New Villages' could ever have succeeded in South Vietnam is another matter. Between a government that regarded them as a literally captive audience for its eccentric ideas of personalism, to the exclusion of more mundane functions, and a US military effort that was only interested in Strategic Hamlets as long as it would allow them, and the Vietnamese Army, to get on with the principal business of killing guerrillas, the answer is, probably, 'no'. Even so, as Duncanson suggests, there may have been hopeful signs. With increased government control 'the yield from land tax doubled from 1961 to 1962. Viet Cong recruitment fell off for perhaps the only time after 1959 and by the spring of 1963 the situation was that the Strategic Hamlets succeeded . . . in facing the Viet Cong with an obstacle they urgently wanted out of the way, and at the same time in bringing the authority of the régime into many South Vietnamese villages for the first time.'[77] But perhaps the fatal blow was that the GVN tried to do too much too fast and as evidence quoted in support of this argument in Osborne's study of Strategic Hamlets is Colonel Pham Ngoc Thau's lecture at Cornell University in May 1964. Colonel Thau, one of the directors of the Strategic Hamlet Programme, was later distinguished by his abortive coup against General Khanh's régime in 1965 but an even greater distinction is that he was also one of the most highly placed Viet Cong agents in the Diem administration. Whether the breakneck speed of the Strategic Hamlet Programme owed something to him as sorcerer's apprentice or whether it would have outrun itself anyway must be a matter of speculation as Colonel Thau was killed shortly after his unsuccessful coup.[78]

What is somewhat less speculative, however, is how the NLF responded to the largely unexpected arrival of US support for Diem in 1962 and how they began to cope, eventually, with US helicopters and with the strategic hamlets. The latter, in fact may have been much more of an inconvenience than the NLF would publicly admit and there is evidence that they were worried enough to ask advice from the North how to tackle the problem. From 1 January 1962, however, what had previously been the southern branch of the Vietnam Workers Party was supposed to have become the autonomous People's Revolutionary Party of South Vietnam and, again, there is some evidence that there was continuing tension between North and South (or at least a divergent assessment of Party interests) in assessing the stage which the revolution had reached. Where the South may originally have launched itself on a variant of the armed struggle out of sheer self-preservation, in the North self-preservation meant safeguarding the achievements of the revolution and this, in turn, meant doing nothing that would provoke a US attack. But with an apparent improvement in the fortunes of the NLF in 1961 it was hardly surprising that this should have been reflected in a new and hopeful party line. At about the same time as Taylor and Rostow were visiting South Vietnam to see how bad things were the Party's Central Office for South Vietnam was apparently making its own assessment of the revolution in the South, decided there was a high tide, and that 'the period of temporary stabilisation of the US–Diem régime had passed and the period of continuous crisis and serious decline has begun'. In practical terms it announced that the 'partial uprising' had already started; that the military phase of the struggle was now dominant in the Central Highlands; but, in other respects, the Party leadership, in rather a Micawber-ish mood, was waiting for something to turn up.[79]

In the event it was the Americans who turned up, in rapidly increasing numbers, to frustrate any hopes of transforming the partial into a general uprising and by the end of 1962 with the situation finely balanced, and in spite of each side believing it had the advantage, something like a stalemate had developed. If the GVN and the US between them had not suppressed a revolution at least they had dampened down a revolutionary war. On the other hand, by 1962 the NLF may have had something like 300,000 members and perhaps a passive following of more than a million.[80] The State Department's Intelligence and Research Bureau put the figure at 100,000 for irregulars and sympathisers but even if, as the GVN claimed, 21,000 Viet Cong *had* been killed that year this still left, on State Department estimates, 23,000 'élite fighting personnel'. Hilsman's presentation of these figures in December 1962 and his appreciation of the multiple factors involved in insurgency made this one of the most sensible and prescient accounts available to policy-makers and, with so much to contradict McNamara's confident assertion that all the objective criteria suggested the US was winning, one had to ask who was reading the reports and what effect, if any, were they having.[81]

Hilsman's memo had been addressed to the Secretary of State. But perhaps the single most important detail in understanding what happened in the Kennedy Administration's approach to Vietnam is that its Secretary of State never went to Vietnam and although it may be argued that any competent Secretary or Minister can get a very good picture by staying at home and evaluating the evidence, nevertheless Rusk's notable absence from Vietnam underlines why so many people felt that the State Department generally and he personally had abdicated responsibility and had turned it over to McNamara, to the Department of Defense and to the military in general. There were, of course, more urgent problems to be dealt with – Berlin in 1961, Cuba in 1962 – and, in any case, someone with the authority of the Army Chief of Staff had announced, in November 1962, that Vietnam was essentially a military problem. Even if that proposition was challenged there was still enough data on which to base hopeful conclusions. For example, in Hilsman's Intelligence and Research survey of December 1962 the VC controlled about 20 per cent of the villages but only 9 per cent of the rural population. Were these figures going up or down and, in either case, how fast? By the end of 1963 there would be bitter disagreement between State and Defense not only on figures and assessments from Vietnam but also on whether the State Department had any entitlement to prepare them – Rusk conceded to McNamara they had not – and with even the 'civilian' component of the American 'country team' in Vietnam telling US reporters that they should 'accentuate the positive' this helped to create a further gap between reality and understanding.

THE PROBLEM OF DIEM

But it seems that even critical observers and analysts continued to offer assessments of at least qualified optimism. Perhaps one might discount the same Army Chief of Staff, General Wheeler, when he said in January 1963 'We are winning slowly' and although, like Hilsman, Michael Forrestal's report from Vietnam in February was particularly perceptive, nevertheless, if one was looking for a bottom line in that report for the President, it was 'We are probably winning'.[82] A month later, on a visit to the US C-in-C Pacific it appears that even Thompson reported: 'One year ago we were neither winning nor losing in RVN. Now we are definitely winning.'[83] Perhaps, also, it was because, having seen what *might* be done, they saw what *should* be done and, having got that far, it became a question of what *could* be done. Thus, for Hilsman, it was essentially a problem of co-ordination; for Forrestal it was mostly a matter of an overall plan; and for Thompson, reporting to Diem, it was a matter of making strategic hamlets a reality rather than a matter of target dates and monthly statistics.[84] For at least two out of the three, however, it was also a matter of personalities: in other words, said Hilsman, it always came back to Ngo Dinh Diem.

US involvement in the coup which led to the assassination of President Diem and his brother, Ngo Dinh Nhu, is still, for many Americans, probably the most painful and controversial episode of the Vietnam War. It is also, arguably, something that was inherent in the logic of US intervention. The US, by virtue of its commitment to South Vietnam and, even more, by its commitment to Diem, had become involved in a revolution. If there was little or no hope that Diem's government could suppress the revolution, if, in fact, it had become an inadequate instrument for carrying out America's political purpose, then, unless the US was prepared to abandon this purpose, there was only one course to be followed. Some matter-of-fact considerations about removing Diem had been aired before the end of Kennedy's first year in office but there was a world of difference between action and speculation and although, after eight years, Diem's family government proved to be less rather than more amenable to US direction the fact that they were still in place, and the struggle had not been lost, entitled them to some respect and support in Washington. But the situation was beginning to change.

One of the more important changes occurred in the State Department in March 1963 when Hilsman became Assistant Secretary of State for the Far East and Harriman became Under Secretary of State for Political Affairs. In six months' time they would mount their own successful Vietnam coup within the Administration but to begin with, the 'balance of forces', as a Viet Cong analyst might have described it, was very much in favour of those such as McNamara, Taylor (now Chairman of the JCS) and Nolting who were prepared to retain Diem or give him, once again, one last chance. Nevertheless, Diem was beginning to lose his support outside the Administration and previous champions such as Senator Mansfield had now become outspoken critics while others, such as Buttinger, were working actively against him. Kennedy, too, is said to have begun to have doubts, mostly on humanitarian grounds, about the way the Vietnamese Army was conducting its 'search and destroy' operations and there had been a notable defeat of ARVN (Army of the Republic of Vietnam) forces, with enormous military and political consequences, in a set-piece battle at Ap-Bac at the beginning of January 1963. Even taken together, however, they did not add up to either an immediate shift of power in Vietnam or a change in US policy. When the stalemate – for both sides in Vietnam, and in Washington – was broken it was in fact largely unexpected and somewhat accidental.

After one of the many superb summaries and analytical prologues in the Gravel edition of the Pentagon Papers, the chronology for the chapter 'The Overthrow of Ngo Dinh Diem' begins: '8 May 1963. Hué incident. Government troops fire on a Buddhist protest demonstration, killing nine and wounding fourteen.' Thus, the Buddhist crisis had begun in which the latent forces of political discontent in South Vietnam were energized and mobilized to the point where they made a government change course; but in Washington, not Saigon. The incident in itself may have seemed trivial: Catholics in Hué had been allowed to fly Papal flags but Buddhists had been forbidden to fly their flags for the Buddha's birthday and although the government response was selective and savage enough on that occasion what really captured world attention was the horrific spectacle a month later of a Buddhist monk burning himself to death in a Saigon street. This, rather than anything else, is what seems to have prompted a profound re-examination of America's commitment to the Diem government. The *New York Times* concluded that if Diem could not genuinely represent a majority then he was not the man to be

President; and in Washington Hilsman, Harriman and the Vietnam Task Force had already devised an improbable plan if the situation became more serious. If there were circumstances, in which the US would play no part, where Diem was 'definitively unable act as President', the US would want to back Vice-President Tho as his constitutional successor. They would deny it if the proposal was leaked but they also wondered whether they should tell Diem about the plan, too.[85]

What the US would do if the Vietnamese themselves were to re-order their government, and whether the US wanted this to happen, was about to become a critical question. As long as Nolting was in Saigon he had shielded Diem from Washington's sharper criticisms and there seemed to be no major differences between him and the US military commander, General Harkins. Even when he had returned to Washington and the crisis there and in Saigon had reached its peak Nolting's benevolence and high regard not only for Diem but for Nhu as well seemed undiminished. At a meeting on 27 August 1963, by which time Nhu and his wife had clearly been identified as the primary US targets, Nolting told the President that Nhu was pro-Vietnamese rather than anti-American. In fact, said Nolting, he was an able person who had been responsible for the success of the strategic hamlet programme and although he was feared by the people the Vietnamese were respectful of those who could command. Nolting's advice was not to fight the internal situation in Vietnam too hard and in response to a question from Kennedy said: 'He thought we should take it slow and easy over the next several weeks.'[86]

By this time Nolting had left Saigon and was to be succeeded as Ambassador by Henry Cabot Lodge, the Republican Vice-Presidential candidate of 1960, one of Kennedy's nicely chosen appointments, who, on his arrival in Vietnam, found himself in the middle of another Buddhist crisis. Taking advantage of the hiatus between the departure of one US Ambassador and the arrival of another, on 21 August Nhu had unleashed his own Special Forces on Buddhist pagodas throughout the country. Aimed at depriving them of their leadership and presumably at presenting Lodge with an accomplished fact, Nhu's action was a violent repudiation of Diem's promises of reconciliation. It was also the act, in Hilsman's opinion, which severed relations between the Diem régime and the US. The announcement which dissociated the one from the other's actions – its 'act of desecration in violation of its pledged word' – was, he said, only the epitaph.[87] Considering what happened next it is understandable and indeed essential that Hilsman should have announced the alliance to be extinct. What the US was about to do was to get rid of the bodies, which were dead only in a political sense, and Hilsman would be one of the prime removers.

THE COUP

'The Cable of August 24', a chapter title in Hilsman's book, is still one of the most controversial episodes of the Vietnam War. The Senate Foreign Relations Committee study devotes ten pages to the cable and its aftermath and hardly anyone who was involved agrees on the details with the others.[88] In brief, the 'end-run' telegram, for those unfamiliar with American football, was a successful attempt to go clean around the opposition and tell the Saigon Embassy that, after reasonable opportunity to remove the Nhus, if Diem remained obdurate, the US was prepared to accept the obvious implication: he could no longer be supported. And, even more important: 'You may also tell appropriate military commanders we will give them direct support in any interim period of breakdown central government mechanism.'[89] Drafted by Hilsman, with support from Harriman, Forrestal and Ball, Hilsman says it was cleared by the President, word for word and with that *imprimatur* it seems that no else felt like objecting at the time.[90] On the Monday following, 26 August 1963 (the cable was sent on the Saturday) there were opportunities for recrimination or, even, remorse and the argument went on for two or three days whether principals such as McNamara or Taylor or McCone (CIA) had been duped but on 29 August when Kennedy polled his advisers one by one they all agreed to stand by the original cable. The US was now committed to supporting a coup but only one which had a good chance of success. By then, or certainly over the next few months, they probably had a whole network of agents in South Vietnam who were actively engaged in plans to replace the existing government. One of the most senior agents had been approached by the newly appointed commander of the Army of the Republic of Vietnam a couple of days after the pagoda raids on 21 August. The CIA man reported that General Don had appeared not to know what to do next but with other contacts being made by the CIA with potentially dissident senior Vietnamese officers, and Ambassador Lodge entering the game with enthusiasm, it looked as if an army coup was imminent.[91] In the event, it was not. General Harkins, for one, made no bones about his continuing support for Diem and his opposition to a coup. Fearing they might be betrayed the Generals called it off, leaving themselves for the moment in limbo and the Kennedy Administration in perhaps even greater disarray.

The coup which should have taken place in a week in fact took another two months to mature. In the meantime although Washington was obviously in two minds about continuing active involvement Kennedy let it be known in an American TV interview that unless the GVN made a greater effort to win popular support he didn't think the war could be won out there but, he added, 'with changes in policy and perhaps with personnel I think it can' and the State Department cabled his comments to Saigon with a note: 'They represent the US Government's attitude towards the situation and should be followed as the official public position.'[92] This at the time (2 September) may have been true but the significant changes, in personnel and even in policy, had by no means been agreed in Washington. In fact the essential deadlock continued with the Administration casting around all over the place for a policy to deal with the Ngo family. Almost all the permutations were tried: with Diem but without Nhu, with Nhu but without Mme Nhu and so on, not forgetting the other brothers as well. After a week of this and on the day before they received Lodge's ominous but euphonious cable from Saigon 'The ship of state is slowly sinking', Kennedy and his advisers called for an on-the-spot report to be made to them in four days' time.[93] When the two antagonists, General Krulak representing Defense and the JCS, and Joseph Mendenhall of the State Department, returned they presented what Krulak claimed were, in effect, the town and the country reports. Whether this was the basis of the difference or not Mendenhall thought the situation was hopeless. Krulak 'believed strongly that we can stagger through to win the war with Nhu (did he really mean Nhu?) in control'. Obviously the NSC (National Security Council) could hardly make its decision if this was the crucial evidence, and after a week of deadlock it decided to send the next two members, Secretary of Defense McNamara and Chairman of the JCS, General Taylor. Again it seems significant that Rusk was not included. To be fair, for Rusk to have been more effective he would probably have to have been Colonial Secretary rather than the Secretary of State. Even though the recommendation, understandable though it is, 'that Ambassador Lodge be told to tell Diem to start acting like the President of Vietnam and get on with the war' seems of little use beyond the nursery door.

Rusk embodied the US dilemma. 'We will not', he said on an earlier occasion, 'pull out of Vietnam until the war is won and we will not run a coup.'[94] When McNamara and Taylor returned to Washington and presented their report to the President on 2 October they suggested the war was being won *but* they implied that a coup might still be necessary, although not yet. Altogether it was rather a neurotic report. The prospects of victory were there, indeed they were scheduled, but Diem and Nhu might, as they say, 'blow it'. Obviously this put the US into a quandary but, beginning with the good news, so sure were McNamara and Taylor of the successes of the strategic hamlets and the soundness of Vietnamese tactics and techniques which 'give promise of ultimate victory' that they proposed withdrawal of 1,000 US military personnel by the end of 1963. Moreover, they believed, the US part in the task of counter-insurgency could be completed by the end of 1965 by which time it seems that victory would have been assured.

> If, by victory, we mean the reduction of the insurgency to something little more than sporadic banditry in outlying districts, it is the view of the vast majority of military commanders consulted that success may be achieved in the I, II and III Corps area by the end of (Calendar Year) 1964. Victory in the IV Corps will take longer – at least well into 1965.[95]

Whatever the reality of this dazzling prospect might have been – and it looked as if McNamara was still locked into his original schedule – it was obviously dimmed by discontent with what they called the Diem/Nhu régime which had now become 'a seething problem'. It was indeed hard to imagine how victory would be achieved in a couple of years, as they reported that: 'The discontent of the élite – reflected chiefly in the progressive loss of responsible men – had now reached the point where it is uncertain that Diem can keep or enlist enough talent to run the war.' As matters stood, political tension was acknowledged to be so high that it could boil over at any time into another cycle of riots, repressions and resignations but this tension would, they thought, disappear in a very short time if Nhu were removed. If this was so, what were the implications? The prospects of what they called 'an early spontaneous replacement' of Diem were not high. Even if there was a 'replacement régime' there was only a 50–50 chance that it would be an improvement. Obviously, clear and explicit US support could make a great difference to the chances of a coup but so far they neither knew 'what acceptable individuals might be brought to the point of action' nor did they know what kind of government would emerge.

> If and when we have a better picture, the choice will still remain difficult whether we would prefer to take our chances on a spontaneous coup (assuming some action by Diem and Nhu would trigger it) or to risk US prestige in having the US hand show with a coup group which appeared likely to be a better alternative government.

At this stage, then, the inferences seem unmistakable: McNamara and Taylor and the Administration in general were afraid of an unsuccessful coup and because of (reciprocal) doubts about the Vietnamese generals were not prepared to 'run' one. Their recommendation was therefore that, having ruled out 'reconciliation' as well, the only way to bring Diem to heel was to use 'selective pressures'. Nevertheless, when the report was debated it seemed that, as a compromise, everyone agreed that, casuistical though it might have been, 'the US would work with the Diem government but not support it'. From here it was not a very big step to a renewal of more active involvement in a coup and, when it happened, one may ask why it happened. There seemed to be three major possibilities. The first, that it was simply deliberate, second, that it was to prevent an accommodation between Nhu and North Vietnam and the third is that it may have been inadvertent.

Considering what was decided on the basis of the McNamara–Taylor report the Senate Foreign Relations Committee analyst has no doubt,

> When Kennedy made the decision on October 5 1963, to reject 'reconciliation', and to apply most of the pressures under the category of phase 2 of the pressure track, he was fully aware not only that these actions were calculated to induce a coup, but that they were the precise signals of US support for a coup that the opposition generals had said they needed to have before proceeding.

And, to reinforce the proposition:

> Thus, October 5, 1963, was the day the President of the United States decided to move against President Ngo Dinh Diem, knowing the result probably would be the overthrow of the Vietnamese President.[96]

An alternative and intriguing explanation has been put forward most recently by Professor George Kahin. Scrupulously honest in his presentation of the evidence, and himself raising the question whether it was US officials who exaggerated or misrepresented his actions, Kahin wonders whether Nhu was serious about at least exploring the possibilities of a cease-fire with North Vietnam.[97] McNamara and Taylor and the State Department member of their mission, William Sullivan, had all been aware of Nhu's 'flirtations' with the communists. Whether Nhu's advances were serious or not was another matter but Chester Cooper, in his CIA role, was wondering whether both Diem and Nhu would seek *rapprochement* with the North simply on the basis of a cease-fire in return for which 'they might seriously entertain the certain minimum DRV demand for the removal of US forces.'[98] Whether, in this case, Nhu believed that Hanoi would respect South Vietnam's neutrality, and whether he assumed that Diem would be in a position to risk an election in which the NLF would compete, suggests, however, for someone as astute as Nhu, a major hallucination. It was, of course, by no means impossible, at least as an overture or an option that might be used to blackmail a fearful US government and one wonders whether it might have been corroborated by internal sources in North Vietnam. Alternatively, and drawing on the same source as Kahin uses, there is perhaps another explanation in the State Department's Intelligence and Research memo 'The Problem of Nhu'. Nhu, it said, was capable of believing that he could manipulate the situation to his advantage, whether through fighting or negotiating with the Communists. His megalomania was manifest and his claim was that only he could save Vietnam but as a partial explanation for his excess of self-confidence and fantasies of power it suggested that, for the past two years, he had been smoking opium.[99] Whatever the cause of his behaviour, and whether he was rational or not, would not have removed US fears that Nhu was trying to cut the ground from under their feet but the question remains whether or not it was sufficient cause for the US once again to have become involved when the Vietnamese generals began their second attempt at the coup. Lodge, perhaps, had been right in August: there really was no turning back once the US had made contact with the dissident generals, no matter how conditional their interest. They might not, in spite of the increasing frequency of CIA contacts, be taking an active part but, bearing in mind that CIA Director McCone was against a coup, it was not a well established position. 'We certainly cannot be in the position of stimulating, approving, or supporting assassination, but on the other hand, we are in no way responsible for stopping every such threat of which we might receive even partial knowledge.' It seems, therefore, to have been a conditional imperative: 'Thou shalt not kill but needst not strive officiously to keep alive.'

All of which argues for premeditation; and when, after last-minute hesitations, the 'high prospect of success' appeared at the end of October, the conditions of support had been set out, and the message that had been received from the White House was that it was in the interest of the US that the coup should succeed, there was that much less evidence to support the third possibility, the idea of an inadvertent commitment to a coup. One wonders, nevertheless, whether Kennedy and his advisers really did mean to start the ball rolling on 5 October or whether, at that point, they still hoped that Diem might prove to be amenable to the powerful influences of the US. Instead, and even if it did not evoke quite the same sense of horror as parricide did in earlier times, the US was eventually involved in the overthrow of a friendly government. Perhaps 'amicide' sounds too flippant but for another Director of the CIA, William Colby, and many others, what he called the American-sponsored overthrow of Diem was the worst mistake of the Vietnam War.

The coup, when it took place on 1 November 1963, was relatively smooth. Diem's loyal forces were blocked or nullified in some masterful chess moves and the assault on the Gia-Long Palace was, to add to the intrigue, led by Colonel Pham Ngoc Thau, the 'Master Spy'. He and his men seemed, moreover, to have been within a hair's breadth of Diem and Nhu when they surrendered. Perhaps that had been his mission all along although whether their fate would have been very different if he had got to them first must, of course, be a matter for speculation. Having escaped from the Palace they eventually surrendered at a French church in the Chinese quarter, were put into the back of an armoured vehicle, and unceremoniously shot. After the event, and as a post-script, there was an interesting exchange of cables between Saigon and Washington. Part of Lodge's 'Eyes Only' telegram of 6 November is quoted by Schlesinger:

> . . . The coup was a Vietnamese and a popular affair, which we could neither manage nor stop after it got started and which we could only have influenced with great difficulty. But it is equally certain that the ground in which the coup seed grew into a robust plant was prepared by us and that the coup would not have happened [as] it did without our preparation . . .
> All this may be a useful lesson in the use of US power . . .[100]

The cable has now been declassified. That particular paragraph continued 'General Don as much as said this to me on 3 November. Our actions made the people who could do something about it start thinking hard about how to get a change of government.' Selection from long cables is obviously a matter of choice and although Schlesinger acknowledges the element of US involvement in the coup it might have seemed stronger still if instead of the '. . .' he had continued Lodge's 'useful lesson in the use of US power'. It went on,

> The President, the State Department, the Military, the AID, the USIS, and the CIA deserve credit for this result. Without united action by the US government, it would not have been possible. Many Americans in Saigon were required suddenly to start thinking differently, a difficult thing to do. The fact that they did so is creditable.[101]

In what was part commentary and part explanation of recent events Lodge had said earlier,

> At the time of the pagoda raids of August 21 USG and GVN seemed to be totally deadlocked. Diem and Nhu evidently thought that the US was hooked. It seemed that we were on the horns of a dilemma in which we were forced either to do nothing or else to injure the war effort and dangerously lower the basic living standard of the people – or else to act like a colonial power. There seemed to be nothing which would hurt Diem and Nhu which would not repeat not hurt us as much, if not more. We were being totally taken for granted by the GVN; we were never asked to do even the smallest favour.

Listing the ways in which 'we began to show our displeasure', Lodge ended the first part of the cable: 'Also, we did not, as we had done in the past, turn over coup information to GVN.' He signed off the second part of his cable to the President: 'My thanks to you and all those associated with you for comprehending and imaginative guidance and support.'
The cable in reply set out the President's position

> As you say, while this was a Vietnamese effort, our own actions made it clear that we wanted improvements, and when these were not forthcoming from the Diem government, we necessarily faced and accepted the possibility that our position might encourage a change of government. We thus have a responsibility to help this new government to be effective in every way that we can, and in these first weeks we may

have more influence and more chance to be helpful than at any time in recent years.

It concluded: 'With renewed appreciation for a fine job, John F. Kennedy.' Just over two weeks later the US would also have a change of government when Kennedy, too, was assassinated.

REFERENCES AND NOTES

1. It is, for example, one of Dr R. B. Smith's notable observations 'It arose not from anything the Americans did in South Vietnam – which Hanoi might dislike but could not effectively counter – but rather from the consequences of American policy in Laos.' *An International History of the Vietnam War Volume I, Revolution Versus Containment, 1955–61* (London 1983). Whether the US, as he suggests, decided to block Chinese ambitions in Laos, or whether they just capitalized on opportunities, one can at least agree that 'the result was that the American presence, without being powerful enough to prevent further communist intervention in Laotian politics, seemed to threaten both Chinese and North Vietnamese interests in Laos'. pp. 80–1.

2. Useful sources on Laos, especially in the context of the Indo-China wars, are Stuart Simmonds, 'Independence and Political Rivalry in Laos, 1945–61' in Saul Rose (ed.) *Politics in Southern Asia* (London 1963) and 'The Evolution of Foreign Policy in Laos Since Independence', *Modern Asian Studies* II, I (1968). Hugh Toye, *Laos. Buffer State or Battleground* (London 1971). Arthur J. Dommen, *Conflict in Laos* (New York 1971). Charles A. Stevenson, *The End of Nowhere* (Boston, Mass. 1973). Bernard B. Fall, *Anatomy of a Crisis* (New York 1969). Marek Thee, *Notes of a Witness* (New York 1973). Michael Field, *The Prevailing Wind* (London 1965).

3. The extent to which their interests were represented by *Pathet Lao* is often overlooked. Concepts of 'nationhood' for peoples whose political range is only three valleys wide – their own, and the valleys on either side – were hard enough to establish at the best of times. They were further impaired by hostility to the ruling, lowland, Lao and by the fact that many of the same tribes lived on the other side of a not very meaningful border with North Vietnam. In 1960 the Federation of Malaya's Adviser on Aborigines, reported from Laos that 60 per cent of *Pathet Lao* forces were *montagnards*. As in Malaya, which had learned during the communist insurrection from the disasters of forcible resettlement, so the one successful *montagnard* resettlement scheme in Laos, in Nam Tha province, had taken eight years.

4. Stephen E. Ambrose, *Eisenhower*, Vol. II, *The President* (New York 1984).

5. Dwight D. Eisenhower, *The White House Years, Waging Peace 1956–1961*, (London 1966), p. 267.

6. Ibid. p. 275.
7. 'The delegation was seen off from the airport by a large crowd which included the heads of diplomatic missions. A notable absentee was the Ambassador of the US. This incident might be dismissed as too trivial to be included in an account of the period were it not for the fact that such studied discourtesies are long remembered in Laos.' Simmonds, 'Independence and Political Rivalry in Laos 1945–61', p. 180.
8. George W. Ball, *The Past Has Another Pattern* (New York 1982).
9. Roger Hilsman, *To Move A Nation* (New York 1967), p 112.
10. Arthur M. Schlesinger, *Robert Kennedy And His Times* (New York 1979), pp. 490–2.
11. In 1963, for example, the total value of exports excluding gold was put at a modest 57 million *Kip*. The value of imports was 2,323 million *Kip*. Budget revenue for the year came to 915 million *Kip*, while budget expenditure came to over 5,000 million. Short, 'The Differential Economy', *Far Eastern Economic Review*, December 24, 1964.
12. Professor Simmonds remarks 'It could be said that both the United States and the Communists now had front organisations in Laos.'
13. Hilsman, op. cit. p. 115.
14. Eisenhower, op. cit. p. 608.
15. Toye, op. cit. p. 142. Colonel Toye is too modest to mention it but the account in his book is based on his conversations with Kong Lé at the time of the coup.
16. According to Schlesinger, *A Thousand Days* (Fawcett 1965), p, 165. McNamara, on the other hand, said, flatly 'President Eisenhower advised against unilateral action in connection with Laos.' McNamara also records a divergence of opinion between Eisenhower and the outgoing Secretary of State, Christian Herter. Herter thought Communist members of a Laotian government would undoubtedly lead to subversion and a communist government. Eisenhower thought that even with communist representatives it might be possible to maintain a coalition government indefinitely. Another apparent discrepancy: according to outgoing Defense Secretary Gates the US could not of course meet two limited war 'situations' going on at the same time. According to McNamara Gates said 'The US can handle any number of small limited war situations at one time.' Also according to McNamara's account, when Kennedy asked what action could be taken to keep the Chinese Communists out of Laos there was no answer from Eisenhower. Among items of interest from Herter's 'memorandum for the record' of the same meeting on 19 January 1961 is that the British were chary about recognizing the 'new' government in Laos but that he, and presumably the State Department, were not; that this legal government now had the right to request SEATO assistance should external aggression be established and that, in their view, such aggression was constituted by the Soviet airlift. McNamara to President, 24 January 1961; Herter memo, 19 January. NSF Country File, Vietnam. Johnson Library. Historically, perhaps, the most interesting item in the McNamara account is 'President Eisenhower stated in the long run the US cannot allow the Castro Government to continue to exist in Cuba.'

17. G. F. Hudson, Richard Lowenthal, Roderick MacFarquhar, *The Sino-Soviet Dispute* (London 1961).
18. Extracts from Khrushchev's speech may be found in David Floyd, *Mao Against Khrushchev*, (London 1964), p. 308.
19. Hilsman, op. cit. p. 414.
20. The memorandum will be found in *US-Vietnam Relations*, Book 11, pp. 1–12.
21. *US-Vietnam Relations*, Book 2, IV A.5, pp. 88–92.
22. W. C. Gibbons, *The US Government and the Vietnam War* (Washington 1984), Part II, p. 14. footnote 31.
23. So far, four eight-man teams had been organized 'for harassment' but had only been used in the South. Counter-insurgency, on the other hand, like the shibboleth it became, was not widely understood but, where it was, it suggested US intervention on a massive scale.
24. Theodore Sorenson, *Kennedy* (London 1965), p. 271.
25. Kennedy's article 'What Should US Do In Indo-China?' (*Foreign Policy Bulletin*, May 15, 1954) hardly answered his own question. Although it struck all the right notes it was difficult to pick out the tune.
26. As Assistant Secretary for Far Eastern Affairs in 1951 Rusk had denounced the 'Peiping' régime as a 'Slavic Manchukuo': tantamount to a colonial Russian government. 'It is not the government of China. It will not pass the first test. It is not Chinese.' Warren Cohen, *Dean Rusk* (The American Secretaries of State and Their Diplomacy, Volume XIX) (New Jersey 1980).
27. Gibbons, op. cit. p. 14.
28. Ibid. pp. 35–6.
29. *Pentagon Papers* (Gravel), II, p. 642.
30. Sorenson, op. cit. p. 301.
31. Gibbons, op. cit. p. 20.
32. Herbert S. Parmet, *JFK* (London 1984), p. 148.
33. This is still according to Robert Kennedy, cited by Parmet. A somewhat different account is given in a 'Pentagon Papers' memorandum, *US-Vietnam Relations*, Book 11, pp. 62–6.
34. Ibid. p. 66.
35. Arthur M. Schlesinger, *Robert Kennedy and His Times* (New York 1978). p. 757.
36. Ibid. p. 758.
37. *US-Vietnam Relations*, Book 11, pp. 159–66.
38. Ibid. p. 132.
39. At a farewell dinner Johnson compared Diem – at least in certain characteristics – to George Washington, Andrew Jackson, Woodrow Wilson and Franklin Roosevelt. Vice-Presidential Security File, Far East Trip, May 1961. Johnson Library. One suspects these were unscheduled references.
40. Later, in his own language, he told a large gathering of Senators 'If a bully can come in and run you out of the yard today, tomorrow he will come back and run you off the porch', Gibbons, op. cit. p. 46.
41. The recommendations are summarized in a memorandum from Rusk to the President, 28 July 1961. Gareth Porter, *Vietnam: The Definitive Documentation of Human Decisions* (London 1979), Vol. 2, p. 112.

42. Pentagon Papers (Gravel) II, pp. 167–73.
43. According to Schlesinger, *A Thousand Days*, Khrushchev again referred to their 'sacred' nature, p. 339.
44. A somewhat ʄuller version than that of the Pentagon Papers is in Porter op. cit. pp. 128–34.
45. Rostow's widely quoted address 'Guerilla Warfare in Under Developed Areas', a paraphrase of Kennedy's inaugural, is a fanfare without many notes and a justification for US intervention in Vietnam. It may be compared with the presentation which Roger Hilsman gave: 'Internal War; The New Communist Tactic' on 1 August 1961; with unmistakable Cold War attitudes and deductions but far more interesting and penetrating than Rostow. The principal parts may be found in T. N. Greene *The Guerilla – And How To Fight Him* (New York 1962).
46. Gibbons, op. cit. p. 91.
47. Ball, op. cit. p. 366.
48. U. Alexis Johnson, *The Right Hand Of Power* (New Jersey 1984), pp. 324–5.
49. Ball, op. cit. p. 364.
50. Gibbons, op. cit. p. 97.
51. Rusk's extraordinary idea that any plan of action in North Vietnam should strike first at any Viet Cong *airlift* into South Vietnam apparently went unchallenged.
52. The Senator Gravel edition of the Pentagon Papers, Vol. II has a superb analysis of 'The Fall Decisions' in the chapter 'The Kennedy Commitments and Programs', 1961.
53. Gravel II, p. 98.
54. *US-Vietnam Relations*, Book 11, p. 419–20. National Security Action Memorandum no. 111, Nov. 22, 1961.
55. Gibbons, op. cit. Part II, pp. 99–100.
56. Ibid. p. 103.
57. Kennedy's letter to Diem on 14 December 1961. In State Department *Bulletin*, 1 Jan. 1962.
58. Below decks there were also US landing craft.
59. Summary report, Laos, 27 March 1961. Vietnam Task Force. Kennedy Library.
60. Gibbons, op. cit. pp. 108–9.
61. As early as May 1961, when he was in Geneva for the opening of the Laotian conference, Rusk had warned 'We cannot now carry out expanded Vietnam program with any hope of reconciling it with restrictions of Geneva clause as interpreted by ICC.' Rusk to State, from Geneva, 14 May 1961. Kennedy Library.
62. McNamara memo to Rusk, 18 December, *US-Vietnam Relations*, Book 11, p. 426.
63. *US-Vietnam Relations*, Book 12, pp. 442–4.
64. RWK memo 20 July 1961, Kennedy Library.
65. Komer's reflections on Vietnam may be found in *Bureaucracy at War* (London 1986).
66. Sir Robert Thompson, *No Exit from Vietnam* (London 1969), Ch. 9, 'Failure of American Strategy'.
67. Thompson to Diem, 13 November 1961, *US-Vietnam Relations*, Book 11, p. 347.

68. *Pentagon Papers* (Gravel), Vol. II, p. 164.
69. *US-Vietnam Relations*, Book 11, p. 408.
70. *US-Vietnam Relations*, Book 12, p. 480.
71. Hilsman, op. cit. p. 444.
72. It first flew south to Singapore, so as not to compromise the Malayan government, and then, from a British base, it flew north.
73. Gibbons, op. cit. p. 116.
74. Quoted in Milton E. Osborne, *Strategic Hamlets in South Vietnam*, South-East Asia Data Paper, p. 35, Cornell University, NY, April 1965.
75. *Pentagon Papers* (Gravel), Vol. II, p. 128.
76. Ibid. p. 151.
77. Duncanson, op. cit. pp. 326–7.
78. Truong Nhu Tang, *Journal of a Vietcong* (London 1986), Ch. 6, 'Albert Pham Ngoc Thau: Master Spy'.
79. Extracts from a resolution of an enlarged conference of COSVN, October, 1961 are in Porter, op. cit. Vol. II, pp. 119–23.
80. The figures taken from North Vietnamese sources, are given in Duiker, op. cit. p. 215.
81. 'The situation and short term prospects in South Vietnam', *US-Vietnam Relations*, Book 12, p. 488.
82. *Pentagon Papers* (Gravel), Vol. II, p. 719.
83. Gibbons, op. cit. p. 140.
84. Three studies of counter-insurgency, and the shortcomings in its application to Vietnam, may be found in Douglas Blaufarb, *The Counter Insurgency Era* (New York 1977); Larry E. Cable, *Conflict of Myths, The Development of American Counter-Insurgency Doctrine in the Vietnam War* (New York 1986); Andrew F. Krepinevich, *The Army and Vietnam* (Baltimore/London 1986).
85. Gibbons, op. cit. p. 145.
86. National Security files, meetings and memoranda, 27 August Conversation with the President, Kennedy Library. Excerpts from this discussion may also be found in George McT. Kahin *Intervention* (New York 1987) (Anchor), pp. 161–3.
87. Hilsman, op. cit. p. 483.
88. Hilsman's account may be compared with that of George Ball, op. cit. and the interleaved reminiscences to be found in Charlton and Moncrieff, op. cit. I am grateful to the late Governor Harriman, and his office, for allowing me to read his Oral History in the Kennedy Library which throws light on this and many other episodes of the US involvement in Laos and Vietnam.
89. *Pentagon Papers* (Gravel) Vol. II, p. 734.
90. Gibbons, op. cit. p. 149.
91. Kahin, op. cit. p. 157.
92. Gibbons, op. cit. p. 163.
93. McNamara was apparently in such a hurry that he ordered his representative to depart within 90 minutes. Hilsman said he had to get the departure delayed until the State Department representative arrived at the airfield. Hilsman, op. cit. p. 501.
94. Kahin, op. cit. p. 166.
95. Memorandum for the President, 2 October 1963. Report of McNamara/

Taylor mission to South Vietnam. NSF Country file, Kennedy Library.

96. Gibbons, op. cit. p. 189.
97. Geoffrey Warner, who interviewed a number of the people concerned, presents a remarkable account in two articles on 'The United States and the Fall of Diem', *Australian Outlook*, December 1974 and April 1975. I am indebted to Professor Warner, also, for a copy of an unpublished lecture on the same subject.
98. Kahin, op. cit. p. 169. See also, Cooper, *The Lost Crusade*. Ch. 9.
99. Director, Intelligence and Research, to Secretary of State, 15 September 1963, meetings and memoranda, Kennedy Library. Harriman recounted 'He had just been down to Morocco: said he was going to settle the differences between Morocco and Algeria. Not well balanced; I don't mean to say he was off his rocker but he wasn't a rational administrator.' Harriman, Oral History, Kennedy Library.
100. Schlesinger, *Robert Kennedy and His Times*, pp. 778–9.
101. NSF Country, Lodge to Secretary of State, 6 November, Kennedy Library.

Chapter 7

JOHNSON'S CHOICE: 1963–1965

President Johnson, for reasons which are totally unclear to me, had
some kind of belief or conviction, I don't know how strong it was, that
because President Kennedy had been in a sense responsible for Diem's
demise, he in turn was assassinated himself. I mean, it was a strange
and rather bizarre view he held. I don't know how convinced he was
about it, but I've heard him say it, and it rather surprised me because
I was wondering exactly how he'd put this together in his head.

That recollection of Richard Helms, whom Johnson eventually
appointed as Director of Central Intelligence, however serious
the President might have been, and however he might have put
it together, is an extraordinary and haunting idea to have come
from one of the least metaphysical of American Presidents.[1] In a
sense, however, they were responsibilities which Johnson himself
carried throughout his presidency. In the first place US involvement
in the coup, even if it was only negative in that they knew but did
not speak of it to Diem, had produced an air of complicity as well
as a renewed stake in the successor government. Johnson had not
approved of the coup but now had to live with its consequences, for
better or for worse. As he also had to live with the consequences of
Kennedy's assassination when he was catapulted from the comparative obscurity of the vice-presidency to assume the mantle and the
legacy of America's youngest, and, so his supporters believed, most
attractive president of the twentieth century. Johnson did not come
out of, nor did he fit, the Kennedy mould. He was, essentially, an
American rather than a world politician and where Truman, coming
like Johnson, unexpectedly, to the presidency had suddenly attained
international stature in the closing months of the Second World War,
Johnson was more inclined to recreate the mood and opportunities of
America in the recovery of the 1930s and the policies of his political
hero before Roosevelt became an international statesman and leader
of the free world.

Johnson's aspirations and achievements may be found in the inside covers of his memoirs, the extraordinary panorama of the 'Landmark Laws of the Lyndon B. Johnson Administration' with which the President and Congress 'wrote a record of hope and opportunity for America'. His more limited knowledge of the world, almost paranoid perception – or, at least presentation – and natural exaggeration may be found in his map of Southeast Asia in 1965 where, on a given Djakarta–Hanoi–Peking–Pyongyang axis, communist pincers are shown to be closing from north and south.[2]

After the event Johnson and his team of writers went to some trouble to present Vietnam as part of the grand design of containment and the rejection of appeasement with which, by implication, Johnson had been associated since before Pearl Harbour. There was to be no doubt that, once the nation's pledge had been given, Johnson was not just a sunshine supporter, someone who would run for cover when the storm broke. 'The protection of American interests in a revolutionary, nuclear world is not for men who want to throw in our hand every time we face a challenge.'[3] Vietnam at the end of 1963 was the obvious challenge: both to US foreign policy and to its continuity. For Johnson it was an inherited problem; and at first it looked like a reflex announcement which suggested that it would be dealt with as the continuation of hereditary policies.

The first of Johnson's presidential decisions on Vietnam, that of 26 November 1963, was contained in National Security Action Memorandum 273 and was described in the Pentagon Papers as 'an interim don't rock-the-boat document'. Before this reaffirmation of policies was issued – and the President had declared, publicly, to a joint session of Congress that the US would honour its commitments from West Berlin to South Vietnam – Johnson had talked to Ambassador Lodge who had been scheduled to meet President Kennedy in Washington. Lodge, perhaps most of all, assumed that the removal of Diem would allow the US to wipe the slate clean and to start again with an effective, responsible and popular régime in South Vietnam. His military counterpart, General Harkins, with whom Lodge was hardly on speaking terms, was worried about the upsurge of Viet Cong activity and the wholesale removal of Vietnamese province chiefs who had been appointed by and were presumably loyal to the old régime but, like Lodge, gave an optimistic account when the principal US policy makers had met in Honolulu on 20 November 1963.

It was at this meeting that planning had begun for a stepped-up programme of what has been described as 'non-attributable hit-and-run' raids against North Vietnam and the *New York Times* commentator, Hedrick Smith, goes on to assert: 'In his first Vietnam policy document, on November 26, President Johnson gave his personal sanction to the planning for these operations.'[4] Probably this may be inferred from the specific NSAM reference:

7. Planning should include different levels of possible increased activity, and in each instance there should be estimates on such factors as:
   a) Resulting damage to North Vietnam;
   b) Plausibility of denial;
   c) Possible North Vietnamese retaliation;
   d) Other international reaction[5].

and, in any event, when McNamara was, once again, dispatched to Saigon on 20 December, the official US Navy historians record that he showed great interest in developing full capacity for early implementation of several actions contemplated under Operation Plan 34A. For more than a year the Kennedy administration, in Washington and in Saigon, had been considering how US motor torpedo boats could be used in coastal raids on North Vietnam; and on one occasion, in May 1962, an American submarine had apparently been used in a co-ordinated operation with South Vietnamese frogmen in an attempt to sink a North Vietnamese gunboat at its base in Qang Khe.[6] Nothing much seems to have come of such operations but with the arrival of faster boats and a new and more amenable government in Saigon McNamara was able to report on 21 December that plans for a wide variety of covert sabotage and psychological operations against North Vietnam had been prepared from which 'we should aim to select those that provide maximum pressure with minimum risk'.

Like Kennedy before him who, in turn, had inherited the Bay of Pigs operation from Eisenhower, Johnson had thus acquired and approved operational plans which, in themselves little more than pin pricks, would nevertheless become US-organized attacks against North Vietnam and the occasion for much more dramatic and momentous events in the Gulf of Tonkin. The new President had, as it were, been put in charge but had also become part of a machine that had been running for years and, as far as direction was concerned, was content, even after the event, to let it be described as 'Steady On Course'. The practically simultaneous deaths of Diem and Kennedy, while they might have provided the opportunity for a major reassessment of US policies and objectives in Vietnam, in the event produced nothing of the kind although it has been suggested that if Kennedy had lived he would have withdrawn the US from Vietnam. After Diem's death and a certain opening up of South Vietnamese society and government many of the shortcomings in 'performance', hitherto concealed, became obvious; but whether or not that would have been enough to persuade Kennedy to change course is open to question. Certainly it was not enough to persuade Kennedy's advisers, most of whom stayed with Johnson, nor the great officers of state who, like Johnson, continued to believe in Kennedy's last public will and testament on Vietnam: that withdrawal would be a great mistake.[7]

For the next six months, from Kennedy's assassination in November

1963 to the drafting of a 30-day scenario in May 1964 showing how the US could simultaneously launch air attacks on North Vietnam and call for a conference on Vietnam, the problem for the US was, without overthrowing the North Vietnamese government or destroying the country, whether what the scenario described as 'DRV-directed Viet Cong terrorism and resistance to pacification efforts in the South' could be stopped. If the government of Vietnam was itself to prove more capable of dealing with the insurgency this would obviously be half the battle won and, just as Diem's government had become the scapegoat of almost everything that had gone wrong so the highest hopes were placed on the ability of his successor, General Minh, to turn things around. A month later, following McNamara's visit to Saigon in December, these hopes seemed to be vanishing but it would have been hard for any president to be sure that he was reading the right signals. Lodge and McNamara, for example, were like weather balloons blowing in opposite directions while McCone, the CIA Director, who could see no basis for optimistic forecasts in November, said he was a little less pessimistic in December than the Secretary of Defense. McNamara, on the basis of his report to Johnson on 21 December, seemed, in one sentence, to go from one end of the scale to the other: 'running scared, hoping for the best' but, in any event, preparing for more forceful moves if the situation did not show early signs of improvement.[8]

Again blaming 'undue reliance on distorted Vietnamese reporting' what in effect McNamara was saying was that he had had no idea until then how bad things were. The strategic hamlet programme was foundering; the Vietnamese generals were preoccupied with politics; the government was indecisive; and if current trends were not reversed in the next two or three months they would lead to neutralization at best and more likely to a communist-controlled state. McNamara conceded that he might be overly pessimistic but presumably believed that 'more forceful moves' would somehow reverse the unfavourable trends. At this stage it is a moot point whether the frailties of South Vietnam could properly be ascribed to the North. The best guess, according to McNamara, was that between 1,000 and 1,500 Viet Cong cadres had entered South Vietnam from Laos in the first nine months of 1963 while the Mekong route was being used for heavier weapons and ammunition. Nevertheless, as far as the Joint Chiefs of Staff and their new Chairman, General Maxwell Taylor, were concerned if North Vietnamese support ceased 'the character of the war in South Vietnam would be substantially and favourably altered'. Their solution to the problem was entirely military although the objective was political. South Vietnam, the pivot 'in our world wide confrontation' with the communists was, said Taylor, the first real test of our determination to defeat the communist wars of national liberation formula; and, in an open-ended version of the domino proposition, he argued that the effects of US failure would be felt in Africa and Latin America as well as in Asia. In order to convince the enemy of US determination 'to see the Vietnam campaign through to a favourable conclusion' it seemed that the US would have to prepare for an equally open-ended commitment and, putting aside many of its self-imposed restrictions, would have to prepare for whatever levels of activity might be required.

In practical terms Taylor wanted, first, to make the US military commander responsible for the total US programme in South Vietnam. Next, he wanted the government of Vietnam to turn over the tactical direction of the war to the US and then, on an ascending scale of aerial bombing, mining the sea approaches and commando raids on North Vietnam, with a final commitment if necessary of US forces in direct operations against the North; any or all of these actions would convince friend and foe alike that the US was determined to win. As he makes plain in his memoirs Taylor deplored the absence of what he called authoritative political guidance and in this case he may well have felt that by providing the means he was forcing the US to face up to the implications of their objectives in Vietnam.[9] Although he said the Joint Chiefs were aware that the focus of the counter-insurgency battle lay in South Vietnam itself, and that the war 'must certainly be fought and won primarily in the minds of the South Vietnamese people', what in fact he was doing was to suggest that the US should fight a different war altogether or, rather, two wars. First, an American war, American style, against the communist forces in the South with at least the implication that US troops might be used and, certainly, that it would be fought under a US commander. Second, the US should co-ordinate the war against the North, and, again, the implication was that in the last resort it would have to be done by US forces. In all of this it would seem that the government of Vietnam was to play a marginal role and although it was on a much later occasion that Taylor signalled 'Not much of a government is required for the GVN to play its role' it could already be seen that it was in danger of becoming a secondary consideration.

THE KHANH COUP

A week after Taylor had sent his memorandum to the Secretary of Defense the government of South Vietnam collapsed. That is to say General Minh, who had succeeded Diem as head of state less than three months before, was himself succeeded by General Khanh in a coup which removed him and, as Taylor said, 'the generals we knew best'. It may also be said that whatever hopes or expectations of increased political stability after the Diem upheaval collapsed with it as the Khanh coup, far more than the removal of Diem, revealed the essential political weakness of South Vietnam. In a New Year message a month before the coup General Minh had been assured by Ambassador Lodge, on Rusk's instructions, that he had the complete support of the US government as *the* leader of Vietnam. A month later the US had to pretend that, although he had been removed, it was an internal reorganization; that it may have been unwelcome; that, unlike the Diem affair, the US had had nothing whatever to do with it; but that it would now make the best of it.

In one respect at least the Khanh government may have been a great relief to the US. Whether or not he took it seriously, whether or not the Americans believed him and whether or not it was just a convenient excuse General Khanh had told the Americans that pro-French, pro-neutralist, generals were planning a palace coup after which they would call for the neutralization of South Vietnam. While all of this may have reflected fears that recent French initiatives – the belated and what for the US was very unwelcome French recognition of Communist China as well as calls for the neutralization of Southeast Asia – might be having their effect in South Vietnam, the striking thing when Khanh evidently made his intentions clear to Ambassador Lodge, was that the Ambassador's first thought was to protest to de Gaulle rather than to warn the GVN and in the event Lodge gave Washington 45 minutes' notice of Khanh's impending coup.[10] For the moment, at any rate, the coup seemed to take care of the dangers of neutralism in South Vietnam but it was in response to a tentative suggestion of neutralization that arose within the US that Johnson's advisers defined their position and, in rejecting it, left practically no alternative than to plan for extended US commitments.

Senator Mansfield, moving over many years from support to opposition, is one of the more reliable barometers of American opinion on the Vietnam experience. In early January 1964 he warned Johnson, 'We are close to the point of no return in Vietnam' and rather than fight another Korean War which might again involve China Mansfield thought there should be more emphasis on Vietnamese rather than US responsibilities and some sort of international effort to bring about a peaceful solution.[11] Whether France could be a key factor in bringing an end to the conflict between North and South Vietnam and whether at the same time, South Vietnam's control of its territory could be strengthened, might have been incompatible objectives which begged a number of further questions; but they were sufficient to require a refutation from Johnson's three principal civilian advisers on whom he would rely in framing his policy on Vietnam. McGeorge Bundy said the US should not be the first to quit in Saigon and warned Johnson that the political damage to Truman and Acheson from the fall of China arose because most Americans came to believe that 'we could and should have done more than we did to prevent it'. Only when we were stronger in South Vietnam, said Bundy, could the US face negotiations. McNamara went further. Even on the existing ground rules, he said, and although the security situation was serious, 'We can still win', whereas any deal to divide or 'neutralise' South Vietnam would inevitably mean a new government in Saigon that would in short order become Communist-dominated. Because the stakes in preserving an anti-Communist South Vietnam were so high the US had to go on bending every effort to win and he was confident that the American people were by and large in favour of a policy of firmness and strength in such situations.[12]

Whether McNamara in fact had sufficient political acumen to make such a confident prediction perhaps turns on what he meant by 'every effort'. It was a concept which Rusk, significantly, chose not to explore although the implications of relying on what the GVN could do were not very hopeful. 'We believe the fight against the Vietcong can be won without major and direct US involvement provided the new South Vietnamese Government takes the proper political, economic and social actions to win the support of the rural people *and* uses its armed forces effectively.'[13] What would happen if it did not was left unsaid. Three weeks later the Khanh coup again threw South Vietnam into political turmoil and the prospects of the government of Vietnam doing the right thing on their own seemed even more remote.

DEBATE AND DECISION IN HANOI

In one respect at least, however, Rusk was almost certainly right when he commented on Senator Mansfield's idea of a diplomatic offensive: it would not work until the North Vietnamese had become convinced that they could not succeed in destroying the Republic of Vietnam by guerrilla warfare. This, however, was almost the exact moment when the North Vietnamese became convinced that they would in fact have to increase their support for the revolution in the South; that, for the moment at least, the prospects of a general uprising against the new régime were almost as bleak as the prospects of the government's stability began to appear to the US; and that, although they would in the long run be able to take advantage of their political strength, the time had come to redress the military balance of power in South Vietnam.

It was a remarkable decision, both nationally and internationally, and for the government of North Vietnam demonstrated its ultimate commitment to the proposition that Vietnam was one and indivisible.

One of the reasons, perhaps, why the Ninth Plenum of the Vietnamese Workers Party Central Committee meeting in Hanoi in December 1963 decided that it would begin to commit its own regular forces may have been that, although they would only be sent in small numbers, it was thought that they would be sufficient to tip the balance in favour of the revolutionary forces; and even if they did not they would make up for any lost momentum if some of the NLF believed that at least one of their objects had been achieved with the overthrow of Diem. Another reason to which this is linked is put forward by Duiker: if further destabilization could be effected in the South, and quickly, the US might be persuaded to disengage. Or, as perhaps some of the early American pessimists such as Senator Mansfield would have argued, there was no longer anything worth fighting for. A third possibility, again suggested by Duiker, is that 'the inherited experience of the Party in leading the Vietnamese revolutionary movement' really did add up to a belief that power grew out of the barrel of a gun.[14] Having comprehensively defeated the forces of French colonialism with that culminating and remarkable set-piece battle at Dien Bien Phu, loosening the grip of the Americans, who were not nearly so well established, politically or economically, and had far less to lose, might not be impossible either.

It seems nevertheless to have been a traumatic decision which came at the end of a heated debate. In effect the Party recognized that North Vietnam, like the US, was about to commit itself to large-scale war in the South with all the unknown suffering which that might involve. Taking the Battle of Ap-Bac as a yardstick, and the demonstrated Viet Cong ability to defeat government forces, they realized that unless the US did decide to withdraw they would probably have to introduce their own fighting forces and if the Americans came in sufficient numbers, turning South Vietnam into a neo-colonial dependency, it would mean another bloody and protracted war, this time against the most powerful nation in the world. Such a daunting prospect alone would have prompted second thoughts but there were ideological differences as well which divided the Party. In general, it was the Chinese who supported the communist struggle in Vietnam and it was the Russians who, in spite of their formulation of wars of national liberation, did not. Not least of North Vietnam's problems therefore was how to avoid taking sides in the Sino–Soviet split: how not to alienate the USSR and how not, conversely, to become enthralled to China. Unmistakably, at least for the moment, they were going to lean to one side: far enough to produce 'rightist deviation' among a number of Party members, identified by Le Duan as mostly intellectuals – and even, reportedly, to a request from some PAVN (People's Army of Vietnam) officers for transfer to the USSR and to the Red Army.[15]

For the rest, however, there was the consoling argument that the US was 'strategically vulnerable' so that even if it did increase its commitment it would have its own problems to deal with. Each side, therefore, at this stage was preparing to do what was necessary to persuade the other that it could not win in South Vietnam and, as it happened, each side was prepared to raise its stakes in a process of reciprocal escalation. Nevertheless it is still somewhat surprising that the North Vietnamese decided to send regular formations to the South in 1964 and thus give the US the opportunity to present it as 'foreign' intervention although, with the equivalent of a full division of Americans in South Vietnam by the end of 1963, it is another moot point who and when began the intervention first.

Coming to its momentous decision to increase its contribution to revolution in the South may have been hard enough for North Vietnam; but while the commitment to South Vietnam was in no doubt it looked as if the US would also have to do more, if only to try to maintain some sort of stability for the government, and it would obviously be more difficult, politically, to go in deeper after it had already been announced that 1,000 US troops were to be withdrawn. Nevertheless, reporting from Saigon after the Khanh coup, Ambassador Lodge declared 'Our side knows how to do it; we have the means with which to do it; we simply need to do it.'[16] Was this true and, in any event, how was it to be done? Even if Lodge and the US military commander in Vietnam, General Harkins, were personally at odds they both managed to arrive at optimistic conclusions from disconcerting data. Thus, according to Harkins, in the last quarter of 1963 and in spite of political turbulence, a satisfactory tempo of operations was maintained: but they were not effective. Training programmes were 'quantitatively satisfactory': but had not developed combat aggressiveness or compensated for the lack of other motivations. In fact, 'If the military aspects of the fourth quarter of calendar year 1963 were viewed in isolation, or could in any way be considered typical, the forecast will be pessimistic in nature and a complete reappraisal of US effort, approach, and even policy would be indicated.'[17]

From other points of view there were much more alarming forecasts although, in retrospect and if one accepts the otherwise gloomy CIA assessment that the 'greatest single positive achievement during three months of post-Diem régime was measurable success of General Minh in establishing himself as popular leader', it would seem as if, before the Khanh coup at the end of January, there had been a moment when a popular government might have had more success with positive and imaginative measures to secure support in the villages. On the other hand, with their vastly superior intelligence (one notes in passing that US military advisers working in intelligence were 'rotated' like everyone else after twelve months: the point at which most foreign intelligence officers began to be useful) and their ability to mount bigger operations with heavier weapons (one of the consequences of the Ninth Plenum seems to have been a standardization and improvement in weapons available in the South) the communist insurgents were doing well compared to the slow-moving and not very heroic ARVN forces; and with the Laotian and Cambodian frontiers practically open the entire pacification effort was compared 'to mopping the floor before turning off the faucet'.

'THE MOST CRITICAL SITUATION'

Thus, with a Special National Intelligence Estimate concluding that unless there was a marked improvement in the effectiveness of the GVN and its armed forces there was only an even chance that it would survive 'during the next few weeks or months', it is not surprising that the Pentagon Papers analyst in turn concluded 'As winter drew to an end in February-March 1964, it was recognised, as it had never been fully recognised before, that the situation in Vietnam was deteriorating so rapidly that the dimensions and kinds of efforts so far invested could not hope to reverse the trend.'[18] When McNamara and Taylor were once again sent out to Saigon they had been told 'RVN faces the most critical situation in nearly ten years of existence'. When they came back after a visit that included deliberate and ostentatious endorsement of General Khanh (Johnson had said he wanted photos of Khanh triumphant, physically supported by Taylor and McNamara, on the front pages of the world press) McNamara's recommendations were adopted word for word in the National Security Action Memorandum (288) which defined US policy. Presumably, as the recommendations were based on the analysis, this was approved as well and it was, probably, the most portentous official US statement on Vietnam since the 1950s. It seemed in fact to echo Taylor in that it was now the fate of all Southeast Asia which turned on whether the US preserved an independent non-communist Vietnam and how the US was seen to respond in this test case of its capacity to meet a communist war of liberation. In his analysis McNamara was walking a tight-rope between pessimism and optimism. Forty per cent of the countryside was under VC control or predominant influence; but the 'military tools and concepts of the GVN/US effort are generally sound and adequate'. The Khanh government was of 'uncertain viability'; on the other hand it had 'a good grasp' of the basic elements of rooting out the Vietcong'. 'Additions in US personnel' were not indicated under current policy but the Vietnamese armed forces would have to be increased by at least 50,000 men and the para-military forces totally reorganized.

Essentially the recommendations were for a middle course, between the extremes of 'neutralisation' and direct military action against North Vietnam, both of which were rejected and while many of them seem sensible enough and undramatic in themselves there were two underlying features that were in fact of overwhelming importance. First, 'The US at all levels must continue to make it emphatically clear that we are prepared to furnish assistance and support for as long as it takes to bring the insurgency under control.' Second, and perhaps less obvious, was that most of the recommendations, in so far as they were designed to support pacification and a new programme for national mobilization in South Vietnam, would have needed years to have had effect. On both counts therefore the US just as much as North Vietnam, was committing itself to protracted war but one which, unlike Vietnam, would be on a time-scale that was largely outside US experience in the 19th and 20th centuries.

WAR PLANS

Unless, that is, a way could be found that would persuade North Vietnam that the revolution would not succeed in the South. This was something which McNamara considered in his memorandum but in practical terms he said it would be directed toward 'collapsing the morale and the self-assurance of the Vietcong cadres now operating in South Vietnam and bolstering the morale of the Khanh regime'. The conditions for 'new and significant pressures against North Vietnam' were, first, if the Khanh government took hold vigorously: inspiring confidence, whether or not it made noteworthy progress or, second, if there was hard information on significantly increased arms supply from the North (it is interesting to note that at this stage there was apparently no anticipation of regular PAVN forces). Khanh himself did not at that stage favour overt actions against the North either so it looked as if the retaliatory actions and 'Graduated Overt Military Pressure' would depend upon the discovery of 'significantly' more or better weapons supplied by the North. But apart from interrupting the supply it was not clear how attacking the North would either 'accelerate the realisation of pacification' or 'denigrate' the morale of the Viet Cong forces.

It was nevertheless on these unexamined assumptions that contingency planning on 30 days' notice for attack on North Vietnam took off. Since the beginning of the year, according to the chairman of the Interagency Task Force on Vietnam, there had been constant suggestions from one of the President's advisers, Walt Rostow, about bombing the North[19] and this was the course favoured by the JCS as well. Either this would get North Vietnam to the conference table or it would warn them to reduce their support for the Viet Cong. Rostow's assumption, reinforced by his experience as an economic historian, was that North Vietnam now had an economy – power stations, railroads, even factories – that was vulnerable to air attack and if they were threatened they would be forced to weigh up the destruction against their dogmatic but expendable objective of revolution in the South: 'Ho Chi Minh is no longer a guerilla leader with nothing to lose'.

Simply to start bombing the North however would need some considerable justification and explanation even if, in the spring and early summer of 1964, there were signs of support. Congressman, later President, Ford, for example, had deplored a reluctance on the part of Administration officials to commit US forces to combat for a Vietnam-US victory; and Senator Fulbright, chairman of the Senate Foreign Relations Committee who was later to turn so violently against the war and against Johnson, reckoned that the only options open were to help the South Vietnamese win the war or else to expand it.[20] Either course seemed to lead to attacks on North Vietnam and when McNamara and Taylor met in an informal, unrecorded session with the Foreign Relations Committee at the end of March Taylor already had an outline of three ways in which force could be applied to North Vietnam: border control operations, a selective programme of retaliation, and an escalation of military pressure. Questioned by the Senators, particularly about the US forces this would seem to involve, McNamara implied that extra ground forces would not be required: the US would attack by air.

Although, in the peculiar circumstances that were reported to them, Congress later gave almost unanimous support to the President in the Tonkin Gulf Resolution, this was not something which Johnson and his advisers could have taken for granted. Senator Morse, for example, one of only two Senators and Congressmen to vote against the resolution, told the Senate in March 'We should never have gone in. We should never have stayed in. We should get out.' And Senator Gruening, who was the other one who voted against it, was equally unequivocal: 'The war in South Vietnam is not and never has been a US war.' There were, of course, Senators who took the opposing view – that the war must be carried to its source in North Vietnam – but the necessity for unmistakable (and undeniable) Congressional support had already occurred to the Administration. A couple of days after the critical remarks of Morse and Gruening the State Department's Vietnam Committee, which was looking at 'Alternatives for Imposition of Measured Pressure Against North Vietnam' had before it as a vital part of the scenario a draft Congressional resolution. The problem, however, was to find an occasion, and a time, when it could be introduced. If the US Administration was thinking about attacking North Vietnam, for however long and however strong the attacks might be, and even if it was only to restore peace or allow the government of Vietnam to suppress what might then revert to indigenous revolution, it would probably require the functional equivalent of a declaration of war. It was arguable that the President as Commander-in-Chief already had the inherent power to commit US forces but even if Congressional sensitivity about what US military advisers were actually doing in Vietnam was not that much in evidence the Administration needed the financial support of the lower house and it would at least be prudent to enlist the Senate as well in such a potentially momentous decision.[21]

Two months later the problem was still there, expressed on this occasion in a message from Rusk to Ambassador Lodge in Saigon on 21 May 1964.

> On the basis of my talks with Congressional leaders and committees and a sensing of public concern about Southeast Asia, I am convinced that the American people will do what has to be done if there is something to support. The prospect that we might strike the North, with all of the attendant risks, only to lose the South is most uninviting.[22]

In the interval Rusk had paid his first visit to Vietnam where he had encountered – and to some extent countered – General Khanh's new-found enthusiasm for an attack on the North. After Rusk had returned to Washington, political stability in the South seemed to have slipped once again and Khanh was casting around desperately for remedies: evacuating two million people from Saigon, suspending civil rights (someone seems to have told him that is what Lincoln did in the Civil War) or even declaring war against North Vietnam. With this last point Lodge appeared to sympathize but it was agreed in Washington that when McNamara was in Saigon a week later he was to tell Khanh that the US had no intention either of supporting or undertaking the military objective of rolling back Communist control in North Vietnam.

This, of course, did not rule out the lesser objective of persuading North Vietnam, in Khanh's words, not to interfere in South Vietnam's internal affairs: to which was added the idea of punishing the North if it continued to do so. This simple calculus of 'carrot and stick' as Lodge called it had been considered during Rusk's visit to Saigon in April and involved a secret ultimatum to be delivered in Hanoi by a third party (Canada was suggested) in which North Vietnam was to be told to call off its support for the Viet Cong. In return the US would make food imports available but if it failed to comply it would suffer punitive strikes to which the US would not admit publicly. In order to provide what Lodge called a 'saleable package' which Ho could in turn present to his people Lodge thought it might be necessary to withdraw some Americans from South Vietnam but although the idea of a Canadian intermediary was followed up, the offer of troop withdrawal seems not to have been made nor, if it had, would one have expected anything to have come of it.

The US at this point was obviously about to enter the unknown in the next stages of its policy. No one knew what it would take to stop North Vietnam (nor, in a sense, to 'start' South Vietnam) and even less could the consequences be predicted. Rusk, during his Saigon visit, had discussed the possibilities of Chinese intervention and, according to the Pentagon Papers commentator 'There was speculation whether the use of nuclear weapons against North Vietnam would bring in the Russians.'[23] On a somewhat less apocalyptic but almost as alarming a note 'Bundy (William) conjectured, for argument's sake, that nukes used in wholly unpopulated areas solely for purposes of interdiction might have a different significance than if otherwise'. The argument does not seem to have been pursued but the question remained: how could North Vietnam be prevented from supporting the southern insurgency and how could the Administration secure popular support for whatever it was it decided to do?

In addition to its Vietnam problems the US was confronted with another: what to do about Laos where things started to fall apart after a major communist offensive in May. By then, however, there were four separate groups in Washington engaged in plans and exercises which ranged from total administrative re-organization – and large-scale US bureaucratic intervention – in South Vietnam to the theory and practice of hurting but not destroying the North. One group was trying to predict 'enemy' reactions and another was drafting alternative forms of a Congressional resolution which would validate whatever was to be done. On 23 May the group that was working on military plans completed its 'Scenario for Strikes on North Vietnam' which assumed that whatever the US did in South Vietnam would not prevent further deterioration there together with Lodge's rather more dubious assumption that firm action against the North was the only way to make a significant improvement in South Vietnam's self-defence. Assuming, further, that the time for action had arrived the scenario began with a recommendation that any conference on Laos or Vietnam should be postponed 'until D-Day' and, after the initial warning to Hanoi, proceeded with a joint Congressional resolution, allied consultation, Khanh's demand that North Vietnam should stop its aggression, and then, using that as the cover, the US would simultaneously attack North Vietnam by air, call for a conference on Vietnam, and go to the UN.

Presumably something similar had been drafted before Britain, France and Israel attacked Egypt in 1956, but this ingenious sequence of events that was to take place over 30 days was a part of US contingency planning rather than an operational directive. Nevertheless many of the proposals found their way into the 'Basic Recommendation and Projected Course of Action on South-East Asia' memorandum of the National Security Council's Executive Committee, sent to the President on 25 May, with its conclusion which could have been a paraphrase of Eden's announcement of the Suez operations: 'This peace-keeping theme will have been at the centre of the whole enterprise from the beginning.' There were risks, of escalation toward major land war or the use of nuclear weapons, as well as Viet Cong responses which would lose South Vietnam to neutralism and so eventually to communism, but it was 'the hope and best estimate of most of your advisers that a decision of this kind can be executed without bringing a major military reply from Red China, and still less from the Soviet Union'.[24] Having touched on many of the same issues as the '30 Day' scenario and based on the proposition that the US could not tolerate the loss of Southeast Asia to communism the Committee had this to say on the matter of a Congressional resolution:

> We agree that no such resolution should be sought until Civil Rights is off the Senate calendar, and we believe that the preceding stages can be conducted in such a way as to leave a free choice on the timing of such a resolution. Some of us recommend that we aim at presenting and passing the resolution between the passage of Civil Rights and the convening of the Republican convention. Others believe that delay may be to our advantage and that we could as well handle the matter later in the summer, in spite of domestic politics.

TONKIN GULF

Between then and November the actions of the US in Vietnam would, increasingly, have to be considered in the context of US politics in an election year. If the Administration was going to organize some sort of attacks on North Vietnam it would be important to have the Congressional resolution; but while this had already been drafted there had been no obvious occasion, no dramatic event or atrocity, which would have ensured overwhelming support had it been presented. Then again there was the question of how long it would take for an attack to produce useful results. Would North Vietnam be deterred? What would happen in the South? When the next conference took place at Honolulu at the beginning of June 1964 between McNamara, Rusk (who had stopped off briefly in Saigon), Lodge, and the new American Military Commander in Vietnam, General Westmoreland, Lodge reckoned that most support for the Viet Cong would fade as soon as some 'counter-terrorism measures', as he called them, were taken against the North. Furthermore, he said, they would bolster morale and give the population in the South a feeling of unity. The two options which he instanced were 'If we bombed Tchepone' (one of the staging points, in Laos, of the Ho Chi Minh trail) and the other was an attack on North Vietnam torpedo boats.[25] Among the actions which had already been considered and at one time, apparently, preferred was a blockade of Haiphong – possibly because of the Cuban precedent although whether this could have been accomplished without some act of war is an open question – and it is conceivable that this accounted for the interest in torpedo boats. There was, however, some feeling in the State Department as McGeorge Bundy told Johnson that the US posture towards Vietnam was 'too McNamara war-like' and, as an interesting side-light, the US had supported a UN condemnation of a British air strike in the Yemen because, according to Adlai Stevenson: 'We have a consistent record of opposition to reprisals of this sort' and 'This particular strike was out of all proportion to the provocation – although the provocation was real.'[26]

The line between provoked and unprovoked US air attacks on North Vietnam was soon to become rather blurred and at the end of August, after the Tonkin Gulf incidents, the Pentagon Papers described a JCS memorandum as calling for deliberate attempts to provoke the DRV into actions which could then be answered by a systematic air campaign.[27] Perhaps this camouflage was thought necessary because their earlier proposal for unprovoked attacks – to which, incidentally, their outgoing chairman, General Taylor, apparently did not subscribe – had been turned down. Ten years after it had first been suggested, the JCS wanted to destroy the new 'target complex' at Dien Bien Phu: which was now reckoned to be one of the key points in moving war materials from North Vietnam into Laos and South Vietnam. Instead of limited attacks to change Hanoi's intentions the JCS wanted to make sure of destroying its capabilities but were apparently prepared to compromise on 'sustained attacks' as an initial measure.[28]

At the other end of the scale on which US decisions were being made was, it might be assumed, negotiation. At the UN, however, the US assumed that there might not be enough support in the Security Council for 'affirmative action' on South Vietnam – 'the one thing we do not want is to take our basic political case to the UN and fail to muster a majority' – but in any event the US seemed more intent to ratify than to negotiate its position on Vietnam.[29] There was of course the possibility that its opponents did not understand what this was so when the new Canadian representative on the practically defunct International Control Commission went to Hanoi in June, 1964 his essential role was that of herald. When he had met the Canadian Prime

Minister, Lester Pearson, in New York at the end of May Johnson had said that his message to Hanoi was that, while he was a man of peace, he did not intend to permit the North Vietnamese to take over Southeast Asia. Even if Hanoi's objective had been the more modest one of South Vietnam it seems that the message which Seaborn was given was that the US position was absolutely non-negotiable. According to one account he had conveyed US determination 'to contain the DRV to the territory allocated it' at Geneva in 1954 and to see the GVN's writ run throughout South Vietnam. He had also been told to remind Hanoi that US patience was 'running thin' and if the conflict should escalate the greatest devastation would of course result for the DRV itself.[30] To underline the seriousness of US intentions Seaborn reminded Pham Van Dong that their commitment to South Vietnam had implications expanding far beyond Southeast Asia. Pham Van Dong, apparently, laughed and said he did indeed appreciate the problem. A US defeat in South Vietnam would in all probability start a chain reaction extending much further.

> The USA is in a difficult position, because Khanh's troops will
> no longer fight. If the war gets worse, we shall suffer greatly but
> we shall win. If we win in the South, the people of the world will
> turn against the USA. Our people will therefore accept the sacrifices,
> whatever they may be.[31]

For North Vietnam therefore, just as much for the US, there seemed to be nothing substantive to negotiate about. According to Pham Van Dong what President Ho Chi Minh had meant by a just solution was, first, that the US should withdraw from Indo-China; second, that the affairs of the South must be arranged by the people of the South; third, it meant reunification of the country. The only concession was time. 'We are in no hurry. We are willing to talk but we should wait until South Vietnam is ready.' As for the war itself Pham Van Dong said he suffered to see it go on, to develop, to intensify: 'Yet our people are determined to struggle. It is impossible, quite impossible (excuse me for saying this) for you Westerners to understand the force of the people's will to resist and to continue.'[32]

Beyond those uncompromising positions, prospects of a government of national coalition, which Pham Van Dong said would 'snowball' in the South, were unimportant but there were two further points of interest. First, his statement that the DRV would not enter the war, second, his assertion: 'We shall not provoke the USA.' Other than deception, two months after the decision may already have been taken to send PAVN units to the South, it is an open question, or perhaps a matter of definition, what Pham Van Dong meant by the first statement. But the second, even if it did not mean that he was aware that the US was looking for provocation, did mean, if it was true, that the US could not rely on North Vietnam to put the American scenario into effect. At least in so far as its own regular forces were concerned; but this did not rule out the irregular forces which, although now under the command of General Westmoreland, were to be used for more or less clandestine operations against North Vietnam.

Whether or not one believes that it was these operations, code name Op Plan 34A, which resulted in the mutually acknowledged encounter between North Vietnamese torpedo boats and a US destroyer and aircraft in the Gulf of Tonkin on 2 August they were, in themselves, the first US-directed attacks on North Vietnam. US servicemen had already been killed in South Vietnam in 1964, US aircraft had been shot down and a US aircraft ferry was mined and sunk at Saigon in May. There was, however, no suggestion that 34A operations were designed on a retaliatory basis. Rather, as the official history of *The US Navy and the Vietnam Conflict* puts it: 'In initiating maritime operations, Washington policy makers sought to send a clear signal to Hanoi of US potential for retribution.' Initially, however, they remark, the communication was muffled; as would be the connection with the US Navy on the high seas. Essentially what was under way was a projected series of covert coastal operations, in unmarked boats, with international crews – Vietnamese, Thai, Taiwanese and, apparently 'European' mercenaries – but, unmistakably, under US direction and control. From the beginning of 1964 they were under the overall command of the US Commander in Vietnam; there was an office in the Department of Defense in Washington which 'kept a tight rein' on the operation; and direct oversight of the Naval programme was exercised by the US Naval Advisory Detachment in Danang, the base used by boats operating on missions to the North.[33]

Desultory operations by South Vietnamese frogmen had begun in February 1964: but the first 'significant success' is reckoned to have come at the end of May with the capture of a North Vietnamese junk and the interrogation of its six passengers. In June and July the attacks increased in frequency and intensity and on at least one occasion resulted in quite a heavy fire fight with North Vietnamese defenders. At the same time, in separate operations, US Air Force fighter bombers based in South Vietnam were attacking targets in Laos and naval aircraft from US carriers were flying photographic reconnaissance over Laos and two of them had been shot down in early June. More serious in its consequences were the 'Desoto Patrols' which had begun in 1962 off the northern coastline of China and which were designed 'to collect intelligence concerning Chicom electronic and naval activity . . . establish and maintain Seventh Fleet presence in area [and] serve as a minor cold war irritant to Chicoms'. They were subsequently extended to cover North Korea, the USSR, North Vietnam and Indonesia but the patrolling destroyers were ordered not to approach within 20 nautical miles of the mainland. In 1964 this was reduced to 12 miles but in the case of Vietnam, and for the first time, the destroyer was authorized to close up to four nautical miles to the mainland. The reason for this drastic reduction was the request from General Harkins' command that the patrol should obtain 'intelligence on DRV forces capable [of resisting] projected operations in conjunction with OPLAN 34A' and the destroyer was to photograph, to monitor junk activity, to provide information on VC supply routes and, perhaps most important, to locate and identify coastal radar transmitters.

When the patrol actually took place in March (it had been postponed so as not to interfere with 34A operations) its operational radius had been changed somewhat – up to eight miles from the North Vietnamese mainland but only four to the offshore islands – but it was a large assumption that, as when the French had left ten years earlier, the limit for territorial waters was still only three miles. Whatever it was in law and whenever it was that North Vietnam laid claim to a 12-mile limit the US Pacific Fleet in the mid-twentieth century, like the French Navy in the nineteenth, did not take the Vietnamese very seriously and even in regard to the USSR its commander, in order 'to assert our traditional belief in the right of free use of international waters', had also requested permission to send a destroyer into the Sea of Okhotsk: close enough to Russia for it not to have been entered by a US warship for the previous ten years.

In respect to the guidelines that were issued for the July/August Desoto Patrol, there was apparently a greater awareness of the risks involved than there had been earlier in the year and on-call air support had been arranged from a US carrier. Whether or not this awareness was because of the coincidence with 34A operations, at the time when the destroyer *Maddox* was off the North Vietnamese coast on the morning of 31 July, it was close enough to see the four fast patrol boats returning from a 34A offshore bombardment of the North Vietnamese island on Hon Me. The following day the *Maddox* was passing five miles away from other North Vietnamese islands and the day after that it appears that the North Vietnamese naval headquarters ordered its coastal forces to prepare for battle. In the generalized account which they themselves have given, the North Vietnamese, having noted various air and sea attacks, made no attempt to conceal what happened. 'At noon on Sunday, 2 August 1964 our Navy's Squadron 3 . . . was ordered to set out to resolutely punish the "acts of piracy" of the US imperialists and to attack the destroyer *Maddox* which had penetrated deep into our coastal waters.'[34] Half an hour later North Vietnamese torpedo boats were close enough to be seen by the *Maddox* and when they finally closed, approximately 25 miles from the Vietnamese coast with the *Maddox* making full speed away, the destroyer opened fire and the North Vietnamese boats launched their torpedoes. After 20 minutes the surface action was over but carrier-borne US aircraft immediately afterwards sank one MTB and two others were damaged and beached.[35]

This much seems generally to have been agreed on both sides. Thereafter on the US side the Pacific Fleet Commander wanted to assert the right of freedom of the seas and to resume the patrols; but the conditions that were imposed were, first, that it should not take place during the next 34A coastal operation and second, that it should stay 12 nautical miles from the North Vietnamese mainland. There was now, apparently, 'concern in the Washington intelligence community that the North Vietnamese considered the 34A and Desoto Patrol operations as one'[36] and having suffered a bloody nose in a brave but fruitless attack it was an open question whether the North Vietnamese would risk another. Probably it was not expected and certainly, by itself, the naval clash on 2 August had not been the occasion for any US retaliation. As Johnson put it: 'we would assume the unprovoked attack has been a mistake.' Over the next week this would emerge as the dominant theme in the US presentation: 'unprovoked attack' together with 'freedom of the seas' and 'innocent passage' and might perhaps have been limited to verbal orchestration had it not been for the event, real or imaginary, that was next reported from the Gulf of Tonkin.

Whatever it was that did or did not happen on the night of 4 August first of all removed the restraint on open and damaging US air attacks against North Vietnam, and to that extent may be said to have been the occasion for starting the war, but also afforded the opportunity for a consummately skilful and successful political operation. It began on the morning of 4 August in Washington, 12 hours behind Saigon time, when McNamara, according to Johnson's account, telephoned him to say that there was a strong indication from an intercepted message of another attack on US ships in the Gulf in Tonkin. If Johnson was waiting for something that would, simultaneously, reveal him as a man of action and a man of prudence this was a remarkable opportunity. Having ordered the Desoto Patrol to return to the Gulf of Tonkin after the encounter on 2 August there had, apparently, been another attack on two US destroyers on the night of 4 August. The details subsequently became more and more obscure but when the first reports reached Johnson during a 'leadership breakfast' with Democratic Senators he presented it, presumably as he received it, as another unprovoked attack on US warships on the high seas. Nine torpedoes had been fired at the US destroyers, according to Johnson, and if this was not outrage enough he contributed his own intensely emotional flight of fancy 'Some of our boys are floating around in the water'. If the US ships had been hit this might well have been true, but, for Johnson, it seems that what was conceivable had become reality.[37]

It was a powerful argument and when Johnson appeared on television later than night to announce that, as he spoke, air action was already under way as a 'positive reply' it was described as the response to a multiple attack. Not only was it deliberate and unprovoked, but it was also, as Rusk said, inexplicable; a sort of mad dog act, one might infer, to which there could only be one response. It was not as if just a few shots had been fired. At one point it seemed as if the attackers had fired 22 torpedoes in an encounter that went on for hours with US retaliation by sea and air which had sunk several of the torpedo boats in a repeat performance of what had happened in broad daylight two days earlier. Only this had happened on rather a dark night and the evidence that it happened collides with the doubts of those who think that in reality it never happened at all.[38]

In February 1968 when the Senate Foreign Relations Committee returned to the events in the Gulf of Tonkin one of the sub-headings in the published account of the Secretary of Defense's exhaustive testimony was 'Monstrous Insinuations'. In the interval it had been suggested, and would be again, that whatever had happened on 4 August had, as McNamara described it, been induced by the US to provide it with an excuse for retaliation. Or, as George Ball, Under Secretary of State at the time suggested ten years later, the Desoto Patrols were intended primarily for provocation.[39]

Leaving that as an open question and assuming, further, that when the first reports arrived in Washington of a second attack on 4 August, they were in good conscience taken at their face value, what does in fact appear as a 'monstrous insinuation' is that there was no known connection between 34A operations and the Desoto Patrols. Senator Morse, who suspected that there was, said as much in the Senate on 5 August but the following day he was told categorically by McNamara in committee:

> First, our Navy played absolutely no part in, was not associated with, was not aware of any South Vietnamese actions, if there were any. I want to make that very clear to you. The Maddox was operating in international waters, was carrying out a routine patrol of the type we carry out all over the world at all times. It was not informed of, was not aware of, had no evidence of, and so far as I know today had no knowledge of, any South Vietnamese actions in connection with the two islands, as Senator Morse referred to.[40]

According to the Senate Foreign Relations Committee study there were in fact four points in the US decision-making system where information about both the proposed Desoto Patrols and the proposed 34A operations was available: in Saigon, in Honolulu, and two in Washington but the division of responsibility for the two programmes, the study suggests, could have been responsible for a compartmentalization of knowledge. Whether it was or not it may be argued that there was no reason why the Pacific Command should *not* have known of Westmoreland's coastal operations, and vice versa, and most of the evidence suggests that they did. Similarly, even if they were not perfectly synchronized they were connected in purpose: and yet it was argued that the North Vietnamese should have known perfectly well that they were entirely separate operations and that, inferentially, they should have observed the same nominal distinctions as the US administration would subsequently claim. As they had not, and as the President had announced it as open aggression on the high seas against the US, he had ordered an attack on the torpedo boat bases and oil storage tanks by over 60 US carrier-borne aircraft. A single strike, it was effective in its limited purpose of destroying or damaging the targets and also perhaps as a warning of further attacks. Whether it would in any way persuade Hanoi to reduce its support for the southern revolution was another matter and if it did not would another act of war be necessary?

Before he became Vice-President it was said of Johnson that there could be no doubt that he was among the most effective and powerful leaders in the history of the US Senate.[41] His role as Senate Majority Leader during the Eisenhower presidency had however been to facilitate rather than to criticize Republican foreign policy: to the point where it was also said that his insistence on subordination to the executive on all issues of national security – even denying the right of Congress to information – seriously reduced the Senate's ability to participate in foreign policy decisions; and that by insisting that the Senate yield to the President he reduced its customary right to share in foreign policy. Having just crossed one major barrier on the road between peace and war by an open attack on North Vietnam, but with the likelihood that something more would be needed, Johnson was about to demonstrate that skill of consensus building and deployment which had been the hallmark of his political life. Of his previous Senate mobilizations it was said they were like Greek drama – most of the action had taken place off-stage – and the passage of the Tonkin Gulf resolution through Congress was no exception. With minimum divulgence of detail that could throw into question the account of unprovoked aggression, and with Democrats and Republicans responding to the same patriotic feelings, the House voted unanimously in favour of the joint resolution.

In the Senate it was to prove more difficult: even if the final score of 88–2 in favour of the resolution suggested a runaway victory. Few questions had been asked at a remarkably brief committee session but in the course of a two-day debate, apart from the poignant warnings of Senator Morse, it was obvious that many Senators had reservations about the US position and US policies in Vietnam but hardly anyone thought that was the occasion to voice them. An unprovoked attack had been made on US ships; there had been an appropriate response; and now it was time to close ranks and support the President. Honour, integrity and vital interests were mentioned but it was a sober, responsible and dignified debate in which almost everyone agreed with Senator Fulbright that the situation had been handled in the best possible way and that the joint resolution in turn was the best way to prevent an escalation or enlargement of the war. The reassurance of Fulbright, who was steering the resolution through the Senate, with the support of Majority and Minority leaders, the more important in the case of someone like Mansfield who was known to have fundamental doubts about US policy, allowed the Senators to believe that, open-ended permission notwithstanding, they were voting to contain rather than to expand the war and the US role therein. Senator Nelson had wanted to make it absolutely explicit by introducing an amendment, part of which read: 'Our continuing policy is to limit our role to the provision of aid, training assistance, and military advice, and it is the sense of Congress that, except when provoked to a greater response, we should continue to attempt to avoid a direct military involvement in the South-East Asian conflict.'[42] On procedural grounds Fulbright regretted that he could not accept the amendment but nevertheless he gave it an endorsement which seemed just as valuable as the amendment itself: 'I believe it is an accurate reflection of what I believe is the President's policy, judging from his own statement.'[43]

Four years later when Fulbright was responsible for re-opening a Senate inquiry into what happened in the Gulf of Tonkin, he said that taking the resolution to the floor of the Senate was something he regretted more than anything he had ever done in his life. In particular he wondered why he had not had the sense to question one particular cable, the authenticity of which seemed to have been the basis of his assurance to Senator Nelson that there was absolutely no connection between the US destroyers and any 34-A operations the South Vietnamese themselves might have conducted. When Nelson and Senator McGovern had gone to see Fulbright before the resolution was passed it was apparently presented as a limited response, rather than a blank cheque, something that would defuse the Vietnam issue during the presidential campaign – and something that would help Johnson against Goldwater. Johnson would later argue that Fulbright knew exactly what he was doing when he steered the resolution through the Senate but on two counts this does not seem to be true. First, Fulbright, like everyone else, had been assured and reassured by McNamara that there was no provocation, no incriminating connection, and no doubt that a second attack had taken place. Second, according to the White House Press Secretary at the time, he had very definite assurances from Johnson that the Tonkin Gulf resolution was not going to be used for anything other than the Tonkin Gulf incident itself.[44] According to Senator Gruening, who voted against the resolution, Johnson had also asked him not to introduce a resolution which would have prevented draftees being sent to Vietnam and had said: 'Listen, if we're not out of there by next January you can do anything you please.'[45]

Gruening, incidentally, like many others, said that Johnson could have been one of the great Presidents had it not been for Vietnam. Averell Harriman said he would have been the greatest and in the famous passage of recrimination related by Doris Kearns, Johnson described how he had to abandon his hopes of building the Great Society in America for 'that bitch of a war' in Vietnam. In the summer and autumn of 1964 it seems possible that Johnson had not yet decided to go to war in Vietnam; that he was waiting upon events; and that, like McNamara, he may have been running scared but was hoping for the best. Whatever he was doing, however, after 10 August Johnson had in his pocket a joint Congressional resolution which said that the maintenance of international peace and security in Southeast Asia was vital to US national interests and to world peace; that the US was prepared to take all necessary steps, including the use of armed force, to assist any member of SEATO or protocol state; and that Congress approved and supported his determination, as C.–in–C., to take all necessary means to repel any armed attack against the forces of the US as well as to prevent further aggression.

It is hardly surprising, therefore, that this was described as the functional equivalent of a declaration of war even if, in the minds of at least some who voted for it, they intended the opposite: that, as Johnson proclaimed, there should be no wider war. Perhaps this was the fatal ambiguity: believing in Fulbright's assurances and at the same time allowing the words to stand which would allow the President to do whatever he wanted until either peace was restored or Congress withdrew its support. Ten years earlier, largely perhaps because Britain would not agree, Senators had refused to write a blank cheque and so the Congressional resolution that would have supported US intervention at Dien Bien Phu stayed as a draft in Dulles's pocket. Now it was in Johnson's pocket: but the difference was that it was signed, sealed and delivered.

What Johnson would do with it was another matter, particularly as he was now entering the last stages of a presidential compaign. The purpose of the Congressional resolution may well have been 'to pull the rug out from under Goldwater' and with the simultaneous implication of firmness and restraint, as in the single-strike retaliation, it could be presented as an appropriate, rather than the wildly disproportionate, response which could so easily be hung around the neck of Johnson's Republican opponent, Senator Goldwater. Whereas Johnson was to profit from the ambiguities of the Tonkin Gulf resolution Goldwater never really recovered from his ambiguity about the use of nuclear weapons and the circumstances in which they could be employed.[46]

Appealing to the precursors of the silent majority, the slogan

'In your heart you know he's right' was cleverly turned into 'In your heart you know he might' and perhaps it was the fear that Goldwater, the Air Force Reserve General, would lead the country over the nuclear precipice which more than anything sent Johnson back to the White House, President in his own right, with 'the greatest vote, the greatest margin and the greatest percentage that any President had ever drawn from the American people.'[47] But perhaps, as Theodore White suggests, the election was over before it began, decided long before, perhaps within minutes of the fatal shot at Dallas, and Johnson had properly succeeded to the Kennedy inheritance and to the Kennedy war.

Johnson had also reached the point where the decisions would finally have to be made whether to fight or to let Vietnam go. In July 1964 General Maxwell Taylor had become a new or rather a different but perhaps an even more important player in the bureaucratic game when he took over from Lodge as US Ambassador in Saigon. His previous position as Chairman of the JCS had allowed him to concentrate military opinion on what should be done in Vietnam, as it were, from first principles. Now that he was in Saigon two halves of US policy came together: reports from the field which had the authority and experience of someone who had commanded military forces at the highest level and an input to strategic decisions that would be based on first-hand experience on the spot. Taylor's first report from Saigon, on 10 August, the day Johnson signed the Tonkin Gulf resolution, was surprisingly optimistic and, as he himself admitted, exceeded the optimism of most senior US officials in Saigon. It was surprising in that it described what was at best a political stalemate, even if there had been an extraordinary but rather dubious statistical improvement. Taylor said that only 20 per cent of rural South Vietnam was under Viet Cong control, i.e. half what McNamara said it was in mid March but the principal hopes were to be pinned on contingency plans for action against North Vietnam and a readiness, by 1 January 1965, to put them into effect. In the meantime opportunities or occasions might present themselves when either or both sides, successively, could take the conflict up another notch. One such event occurred on 1 November 1964 at Bien Hoa airfield.

At the same time as the attack was made on the North Vietnamese naval bases on 6 August squadrons of US aircraft began to move up and into mainland Southeast Asia, some to Thailand, but most into South Vietnam with the heaviest concentration, of B-57s (originally the British 'Canberra' medium bomber), stationed at Bien Hoa. As they did not start bombing attacks (and then on South rather than North Vietnam) until the following February their presence which was no doubt intended as a gesture of reassurance and determination also constituted a standing temptation to the guerrillas. So much so that one of Johnson's civilian advisers, Michael Forrestal, wondered whether the Air Force had not deliberately set it up so that they could retaliate.

> They moved these airplanes in when they had no reason to, not the faint-est tactical, strategic, logistical, political reason . . . to move these obsolete jets out of the Philippines and park them all in a row undefended on Bien Hoa airfield. And if you knew, if you had studied, the Vietcong for very long this was something they had to attack, they couldn't restrain themselves. We made all these arguments to the Defense Department . . . but for reasons of their own they went ahead and the President didn't think that was important enough to tackle the Defense Department on. Then they were all blown up.[48]

In the event they were not all blown up but a VC mortar attack destroyed five and damaged thirteen B-57s, killed four Americans and wounded 72. Taylor in Saigon and the JCS in Washington recommended immediate retaliation but, two days before the US election, the answer was, predictably, 'no'. That the US service chiefs were anxious to begin attacks on North Vietnam is borne out by a previous example. Desoto Patrols in the Gulf of Tonkin had been resumed on 17 September. On the following night there seemed to be a repeat performance of what had been reported on 4 August: destroyers manoeuvring to avoid torpedoes, a two-hour engagement, hundred of rounds fired, enemy craft apparently sunk but no corroborating evidence that the US ships had been attacked. Nevertheless the JCS wanted to use the occasion, such as it was, to attack more oil installations, this time in Hanoi and Haiphong, and at the same time to use the not yet destroyed B-57s from Bien Hoa to attack some 40 Chinese MIG fighters which had been flown in to an airfield north of Hanoi at the same time as US aircraft had been deployed to South Vietnam.[49]

HOW TO HELP THE SOUTH

On this occasion, however, Johnson and his civilian advisers were sceptical: and the President made it clear that he was not interested in rapid escalation on such frail evidence and with such a fragile government in South Vietnam. Preoccupation with the impending election apart the weakness of the GVN was to provide the principal limitation on the development of Johnson's policies. As he told his principal advisers on 9 September, he did not wish to enter the patient in a ten-round bout when he was in no shape to hold out for even one. That was already an accurate analogy in the summer of 1964 – 'An absolute shambles. Public law and order broke down in Saigon itself . . . some days when we couldn't find the government'[50] – and with Khanh going around in the revolving door of government – some days he was in power, some days he was not – US frustration was becoming more obvious. Taylor, for example, hardly concealed his disdain for the GVN:

> A group of men who turned off their hearing aids in the face of appeals to the public weal. These people simply did not have the sense of responsibility for the public interest to which we were accustomed, and regularly estimated matters in terms of their own personal gains and losses.[51]

But faced with what the Director of the CIA said was a disturbing prospect of increasing support in South Vietnam for negotiation, Taylor's conclusion was that: 'As long as the armed forces are solid, the real power is secure.' This might have been by way of rejoinder not only to Johnson, who asked what would happen if the GVN got weaker and weaker, but also to McCone who said that they might find that the original US purposes, as set out in Eisenhower's letter of 1954, 'were no longer supported by the people of Vietnam themselves'. It could, also, have been the point where and when the GVN became secondary to US purposes. Taylor was to look more and more like a shadow Governor-General even though at this point he did not seem to realize how bad things were in the countryside and relied instead on Khanh's regular reassurances. When he did, eventually, the solution was to introduce more US forces but for the moment the answer to the problem was money rather than men. Money, said McNamara, was no object. It would, said Rusk, be worth any amount to win and if as he said, the cost of the anti-Communist struggle in Greece had worked out at $50,000 a guerrilla, the thought of a similar fixed-price operation must have been reassuring at what was otherwise rather a disturbing time.

Rusk and McCone, incidentally, did not seem to agree on this occasion whether the Sino–Soviet split would inhibit adventures by Peking and Hanoi – McCone said it would not: 'Hanoi and Peking now believed they were doing very well' – but on the eve of the first Chinese nuclear test there seemed to be a possibility of Russo–American convergence which could conceivably have affected Vietnam. At a meeting on 15 September it was agreed at the highest level that it would be better not to prevent a Chinese nuclear test by an attack on their nuclear installations but in certain circumstances there could be 'a possible agreement to cooperate in preventive military action. We therefore agreed that it would be most desirable for the Secretary of State to explore this matter very privately with Ambassador Dobrynin as soon as possible.'[52]

Fear of China was the theme that Johnson later developed, or allowed to be presented, in his memoirs which gave an alarming picture of how the Far East might have looked to him at the end of 1964. The possibilities of what Johnson described as a

Djakarta–Hanoi–Peking–Pyongyang axis may well have been there and if they were, no further justification of a steadfast US policy in Vietnam would seem to have been required. As far as new US initiatives were concerned Johnson in particular seemed hesitant and uncertain. Having rejected proposals for retaliation after the Bien Hoa fiasco and having had Taylor's November report that they were in a losing game in Vietnam Johnson was beginning to be confronted, and perhaps now to confront himself, with agonizing choices. On a reading of at least one paragraph of Taylor's report what he described as 'the minimum government' had almost ceased to exist; and although Taylor toyed with the idea that US officials might take over operational control of the GVN and the US 'might do better to carry forward the war on a purely unilateral basis' these seemed little more than talking points. In fact Taylor had nothing tangible to recommend for strengthening or even preserving the GVN, but as it seemed to be a matter of confidence and morale as much as anything else, Taylor was in favour of increasing covert sea and air operations as a means to this end. The main thrust of Taylor's argument however was towards air attacks on North Vietnam: as an imposed cost of their 'nefarious actions', as a means of reducing their operational support and as a bargaining counter with the GVN so that it would become more effective.

The stark contrast with these changes that were to be induced by the US, which was now beginning to appear as the prime mover, was to be seen in Taylor's honest but puzzled account of the strength of the revolutionary forces in South Vietnam, who, even if they were directed, supplied and supported by the North, were obviously formidable opponents in themselves.

> The ability of the Viet-Cong continuously to rebuild their units and to make good their losses is one of the mysteries of this guerrilla war. We are aware of the recruiting methods by which local boys are induced or compelled to join the Viet-Cong ranks and have some general appreciation of the amount of infiltration of personnel from the outside. But taking both of these sources into account, we still find no plausible explanation of the continued strength of the Viet-Cong if our data on Viet-Cong losses are even approximately correct. Not only do the Viet-Cong units have the recuperative powers of the phoenix, but they have an amazing ability to maintain morale. Only in rare cases have we found evidences of bad morale among Viet-Cong prisoners or recorded in captured Viet-Cong documents.[53]

'OFF TO THE RACES'

If, as Taylor argued, there was little to say about the counter-insurgency programme except to recognize that it depended entirely on the GVN there was equally little that the US could do, at least in the short term, which was likely to affect the balance of forces in the South except to carry the war to the North. This was what Taylor wanted. For him it was an inevitable choice. Either the US took military action against North Vietnam or it ran 'a very real risk of failing disastrously in South-East Asia'. But Taylor's audience in Washington while, as he put it, sympathetic was 'still not ready to bite the bullet'.[54] This may have been true in that air attacks had not begun immediately but on 1 December 1964 the manuscript record of the executive committee on South Vietnam shows that the policy decision was made by the President: 'There will be reprisals but decide exactly what at the time.'[55] In a sense this was Johnson's version of 'massive retaliation: at times and places of our choosing' and it allowed the President not only to decide on what would be done but also to postpone immediate actions. In the meantime, having taken the critical decision, was there any chance that anything less than air attacks on the North would be enough to hold South Vietnam together? The impression of this meeting was that the President was at his wits end, casting around desperately, clutching at straws, prepared, as he said, to try everything 'before Wheeler (the Chairman of the JCS) saddles up'. How could 34,000 hard-core VC, he asked, lick 200,000 ARVN regulars? Why not say 'This is it!'? Not send Johnson City boy out to die if they acting as they are.'

To this last and perhaps rhetorical question there was no recorded response but McNamara confirmed the essential proposition that it was 'downhill in South Vietnam no matter what we do *in* country'. Obviously the situation was getting worse but, given the state of South Vietnam, Johnson still hesitated. They did not, he said, 'want to send widow woman to slap Jack Dempsey. DRV will bomb Saigon once. Then we are off to the races'. The day of reckoning was coming and Johnson added 'We want to be sure we've done everything we can'. Help from almost all quarters was considered. Within South Vietnam, having been told by Taylor in effect to write off the Buddhists and the French, Johnson asked whether the Pope could not straighten things out with the Catholics. Why could not they get ambitious politicos into the act? Why not use Chinese Nationalist forces? Anything to be got from India? Or Pakistan? Or even, suggested Rusk, the Germans: although he was reminded by McNamara that would not be popular domestically (whether that meant in West Germany, in the US, or South Vietnam was not entirely clear). Like Dulles before the fall of Dien Bien Phu, Johnson was obviously intent on mobilizing allied or 'third country' support. Rusk was certain that the British could do more – 'Hit Wilson' was another of his suggestions – while McNamara said that 1,000 men from the Philippines and Australia as well as the UK would have a political effect out of all proportion to their numbers.

With the hope therefore that somehow the US would be able to put out more flags Taylor was sent back to Saigon to be given one last chance. He was now authorized to start planning attacks against the North with the GVN: although they were told that this did not imply any US commitment. Roughly the same thing could be said of the planning that was going on in Washington. While it may have been astute of policy framers such as the Bundy brothers to present Johnson with options based on what George Ball called the Goldilocks principle – too hard, too soft, just right – and while this may not have taken in the full range of possibilities, even from what he was offered Johnson was having difficulty choosing. The planning which began on 3 November, the day of Johnson's election, with the establishment of a Working Group of the National Security Council under the Chairmanship of William Bundy, had produced three rather blurred options. The first was a continuation (and some intensification) of existing operations. The second, 'fast/full squeeze', involved heavy and uninterrupted bombing until North Vietnam agreed to call off its support and/or operations in South Vietnam and Laos. The third, more deliberate, 'progressive squeeze and talks', would gradually intensify the attacks on the North and was 'designed to give the US the option at any time to proceed or not, to escalate or not and to quicken the pace or not'.[56]

Perhaps, because it seemed to suggest that the President would still be in control, this was why the third option appealed to Johnson. Rather than the open-ended war of Option B this was somewhere between game strategy and a management exercise but, even so, it was not enough to secure Johnson's irrevocable commitment: beyond, that is, his decision on 1 December that there would be reprisals: but he would decide exactly what at the time. Throughout November when the most intensive planning for some sort of war was taking place the President had been under equally intense pressure, directly and indirectly, from the JCS who, on four different occasions, submitted formal proposals for attacks against North Vietnam.[57] 'Every time' Johnson cabled Taylor at the end of December 'I get a military recommendation it seems to me that it calls for large-scale bombing. I have never felt that this war will be won from the air and it seems to me that what is much more needed and would be more effective is the larger and stronger use of Rangers and Special Forces and Marines or other appropriate military strength on the ground and on the scene.'[58] This was the kind of war, Johnson said, which the US had been building up its strength to fight since 1961, and, by implication, was the sort of war he was prepared to fight in South Vietnam. Here he was at odds with Taylor who resisted the commitment of US battalions to South Vietnam until the moment they arrived and was wholly in favour of air attacks on the North but one of the problems with Johnson's preferred policy was that, by increasing the number of US troops, élite forces though they might be, he would be increasing the number of targets for VC attacks. Following the attack on US aircraft at Bien Hoa airfield in early November, an attack on a US officers' billet in Saigon on Christmas Eve killed two Americans and injured another 60. Again, as after Bien Hoa, Taylor recommended an immediate 'reprisal' air attack against North Vietnam and again Johnson demurred.[59] One point on which Johnson and Taylor had however originally agreed was that, because of the danger of a North Vietnamese response to US air attacks, South Vietnam would have to be in better shape than when Taylor had returned to Saigon in early December. By the end of December, it was, if anything, worse and this was one of the reasons why Johnson did not respond to the attack on Christmas Eve. By then, and in spite of explicit warnings from Taylor, General Khanh and a group of young generals had overthrown the civilian government and announced their Armed Forces Council as the new rulers of South Vietnam. The upshot was that Taylor asked Khanh to resign and leave the country; while Khanh and his colleagues, after some astute manoeuvres, were on the point of asking Taylor to do the same. Before long the US would be involved with Khanh in a second, briefer and less sanguinary performance of their saga with Diem and Taylor and Khanh would be in open opposition. Other Americans, such as McGeorge Bundy who described Khanh as the focus of raw power, were convinced that there was no one else in sight although some might have remembered that, for years, exactly the same was said of Diem, and even of Bao Dai before him. Eventually, and only two weeks after Bundy's endorsement, Khanh was removed from power and, on 25 February 1965 to Taylor's intense satisfaction, he was shipped off to indefinite exile.

Problems such as this were of course far more serious than who was in and who was out in what was called 'a revolving junta' in South Vietnam. Apart from the uncertainties of political direction, and the inevitable questions that were raised about its alliance-worthiness, abrupt and eccentric changes in administration such as this led to even greater enfeeblement of the 'pacification' programme. Generals who are playing politics as well as playing soldiers seldom manage to do both successfully but the example is there to be copied. On one occasion, for example, a Vietnamese battalion, having run into a minefield, broke off contact and, to the amazement of its US advisers, headed back towards Saigon. When next located it was in the middle of Saigon participating in an abortive coup. This was in September 1964 and the operation had been in support of an intensive pacification effort in the provinces around Saigon. A year later an inquiry into this particular programme (*Hop Tac*: 'Cooperation') which was supposed to have been a show piece of US – Vietnamese planning said, among other things, that in the eyes of many Vietnamese it was 'the plan of the Americans': something which perhaps Khanh had done to keep the US happy. Whether and to what extent the Vietnamese would support other US plans and what the effect would be if US soldiers were introduced to help fight a war for which the Vietnamese were thought to be inadequate or insufficient was the dilemma which faced the US in 1965. Reluctant to commit himself yet to attacking North Vietnam, but with little interest being shown by Taylor in more US forces, Johnson did not seem to know what to do next and, in the absence of agreement, perhaps instinctively, did nothing.

At the end of January two of his principal officers confronted Johnson with the consequences of temporization. McGeorge Bundy and McNamara had asked to see the President and were going to tell him that 'Both of us are now pretty well convinced that our current policy could lead only to disastrous defeat'. Having supported Johnson's unwillingness in earlier months to move out of the middle course, and while they agreed that every effort should still be made to improve operations on the ground and to prop up the authorities as best they could, none of this was enough and the time had come for harder choices. Again there appeared to be three options. One was 'to deploy all our resources along a track of negotiation, aimed at salvaging what little can be preserved with no major addition to our present military risks'. The second appeared to be the 'middle course' but was in fact the one which Bundy and McNamara thought was the worst: 'to continue in this essentially passive role which can only lead to eventual defeat and an invitation to get out in humiliating circumstances'. This option being discarded there was therefore only one alternative to negotiation: 'to use our military power in the Far East and to force a change of Communist policy'. Or, if one assumes that a negotiated defeat was a non-option, there was only one course and Johnson was being asked to take it.[60]

At this point it would seem that the initiative was very much with Bundy and McNamara and, if Bundy's account is to be believed, the position of pre-eminence was theirs by default. Rusk, apparently, had nothing left to offer. He did not disagree that things were going very badly and that they would get worse. But the consequences of both escalation and withdrawal were so bad that they simply had to find a way of making the present policy work. 'This would be good if it was possible. Bob and I do not think it is.' Whether or not Johnson agreed with the logic of this presentation or whether Johnson instinctively agreed with Rusk, Bundy was soon on his way to Saigon. Just as in earlier years Taylor–Rostow or McNamara–Taylor visits led to enhanced US commitment and effort so the Bundy trip might well have done the same but, coinciding with the Viet-Cong's own escalation, it made for an inevitable and momentous conclusion. On the last day of Bundy's visit, 7 February 1965, a Viet-Cong 'spectacular' at Pleiku killed eight Americans, wounded more than 100 and destroyed a number of US helicopters on an adjacent base. It was the sort of attack to which Johnson could hardly not have responded and the significance of Bundy's remark 'Pleikus are like streetcars' lay in the opportunities which had hitherto not been taken. This time, with Bundy telephoning in the details to Washington and after a brief meeting of an augmented NSC, Johnson ordered a retaliation attack and on successive days US Navy and Air Force planes, augmented by SVNAF (South Vietnamese Air Force) aircraft, attacked military targets in North Vietnam. On 10 February another Viet-Cong attack at Qui Nhon killed 23 Americans and, again, the US responded with attacks with 100+ aircraft. A week later the first US bombing attacks, as distinct from close-support gunship attacks, were made on South Vietnamese targets and, even more ominously, squadrons of Strategic Air Command B-52s were moved to the US base at Guam, within striking distance of Vietnam.

WAS THE US AT WAR?

Part of the significance of this second US response was that it was no longer advertised in terms of reprisal and retaliation. Hanoi was now held to be responsible, as Bundy suggested, for 'the whole VC campaign of violence and terror in the South' and it was for this reason that the Pentagon Papers analyst described the second set of air strikes on 11 February as constituting a much sharper break with past policy than any previous US action in Vietnam.[61] Could the US now be said to be at war? This was a question to which even Bundy did not seem to know the answer although it may perhaps have been because Johnson refused to ask the question. On 13 February Johnson agreed to start a programme of limited but sustained air attacks against North Vietnam: once or twice a week, hitting two or three targets at a time. At least this was the message to Taylor; but, three days later, recognizing that continuing military action against the North was a watershed decision, Bundy was writing to tell Johnson: 'There is a deep-seated need for assurance that the decision has in fact been taken.' For one thing 'Bob McNamara repeatedly stated that he simply has to know what the policy is so that he can make his military plans and give his military orders' and it seemed essential to McNamara and Bundy 'that there should be an absolutely firm and clear internal decision of the US government that this decision be known and understood by enough people to permit its orderly execution'.[62] Having apparently made up his mind in council and having given his orders, as it were, in the presence of credible witnesses it does seem extraordinary that Bundy should have needed to nail Johnson down on his decision. In large part it seems to have been because Johnson, as Bundy put it, did not want to give a loud public signal of a major change in policy 'right now'; and in smaller part it may have been because Johnson was reluctant to recognize that he might already have gone to war. In intention, at any rate, it was not supposed to be a war. It was supposed to be a signal both to North and South Vietnam of US determination to prevent a Communist victory in the South and a warning to the government in Hanoi to abandon its support for the southern revolution; but even this, involving as it did unmistakable acts of war, was something which Johnson seemed loath to admit. He was, rather, anxious to assure the Russians and the Chinese that the US in fact had no aggressive intentions towards the DRV even though the US as a whole would sooner or later realize that it was going to war if only to maintain peace.

Perhaps this would have been easier if the US had not been engaged in regular air attacks on North Vietnam but, in any event, the air attacks themselves contributed to the other definitive commitment: the deployment of US ground forces. In one sense they appeared to be alternatives: either ground forces in the South or air attacks on the North but while the planning for each may have been independent of the other, as a means to the same end they were almost bound to touch at some point. In the 40-page war plan/war game 'Courses of Action in South-East Asia' which McNaughton and William Bundy had prepared at the end of 1964 when it was understood there was a list of 94 targets that might be attacked in North Vietnam, two triangles were superimposed on a map of Vietnam. One had its apex at a Chinese airfield on Hainan and the other at Phuc Yen just north of Hanoi where squadrons of Chinese MIGs were deployed after the first US air attack in August. In February 1965 the first SAM sites were observed in North Vietnam and in the same month the first US surface-to-air missiles arrived at Danang to protect its airfield and what was becoming the principal US base in South Vietnam. Whether or not there was any intention in Hanoi or Peking of attacking Danang its protection posed another problem. In a simple sequence described by U. Alexis Johnson, Taylor's deputy in Saigon: 'for the Hawks (the US anti-aircraft missile) to be effective they had to be on the hills around Danang. To protect the Hawks you had to bring in the Marines.' At the time, he says, they were not contemplating any massive introduction of US forces – 'and, frankly, this grew, somewhat like Topsy'.[63]

Presumably operational requirements such as this had been considered by the President's advisers in their plans in which the US always appeared to be in control of events but once the Marines had been put ashore – two battalions at Danang on 6 March – what happened next would not necessarily be under US control. In any event, with the first commitment of regular US forces the Administration, whether it realized it or not, had gone through a sort of sound barrier. Other airfields apart from Danang would probably have to be defended as well. Rules of engagement would be changed so that Marines could go on limited offensive operations or help ARVN units that were under attack and, in another manifestation of Catch 22, the more the US was prepared to do the less anxious might South Vietnamese forces be to fight, particularly if it seemed to be an American war, and the US might end up doing even more.

The fact that this, in the end, is what happened, with the US taking over the greater part of the war, does not of course mean that this was what was intended. Johnson, for example, may have wanted to limit the US commitment to 100,000 men, something which he could have reached in stages without confronting the obstacle of a two-thirds majority in the Senate who were needed to approve a declaration of war. His powers as Commander-in-Chief, demonstrated in the sudden intervention in the Dominican Republic in April, could in such an event be quite overwhelming and apparently successful and although the challenge of Vietnam was of quite a different order there were not enough people telling him that it could not be done. Too many, in fact, telling him that it could and, in any case, that it had to be done. McNamara, for example, working out that by keeping Viet-Cong on the move or forcing them to fight there would be a quantum leap in the supplies they would need from the North and the more supplies they needed the greater would be the proportion which the US would destroy in transit. Rusk, less certain that fire power and mobility and logistic supremacy would win, asserted that the US had a commitment to South Vietnam and that commitment must be honoured. The JCS, looking at war uncomplicated by political considerations, took it as a problem of applied US power, had no reason to believe that North Vietnam would be able to withstand US pressure and, because they believed in their own ultimate supremacy, did not seem to care much whether China and the USSR intervened or not.

Even at the point when it looked as if decisions were being taken and Senators such as Fulbright and McGovern were warning against any expansion of the war it could well have been Johnson rather than McGovern who said: 'We cannot simply walk out and permit the Vietcong to march into Saigon.' Within the Administration, Under Secretary of State George Ball ultimately led a last-ditch resistance to the troop commitments of July 1965 and after producing a 40-page memorandum in October 1964 was regarded as the in-house dissident. His 'sceptical thoughts' on US policy included such hopeful objectives of a negotiated settlement as 'the effective commitment of North Vietnam to stop the insurgency in the South' but while, effectively, it seemed to be a plan for a negotiated capitulation he assumed that the pre-condition would be an agreement for a cease-fire. Adlai Stevenson, US representative on the UN Security Council, had also been associated with last-minute attempts to find the basis for a negotiated settlement and while he discovered that Secretary-General U Thant favoured a cease-fire too, US insistence that North Vietnam's infiltration must cease and South Vietnam's independence must be guaranteed meant that there were no grounds for negotiation at least on the US side.

On the North Vietnamese side however it has been suggested that as late as March or even April they were prepared to negotiate rather than fight: thus, by implication, that the war would have been avoidable.[64] Whether they, also, would have agreed to a cease-fire, as they had been compelled to agree in 1954, whether the GVN would have agreed, whether it would have been observed and what the other implications would have been are questions which would still have had to be answered if either side, or any one of the four sides – US, GVN, DRV, NLF – had shown any sign of compromise but at least in their public positions there was virtually none.

THE POINT OF NO RETURN

By February 1965, then, and whether or not previous attacks of one against the other could have been written off as being impetuous, inadvertent or ill-informed, both the US and North Vietnam had now reached the point of no return. To revert for a moment to Hobbes, the nature of war 'consisteth in a tract of time wherein the will to contend by battel is sufficiently known not so much in actual fighting, but in the known disposition thereto': something that was revealed by the way in which each side made peace so conditional that war became inevitable. An appeal from the leaders of 17 non-aligned nations for an end to the conflict through negotiations allowed the US to re-state the conditions for 'unconditional' discussions and, at the same time, gave Johnson the opportunity of delivering his most characteristic, imaginative and pointless proposals. Essentially it transformed the Mekong into the Tennessee Valley and converted a revolution into a problem of development. Speaking at Johns Hopkins University on 7 April Johnson's 'pattern for peace' in Southeast Asia in a sense admitted that the war had already begun and 400 young Americans had already been killed to defend the national pledge that every US President had made since 1954. Everything that the US was doing, however, was to convince the leaders of North Vietnam 'of a simple fact': the US would not be defeated, would not grow tired, would not withdraw 'either openly or under the cloak of a meaningless agreement'. US resources were equal to any challenge. Once that was conceded, as well as an independent South Vietnam, the only path for reasonable men was that of peaceful settlement and for Johnson the 'terrible irony' lay in the fact that what the people of North Vietnam really wanted was the same as all the other poor people in Southeast Asia. Hinting that North Vietnam might take its place in some sort of American Marshall Plan Johnson pledged himself to ask Congress to provide a billion dollars to support a UN development programme in Southeast Asia in which healthy children, abundant harvests and electricity would be the common objective. The fact that Vietnam was still divided would in itself no longer be divisive.[65]

It was an ingenuous approach, a balance of threat and promise, but with restricted appeal in Hanoi whose perspectives were entirely different. On the same day that Johnson spoke at Johns Hopkins the Central Committee in Hanoi had given different dimensions for peace: that the US must withdraw completely from South Vietnam and that the peaceful reunification of Vietnam was to be achieved with no foreign interference. Essentially it returned to Geneva, 1954 and where the US took for granted that there were now two Vietnams the Central Committee, claiming to speak as always for the Vietnamese people, reasserted its proposition that Vietnam was one and indivisible. Although, rather tritely, they could be presented as differences of perception it is hard to understand how either presentation could have encouraged the other side to believe that there was any basis for serious negotiation. Quite apart from the fact that North Vietnam was being attacked regularly by US aircraft and Americans in South Vietnam were subject to intermittent attacks, for any dialogue to have begun would have required one side or the other to abandon its position. Publicly, neither side was prepared to compromise. Privately, both sides were putting forces into position in South Vietnam. Towards the end of April US intelligence confirmed the presence of a regiment of the 325th PAVN Division in Kontum Province which had been there since February. Altogether regular PAVN units totalling 8,500 men were subsequently identified as having arrived in South Vietnam by the end of April – 2,500 by the end of 1964[66] – and although their full strength was unknown to them at the time the US was already planning to put 90,000 men, most of them American, into South Vietnam in order to hold the country together.

Not everyone agreed that such numbers would be necessary but as McNamara had minuted on the report of the Army Chief of Staff in March: 'Policy is: anything that will strengthen the position of the GVN will be sent . . . '[67] and even though the formal decisions had not yet been taken which would send the total of US forces in South Vietnam up to nearly 200,000 by the end of the year the US was, logically at least, becoming involved in an open-ended commitment. If air attacks on the North had not yet persuaded them to abandon the revolution in the South, and if that revolution was itself on the brink of success, was there some level of US commitment, some size of US forces and some appropriate US strategy that would persuade Hanoi – and the NLF – that they could not win? When the US were concerned to try to keep out of the ground war in South Vietnam, US battalions were deployed principally to provide security for US air bases but, having arrived, they were soon to be the means to more ambitious ends. If US forces were more or less permanently in position in South Vietnam would this in effect 'deny' victory to the Communist forces? The 'enclave' strategy as it was known was, as the Pentagon Papers analysts describe it, a masterpiece of ambiguity but the existence of heavily fortified but diminished areas would seem to have offered little more hope of success than Corregidor, Tobruk or Stirling Castle. In any event, the arrival of US battalions seemed to provide their own momentum and to offer the hope of seizing the initiative from the enemy (as well, it might be said, as from the South Vietnamese Army).

The US Military Commander in Vietnam, General Westmoreland, now began to assume a position that was at least equal in importance to that of the US Ambassador, General Taylor. Convinced that the enclave strategy would lead to disaster, the alternative of 'search and destroy' which was given Presidential approval in the summer of 1965 was, as the Pentagon Papers analysts observed, articulated by both Westmoreland and the JCS 'in keeping with sound military principles garnered by men accustomed to winning'.

> Accompanying the strategy was a subtle change of emphasis – instead of simply denying the enemy victory and convincing him that he could not win, the thrust became defeating the enemy in the South. This was sanctioned implicitly as the only way to achieve the US objective of a non-communist South Vietnam.[68]

Thus, in June, '"Rolling Thunder" [the US air attacks on the North] and the ground strategy switched places in the order of priorities as far as achieving US objectives was concerned' and the day after it was announced in Washington that 'American forces would be available for combat support . . . when and if necessary' an editorial comment seems to have been apropriate: 'The American people were told by a minor State Department official yesterday that, in effect, they were in a land war on the continent of Asia.'[69]

It was a situation which Johnson still seemed loath to acknowledge but at this point the government of South Vietnam was crumbling. Six district capitals had been abandoned since May. After fierce fighting as well as steady attrition 20 ARVN battalions were no longer combat-effective and in the middle of June the flamboyant

Air Vice-Marshal Ky and the more sober General Thieu overturned the last civilian government. US air attacks on the North intensified and as a measure of terrible first-aid American B-52s began bombing South Vietnam in support of what was about to be described by McNamara as a 'non-government'. As if all this was not bad enough it was at this point also that General Westmoreland tendered his estimate: 44 US or 'third country' battalions, a total of 175,000 men, would be needed by the end of 1965. And when asked by the JCS whether that would be enough to persuade Hanoi and the NLF that they could not win Westmoreland could give no assurance over the next six months although it would establish, he said, a favourable balance of power by the end of the year.

It was perhaps at this point, too, that it could be seen that in order to save itself from defeat in South Vietnam the US was going to war for its own purposes. In March, in a frequently quoted memorandum for McNamara, the Assistant Secretary of Defense, John McNaughton, had quantified US aims in Vietnam: 'seventy per cent to avoid a humiliating US defeat (to our reputation as a guarantor). Twenty per cent to keep South Vietnam (and the adjacent) territory from Chinese hands. Ten per cent to permit the people of South Vietnam to enjoy a better, freer way of life.'[70] If McNaughton's memo seemed unduly cynical at the time, the last stages of America's entry into full-scale but limited war suggest unmistakably that South Vietnam was once again an object rather than a subject of international relations. Specifically, its government was not expected to last until the end of the year. Generally, it was described by McNamara as a 'non-government'; a government, said Lodge, (who was shortly to replace Taylor as Ambassador in Saigon) which should not be taken too seriously: 'If the area is important to us we must do what is necessary regardless of the government.'[71]

Whatever it was now in relation to the US, the assumption of most of Johnson's advisers at the end of July 1965 was that, unless the US did something about it, the GVN would soon cease to exist. Whether or not the war was about to enter the 'third stage' in which, according to the Maoist sequence, guerrillas would emerge as conventional forces in sufficient strength to defeat the government, the situation was obviously critical but, equally obvious from McNamara's presentation, this was exactly the war that the US could hope to win or, in McNamara's less sensational grammar and other things being equal, they stood 'a good chance of achieving an acceptable outcome within a reasonable time'. Given the almost unrelieved gloom that surrounded his assessment of South Vietnam which looked as if it could do practically nothing to help itself it became clear from his exposition that it was marvellously dispelled by a confidence in US dynamics: that it was about to take over the war and that US forces could fight guerrillas and 'main force' units with equal facility. It was, one might say, on the point of becoming a McNamara-type war in which it would be easier to identify, locate and attack the enemy or, as General Wheeler put it, the Viet Cong would have to come out and fight. And then, as the French believed before the battle began at Dien Bien Phu, the outcome could be in no doubt.

On the assumption that the military projection was correct McNamara might have had no doubts either. Wheeler, hopeful, said the commitment of large-scale PAVN forces would be a favourable development for the US. They would be unlikely to send more than 25 per cent of their forces into the South: some 60,000 men. McNamara was asking for another 100,000 – and perhaps another 100,000 in six months' time – but having forced the enemy to fight and die beyond his means, he, too, took it for granted, or else it was a confession of faith, that the VC/DRV main force units would be destroyed. After which the South Vietnamese could go back to their programme of rural reconstruction. Obviously there were certain costs attached. Altogether US armed forces would have to be increased by 375,000 men. Congress would have to authorize a call-up of the Reserves and National Guard and an increase in the draft. By the end of the year the US could expect to have 500 men killed in action every month but McNamara believed that the US people would support the course of action which he proposed because it was 'a sensible and courageous military-political program designed and likely to bring about a success in Vietnam.'

CONSENSUS

It was, in its way, a business-like forecast: this is what has to be done and this is how much it will cost to get the job done properly. In these terms it was a matter of how much more was needed to complete a job that had already been begun; and, apart from the fact that modern Secretaries, or Ministries, of Defense tend not to talk about going to war, the job in this case was identified by McNamara as 'demonstrating to the VC/DRV that the odds are against their winning'. So, in a way, the US was not really going to war but simply moving further up the Clausewitz scale by using more force. The only question that remained was how far it would have to go and how soon. Johnson's inclination undoubtedly was to move up in stages, avoiding crises and confrontation, and when the time came for him to muster the final consensus this in fact was the way in which it was presented.

The two meetings at which the options were presented and the choice confirmed took place on the evening of 27 July 1965. The first, a meeting of the National Security Council, lasted 40 minutes and the second took place ten minutes later between members of the NSC and the Joint Leadership of Congress. Allowing for differences of tone and reporting on both occasions the President offered the same five choices. The first, with its more dramatic coda, was to use the massive power of the US, including the Strategic Air Command, to bring the enemy to his knees – 'blowing him out of the water tonight'. That, said Johnson, was a course which was favoured by less than 10 per cent of the country. The second course was to get out 'on the grounds we don't belong there' and 'ought not to have been there'. Not many people felt that way about Vietnam. Commitments had been made by three Presidents. 'Most feel that our national honor is at stake and we must keep our commitments there.' The third choice was to stay where they were with 80,000 men, taking casualties and doing nothing. Or, as Johnson told the Congressional leaders, 'get Lodge out there and see if he can pull a rabbit out of the hat'. Not surprisingly, no one was recommending that course so it seemed in effect to be a straight choice between options 4 and 5.

The fourth choice, said Johnson, was to declare an emergency: 'Call in the reserves, thousands of men and the billions of dollars – tell the country that our best guess was Y billion dollars and X thousand men, and ask for it.' It was something which, Johnson told the Congressional leaders, had a good deal of appeal to him as President but accounts of both meetings emphasized Johnson's concern with the Russian as well as the Chinese reactions if the US were to take that course. In February, whether or not they had considered the implications, the US had bombed North Vietnam when Premier Kosygin was in Hanoi and although this had not produced a violent response, the USSR since the fall of Khrushchev the previous autumn had been taking a renewed and lively interest in North Vietnam even though Khrushchev himself seemed to have lost interest in his wars of national liberation. It would have been an obvious risk to count on continued USSR quiescence – Johnson mentioned hints which the USSR had given and the special problem of the surface-to-air missile sites – and at the back of everyone's mind and in most intelligence appreciations and policy projections there was the unknown and ominous factor of Chinese intervention. Whether this was the prime factor, or whether Johnson's caution was founded on native political calculus, the alternative to what he himself called a provocative and dramatic approach would be simply 'to give the commanders the men and materials they say they need from existing forces, to use money under a transfer authority – to try not to bluff or brag or thunder – and at the same time to get Ambassador Goldberg (America's new representative at the UN) and Secretary Rusk to go and work for a diplomatic position.' That would at least see them through the critical monsoon season and although it meant using up the manpower reserves they would quietly push them back up. So, as Johnson told the Congressional leaders in recommending this course, 'before he went into the districts of the Congressmen and Senators he would have do.e what Westy and Wheeler want done'.

The choice, in fact, had already been made a few minutes before in the NSC meeting and in one sense was the peak of Johnson's consensus-building achievement. In the final ascent, when the President and his advisers were considering McNamara's report, only George Ball and Clark Clifford, Chairman of the Foreign Intelligence Advisory Board, had urged the President to draw back in face of impending disaster but even Ball had apparently said he 'would go along with' the report.[72] *In extremis*, Mansfield, too, said that as a Senator and as Majority leader he would support the President's position: even though he had been bombarding the White House with dire and accurate prophecies and had read a statement to the Congressional leadership meeting which seemed on the verge of dissent. Fulbright, if not now irreconcilable, was at least excluded from the President's consultative circle but Johnson had perhaps more than made up for this with his historical consensus. In June and July two of the principal architects of US Vietnam policy had been invited to give their opinions. As one of the 'Elder Statesmen' (General Bradley and the Marshall Plan Administrator, Paul Hoffman, were two of the others) former Secretary of State Dean Acheson had joined with the others in saying 'You have got to face up to this and do whatever is necessary even if it gets you into a Korean scale of war'[73] and when General Goodpaster had been sent to brief the former President on the latest development in Vietnam he reported:

> General Eisenhower considered the matter at some length. The first question to consider is what the end of all this can be. He commented that we have now 'appealed to force' in South Vietnam, and therefore 'we have got to win'.[74]

With the weight of this historical consensus behind him Johnson's meeting with the Congressional leadership took on the nature of a national rally. A few minutes earlier, at the end of the NSC meeting, the President had asked whether anyone in the room opposed the course of action decided on. There was no response. Now it was an occasion for presenting and enlisting the right amount of determination, for a certain amount of dissembling or equivocation, for historical allusions, and for a great deal of patriotism. Where Westmoreland had asked for 44 battalions, McNamara translated this into 'an immediate requirement' for only 13. Where the ratio of soldiers to guerrillas was thought of as 10 to 1, General Wheeler reduced it to 4 to 1. Where McNamara asserted there had been no major defection of GVN forces, Wheeler, who knew that was not true, said nothing. For those who were looking for historical precedents and analogies Johnson read from Eisenhower's letter to Churchill during the battle of Dien Bien Phu (perhaps it was the part about the failure to halt Hirohito, Mussolini and Hitler) and Ambassador Lodge, pitching it rather steep, said that to pull out of Vietnam (alternative 2) would be worse than a victory for the Kaiser or Hitler in the two World Wars.

Almost everything therefore seemed to point to alternative 5, rather than 4: asking, undramatically, for what was needed for the next five or six months but, either way, said Johnson, he would give General Westmoreland what he wants. Likening his position during the 1954 crisis to that of one of the Senators at the meeting, Johnson said he had supported the decisions then without approving them but now, perhaps in case anyone had missed the point, he added 'There were 80 to 90,000 men out there asking for help and his answer was "yes".' An historic meeting, said the Speaker. The President would have the support of all true Americans. The following day, 28 July, in the course of a mid-day press conference, Johnson rehearsed his understanding of the lesson of Munich and announced that 50,000 troops would be added to US fighting strength in Vietnam although unconditional negotiations would, as always, be welcome. The text of the President's statement was widely distributed under the title 'Peace With Honor'. For those who remembered what Chamberlain said when he returned from Munich it may not have been very encouraging. But perhaps Mr Johnson was thinking of Disraeli.

For his part, in confirming the intentions of one side in the culminating and principal phase of the Vietnam war, Johnson believed, and like Hobson it may have appeared, that he had no choice. Continuity if not integrity had to be maintained so, with Rusk taking the US commitment for granted, McNamara taking it on as a problem-solving exercise or some sort of crisis management, the JCS eager to employ their expertise and resources, most of his advisers closing down the options and no absence, initially, of popular support, one may argue that unless South Vietnam was to collapse under the strain of war and revolution Johnson, if he did not want to go backwards, had to go on. His attempts so far to 'demonstrate the odds to Hanoi' might have been too inconsistent to constitute an effective warning but even if there had been a perfect translation from intention to action the question of whether it would have deflected North Vietnam from what looked like its sacred purpose of reunification remains unanswered but the odds are that it would not have been accomplished without the destruction of its government and a large part of its country and people.

This probably being unknown at the time, the US set out to meet what its government saw as challenges and commitments. Its generals, like those of Athens, were for the time being 'empowered to act as they thought best in the interest of the state respecting the

numbers of the army'[75] (although they would object that, unlike
the Athenian generals, they were not entrusted with the whole
management of the expedition) and one wonders whether Maxwell
Taylor, the classicist general, who did not aspire to the role of an
American Xenophon leading a retreat to the sea, ever pondered on
Thucydides' description of the Sicilian expedition when it set out.

> Indeed the expedition was not less famous from wonder at its boldness
> and by the splendour of its appearance than for its overwhelming strength
> as compared with the peoples against whom it was directed; and for the
> fact that this was the longest passage from home hitherto attempted and
> the most ambitious in its objects, considering the resources of those who
> undertook it.[76]

REFERENCES AND NOTES

1. The quotation is from Richard Helms, Oral History, Johnson
    Library. Thomas Powers in his book about Helms, *The Man Who
    Kept The Secrets* (New York 1979), reports Johnson's conviction that
    the two assassinations were related: 'they' got Kennedy in retribution
    for Diem. p. 152.
2. A very minor incident during 'Confrontation' is likewise turned
    into the sensational and inaccurate 'In December 1964 Indonesian
    and Australian gunboats fought off Singapore' and the subsequent
    British organization of a 'war fleet'.
3. *The Vantage Point* (New York 1971), p. 50.
4. *Pentagon Papers* (*New York Times*), 1971, p. 189.
5. Gareth Porter, *Vietnam: The Definitive Documentation of Human
    Decisions* (London 1979), Vol. 2, p. 222.
6. Edward J. Marolda and Oscar P. Fitzgerald, *The United States
    Navy and the Vietnam Conflict*, Vol. 2, Naval Historical Center,
    Department of the Navy, Washington DC, 1986, pp. 202–3.
7. On the day he was shot, with terrible irony, Kennedy had told a
    Fort Worth Chamber of Commerce breakfast 'The Iroquois helicopter
    from Fort Worth is a mainstay in our fight against the guerrillas in
    South Vietnam. So wherever the confrontation may occur . . . the
    products of Fort Worth and the men of Fort Worth provide us with
    a sense of security.'
8. W.C. Gibbons, *The US Government and the Vietnam War* (Washington
    1984), Vol. 2, pp. 209–11.
9. Maxwell Taylor, *Swords and Plowshares*, (New York 1972).
10. *Pentagon Papers* (Gravel) Volume III, pp. 37–8. For an account of
    what happened from the point of view of the deposed generals see
    Tran Van Don, *Our Endless War*, (London 1978), Ch. 8.
11. Gibbons, op. cit. Vol. 2, pp. 215–16.
12. Ibid. p. 217.

13. Ibid.
14. William J. Duiker, *The Communist Road to Power in Vietnam* (Boulder, Colorado 1981), p. 226.
15. William S. Turley, *The Second Indo-China War* (London 1986), p. 57.
16. *Pentagon Papers* (Gravel), Volume III, p. 39.
17. Ibid. p. 40.
18. *Pentagon Papers* (Gravel), Volume III, p. 42.
19. William H. Sullivan, Oral History, Johnson Library.
20. Gibbons, op. cit. p. 242.
21. Although, as Kaufman points out, Johnson's request in May for $125 m. in additional economic and military assistance for South Vietnam troubled some Congressmen, for the first time in the 19-year history of the Foreign Aid Programme the House Foreign Affairs Committee approved the President's full request for funding, including the additional aid for Vietnam. Furthermore, the final appropriation of $3.25 billion was only $267 m., or 7.6 per cent less than the original request: the lowest pecentage cut in the entire history of the Aid Programme. Burton I. Kaufman, 'Foreign Aid and the Balance of Payments Problem: Vietnam and Johnson's Foreign Economic Policy' in Robert A. Divine (ed.), *The Johnson Years* (Lawrence, Kansas 1987) Vol. 2, p. 84.
22. Gibbons, op. cit. p. 253.
23. *Pentagon Papers* (Gravel), Volume III, pp. 65, 163.
24. NSF Aides – memo for President, Vol. 4, Johnson Library.
25. *Pentagon Papers* (Gravel), Volume III, P. 173.
26. Bundy Memos Vol. 3, 9 April 1964, Johnson Library.
27. *US-Vietnam Relations*, Book 4, pp. 6–7.
28. *Pentagon Papers* (Gravel), Vol. 3, pp. 172–3.
29. NSF Aides – Memos for President. Vol. 4, May 25, Johnson Library.
30. George C. Herring (ed.), *The Secret Diplomacy of the Vietnam War: The Negotiating Volumes of the Pentagon Papers* (Austin 1983), pp. 19, 7.
31. Ibid. p. 33.
32. Ibid. p. 32.
33. Edward J. Marolda and Oscar P. Fitzgerald, op. cit. p. 338.
34. *The Anti-US Resistance War For National Salvation 1954–1975* (JPRS Washington 1982). By way of comparison, in October 1946 in the course of a dispute between Britain and Albania two British destroyers struck mines in the Corfu Channel. One was sunk, the other damaged, and 44 British sailors were killed or drowned. Among other things the British ships, having previously been fired on by Albanian shore batteries, were studying Albanian coastal defences. The International Court, with dissenting opinions, gave judgment against the People's Republic of Albania although they recognized that their sovereignty had been violated. Compensation of $2 m. was never paid. Nor was Albania bombed or shelled in reprisal.
35. Four books have been written on the Tonkin Gulf episode and its aftermath. In addition to John Galloway, *The Gulf of Tonkin Resolution* (Rutherford, N.J. 1970) they are Anthony Austin, *The President's War* (Philadelphia 1971); Joseph C. Goulden, *Truth is the*

First Casualty (Chicago 1969); and Eugene G. Windchy, *Tonkin Gulf* (New York 1971). Gibbons, op. cit. Vol. 2, provides one of the latest collations; and the Senate Foreign Relations Committee produced two sets of Hearings when they re-opened the question in 1968 (20 Feb, 16 Dec) and more evidence for the 'Termination of South-East Asia Resolution' in May 1970. The original Hearings were at a joint meeting of the Committee on Foreign Relations and the Committee on Armed Services, South-East Asia Resolution, 6 August 1964. *US News and World Report* on 23 July 1984 had an article 'The "Phantom Battle" That Led to War' which uses documents from the Johnson Library although two of the meetings seem to be elided.

36. Marolda and Fitzgerald, op. cit. p. 422.
37. LBJ Papers. President. Meeting notes, 4 August. Johnson had begun with his favourite opening: 'I want to counsel with you.' When the meeting ended Senator Aiken remarked: 'By the time you send it up there won't be anything for us to do but support you.' See also Mark A. Stoler, 'Aiken, Mansfield and the Tonkin Gulf Crisis', *Vermont History*, Spring, 1982.
38. Among those who were convinced that it was an illusion was Commander James B. Stockdale. With first-hand experience of the events of 4 August, and convinced then that nothing had happened, he was, by ironic coincidence, ordered to lead the attack the following day. A year later he was shot down leading a similar attack and spent the rest of the war in a North Vietnamese prison. He was subsequently awarded the Congressional Medal of Honor for conspicuous bravery in captivity. James and Sibyl Stockdale, *In Love and War* (New York 1984).
39. Michael Charlton and Anthony Moncrieff, *Many Reasons Why* (London 1978), p. 108.
40. Gibbons, op. cit. Part 2, p. 312.
41. Doris Kearns, *Lyndon Johnson and the American Dream* (Signet 1976) p. 165.
42. Gibbons, op. cit., p. 327.
43. Ibid. p. 328.
44. Ibid. p. 334.
45. Gruening, Oral History, Johnson Library.
46. Some indication of Goldwater's alarming ideas and understanding was his argument that the war should have been carried to North Vietnam ten years before and his speculation that, at the same time, a low-yield atom bomb might have been dropped on North Vietnam as a defoliation project. Theodore H. White, *The Making of the President* (London 1964), p. 106.
47. Ibid. p. 380.
48. Michael V. Forrestal, Oral History, Johnson Library. For another account of what happened see Townsend Hoopes, *The Limits of Intervention* (New York 1970).
49. NSF Aides memoranda for the President (McGeorge Bundy), vol. 5, Gulf of Tonkin incident, 18 September, Johnson Library.
50. William H. Sullivan, *Oral History*, Johnson Library. There is a useful summary of government upheaval in Larry Berman, *Planning a Tragedy* (New York 1982), p. 161.

51. NSF Files, McGeorge Bundy memoranda for the President, 14 September, 1964, Johnson Library.
52. Bundy, memos 'Chinese Nuclear Weapons', 15 September, 1964. Johnson Library.
53. Taylor, 'The Current Situation in South Vietnam, November 1964', NSF files, Johnson Library.
54. Taylor, op. cit., p. 327.
55. Cabinet Room – Ex-Com (SVN) 12/1/64 (1139), NSF Files, Johnson Library.
56. *Pentagon Papers* (Gravel), Vol. III, p. 224.
57. Ibid. p. 231.
58. Gibbons, Vol. 2, op. cit. quoting cable, p. 383.
59. On the matter of appropriate reprisals, apart from the *reductio ad absurdum* problem in developing a tit-for-tat strategy ('They blow up a restaurant – what the hell you going to do? Try to bomb a restaurant?') noted by Chester Cooper in his 'Oral History' (Johnson Library), the connotation and comparisons with what happened in Nazi-occupied Europe does not seem to have occurred to US policy makers. Civilians who would be killed, incidentally, in reprisal attacks on North Vietnam would be just as innocent, or guilty, depending on how one looked at it.
60. NSF File Bundy Memorandum for the President, 27 January, 1965.
61. *Pentagon Papers* (Gravel), Vol. III, p. 307.
62. Bundy Memoranda for the President, 16 February, Johnson Library.
63. U. Alexis Johnson, Oral History, Johnson Library.
64. This is the general thrust and implication of Professor Kahin's argument, *Intervention* (New York 1987), Ch. 12.
65. *US-Vietnam Relations*, Book 12, pp. 12–15.
66. I am grateful to Professor William S. Turley for correspondence on this point and am indebted to him for a copy of a MACV Combined Intelligence Center paper 'The NVA Soldier in South Vietnam', 3 October, 1966, Appendix A.
67. *Pentagon Papers*, Vol. III, p. 404.
68. Ibid. p. 395.
69. Quoted in Herbert Y. Schandler, *Lyndon Johnson and Vietnam* (Princeton 1977), p. 22.
70. *Pentagon Papers*, Vol. III, p. 695.
71. Memorandum for the record, 22 July, 1965 'Meetings on Vietnam', 21 July Meeting Notes File, Johnson Library. Other sources for the late July decisions are: Secretary of Defense Memorandum for the President 20 July 1965; summary notes of 53rd NSC meeting, 27 July; memorandum of the same meeting prepared on 2 November 1968, from notes dated 27 July 1965; and NSC: meeting with Joint Leadership 27 July 1965 prepared in December 1968. All Johnson Library. Kahin op. cit. gives detailed comparative accounts. See, also, Robert L. Gallucci, *Neither Peace Nor Honor*, (Baltimore 1975); Larry Berman, *Planning A Tragedy* (New York 1982); Wallace J. Thies, *When Governments Collide* (Berkeley 1980); and for a first-hand account George W. Ball, *The Past Has Another Pattern* (London 1982).
72. This is the account given in Chester Cooper's memorandum, op.

cit., 22 July. It is not mentioned by Kahin but flatly contradicted in the account given by Valenti. Kahin, op. cit. p. 372.

73. William Bundy, Oral History, Johnson Library.
74. The Eisenhower Briefings, Johnson Library.
75. Thucydides, *The History of the Peloponnesian War*, trans. Jowett.
76. Thucydides, op. cit. trans., Richard Crawley (London, 1874).

CONCLUSION

In this account of the origins of the Vietnam War, as at the Geneva Conference of 1954, it is easy to overlook the presence of the Vietnamese; and, by comparison with France or the US harder to remember that they were involved in civil war and revolution as well as a 30 year struggle to decide the political configuration of their country. Again, by comparison, other countries whose power was projected onto Vietnam may be seen as superior in strength until the issue was eventually decided between one of these powers, France, and Vietnam; and issue was joined between Vietnam and the US. In both cases it was complicated by the divisions in Vietnam itself; in the first instance between those who believed the French would provide genuine independence and those who did not. In the second instance by a partition which could have suggested that Vietnam was two countries rather than one.

The origins of war may therefore be sought, in the first place, in the relationship between France and Vietnam. In general terms it was the relationship that was familiar in all parts of Africa as well as Asia between a strong, confident and ambitious 19th-century European power and a comparatively weak and disorganized state. Conflict of varying intensity was endemic in this relationship but successful national resistance depended upon organization and opportunity. In Vietnam, unlike any other part of Southeast Asia, it was complicated by proximity and relations with China; to the point where the outcome of the French war in Vietnam was decided by what had happened in China in 1949. Well before the communist victory in the Chinese civil war, however, occasional projections of Chinese power – whether in the late 19th century or at the end of the Second World War – had led to the discomfiture of France and provided a third dimension to French relations with Vietnam. It is conceivable that incipient and indigenous resistance to French re-occupation of Vietnam after the war would have happened anyway but the ability of Ho Chi Minh to slip backwards and forwards across the Chinese border, with growing approbation from his US friends, allowed that resistance in Tonkin, small and passive though it was, to be organized on communist lines. When, therefore, the surrender of Japan in August 1945 created an immediate political vacuum it was filled with exultant and so far unchallenged forces of Vietnamese nationalism orchestrated if not organized by the leaders of a communist party.

It was this, communist, factor that distinguished Vietnam from another part of Southeast Asia, Indonesia, where the Japanese surrender, and some Japanese encouragement, had put nationalist forces in power to challenge the resumption of Dutch rule but where the communist component did not surface until 1948: and was then removed by the Indonesians themselves. In Vietnam, nationalism and communism – at least in so far as an effective alternative to the French was concerned – were interlocked and, although the French sponsored and virtually created a non-communist variant of monarchical nationalism, until such time as they were prepared to concede significant independence it was easier to portray their Vietnamese allies as collaborators rather than patriots.

Even without the communist tinge to Vietnamese nationalism, however, it is inconceivable that in 1945 France would voluntarily have given up Vietnam or, indeed, any of her overseas territories. De Gaulle's version of the grandeur of France is well known but even the communist leader, Thorez, like Churchill a propos India, said he had no intention of being remembered as the liquidator of French power in Indo-China. Those, especially Americans, who see the origins of war in 1945 and 1946 when France was 'allowed' to return to Vietnam may remember that Free France under de Gaulle was an allied and victorious power. By what right could she have been denied access to Vietnam or to any of her colonies? Perhaps by the right of appeal to the somewhat abstract principles of self-determination in the Atlantic Charter or the Charter of the United Nations. In which case the French could claim that the Vietminh were not properly representative of Vietnamese nationalism and, in any event, Vietnam *was* recognized as a free state – within the French Union.

The 'legitimacy' of French possession of Vietnam had indeed been compromised by the Vichy experience and collaboration with both Germans and Japanese but, while this was sufficient to create the ambivalence of Roosevelt's feelings, the legitimacy of Vietnamese nationalism was itself compromised by its communist leadership. It can be argued that had it not been for intransigence on both sides the French Union *might* have become the matrix for an independent Vietnam but as it turned out the French Union was neither a bold nor imaginative concept and it was impossible within this structure for the French government to pronounce the one word which Ho Chi Minh said was needed: 'independence'. With innumerable changes of government France in fact never conceded more than a heavily circumscribed independence, even to her own client, until it was too late: precisely, not until April 1954 when the Vietminh were on the brink of their astounding victory.

The struggle for Vietnamese independence and the terms and conditions on which it would be achieved had instead taken on the form of ordeal by battle and Dien Bien Phu, one of the decisive battles of the 20th century, was one of the greatest defeats ever suffered by a colonial power. In other circumstances it would have meant the end of the Vietnam war but, by then, what had arguably but essentially been a colonial war had been transformed, at least in the understanding of the US, into the most important secondary conflict of the Cold War.

As long as they had wanted to stay in the war, or until such time as a government was prepared to get out, the French had done their best to convince everyone that in Vietnam they were fighting in the front line of the free world. Indispensable as an ally in Europe the US seemed to take France at its word and after China's entry into the Korean War, no matter what prompted it, it was comparatively easy for the French and for the US to describe Vietnam and Korea as one war. What was more difficult was to enhance the importance of Vietnam to the point where it was vital to the security of the US but in the first instance, in 1950, it was seen as a vital sector in a policy of total containment. In the first instance, too, the French were seen to be containing China rather than Vietnam and in looking at Vietnam from 1950 onwards the US never lost sight of the Chinese connection.[1]

However, provided China might be deterred from open intervention by the nuclear power of the US, it was not yet obvious that France was going to lose its Vietnam war and as long as they were willing to fight the US was willing to pay. Right up until the Vietminh opened their attack on Dien Bien Phu in March 1954 it was by no means certain how the war was going to end. French – and American – premises may have been shaky and French plans defective but if, as was not absolutely inconceivable, their casualties or logistics had made the Vietminh call off their attack, it is also conceivable that peace would have emerged from mutual exhaustion. In the event, French defeat put them in the weakest of positions when the Geneva Conference began but in spite of that, and Mendès France's self-imposed deadline, the war had not ended in outright victory or defeat: at least not in the settlement that was made at Geneva.

The Geneva agreements of 1954 are among the most curious, controversial and unsatisfactory compromises of modern international relations. Perhaps the essential flaw was to have internationalized the peace without in any way guaranteeing it but they were ambiguously if not carelessly worded so that the French could make peace without anyone else being involved in the war. What happened next would be open to interpretation but there were enough pointers to suggest that the supreme irony was that if the US had signed the agreement both China and the USSR, as well as France and Britain, might have guaranteed a settlement in which Vietnam was partitioned for an indefinite period. By refusing to join in any guarantee with communist states one has to ask whether Dulles rejected a finite end to the first Vietnam War and, in so doing, doomed the US to participation in the second. As it happened, however, the opportunity presented itself to create a state in South Vietnam which would survive as long as it had US support but would collapse when that support was removed. In 1954, although the Vietminh felt they had been robbed of victory, Russia and China may have been more disposed to partition; the North Vietnamese might have been forced to settle down to a resentful co-existence; and the two Vietnams, like the two Koreas, could have gone their separate, authoritarian, ways.

In the absence of any guaranteed agreement, however, the open question and starting point for the second Vietnam War was whether Vietnam was one state or two. If it was one, then, if enough people had enough determination, reunification on national, if not ideological, grounds demanded an end to the artificial government in the South. If it was two, then the US and everyone else who respected the sovereign integrity of a small country was entitled to defend it against communist aggression. On balance this account has suggested that it was one and, with the exception of the US and the nominally independent state of Vietnam represented by Bao Dai, that is what the Geneva powers had assumed. Alternatively, if the temporary state of South Vietnam or non-communist parties in the South had been able to mobilize such support in the scheduled elections of 1956 as to call this assumption into question then a more or less legitimate partition might have continued.

In the event Ngo Dinh Diem was not encouraged to put these considerations to the test. An interesting but ultimately unfortunate choice of client, the nature of the US commitment linked his personal fortunes with those of the US; while US optimism and capabilities convinced them that with enough US support South Vietnam, with or without Diem, was a viable state which deserved to survive. Generalizations such as this about 'the United States' beg the question of dissent over US purposes in Vietnam, whether or not government represented the people, and, at least, whether the wrong policies may not have been followed for the right reasons. Not only in hindsight can one see that in Cambodia, Laos and Vietnam there might have been more agreeable alternatives to the triumph of communist parties. But in spite of the arguments of those who claim that the evidence was concealed, the warnings ignored and the failure of US policy stemmed from some sort of continuing governmental aberration, in its origins, long drawn out as they were, there was in every US government since the war a general disposition to intervene. In part this originated with the idea of containment but there was so much confidence in US ability to handle a small war, such as and for so long as Vietnam seemed to be, that at first sight it would have been particularly obstinate or dogmatic to believe that the US would not win its contest with North Vietnam and the National Liberation Front. When America shoved the other fellow damn well moved. Equally dogmatic, this assumption underlay the incremental additions to US power and commitment in Vietnam on a continuum in which the rational use of limited war was a familiar if not entirely normal instrument of national policy.

Perhaps there should have been a clear distinction between peace and war or, at least, Congress should have been asked for a formal declaration of war: although that may be to misunderstand the nature of revolutionary war. It would, however, have confronted the US with the necessity of defining vital interest and national security on the basis of popular decisions. In its absence successive governments were able to assume that they were entitled to define what was of vital importance even if they did not appreciate how many would die in order to sustain their definition. However many it might have been expected to be the object of maintaining two Vietnams can hardly have been, for Americans, of the same importance as it was for Vietnamese. The US defence of South Vietnam, while of considerable interest and benefit to many South Vietnamese, ultimately became, in itself, a US purpose; and at that point one may say the US was fighting principally in its own interest.

In its own way, so, it may be argued, was North Vietnam. There was, at first sight, no inherent and irrefutable reason why Vietnam had to be one state rather than two. Like two Germanies or two Koreas temporary partition could have hardened into indefinite division but the premise for this construction is that most people in at least one half of the country were in favour. In South Vietnam it was difficult to tell, if only because it had not been put to the test in 1956, and if the insurgency when it began in the South was not entirely the work of North Vietnam, which it did not seem to be, then there must have been a significant number of people in South Vietnam who were prepared to challenge this assumption at the risk of their lives.

In the end, and if one has to find a basic cause, perhaps it makes more sense in understanding the origins of the Vietnam war to see it in terms of ambition, more like the 19th-century wars for the unification of Italy and Germany, than in the more anaemic, 20th-century, concept of self-determination. North Vietnam and the National Liberation Front were going to war, as Vietnamese, to unite Vietnam under the leadership of the communist party. The

United States were going to war, as Americans, to prevent that happening.

NOTE

As late as 8 November 1967, in a meeting of the National Security Council, Senator Fulbright was trying to get Vice-President Humphrey to answer the question 'Who is the enemy – Peking or Ho Chi Minh?' Humphrey's reply was 'sanitised' – and remains so. (Johnson Library).

SOURCES AND
FURTHER READING

Particular sources are given at the end of each chapter. Two invaluable bibliographies are Richard Dean Burns and Milton Leitenberg *The Wars in Vietnam, Cambodia and Laos, 1945–1982* (Oxford 1984) and Christopher L. Sugnet and John T. Hickey *Vietnam War Bibliography* (Lexington, Mass. 1983). There is a bibliographical essay 'Suggested Readings' in William S. Turley *The Second Indo-China War* (London 1986). George McT. Kahin has a hundred pages of notes and bibliographical references in *Intervention* (New York 1987).

GENERAL

(i) US Department of State, *Foreign Relations of the United States.*
US Department of Defense, *United States–Vietnam Relations* 1945–1967 (12 volumes) 1971.
The Pentagon Papers (the Senator Gravel Edition) 5 volumes, Boston 1971.
The New York Times, *The Pentagon Papers* (New York 1971).
Congressional Research Service, Library of Congress, *The US Government and the Vietnam War Executive and Legislative Roles and Relationships Part 1 1945–1961, Part 2 1961–1964* (Washington 1984).
Committee on Foreign Relations, United States Senate, *Background Information Relating to South-East Asia and Vietnam*, Washington 1966; and *Causes, Origins, and Lessons of the Vietnam War* (Washington 1973).

(ii) Allan W. Cameron (ed.), *Vietnam Crisis: a Documentary History, 1940–1956* (Ithaca N.Y. 1971).
A.B. Cole et al. (eds.), *Conflict in Indo-China and International Repercussions: a Documentary History 1945–1955* (Ithaca N.Y. 1956).
Gareth Porter, *Vietnam: The Definitive Documentation of Human Decisions*, (2 volumes) (London 1979).

(iii) Marvin E. Gettleman (ed.), *Vietnam: History, Documents and Opinions on a Major World Crisis* (London 1966).
  Marcus G. Raskin and Bernard B. Fall (eds.), *The Vietnam Reader: Articles and Documents on American Foreign Policy and the Vietnam Crisis* (New York 1965).

(iv) Michael Charlton and Anthony Moncrieff, *Many Reasons Why* (London 1978).
  Frances FitzGerald, *Fire in the Lake* (Boston 1972).
  Stanley Karnow, *Vietnam: A History* (London 1983).

THE FRENCH WAR

Peter Dennis, *Troubled Days of Peace: Mountbatten and South-East Asia Command, 1945–46* (Manchester 1987).
Philippe Devillers, *Histoire du Viêt-Nam* (Paris 1952).
Philippe Devillers and Jean Lacouture, *End of a War: Indo-China, 1954* (London 1969).
Dennis J. Duncanson, *Government and Revolution in Vietnam* (London 1968).
Peter M. Dunn, *The First Vietnam War* (London 1985).
Bernard B. Fall, *Street Without Joy* (London 1963).
Bernard B. Fall, *The Two Vietnams* (London 1963).
Bernard B. Fall, *Vietnam Witness* (London 1966).
Bernard B. Fall, *Hell in a Very Small Place* (London 1967).
Ellen J. Hammer, *The Struggle for Indo-China* (Stanford 1954).
R.E.M. Irving, *The First Indochina War (London 1975)*.
George Armstrong Kelly, *Lost Soldiers: The French Army and Empire in Crisis, 1947–1962* (Cambridge, Mass. 1965).
Donald Lancaster, *The Emancipation of French Indo-China* (London 1961).
Henri Navarre, *Agonie de l'Indochine, 1953–1955* (Paris 1956).
Jules Roy, *The Battle of Dien Bien Phu* (London 1965).
Jean Sainteny, *Histoire d'une paix manquée* (Paris 1953).
Stein Tønnesson, *1946: Déclenchement de la guerre d'Indochine* (Paris 1987).

James Cable, *The Geneva Conference of 1954 on Indochina* (London 1986).
Anthony Eden, *Full Circle* (London 1960).
Richard A. Falk, *The Vietnam War and International Law* (Princeton, 1968–1976) (4 vols.).
Francois Joyaux, *La Chine et le Réglement du Premier Conflit d'Indochine (Geneve 1954)* (Paris 1979).
Robert F. Randall, *Geneva, 1954* (Princeton 1969).

VIETNAM

Sources on Vietnam, as a subject in its own right as well as the object or reflection of French and American attentions, may be found in other sections as well as this. Vietnamese communist sources available in English for this period, in so far as they may have been intended for propaganda purposes, tended towards the didactic and polemical; and one may take, for example, the simple assertion of Le Duan, 'Under the leadership of the Party, the entire Vietnamese people took to arms and resolutely waged an all-out and protracted war.' *Forward Under the Glorious Banner of Revolution* (Hanoi 1967). General Vo Nguyen Giap's *Unforgettable Days* (Hanoi 1975) provides an extended prologue to the start of the war with France; and periodicals such as *Vietnamese Studies* have numbers devoted to particular issues eg. Dien Bien Phu.

A useful source, that has been translated, is the chronology *The Anti-US Resistance War For National Salvation 1954–1975*, Joint Publications Research Service (Washington 1982). *Vietnam Documents and Research Notes*, translations of captured documents, was published by the US Embassy in Saigon between 1967 and 1972 but a lot of the material deals with earlier periods.

Joseph Buttinger, *The Smaller Dragon: A Political History of Vietnam* (New York 1958).

Joseph Buttinger, *Vietnam: A Dragon Embattled*, (2 vols.) (New York 1967).

William J. Duiker, *The Communist Road to Power in Vietnam* (Boulder, Colorado 1981).

James Pinckney Harrison, *The Endless War: Vietnam's Struggle for Independence* (New York 1982).

John T. McAlister, *Vietnam: Origins of Revolution* (New York 1969).

John T. McAlister and Paul Mus, *The Vietnamese and Their Revolution*, (New York 1970).

David G. Marr, *Vietnamese Anti-Colonialism*, 1885–1925 (Berkeley 1971).

Douglas Pike, *Viet Cong* (Cambridge, Mass. 1966).

Douglas Pike, *History of Vietnamese Communism, 1925–1976* (Stanford 1978).

Jeffrey Race, *War Comes to Long An* (Berkeley 1972).

Robert Scigliano, *South Vietnam: Nation Under Stress* (Boston 1964).

Ralph Smith, *Viet-Nam and the West* (London 1968).

Robert F. Turner, *Vietnamese Communism: Its Origins and Development* (Stanford 1975).

Denis Warner, *The Last Confucian* (New York 1963).

For an interesting retrospective, one of the Indochina monographs based on the 'debriefing' of senior South Vietnamese Officers, see Nguyen Duy Hinh and Tran Dinh Tho, *The South Vietnamese Society*, US Army Center of Military History (Washington 1980).

UNITED STATES

George W. Ball, *The Past Has Another Pattern* (New York 1982).

Larry Berman, *Planning a Tragedy: The Americanisation of the War in Vietnam* (New York 1982).

Robert M. Blum, *Drawing the Line: The Origin of the American Containment Policy in East Asia* (New York 1982).

Warren I. Cohen, *Dean Rusk*,(Totowa, New Jersey 1980).

Chester L. Cooper, *The Last Crusade* (London 1971).

Daniel Ellsberg, *Papers on the War* (New York 1972).

John Lewis Gaddis, *Strategies of Containment* (New York 1982).

Robert L. Gallucci, *Neither Peace Nor Honour: The Politics of American Military Policy in Vietnam* (Baltimore 1975).

Leslie H. Gelb with Richard K. Betts, *The Irony of Vietnam: The System Worked* (Washington 1979).

David Halberstam, *The Best and the Brightest* (New York 1969).

George C. Herring, *America's Longest War: The United States and Vietnam, 1950–1975* (New York 1979).

Roger Hilsman, *To Move A Nation* (New York 1964).

Lyndon B. Johnson, *The Vantage Point* (New York 1971).

George M. Kahin and John W. Lewis, *The United States in Vietnam* (New York 1966).

Geoge M. Kahin, *Intervention* (New York 1987).

Marvin Kalb and Elie Abel, *Roots of Involvement: The US in Asia 1784–1971*, (London 1971).

Gabriel Kolko, *Anatomy of a War* (New York 1985).

Herbert Y. Schandler, *The Unmaking of a President: Lyndon Johnson and Vietnam* (Princeton 1977).

Arthur M. Schlesinger, *A Thousand Days* (New York 1965).

Arthur M. Schlesinger, *Robert Kennedy and His Times* (New York 1978).

Arthur M. Schlesinger, *The Imperial Presidency* (New York 1973).

Arthur M. Schlesinger, *The Bitter Heritage* (London 1967).

R.B. Smith, *An International History of the Vietnam War* Volume I, *Revolution Versus Containment, 1955–61*, (London 1983), Volume II, *The Struggle for Southeast Asia 1961–65*, (London 1985).

Theodore C. Sorensen, *Kennedy* (New York 1965).

Ronald H. Spector, *United States Army in Vietnam. Advice and Support: The Early Years 1941–1960* (Washington 1983).

Wallace J. Thies, *When Governments Collide* (Berkeley 1980).

William S. Turley, *The Second Indo-China War* (London 1986).

INDEX

Note: In this index subheadings are in chronological order.